An Interdependency Model of

Homelessness

Front cover:
PHOTO © MAUREEN FENNELLI
"SHADOW", from NYC SERIES 1980-96

AN INTERDEPENDENCY MODEL OF HOMELESSNESS

The Dynamics of Social Disintegration

HV
4505
.H83
seab

Christopher G. Hudson

Symposium Series
Volume 48

The Edwin Mellen Press
Lewiston•Queenston•Lampeter

Library of Congress Cataloging-in-Publication Data

Hudson, Christopher G.
An interdependency model of homelessness : the dynamics of social
disintegration / Christopher G. Hudson.
   p. cm. -- [Symposium series ; v. 48]
   Includes bibliographical references (p.   ) and index.
   ISBN 0-7734-8288-1 (hardcover)
   1. Homelessness--United States. 2. Homeless persons--United
States. 3. United States--Social conditions. I. Title.
HV4505.H854   1998
362.5--dc21   98-20712
                                                     CIP

This is volume 48 in the continuing series
Symposium Series
Volume 48 ISBN 0-7734-8288-1
Symposium Series ISBN 0-88946-989-X

A CIP catalog record for this book is available from the British Library.

The Edwin Mellen Press
Box 450
Lewiston, New York
USA 14092-0450

The Edwin Mellen Press
Box 67
Queenston, Ontario
CANADA L0S 1L0

The Edwin Mellen Press, Ltd.
Lampeter, Ceredigion, Wales
UNITED KINGDOM SA48 8LT

Printed in the United States of America

In Memory of my Parents

Jean Barlow Hudson

and

Benjamin Rexford Hudson

Seagulls Over an Inland Field[1]

Why come you, white seagulls, dipping and soaring
over the barren stubble of an inland field?
Why have you left white wave caps, the gleaming form,
and sea-bright air to wander on some nameless quest
through wood and alien field?
In here where skies and soil must, voiceless, tasteless,
be of all the ways of home?

Go back, wild birds!
Whatever it is you seek so far,
it will not recompense be for the high salt spume,
for the waves beating upon the reefs,
the leap and plunge of sea life,
the sands bleached by the kisses of the spray.
Go back, before the grip of home is hurting,
and you have flown too far, too far away!

Jean Barlow Hudson
Early 1940s

---

[1] Hudson, Rexford A.(ed.). <u>Foreverness: The Collected Poems of Jean Barlow Hudson</u> (Yellow Springs, OH: Fallen Timbers Press, 1993).

Contents

Figures

Tables

FOREWORD

For individuals caught in the web of homelessness, it often matters little whether they perceive themselves as trapped by factors economic, social, or psychological. For their sense of immobility, impotence and distrust is felt almost existentially as an inner sense of *unheimlich* -- not "at home" -- and also as an environmental predicament which has placed them in a particular kind of psychosocial, ecological niche. While many practitioners and clinicians in the health and human services domain have long recognized the multi-determined nature of both the state and status of homelessness, it has been for health policy and social welfare planners a more circuitous process to reach the same conclusion concerning the multiple causations of this most palpable and visible outcome. Herein this book by Professor Hudson, discussed eloquently and with impressive empirical foundations, we comprehend the intricate web of interdependencies brought into stark relief and appearing like a spider's web under a magnifying glass. To focus our attention on but one corner of this extensive web, I will use the complex and controversial interrelationship of homelessness and mental illness to assay the dilemma and Professor Hudson's trenchant approach to psychosocial analysis.

There is wide disparity in the results of studies to examine the relationship between homelessness and mental illness in society. The purely epidemiologic approach usually results in identifying a discrete subgroup of homeless persons in the United States who have suffered, or are suffering, from major psychiatric disorder, perhaps as high as one-third of an urban homeless population. On the other hand, investigators who cast a wider net, relying on a broader definition of mental illness to include anxiety, depression and delayed social development, argue that as many as one-half to three-quarters of homeless persons have experienced marked psychological distress. In this book Professor Hudson proposes a model to identify the multiple dimensions and causal relationships among many sociodemographic variables interacting in a dynamic social system so as to bring coherence, both at the clinical or societal level.

There are at least two major reasons why the contributions of this book are important to the future studies of, and policies for, homelessness. First, the model developed by Professor Hudson provides an excellent example of how epidemiologic and population-based data can be used to understand the dynamics of homelessness and to develop social policy responses to the process of social disintegration underlying the homeless state. The rigorous testing of various hypotheses related to the causes of homelessness, using a multivariate statistical analysis, permits us to link epidemiologic and policy research. By this process, some assertions concerning the causes of homelessness are confirmed, and others are diminished, once other variables are controlled for in his model. Professor Hudson does a thorough job of providing alternative interpretations for the findings from his model and, importantly, relates them to competing theories of homelessness introduced at the beginning of the book.

Especially useful is the sociodemographic map of variables such as housing, employment, family structure and fragmentation, institutional involvement and supports, and the adequacy of the supply of social services in the communities (counties). One way to look at this approach is that we have here a broad map from which to work in pursuing detailed analysis, examination and hypothesis testing concerning each of these larger factors. For example, the work of Bassuk and colleagues[2] focuses more on the importance of individual characteristics of individuals who are homeless and probably would be characterized by Professor Hudson as deriving from "disaffiliation theory."

---

[2] Bassuk, E.L., Buckner, J.C., Weinreb, L.F., Browne A. Bassuk, S.S., Dawson R., and Perloff, J.N. (1977). Homelessness in Female-Headed Families: Childhood and Adult Risk and Protective Factors. American Journal of Public Health, 87(2), 241-248.

In such an approach, factors like early childhood violence, previous foster care or out-of-home placement contribute to disruptions in the ability of children to form primary social attachments. These disturbed attachments may be manifest in a variety of ways, such as expressions of violence, lack of engagement with social supports, and lack of willingness in help-seeking; for some proportion of individuals, as they pass through adolescence and early adulthood, there may be evidence of frank psychiatric disorder and impaired health and social functioning. All of these individual characteristics may moderate between the homeless person and efforts to provide him or her with appropriate health and human services. As is true with many social conditions -- paranoid schizophrenia, hard-core drug abuse -- those who are most in need of services may be those most likely to seek them. The model proposed here permits movement of the focus of analysis from macro to micro causation.

Extricating an individual from his or her status of being trapped in a web of dysfunctional psychosocial entanglements is a daunting enough task. Understanding all the dynamics involved in both individual and societal interactions related to homelessness is an even more difficult task.[3] In this book, Professor Hudson takes a major step toward furthering our understanding of homelessness and toward laying the groundwork for future investigators. In addition, he makes many well-founded social policy recommendations, which go to the basic assumptions and the frailties or failings of contemporary American society. Those who would enter into the battle to bring about social change, and to advocate for improvements to reduce the national epidemic and disgrace of homelessness, would be well advised first to be armed with the sense of social context, the array and diversity of facts, and the hard-won insights presented in this comprehensive study.

Robert A. Dorwart, M.D., M.P.H.

Professor of Psychiatry and Social Medicine
Harvard Medical School and the
John F. Kennedy School of Government,
Harvard University

---

[3] Jencks, C. The Homeless. Cambridge, MA: Harvard University. 1994.

PREFACE

This book is an outgrowth of several previous studies which I have conducted on both mental health policy and homelessness. In the 1980s and early 1990s, I was involved in research on the spending behavior of state mental health authorities as well as the decision making procedures used in these institutions.[4] Although this research taught me about the possibilities of achieving a broad national focus with limited research funds, I missed the chance to trace the impact of policy developments in mental health to consumers. One of the findings which particularly concerned me was the very minimal association between expenditure levels and the rated quality of state programs. At about this same time in the late 1980s, I conducted an initial qualitative, exploratory study of policy development for the homeless in Chicago and Illinois with a view to identifying areas of needed research.[5] One of my conclusions was that what was needed was a national study which would collect data in hundreds of localities across the nation so as to permit a multivariate examination of the impact of various types of programs and policies. This was another reflection of my growing interest in linking epidemiological and policy research, a task which is infrequently accomplished.

Although a funded research project of this magnitude was not in the cards, either for myself or any other researchers, in 1990 the U.S. Census Bureau undertook a special enumeration of homeless persons, referred to as the "S-Night" Count.

---

[4] See, for example, Hudson, C.G., Salloway, J., and Vissing, Y.M. (1992). The impact of state administrative practices on community mental health. Administration and Policy in Mental Health, 19, 6, pp. 417-436

[5] Hudson, C.G. (Winter 1988). The development of policy for the homeless: The role of research. Social Thought, XIV (1), pp. 3-15.

Realizing that such data would be aggregated to various levels, such as cities and counties, it occurred to me that the study I initially proposed may be possible through a secondary analysis of the data from the S-Night effort. At the same time I was aware of the various problems of reliability inherent in such a massive project, which the National Coalition for the Homeless has so effectively documented.[6] Before making any final decisions to proceed with the analysis of the S-Night data, I struggled for a year or two about ways to assess and correct for sources of random and systematic error in this data. In this process, I discovered that the Census Bureau had not only collected substantial statistics on this enumeration effort, but also had conducted a survey of the thousands of enumerators who were used right after data collection. After several informal efforts to obtain these data files, I submitted a Freedom of Information Request which after about a year resulted in the release of the necessary files. These in turn required substantial restructuring to convert them from a district office to a county-level basis so as to correlate these various indicators of possible bias with the actual results of the enumeration of homeless persons. At the same time I was having to learn structural equation modeling which provides the researcher with specific tools for testing complex theoretical models and incorporating measurement error into the models.

But still I proceeded cautiously to test out a few of my earlier and somewhat cruder methodologies on the Massachusetts data.[7] The resulting adjustments for undercounting corresponded remarkably well with the counts conducted by several independent political entities in the state, encouraging me to attempt a similar but more sophisticated study on a national level.

What also encouraged me to pursue research in this field was my both experience as a clinical social worker in the 1970s and my foreign travels. Whether I worked on an inpatient psychiatric unit or with the Jewish Family and Community

---

[6] National Coalition for the Homeless, Fatally Flawed, 1991.

[7] Hudson, C.G. (Spring/Summer 1993). The homeless of Massachusetts: An analysis of the 1990 U.S. Census S-Night Data. New England Journal of Public Policy 9 (1), pp. 79-100.

Services, I almost always had a few homeless persons on my caseload, sometimes against the advise of my supervisors. The seeming hopelessness and helplessness of some of these clients suggested to me a universal, timeless, even archetypal struggle which I hoped to share in, learn from, and contribute something to its resolution. Also, having spent about half my childhood living in various developing nations, as well as having regularly visited India over the last twenty-five years, I have always struggled with the meaning of extreme poverty and homelessness, whether it be from a spiritual, psychological, political, or economic viewpoint.[8]

Although I have moved away from clinical practice since the early 1980s and into the discipline of an academic life, one of my ambitions has been to better understand the homeless and possible avenues for their reintegration into community life. The work that follows I hope will contribute to this end. Several of my initial hypotheses were not confirmed, and I was not able to incorporate that some of the more interesting preliminary findings, such as the non-linear relationships between services and homeless rates, into the final structural model. But still I believe that this work will in some small ways advance our understanding of the homeless, needed programs and policies, as well as additional methodologies that others can use in advancing these same interests.

---

[8] See Meher Baba. Listen, Humanity. (New York: Dodd, Mead, & Company, 1967).

ACKNOWLEDGEMENTS

Although this book represents primarily the efforts of its single author, numerous individuals have provided invaluable input and support in its development. Several experts in the field have kindly reviewed and provided valuable suggestions on drafts of the book or its selected chapters. These include Robert Dorwart, Harvard University; Peter Rossi, University of Massachusetts; Joel Blau, University of New York at Stony Brook; and Richard First, Ohio State University. I would like to particularly thank Yvonne Vissing, Salem State College, and Jeffrey Salloway, Univerisity of New Hampshire, for their very thorough reviews and support of the project. Although she did not review any of the written materials, Martha Burt, of the Urban Insitute, provided insightful suggestions during the planning stages of the project.

This project was for the most part unfunded. However, several institutions provided funds either for expenses or various inkind supports. The Schools of Human Services, Salem State College, through Dean Diane Lapkin, generously paid for a key dataset. The Bureau of User Services, of the U.S. Bureau of the Census, waived considerable fees in the preparation of extracts from the STF-2C tape series. The University of Massachusetts computer services provided the project access to LISREL on one of their mainframes before I was able to obtain my own copy. Last, but not least are colleagues, particularly John Carrier, at the Department of Social Administration, London School of Economics, who provided an honorary academic appointment at their institution during my Sabbatical in London, including access to library and computer services, at which time I drafted the first half of the book. Furthermore, John Carrier and his colleagues provided invaluable support and input during our seminars and more informal gatherings. I should also note the generousity of Fred Karnas, of the National Coalition for the Homeless, who provided critical documents on the S-Night effort.

Particularly valuable help was provided by several graduate assistants. Jo Anne Devito was very thorough in her preparation of a few of the datasets, such that obtained from the U.S. Weather Service. More recently, Jennifer Wargacka provided proofreading services, as well as invaluable assistance in the preparation of the references and index.

Finally, I would like to thank my family for their encouragement and support of the project, especially my wife, Barbara. My children, Daniel and Elisabeth, were particularly patient with my monopolizing our personal computer.

Chapter I

INTRODUCTION

"Home is the sacred refuge of our life."

Dryden

The home is also a metaphor. Its physical embodiment in a house has come to represent the attainment of the American dream. The home at once connotes security and independence as well as inclusion in the life of the family and community. Without a home, one is in exile. The homeless, thus, have become not only a painful reality, but a fearsome symbol of a failure of the American dream. Their increasing visibility on the streets of major cities serves as a stark reminder of the consequences of personal and societal breakdown. Other categories of social breakdown, most notably poverty, have become abstractions to which many Americans have become hardened or indifferent. But the spectacle of disheveled, wandering, and hungry men, women, and children puncture this indifference, forcing reaction, whether it be one of caring, curiosity, or condemnation. And as with other tragedies, it forces the question of why.

Homelessness is a symptom of social disintegration, of the breakdown of societal safety nets and preferred means of individual coping, and of relationships with significant others. As a symptom, homelessness at once reveals these breakdowns and camouflages them. It reveals a litany of social problems--housing unaffordability, family breakdown, untreated mental illness, unemployment--but it also obscures their specific interrelationships. By the time an individual or a group becomes homeless, their story has become a fragmented admixture of circumstances, injustices, and pathologies. For this reason, most analyses of homelessness, whether qualitative or

1

quantitative, rarely have been able to move beyond the usual list of causes to provide a coherent account or model of how these forces conspire and dynamically interact to leave an individual or population homeless. This is unfortunate as it has often been observed that homelessness represents a confluence of a wide array of social problems, providing what is a particularly revealing window to the nature of breakdowns in American society.

Central to any attempt to research and understand homelessness is the question of definition, that of who should be considered homeless: those living on the streets? in institutions? in shelters? doubled up with friends? Social liberals usually prefer to define the homeless broadly to include those precariously housed as well as many others, and thus, focus on structural and policy issues in their conceptualization of causes and preferred policies. In contrast, conservatives have sought to delimit the definition to those literally living on the streets and in homeless shelters, and thus focus on individual deficits and an emergency short-term response. Who we consider to be homeless depends on how we define the home, whether as a secure haven in a supportive community, or merely a physical domicile. Webster's dictionary contains several of the more common definitions of the word home:

> ... A dwelling place; the place in which one resides; the seat of domestic life and interests...abiding place of one's affections; a place where one likes to be; restful or congenial place, as home is where the heart..The members of a family [are]; household; as the Depression ruined many homes.[9]

To be homeless, therefore, means more than the lack of a domicile; it means the lack of residence which is safe and secure by virtue of a person's supportive and interdependent relationships with family and community. Ties to family may mean a relationship with a spouse, parent, or trusted partner; and ties with community involve a range of informal and formal affiliations, including participation in churches, social clubs, as well as employment or income maintenance programs. In contrast, Rossi's definition of homelessness typifies the reluctant but understandable decision of most

---

[9]   Webster's New World Dictionary of the American Language (Cleveland: World Publishing Company, 1962).

2

researchers to limit the term to the undomiciled homeless:

> ...any person who does not own or rent a dwelling and is not a regular member of a household that does is homeless...this definition excludes inhabitants of hospitals, jails, prisons, and nursing homes.[10]

Research on the domiciled homeless, who are sometimes referred to as the precariously housed, is often not methodologically feasible, and for this reason most studies have focused on the undomiciled homeless, the 'literally homeless', and these people include those in homeless shelters and flophouse, as well as those found living on the street, as well as abandoned buildings, bus stations and airports, among other locations. While much of this study focuses on the undomiciled homeless, it reviews in Chapter 3 and in the subsequent chapters data which is pertinent to estimating the extent and causes of homelessness generally.

Homelessness is not only a defined state which one enters or leaves, but more importantly, it is a process of social disintegration, one which may be brief, intermittent, or prolonged, and sometimes terminal. One of the more common typologies classifies the homeless into the groups of Marginal, Recent, and Chronically homeless.[11] The fact that the dividing lines between these groups may be almost impossible to define highlights the need to understand the process by which many of the extremely poor are progressively marginalized--economically, socially, and psychologically.

Only a few studies have been able to analyze variations in the size and characteristic of homeless populations between various jurisdictions using counts of persons in homeless shelters.[12] The study which this book is based on goes beyond

---

[10] Peter H. Rossi, Down and Out in America: The Origins of Homelessness (Chicago: The University of Chicago Press, 1989), p. 9.

[11] John Belcher, "Three stages of homelessness: A conceptual model for social workers in health care," Health and Social Work 16 (2), pp. 87-93.

[12] Martha Burt, Over The Edge (New York: Russell Sage Foundation, 1992); Marta Elliott and Lauren J. Krivo, "Structural determinants of homelessness in the United States," Social Problems 38 (1), February 199; Christopher Hudson, "The homeless of Massachusetts: An analysis of the 1990 U.S. Census S-Night data," New England Journal of Public Policy 9 (1), 1992, pp. 79-100; William

this by analyzing variations in the overall level of both the sheltered and street homeless throughout the 3,141 counties in the United States. Prevalence or overall rates, however, result from both the incidence or rate at which people become homeless in a designated period of time and the incidence at which people cease to be homeless, or, the length of the average episode. It has been pointed out that the reasons that people become homeless may be very different from the reasons they are able to exit homelessness.[13] Some presumed causes, such as natural disasters, are more specifically influential in the precipitation of homelessness; others, such as the provision of services, in shortening episodes of homelessness; however, many causes such as the decline of income maintenance or housing benefits, or unemployment, can be assumed to impact on both the initial development and the termination of the homeless experience. The model investigated in this research is, out of necessity, based on an analysis of overall prevalence rates. Until more specific incidence data can be developed, decisions about which factors are most influential at particular stages of the homeless experience must be addressed through the interpretation of the aggregated data.

This study aims to identify some of the ways that individual and societal conditions dynamically interact to create that particularly insidious type of social disintegration which we have come to know as homelessness. It does this through the presentation, testing, and refinement of what will be referred as a Social Interdependency Model of extreme poverty and homelessness. This is a model which, while drawing significantly from the social disjunction theories of Robert Merton and the later social dislocation model of William J. Wilson,[14] considers also the role of changes in social services such as the deinstitutionalization of mental health services

---

Tucker, "Where do the homeless come from?" National Review, September 25, 1987, p. 35.

[13] Herb Westerfelt, "The ins and outs of homelessness: Exit patterns and predictions," Ph.D. Dissertation, The University of Wisconsin at Madison, 1990.

[14] William J. Wilson, The Truly Disadvantaged, (Chicago: The University of Chicago Press, 1987).

4

and changes in the housing market. But most important, it represents a theoretically-guided, comprehensive, and simultaneous analysis of data pertinent to most of the identified causes of homelessness. This data on the 3,141 U.S. counties includes results from the U.S. Census 1990 S-Night enumeration of homeless persons, as well as over 600 additional variables from various governmental and private sources on a range of social conditions, policies, and services (see appendix 1). The focus of this study is, therefore, the problem of homelessness itself rather than the policies and programs which are needed to eliminate it. Nonetheless, a strategy for this is outlined in the final chapter.

This is largely a cross-sectional study, based on data from 1990, although whenever possible, it has been supplemented by data from earlier time periods. The study, therefore, provides a comprehensive profile of homelessness in the United States in 1990. As a picture taken at one point in time, it is necessarily two-dimensional, but like any portrait, the dimension of depth--in this case time order of causal processes--can often be inferred from its substance and context in the same way that a geologist might infer the age of various strata from their content and relative positions.

Theories of Homelessness: An Overview

Most writers and researchers concerned with homelessness have assiduously avoided anything which has resembled formal theory, no doubt to maintain a focus on the reality and humanity of homeless individuals. But most have not been reluctant to propose one or a combination of conditions as the primary or secondary causes of the rise of homelessness in recent years. Each of these when taken in isolation provide only a partial view, but they will form the building blocks to the model which will be presented in the following section and which will constitute the core thesis of this work.

The most commonly cited cause of homelessness in recent years is unaffordable housing. Because of the very definition of homelessness, it is not surprising that the lack of housing is the most universally reported problem of

5

homeless individuals. Robert Hayes, the advocate who in the late 1970s and early 1980s played a central role in bringing the homeless of New York to public attention, summarized the problem succinctly, as "Housing, housing, housing".[15]

It has been well documented that there have been dramatic declines in low-income housing units, especially single resident occupancy (SRO) units, at the same time that homelessness has been on the rise. Much of this decline has been attributed to urban renewal and the gentrification of inner city neighborhoods. This has involved massive rehabilitation and conversion of units to condominiums. It has been buttressed by tax incentives which have favored such conversions and the running down, or "milking" of low-income rental properties, and their eventual destruction, whether by arson or by more formal means.

A second component of the decline of low-income housing has been the disinvestment by the federal government in assisted housing. Between 1980 and 1990 the U.S. Department of Housing and Urban Development's assisted housing budget declined from $32 billion to $7.5 billion per year, a decline of 80% in real dollars.[16] Implicit in the various interpretations of the housing problem is the idea that the tax structure, which favors higher income groups and declining federal investment, has led to a significant decline in available low-income rental housing, thus, driving the relative cost of the remaining housing up to unaffordable levels. Rarely discussed in analyses of the decline in low-income housing is the impact of declining resources of low-income persons.

A second approach to homelessness has focused on the income side of the equation, and has emphasized broader macroeconomic changes in the structure of the economy and job market. It has sought to explain not so much the increasing cost of housing, but declining incomes of the poor which have impacted on the affordability

---

[15] Quoted in, David A. Rochefort and Roger W. Cobb, "Framing and claiming the homelessness problem," New England Journal of Public Policy 8 (1), pp. 55.

[16] Jim Tull, "Homelessness: An overview," New England Journal of Public Policy, 8 (1), pp. 25-48 (Spring 1992), p. 33.

of housing. The most common and general account involves deindustrialization and economic restructuring, or the decline in manufacturing industries and jobs, their shift to third world nations, and their replacement with lower paying service jobs. For instance, it is argued that,

> There are multiple causes for homelessness and persistent poverty in this country. Rapid changes in the economy account for much of the uprootedness. As the U.S. economy changes very rapidly to a world economy, corporations find and take opportunities to move manufacturing facilities outside the U.S. ... Plants close without notice. Mass layoffs, production slowdowns, corporate buy-outs, and product changes are all considered management decisions in spite of the fact that they can have devastating effects on the lives of the workers and their families.[17]

There is little disagreement that this process, however it may be interpreted, has taken place on a massive scale and has disproportionately impacted on black males and other low-income groups in the inner cities.[18] Rossi is one of the few researchers to apply the dislocation theory of Wilson's to understanding homelessness:

> The abrupt rise in female-headed households from 1968 to 1984 in part reflects on the uncertain fate of young men, who thereby become less attractive as mates, less willing to become household heads, and less able to fulfill the economic role of husband and father when marriage does take place.[19]

Dislocation theory argues that there is a critical and growing mismatch between both the type and location of jobs and the available inner city workforce, and that these processes have especially impacted on black men in the inner cities. Unskilled and semi-skilled jobs are disappearing due to both automation and the exodus of manufacturing, and these are being replaced by both minimum wage service jobs, often in distant suburbs, and more often, by technical and professional jobs requiring higher levels of education. Unskilled and semi-skilled jobs are being lost to the third world where corporations are able to employ workers at a fraction of the cost.

---

[17] Friends Committee on National Legislation, Washington Newsletter, July 1988.

[18] William J. Wilson, The Truly Disadvantaged.

[19] Peter Rossi, Down and Out in America, p. 187.

7

Deindustrialization is linked, then, with the globalization of economic activity. In their ownership, operations, and loyalties, major corporations are becoming multi-national, and in doing so, production and thus employment is becoming increasingly specialized. Reich points out that the developed Western nations are attractive to these corporations for managerial and scientific tasks, and the third world, for routine production.[20] For this reason, there has been little political support for the maintenance of the minimum wage, especially among the business community. As the minimum wage stagnates, income maintenance benefits have declined due to the 'principle of least eligibility' which dictates that such benefits must always be less than the lowest paying jobs so as to maintain the work ethic.[21]

Many commentators have de-emphasized economic trends, whether involving housing or jobs, and have instead focused on social and family fragmentation as being either an important moderating variable, or even the cause of homelessness. Perhaps one of the most prominent has been Bahr who has proposed the theory of disaffiliation:

> Homelessness, narrowly defined as literal homelessness, is a condition of disaffiliation, a lack of bonds, a pathology of connectedness, and not an absence of proper housing, or a necessary concomitant of abject poverty or of deviant life-styles.[22]

A similar theory is proposed by Bassuk:

> While there is no uniform profile for homeless families our research uncovered patterns common to many. The majority of women had lived in unstable situations before coming to the shelter. The sheltering facilities were brief stops in patterns of instability and family disruption.[23]

---

[20] Robert B. Reich, The Work of Nations: Preparing Ourselves for 21st Century Capitalism (New York: Vintage Books, 1992).

[21] Joel Blau, The Visible Poor: Homelessness in The United States (New York: Oxford University Press, 1992).

[22] Howard Bahr, "Introduction," in Jamshid Momeni, (ed.), Homelessness in the United States: State Surveys (New York: Praeger, 1990), pp. xxi.

[23] Ellen L. Bassuk, Alison, S. Lauriat, and Lee Rubin, Homelessness: Critical Issues for Policy and Practice e, 1987.

Many researchers, while acknowledging the importance of the breakdown of family relationships, have placed this trend in the context of other proposed causes. At two extremes, are Wilson and McMurry. Wilson argues that macroeconomic changes, leading to extensive unemployment of black males, serves to cause black women to both delay marriage and to stay married for shorter periods of time. In contrast, McMurry minimizes the economic dimension, and casts problems of family fragmentation in the context of individual pathology:

> And in most cases, alcoholism combined with poverty, or mental disadvantage combined with alcoholism are not enough to land the unfortunate out on the street. The proximate cause of homelessness, and what accounts most for the explosion in their numbers, then, is fractured relationships.[24]

Family fragmentation, including the delayed formation of families, may be both a cause and a consequence of other conditions responsible for homelessness. While macro-economic forces clearly place dramatic pressures on low-income individuals and families, the presence of high rates of single parent and one person families in turn complicates not only the employment market but also places significant demands on the housing market, as these families typically require two instead of one housing unit.

The theory that family and community fragmentation places people at risk of homelessness is a theory of the breakdown of primary supports. In contrast, others have emphasized that the breakdown of secondary supports--typically formal social or mental health services--has been particularly critical. In the early and mid-1980s, the most fashionable theory was that the deinstitutionalization of mental health services was the main culprit. Since the mid-1950s there has been a major depopulation of state and county hospitals resulting from such disparate forces as the development of psychotropic medication, new and stricter commitment laws requiring dangerousness, financial problems of the states as well as incentives from the federal

---

[24] Dan McMurray, Chapter 4, "Family breakdown causes homelessness," in Lisa Orr, (ed.), The Homeless: Opposing Viewpoints (San Diego: Greenhaven, 1990), p. 74.

government to discharge mental patients, as well as the philosophy of community care. Many analysts have concluded this process was largely unplanned and precipitous, usually occurring before ample community resources and services could be put in place for the discharged patients.[25] As result, many patients ended up on the streets, as well as 'trans-institutionalized' to jails, nursing homes, and homeless shelters. Belcher and Toomey, for example, found that a substantial portion of discharged mental patients in one Midwestern city became homeless within six months of their discharge, however, they have been careful not to use deinstitutionalization as a primary explanation and in Belcher's more recent writing, he has also emphasized the role of economic dislocation.[26] In contrast, commentators such as Lamb and Torrey have focused more exclusively on personal vulnerabilities and breakdown of or failure to develop secondary supports in the community:

> I want to focus on the seriously mentally ill. These people became homeless because we emptied out the state mental hospitals. ... We thought that all you had to do was empty the hospitals out, open up the gates, and they would live happily ever after. Well, if you drive around downtown Washington, you will see that they are not living happily ever after. These people have brain diseases.[27]

Declining income maintenance benefits have also been frequently cited as a major cause of homelessness. Federal income benefits under the social security act have been indexed to inflation since the early 1970s, and have not declined, and thus are often cited as the single most important reason for the drop in the poverty rate of older Americans. However, those benefits administered and either partially or fully funded by the states, AFDC and general assistance, have seen a dramatic decline. For

---

[25] See Ann Braden Johnson, Out of Bedlam: The Truth About Deinstitutionalization (Basic Books, 1990).

[26] John Belcher and Beverly G. Toomey, "Relationship between the deinstitutionalization model, psychiatric disability, and homelessness," Health and Social Work 13 (2), September 1988; John R. Belcher and Frederick A. DiBlasio, Helping the Homeless: Where Do We Go from Here? Lexington, KY: Lexington Books, 1990..

[27] E. Fuller Torrey, Martha Burt, Ken Beirne, and William Tucker, "Who are the homeless and why are they on the streets?" The Heritage Lectures: Rethinking Policy on Homelessness, December 14, 1988.

example, between 1970 and 1989 the real value of the average AFDC benefit dropped from $568 to $381 (1989 Dollars), or 32.9%.[28] Even more precipitous has been the drop and frequent elimination of general assistance. Burt hypothesizes that this may be a central reason for the precipitous increase in unattached person's among the homeless, and the relatively small number of aged.[29]

Closely related to the idea that breakdown of secondary supports is the central cause of homelessness, is the hypothesis that high levels of personal disabilities is the most critical cause. Many researchers have preferred to reserve judgement on the causative role of personal disabilities, and simply document their pervasiveness among the homeless:

> Recent studies estimate that about one half to three fourths of homeless adults have at least one ADM [alcoholism, drug abuse, or mental health] disorder: Between 12% and 39% have an alcohol problem only, from 5% to 40% are mentally ill without associated alcohol or drug problems, and between 3% and 7% have drug problems. Dual diagnoses range from 2% to 34%, with as many as one third having concurrent alcohol and mental disorders, about 3% having both mental and drug disorders, and perhaps 7% suffering from alcohol, drug, and mental problems in combination.[30]

Likewise, Rossi presents data which indicates that over 96% of the respondents in the 1986 Chicago survey of the homeless reported one or more problems which might be considered disabilities, such as mental illness, substance abuse, medical problems, or a criminal record. He is, however, careful to emphasize that these are not causes as much as risk factors.[31] Although such surveys can do little to disentangle what is a cause of and what is a consequence of the homeless

---

[28] U.S. House of Representatives, Committee on Ways and Means, Background Material and Data on Programs Within the Jurisdiction of the Committee on Ways and Means, Washington, D.C., Government Printing Office, 1990, p. 563.

[29] Martha Burt, Over The Edge, pp. 82-106.

[30] Pamela J. Fischer and William R. Breakey, "The epidemiology of alcohol, drug, and mental disorders among homeless persons, American Psychologist 46 (11), November 1991, p. 1116.

[31] Peter Rossi, Down and Out in America, p. 77.

experience, some research suggests that extensive personal difficulties and disabilities both predate the homeless experience and in turn are exacerbated by it. For instance, the longitudinal research of Cohen showed,

> ...that moderate and heavy alcohol consumption preceded by nearly a decade a man's permanent arrival on the Bowery...Marginal poverty and periodic unemployment created personal and family stressors which in turn produce increased exposure and desire for alcohol; increased alcohol consumption makes it more difficult to hold a job, as well as further exacerbating family strain.[32]

What can be assumed is that disability, whether physical, psychiatric, behavioral, or social, places people at risk of homelessness, a risk which no doubt becomes exacerbated and dangerously high when combined with unemployment, an expensive housing market, family breakup, and inaccessibility of services and concrete supports.

One of the few comprehensive attempts to model homelessness was undertaken by Burt of the Urban Institute. On one hand she emphasizes the role of interest rates, tax policy, and government housing policy in determining the availability of housing, and on the other hand, unemployment, household resources, and social policy in determining the level of available income of the poor and other vulnerable groups. She tested this model in explaining shelter rates in a selected group of urban areas, and concluded that in high growth cities the traditional income maintenance programs, although providing higher benefits, could not overcome the impact of the high cost of living, housing unaffordability, and encroaching gentrification. The study offers evidence to indicate that de-industrialization, the shift of jobs from the manufacturing to the service sectors, has contributed to homelessness, especially in low-growth cities.[33]

This overview of theoretical explanations of homelessness exemplifies the minimal extent that most researchers have been able to generate an explicit and

---

[32] Carl I. Cohen and Jay Sokolovsky, Chapter 5, "Alcoholism contributes to homelessness," in Orr, (ed.), The Homeless, p. 80.

[33] Martha Burt, Over The Edge, pp. 216-219.

comprehensive theory of contemporary homelessness. Most have advanced key arguments relating typically two or three of the major dimensions reviewed here, such as housing unaffordability, economic dislocation, family and community breakup, decline in secondary supports, or high levels of personal disability. With the exception of Burt's analysis, and Wilson's dislocation theory which has rarely been used to understand homelessness *per se*, there is virtually no consideration of race and of major demographic trends, such as the aging of the baby boom generation. The arguments, when advanced, are typically supported by only anecdotal data, and sometimes with survey data with limited generalizeability.

A Social Interdependency Model

Social disintegration, as exemplified by the experience of homelessness, is by definition an experience of fragmentation, of the breakup many of the economically, socially, and psychologically interdependent relationships which sustain people. Relationships entail ongoing transactions, which often involve multiple and reciprocal dependencies. Dependency is a broad term which has meaning only in relation to the content of expectations, as well as their context. Employers are dependent on their employees for services, who are in turn dependent on their employing organizations for income and benefits. The concept of interdependency is, thus, central to this model. It is a statement that individuals are for the most part neither victims of circumstances, nor the primary instigators of their failures, but that responsibility almost always needs to be collectively shared.

Among the most central of these interdependent relationships are those which involve work, whether it is for pay, that in support of a family, or other work which contributes to society. Thus, at the heart of the model, which is investigated here, is the relationship of the individual, with whatever capabilities and disabilities, and the existing structure of work and other economic opportunities (see figure 1). There is a reciprocal relationship between the aggregate of individual capabilities and available job opportunities. The presence of many job opportunities provides job experience and training; conversely, a capable work force attracts and creates business.[34] In contrast, the absence of business activity and high unemployment leads to anomie and even increased rates of mental illness,[35] and a workforce with minimal education or high levels of disability risks the exodus of business to competing locales.

The outcome of the many transactions between an area's workforce and its employers, especially if these result in extensive unemployment, is then moderated by the presence of both primary and secondary social supports. Intact and extended families provide primary support and buffering against the economic and emotional assaults of unemployment, especially when there are two wage earners in a family. Failing the support of other family members as well as savings, the unemployed individual must then fall back on secondary or institutional supports, such as mental health services, unemployment compensation, social security disability, or AFDC. These supports, in turn, modify individuals' job aspirations, capabilities, and opportunities. Family support engenders heightened motivation for career advancement; similarly, the availability of rehabilitation and training services create feedback loops involving enhanced job capabilities.

The extent that income is generated through the reciprocal transactions between an area's workforce and its businesses, and then supplemented by primary family and secondary institutional supports, determines a population's ability to rent or purchase housing. Low wages and high unemployment, with few family supports, and scant support from income maintenance programs, makes housing unaffordable. Similarly, extensive disability and associated unemployment contributes to delayed family formation and high divorce rates, increasing the number of one person and single parent households, thus intensifying the demand on the housing market and driving up prices.

Figure 1 provides a simplified rendition of the most central concepts and

---

[34] See Robert Reich, The Work of Nations.

[35] See M. Harvey Brenner, Mental Illness and The Economy (Cambridge: Harvard University Press, 1973).

14

relationships proposed in this model. Those causal relationships included, as indicated by the lines, represent the most critical ones. There are many feedback and reciprocal relationships which could have been included, however, to do so would be to obscure the idea that the accumulated success or failure of the various relationships--between individual capabilities and job opportunities for instance--best explains the level of homelessness in a community.

Individual aspirations, as well as capabilities, disabilities, and available economic opportunities do not exist in a vacuum, but are defined and molded by a range of historical, cultural, political, and environmental conditions.[36] Capabilities and opportunities, most importantly, are developed out of those created by past generations. A few of these conditions which may be most critical to understanding homelessness include racism, the aging of the baby boom generation, and the epidemological transition involving the overall aging of society. Central to the globalization of economic activity, deindustrialization, servicetization, and restructuring are the many technological developments which are dramatically impacting on the demand for unskilled and semi-skilled work. Each of these conditions, to be discussed in chapter 4, complicates one or more of the components of the network of economic opportunities, family supports, or social services outlined in this model.

---

[36] Robert Merton, Contemporary Social Problems (New York: Harcourt Brace Jovanovitsky, 1976).

Figure 1-1. An Interdependency Model of Social Conditions Predictive of Levels of Homelessness

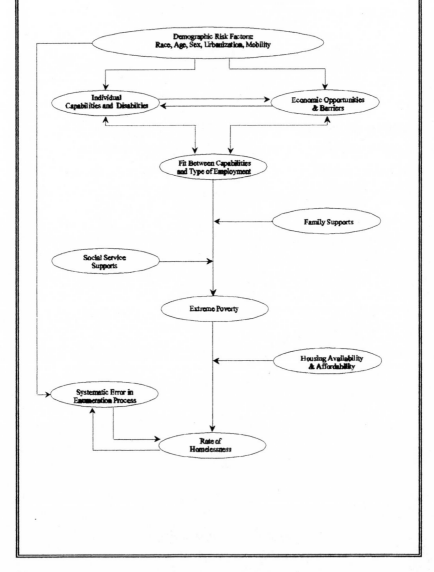

The interdependency model on which this study is based is an old wine in a new bottle. The concepts have been used extensively, and primary credit goes to such people as Robert Merton and William J. Wilson in sociology, and Lillian Ripple and Carol Germain in social work.[37] But it is surprising how infrequently these concepts have guided the study of homelessness and the extent to which research has focused on only one or a few of these dimensions at any one time. The term interdependency has developed several meanings in recent years. One emerges out of functionalism and refers to multiple functions which individuals perform for one another and society as a whole, often cutting across multiple domains of activity such as the economic and personal. Another more developmental as well as prescriptive interpretation has been advanced by Stephen Covey who has suggested that individuals only become capable of consciously and effectively functioning in interdependent relationships after they have mastered early dependencies, and achieved a sense of independence. The ability to manage interdependent relationships is a stage of development beyond independence which American's sense of individualism too often blocks.[38] While the first meaning informs many of the structural analyses conducted in this study, the second underlies the translation of these findings to policy recommendations in the final chapter.

The central aim of this study is, therefore, to test a theory concerning the breakdown of social interdependencies. Specifically, it tests the hypothesis that to the extent that the capabilities of an area's workforce is mismatched with the structure of available job opportunities, and there are minimal and declining levels of primary family and secondary institutional supports, that housing will become unaffordable for many, and these progressively accumulating societal and individual failures result in

---

[37] Robert Merton, Contemporary Social Problems; William J.Wilson, TheTruly Disadvantaged; Lillian Ripple, Motivation. Capacity. and Opportunity: Studies in Casework Theory and Practice (Chicago: School of Social Service Administration, The University of Chicago, 1969); Carel Germain, The Life Model of Social Work Practice (New York: Columbia University Press, 1980).

[38] Stephen R. Covey, The 7 Habits of Highly Effective People (New York: Simon and Schuster, 1989).

high rates of homelessness. It is also hypothesized that the extent of this mismatch, and the resulting homelessness, have been exacerbated by the overall decline in manufacturing jobs, the degree of urbanization, the racial diversity of the area, and the rapid growth of the younger working population due to the aging of the baby boom generation.

Although the hypothesized model does not specify the strength of the relationships between the various components, it does suggest that the most powerful cause of homelessness will be the degree of mismatch between the preparation of the workforce and the available job opportunities. Nonetheless, such a mismatch is probably a necessary but not sufficient condition, one which needs to be accompanied with some combination of family fragmentation, inadequate institutional supports, and a tight housing market, for significant levels of poverty and homelessness to arise. By determining the relative saliency of each of these hypothesized conditions through structural modeling techniques, it is possible to identify points of intervention at which the greatest impact could be expected for a given level of resource allocation. This permits answering a range of questions. For instance, what combination of job training, improvement of general assistance levels, provision of family support or community mental health programs, or funding of Section 8 assisted housing certificates would have the greatest impact on reducing levels of homelessness, nationally and in particular types of communities? Because these hypotheses are tested mainly with cross-sectional data, from one point in time, definitive predictions about such impacts can not be made. Yet when a range of alternative explanations for variations in homeless levels are tested for, such modeling provides one of the strongest bases available for the development of comprehensive and rationale approaches to such multi-dimensional problems such as homelessness.

Plan of the Book

This book presents, tests, and applies the foregoing social interdependency model to understanding variations in homelessness populations throughout the nation, as well as proposing possible remedies based on the findings and on past research. Those familiar with social policy research as well as techniques of structural equation modeling will be interested in reviewing appendix 1, which contains an account of the data on which this model is based, the preliminary transformations and adjustments in it designed to deal with the known problem of the undercount of homeless persons in the 1990 U.S. census, as well as the overall analytic strategy.

Other readers will want to proceed directly to chapter 2 which reviews what is known about the distribution of homeless persons throughout the United States, their characteristics, and the role of major demographic features of the U.S. population, such as its racial diversity, the baby boom generation, immigration, among others, in accounting for observed pattern.

Readers with specialized interests will want to selectively read chapters 3 through 7 which review the evidence for the role of the major dimensions included in the interdependency model: personal disabilities (chapter 3), the job market structure (chapter 4), primary family and other social supports (chapter 5), secondary institutional supports (chapter 6), and housing (chapter 7). The first part of each of these chapters reviews and synthesizes previous research, and is followed by the presentation and analysis of new data.

In chapter 8, the results of a final test of the complete model is presented and interpreted. Although the data does not confirm the model as originally hypothesized and structured in this chapter, it substantially accounts for contemporary levels of homelessness throughout the United States, clearly supporting the role of each of the hypothesized dimensions. However, the analysis reveals a far more modest role for individual disabilities and secondary institutional supports than initially expected. Also included in this chapter are the results of a secondary testing of a simplified or predictive version of the model through comparisons with independent studies, as well as projections of homeless levels to the mid-1990s.

Chapter 9 completes the book by outlining a comprehensive policy initiative which draws on the results of the final testing of the model. The final recom-

mendations involve a linked social development strategy, based on the interdependency model, which integrates individual competency-building and with larger-
scale community-building initiatives through both micro- and meta-linkage
methodologies. It argues for a change in the focus of the current emergency, shelter-
based service system, to one structured around a system of community lodges and an
associated array of housing and rehabilitative options, as well as several initially
targeted policy initiatives designed to grow into more universal social insurance
programs.

Chapter II

THE DIMENSIONS AND CONTEXT OF HOMELESSNESS

Just as an individual's experience is shaped by his or her most visible features, such as age, gender, and race, descriptions of homeless populations ordinarily begin with these same visible characteristics. To the extent that social roles and statuses are shaped by these features, they will affect the likelihood that any given individual will experience homelessness. They are among the risk factors associated with the every day stresses with which an individual might successfully or unsuccessfully cope. Many models of human behavior begin with general risk factors which predispose the individual to particular kinds of problems. This chapter, however, will be restricted mostly to only demographic risk factors, such as age, sex, and race. Other risk factors, such as lack of education or employment, will be examined in subsequent chapters. Demographic risk factors represent an amalgam of diverse influences, ranging from the genetic to the cultural, which although they often can not be specifically measured, collectively create significant risks for both poverty and homelessness.

This chapter, as well as this book, is based on the notion that the development of an understanding of homelessness requires, in part, the measurement or quantification of this problem and its association with various proposed causes. Compassion does not require such measurement, obviously. However, the societal response, whether it is in the form of policies, budgetary allocations, or assignment of staff, is necessarily a measured response and is one which must, as a social investment, have a demonstrably favorable balance of benefits and costs. Anecdotal appeals to compassion, by themselves, probably can at best only convince voters to support a short-term emergency response to the problem.

Counting the Homeless

Throughout the 1980s and early 1990s, there have been numerous attempts to estimate the size of the population of homeless persons, resulting in divergent estimates. In 1982 the Community for Creative Non-Violence pegged the level at over one percent of the population,[39] whereas in 1984 the Department of Housing and Urban Development estimated it at about 0.1 percent, or at the 250 thousand to 350 thousand level.[40] This figure was based on an overall assessment of the relative strength of the results of four estimation methodologies: (I) extrapolation from the highest published estimates; (ii) extrapolation from estimates in 60 cities obtained through 500 local interviews; (iii) extrapolation of estimates from a national sample of 125 shelter operators; and, (iv) a count of the shelter population and local area street count.[41] Three major criticisms have been levied against this effort, and these involve the snowball sampling methods used, lack of specificity in the requests for estimates, and an inappropriate use of RMA population figures to develop national figures. Each of these estimates have been widely discounted because of their methodological flaws, most commonly those involving an attempt to aggregate local guesstimates. Even Mitch Sander, the founder of the Community for Creative Non-Violence, admitted, "...these numbers are in fact meaningless. We have tried to satisfy you gnawing curiosity because we are Americans with little Western minds wanting to quantify everything in sight, whether we can or not."[42]

In one of the very few national studies, the Urban Institute in 1987 utilized

---

[39] Mitch Snyder and Mary Ellen Hombs, Homelessness in America: The Forced March to Nowhere (Washington, D.C.: The Community for Creative Nonviolence, 1983).

[40] U.S. Congress, Joint Hearing before the Subcommittee on Housing and Urban Development of the Committee on Banking, Finance, and Urban Affairs and the Subcommittee on Manpower and Housing of the Committee of Government Operations, HUD Report on Homelessness, 90th Congress, Second Session. May 24, 1984.

[41] See Joel Blau, The Visible Poor: Homelessness in the United States (New York: Oxford University Press, 1992), pp. 21-22.

[42] Ibid., p. 24.

22

random sampling methods in 20 cities throughout the United States and extrapolated from these data that over 0.2 percent of the population was homeless, or between 500 thousand and 600 thousand persons.[43] These data indicated that a disproportionate number of the homeless were single males (73%) and that the findings that families make up a third to a half of the homeless are exaggerated. This data usually originates from shelter-based studies where families are more likely to be found compared to the streets. It has been suggested that this estimate may be comparable with the earlier HUD figures, and if so, it would represent a 22 percent annual increase during the mid-1980s in homelessness.[44]

More recent estimates have typically fallen in the 300 to 800 thousand range (see table 8-2). Two re-analyses of the 1984 HUD study place the figure in the upper end of this range. While the National Alliance to End Homelessness placed it at 735 thousand,[45] that same year HUD adjusted its estimate to 500 to 600 thousand.[46] One of the most recently published estimates is that of Jencks' who used information from Burt's research on the ratio of street to shelter homeless as well as the 1990 U.S. Census count of homeless persons in shelters to estimate the total number at 324 thousand.[47] In contrast, the model to be reported in this book indicates that in 1990 there were at least 480 thousand homeless persons, and 699 thousand if migrants and other persons with no usual home elsewhere are included. This figure uses an adjustment of the 240,140 actually counted, based on known sources of systematic error incorporated into the model (see appendix 1 and chapter 8).

Advocates for the homeless have often argued that any attempt to count the

[43] Martha R. Burt and Barbara E. Cohen, America's Homeless: Numbers, Characteristics, and the Programs that Service Them (Washington, D.C.: Urban Institute Press, 1988).

[44] Martha Burt, Over The Edge, p. 3.

[45] See Institute of Medicine, Homelessness, Health, and Human Needs (Washington, D.C.: National Academy Press, 1988).

[46] Joel Blau, The Visible Poor, p. 24.

[47] Christopher Jencks, The Homeless, (Cambridge: Harvard University Press, 1994), p. 17.

homeless is futile and represents an obfuscation of the problem. Yet, one of the first steps in understanding any social problem is determining who is experiencing it, their personal characteristics and social environments. Enumeration is an inescapable part of understanding, though it should be only a preliminary step. Without baseline data on numbers and characteristics of the homeless in various localities, it is not possible to develop and test models about the interaction of multiple causal factors and determine the most efficacious ways of altering them.

Efforts to enumerate the homeless have been beset with definitional and methodological problems. While most agree that the homeless include those living on the streets and in homeless shelters, there have been recurrent controversies about whether the homeless also include people living in cheap, inexpensive flop houses, those who are institutionalized and who have no other home, and those who are doubled up with friends and relatives. Many who share homes do so simply out of a desire for companionship, however, others do so because of economic necessity. Because of the obvious difficulties of defining and enumerating these later subgroups, most researchers have typically restricted their efforts to the homeless found in shelters and on the streets.

The most intransigent methodological problems have arisen whenever researchers have attempted to count the homeless living on the streets, in abandoned buildings, and other public and semi-public places. Living on the street is inherently dangerous, for this reason, most who do so seek to hide themselves, especially at night. Thus, any attempts to enumerate a complete population of street homeless, is fraught with uncertainty. Several researchers have proposed daytime counts in locations such as soup kitchens. While this is a preferable strategy to night counts, problems remain in that during the day homeless individuals are highly mobile, and this creates the problem of duplicated counting at adjacent locations.

In 1990, the U.S. Census located 240,140 persons, or just under a tenth of a percent (0.096%) of the nation's population, who most would agree were homeless. Most of these (190,406 or 79%) were enumerated in shelters, most commonly those specifically designated for the homeless (see table 2-1). Smaller numbers were found in shelters for runaways (10,329 or 5.4% of sheltered group) and abused women (11,768 or 6.2%). The remaining fifth (49,734 or 21%) were counted on the streets. This is a short-hand term which has come to refer to those homeless found not only literally living on the streets and park benches, but in abandoned buildings, sleeping in cars, bus stations, under viaducts, and in flop houses charging under $12 a night. This has been the most controversial part of the S-Night counts, for which there is strong evidence of a considerable undercount (see appendix 1).

A controversial figure, which has been the basis for numerous national estimates, has been the ratio of the shelter to street population. There is considerable evidence that the U.S. 1990 Census under counted the street population. The ratio of its shelter to street counts was 3.8, which is even higher than what Rossi found in Chicago during the Winter of 1986, 2.8.[48] Both of these, in turn, are greater than the 2.2 which Freeman and Hall used and the 1.8 from the HUD study.[49]

A few years after the Census Bureau released the initial counts, the agency released the counts of a less well known effort to enumerate persons in group quarters "with no usual home elsewhere" (see table 2-1).[50] These are individuals who are technically domiciled, but who few would argue have a home in the usual sense of the term. They are people in "homes" for unwed mothers, drug and alcohol centers, migrant worker dorms, group homes for the mentally ill, among others. These domiciled homeless represent almost as many people as the undomiciled homeless (219,075 or 0.088%). It may be argued that some of these people, such as residents in some group homes for the mentally ill, are in facilities which are sufficiently

[48] Peter H. Rossi, Down and Out in America (Chicago: The University of Chicago Press, 1989), p. 88.

[49] See Richard B. Freeman and Brian Hall, Permanent Homelessness in America? (Cambridge, MA: National Bureau of Economic Research, 1986).

[50] U.S. Bureau of the Census, "Fact sheet for 1990 decennial census counts of persons in selected locations where homeless persons are found," (CPH-L-87), pp. 3-4.

Table 2-1. Overview of Levels of Income Poverty and Homelessness, 1990

Indicator	Number	Percentage
POOR HOUSEHOLDS	11,683,185	12.7%
POOR FAMILIES	6,487,515	10.0%
POOR INDIVIDUALS	31,742,864	13.1%
Poor (75-99% Poverty Level)	9,636,880	4.0%
Very Poor (50-74%)	8,094,306	3.3%
Extremely Poor (Under 50%)	14,011,678	5.8%
KNOWN HOMELESS STATUS	459,215	0.18%
Domiciled (No Usual Home Elsewhere)	219,075	0.09%
Homes for Unwed Mothers	1,682	
Drug/Alcohol Centers	52,038	
Migrant Workers Dorms	35,280	
Group Homes for Mentally Ill	32,348	
Other Non-Household	97,727	
Undomiciled	240,140	0.10%
Emergency Homeless Shelters	168,309	
Shelters for Runaways	10,329	
Shelters for Abused Women	11,768	
Visible on Streets	49,734	
UNKNOWN HOMELESS STATUS		
Non-Family in family households ("Doubled up")	16,146,113	6.50%
Doubled up because of extreme poverty Estimate	1,190,943	0.48%

SOURCE: Computed from U.S. Census STF-1C, STF-3C Data Tapes; Fact Sheet for 1990 Decennial Census Counts of Persons in Selected Locations Where Homeless are Found (CPH-L-87).

homelike that they should not be considered homeless. However homelike some of these places may be, few would contend that they provide the permanence, privacy, security, and affiliations which most associate with the concept of a home. In total, the Census Bureau counted 459,215 persons (0.185%) in 1990 who were homeless, whether domiciled or undomiciled. This figure does not include any adjustments for the undercounting of homeless persons living on the street.

There are several other groups that some have argued are homeless, but others have characterized as the "precariously housed".[51] The Census Bureau includes a category of "non-family in family households" in the decennial census. This group is further subdivided by the relationship between the non-family and the primary family unit, based on whether the persons involved are relatives or non-relatives. This group clearly includes some people who double up because of financial and other emergencies, whether these involve eviction or destruction of a home due to natural disasters, and who would otherwise be completely undomiciled. But undoubtedly the larger part of this group consists of individuals "doubled up" out of a desire for each other's company, or for other non-urgent reasons, including practicality. These include a family putting up an aged parent, a recent college graduate living with his parents to save money, or a family providing a room to an *au par* in return for child care. Almost one out every 15 Americans lives in such a household (16,146,113 or 6.5%), of whom three-quarters (74.0%) are related, and the remaining quarter, not related (table 2-1).

There is currently no certain way to determine what proportion of the doubled-up population are homeless, those who are temporarily doubling up because of a financial emergency and have no usual home elsewhere. Table 2-2 provides data which permit a rough estimate of the size of this population. The table breaks down the rates of doubling-up by the degree of extreme poverty (defined as the proportion of persons under 50% of the poverty line) within the immediate county area. For instance, in those 661 counties where the extreme poverty rate is 3.75% or less, 5.3%

---

[51] Peter Rossi, Down and Out in America, p. 9.

of the population is doubled up. The overall rate of doubling up increases progressively the higher the rate of extreme poverty, until it reaches 9.7% or a tenth of the population in the 78 counties where the extreme poverty rate is over 18%. These data clearly suggest that while many do not double up due to financial exigency, over a million do so as indicated by the strong and significant correlation between the local poverty and doubling up rates. Even in the richest counties some double up because of financial distress. If we assume that the rate of doubling up in these areas (5.3%) represents a close estimate of the proportion of the population who double up for non-emergency reasons, we can calculate the excess over this rate in each of the other five types of areas, in each case apply this rate to the combined population, and then sum the estimates for each of the five types of counties. Then, if we assume that half these people have a regular home and are serving as hosts to the other half who do not, we need to half the resulting estimate. This procedure yields an estimate of 1.2 million, or a scant 7.4% of the doubled up, who are in this state because of extreme poverty and who have no regular home. This estimate is not markedly different from one based on a fairly conservative alternative method. Even if we assume that the extremely poor are no more likely than others to double up, and apply the extreme poverty rate of 5.8% to the doubled up population, we find that there may be over 930 thousand doubled up who are extremely poor.

It should be cautioned that a million doubled up homeless persons is a rough estimate, albeit a conservative one, based on several assumptions. For example, the increasing doubling up in counties with higher levels of extreme poverty may be because these counties are also more rural and the culture may be more supportive of shared households, whether or not there is a financial exigency. This hypothesis was tested through the computation of partial correlation coefficients which permits control for a third variable. While the uncontrolled bivariate correlation between extreme poverty and doubling up is a modest 0.25, this does not decrease, but instead becomes a slightly stronger 0.28 when the level of urbanization is controlled for.

Table 2-2. Relationship of Concentrations of
Extreme Poverty With Doubled-Up Households and Homelessness

Percent Extremely Poor	# Counties; Population; % Nat'l Pop.	Home-less Rate Per 10,000	Doubled-up Households Percent		
			Relatives	Non-Relatives	Total
LOW 3.75 & Under	661 68,785,840 27.7%	5.9	3.8%	1.5%	5.3%
AVERAGE 3.76- 6.25%	1,165 88,968,954 35.8%	8.8	4.2%	1.7%	5.9%
ABOVE AVERAGE 6.25- 8.75%	626 56,104,367 22.6%	9.6	5.9%	1.9%	6.8%
HIGH 8.76- 11.2%	342 19,573,406 7.9%	18.9	6.0%	1.6%	7.6%
VERY HIGH 11.21- 18.0%	267 12,875,098 5.2%	11.1	7.0%	1.8%	8.8%
EXTREME 18.1 & Above	78 2,402,049 1.0%	7.2	8.2%	1.5%	9.7%

Nonetheless, because of these assumptions, it would be premature to characterize this as a firm estimate of the number of homeless persons among the doubled-up, but rather as an estimate of the proportion of those of unknown homeless status who would most likely be literally homeless were it not for the generosity of their relatives or friends. Another group whose homeless status is unknown are those in institutions, such as nursing homes, mental hospitals, and jails. Many of these people, if institutionalized on a short-term basis, maintain a home to which they expect to return. But perhaps the majority, especially those institutionalized on an ongoing or long term basis, have no other place of residence, and some of these lack the financial or personal capabilities to create a home upon their discharge. Whatever the size of this group, they would appreciably increase the size of the domiciled homeless, as it would be difficult to argue that any of these institutions constitute homes in the usual sense of the term.

An ongoing controversy has involved the relationship of homelessness and poverty. On one hand, there are those who would have us believe that poor and non-poor are equally liable to become homeless. On the other hand, there is the view that homelessness is specifically a problem of the extremely poor, and that these conditions are highly correlated. With the exception of those like the famous bag lady who was discovered to be carrying around hundreds of thousands of dollars in paper sacks, it is well established that the homeless are overwhelmingly and extremely poor. It has been estimated that the average homeless persons survives on a budget of between 25% and 40% of the poverty level.[52] It has also been found that,

> The job histories of the homeless show them to have been among the extremely poor and unemployed for years. On the average, it was more than 4.5 years since their last steady full-time job, with a median being 3.3 years. However, the homeless had been unemployed much longer than they had been homeless, by an average of about 3 years.[53]

In this respect, poverty and homelessness are strongly associated in that poverty can reliably be predicted from a person's homeless status. But the reverse is not true, as only 1.4 percent of people who are poor are also homeless.

In 1990, more than an eighth (13.1%) of the U.S. population or 31.7 million persons fell below the poverty level. These individuals typically had incomes dramatically below the poverty line: while less than a third (30.4%) had incomes between 75% and 99% of the poverty level, four-ninths (44.1%) had incomes less than 50% of the official poverty line. Close to an equal proportion of households fell below the poverty line (12.7%), and a lower one-tenth (10.0%) of all family units

---

[52] James Wright, Address Unknown: The Homeless in America (New York: Aldine, 1989), p. 130.

[53] Ibid., p. 72.

experienced the same (see table 2-1).

The question about the association between poverty and homelessness is usually posed as a question of their association on the aggregate or community level. Considered from this perspective, there is only an almost negligible 0.12 ($\alpha < 0.01$) correlation of county homeless rates with their poverty rates. The zero-order correlation of homelessness with the rate of extreme poverty, however, is clearly evident at 0.20 ($\alpha < 0.01$), and of particular concern is the 0.38 ($\alpha < 0.01$) correlation of homelessness with the minority poverty rate.

Table 2-2 provides a more in depth view. When rates of homelessness are calculated for counties with various levels of extreme poverty, it becomes clear that there is not a linear, but a curvilinear relationship between poverty and homelessness. In the counties with the lowest rates of poverty, there are 5.9 homeless persons per 10 thousand persons. This rate grows progressively to 18.9 in the areas with relatively high poverty. But in those counties with very high (11.2%-18%) and extreme levels (over 18%) of people living under half the poverty level, the homeless rate drops progressively to 7.2%. There may be several reasons for this. When the poverty of a community reaches a threshold level of visibility, the homeless decide to leave their home town for more urban areas. A somewhat less plausible hypothesis would be that, with poverty so pervasive, the community is less inclined to blame the individual and, therefore, more likely to provide formal and informal supports. When computed as a curvilinear relationship, the 0.20 correlation increases significantly to 0.23.

The association of poverty with urban conditions is less pronounced, but nevertheless reveals a similar pattern as does homelessness. Figure 2-1 reveals the highest levels of overall poverty, and the second highest levels of extreme poverty, in the most rural areas (16.4% and 6.4%). These dip progressively to 10.7% and 5.0% in areas with intermediate levels of urbanization, and then rebound to the second highest level (14%) of overall poverty and the highest level of extreme poverty (7.5%) in areas which are highly urbanized. These data indicate that the highest levels of poverty are in the most rural and the most urbanized parts of the country.

Nonetheless, when poverty is found it is most extreme in the most urbanized areas. In entirely rural areas, just under two-fifths (38.9%) of the poor receive less than half the poverty-line income. This proportion increases progressively as urbanization increases: in the most urbanized counties, just over half of the poor (50.1%) receive a similar abysmal level of income.

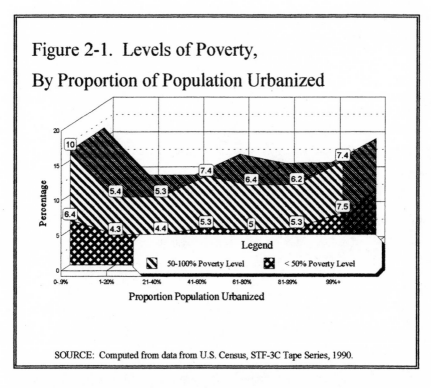

Figure 2-1. Levels of Poverty, By Proportion of Population Urbanized

SOURCE: Computed from data from U.S. Census, STF-3C Tape Series, 1990.

One of the most apparent features of the overall geographic distribution of homeless persons in the United States is its strong association with the major urban areas in the Northeast, West, and Midwest. Figure 2-2 plots the mean levels of homelessness among counties with varying levels of urbanization. Urbanization, for the purpose of this analysis, is regarded as the percentage of a county's population which resides in an urbanized area as defined by the U.S. Bureau of the Census. It

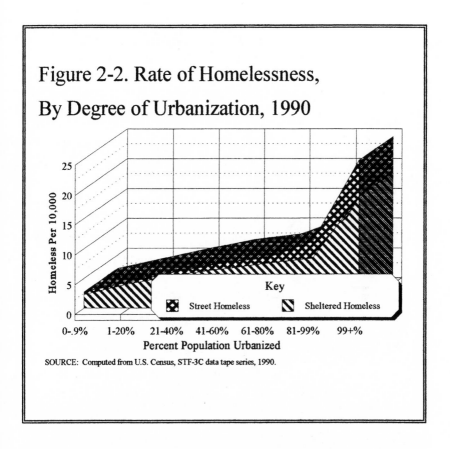

Figure 2-2. Rate of Homelessness,
By Degree of Urbanization, 1990

Homeless Per 10,000

Key
Street Homeless   Sheltered Homeless

0-.9%   1-20%   21-40%   41-60%   61-80%   81-99%   99+%
Percent Population Urbanized

SOURCE: Computed from U.S. Census, STF-3C data tape series, 1990.

is a broad definition which goes beyond the confines of the inner city to include suburban areas. Overall levels of homeless persons per 10,000 population increase about nine-fold, from 2.8 to 24.7, as urbanization increases from the lowest to highest levels. This pattern is most apparent when the street counts are considered, as the level increases by a factor of 15, from 0.4 to 6.0. In contrast, the sheltered differential is about 8, increasing from 2.3 to 18.7. These data suggest that while homelessness is primarily an urban problem, urban areas have done more to provide emergency shelter services for the homeless.

33

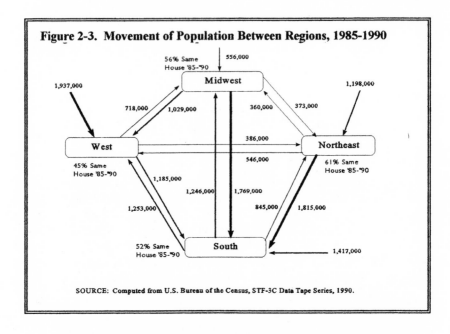

Figure 2-3. Movement of Population Between Regions, 1985-1990

56% Same House '85-'90 556,000

Midwest

1,937,000   1,198,000

718,000   1,029,000   360,000   373,000

West   Northeast

45% Same House '85-'90   386,000   61% Same House '85-'90

546,000

1,185,000

1,246,000   1,769,000

1,253,000   845,000   1,815,000

52% Same House '85-'90   South   1,417,000

SOURCE: Computed from U.S. Bureau of the Census, STF-3C Data Tape Series, 1990.

The same pattern is found regardless of the way county urbanization is defined. For instance, as population density increases from the 1st to the 10th decile, the rate of homelessness increases from 3.4 to 13.1. Similarly, if the absolute population size is considered, homelessness increases from 1.1 in counties of less than 10,000 population to 16.8 in those with a million or more. While the correlation with population size is a modest ($r = 0.28$), that with population density is moderately strong ($r = 0.57$). These correlations no doubt understate the magnitude of what is actually a curvilinear relationship, as revealed in figure 2-2. How much of this apparent association of homelessness with urban areas is a reflection of the greater search efforts undertaken by the U.S. Census in urban areas is unknown. However, it is implausible that such a strong and consistent association could be entirely accounted for by such systematic measurement error, a hypothesis which is tested in this study (see concluding section of this chapter).

The association of homelessness with urban conditions provides an important clue for disentangling the underlying causal nexus. A key demographic feature of urban areas is social mobility. Homelessness is by definition a condition involving the breakdown in patterns of social mobility: people are forced to move, but have no place to move to. If everyone who had a home did not move, the generation of new homeless persons would be brought to a standstill (excepting the experience of immigrants and refugees, and other new population growth). Figure 2-3, based on 1990 census data, illustrates the overall regional shifts of population between 1985 and 1990. It illustrates the continuing shifts of populations to the South and West. It also indicates the relatively greater residential stability in the Northeast, as 61% of the population were in the same home over the five years, in contrast to the moderate levels of 56% in the Midwest and 52% in the South, and the low level in the West of 45%. The pattern revealed here has a moderately small association with the observed distribution of homeless persons. On the county level, there is a -0.26 correlation between the proportion of a county's population which was in the same house in 1985 as in 1990, with the rate of homelessness, indicating that the greater the residential stability, the fewer the homeless. Two other more specific indicators, however, reveal a similar pattern. Just as the greater the percentage of people who were born in their state of residence is associated with lower levels of homelessness (r = -0.29), the more foreign born, the more homeless (r = 0.61). Each of these associations suggest that the more people move, the more they risk losing a permanent home.

Data from previous surveys of homeless persons indicate that the homeless, while mobile, are largely stable within their city and state of residence. For instance, close to half (45.8%) the subjects Rossi interviewed in Chicago were born in Illinois.[54] It has been reported that nationally, 76 percent of the sheltered population have lived for more than one year in the area of their shelter.[55]

---

[54] Peter Rossi, Down and Out in America, p. 126.

[55] Joel Blau, The Visible Poor, p. 28.

35

The Geographic Distribution

The role of urbanization in the distribution of homeless persons throughout the United States is particularly apparent when the relative rates are depicted on a map of the nation. Figure 2-4 contains these results and reveals that the highest rates are not merely in urban areas, but in the coastal urban areas of the Northeast, Florida, and Pacific regions, and to a lesser degree, the urban areas adjacent to the Great Lakes. These are all areas which have seen considerable growth as a result of the globalization of economic activity, a rapid expansion of the service sector of the economies, accompanied by dramatic reductions in opportunities for unskilled labor and low-cost housing, topics which will be explored in subsequent chapters.

Had the actual numbers of homeless, rather than the rates, been plotted on this map, the preponderance of the homeless in urban areas would be particularly dramatic. The county-level map, with an overlay of the state boundaries, reveals little systematic variation between states *per se*, with the exception of a few of those in the southwest where some of the state borders suggest systematic changes in the rates, and thus, risk of homelessness.

Unlike the distribution of homeless persons throughout the nation, the distribution of extremely poor persons is associated with less accessible rural areas, especially those with oppressed minorities groups. Figure 2-5 maps these rates, revealing that the poorest areas consist predominantly of the Appalachian region of Kentucky and West Virginia, the deep South areas of consisting of many low-income blacks, the Rio Grande area, and the Indian Reservations of the Four Corners of the South West, as well as the Sioux reservations of the Dakotas. Because literal homelessness is relatively low in many of these areas, perhaps because of the availability of low-cost housing, there is only a weak association between the rates of homelessness and extreme poverty, as noted in the foregoing section. However, the reader should be reminded that national maps such as these are of such a scale that they can not reflect the extreme but highly localized poverty and homelessness characteristic of the poorest tracts of the inner city.

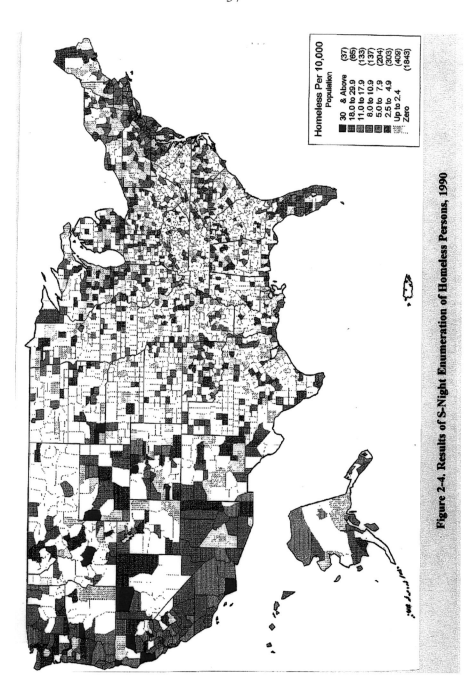

Figure 2-4. Results of S-Night Enumeration of Homeless Persons, 1990

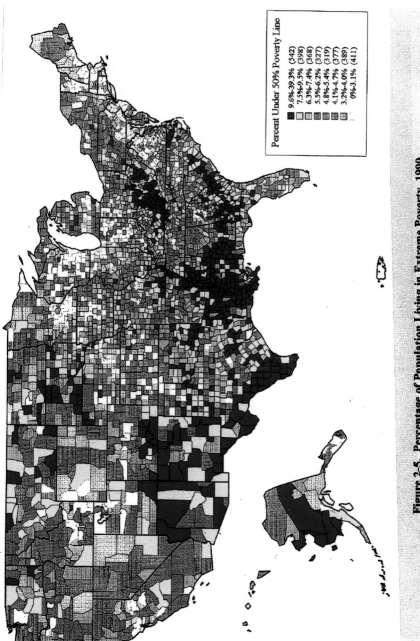

Figure 2-5. Percentage of Population Living in Extreme Poverty, 1990

Percent Under 50% Poverty Line
- 9.6%-39.3% (542)
- 7.5%-9.5% (398)
- 6.3%-7.4% (368)
- 5.5%-6.2% (327)
- 4.8%-5.4% (319)
- 4.1%-4.7% (377)
- 3.2%-4.0% (389)
- 0%-3.1% (411)

Subgroups of the Homeless

Although the homeless represent a diverse population, representing major demographic groups in American society, several subgroups are disproportionately represented. Males, minorities of color, young people in the 18 to 34 age range, and the never married are the groups greatest risk of experiencing homelessness, especially in urban areas. The data supporting this profile comes from the 1990 U.S. Census, as well as a series of multi-city and state studies, sources which demonstrate a remarkable level of agreement in a field of research known for its disparate findings.

While close to a fifth (18.8%) of the homeless are children or adolescents, two-fifths (39.2%) are young adults in the 18 to 34 age range, and the remaining two-fifths (41.9%) are either middle aged or older adults (see table 2-3). The mix of ages varies considerably between homeless shelters where upwards of a half (45.3%) are in the over 35 age group. In contrast, of those visible on the street, over a half (50.5%) are in the over 35 age group and relatively few are children (4.9%). These percentages, based on 1990 Census data, are almost identical to those from a multi-city survey of shelter and street homeless in 1987 conducted by the Urban Institute.[56] Excluding children, the Census revealed a 49.0% to 51.0% split between the two adult categories, almost the same as a 50.5% to 50.1% split found in the Urban Institute study which also excluded children.[57]

Most reviews of the research place both the mean and median age at the same level as the above figures. Rossi review of 23 studies placed it at 36.1, and from another 21 studies, the mean was the same.[58] There is extremely little variation between regions. Several studies from New York all place the average at this same level, as well as research from Ohio, St. Louis, Minneapolis, and Los Angeles.[59]

---

[56] Computed from Martha Burt, Over the Edge, pp. 14-15.

[57] Ibid., pp. 14-15.

[58] Peter Rossi, Down and Out in America, p. 121.

[59] Joel Blau, The Visible Poor, p. 25.

Table 2-3. Percentage of Homeless Persons in Selected Groups, By Type of Site

	Homeless Shelters	Shelters for Runaways	Visible on Street	Battered Women's Shelters	Total
AGE					
0-17	17.1	82.3	4.9	47.7	18.9
18-34	37.6	15.5	50.5	35.6	39.2
35+	45.3	2.1	44.6	16.6	41.9
GENDER					
Male	69.9	54.5	78.9	21.5	68.8
Female	30.1	45.5	21.1	78.5	31.2
RACE-GENDER					
White Male	35.7	28.5	38.7	11.7	34.8
White Female	13.3	24.2	9.4	46.5	14.6
Minority Male	34.3	26.0	40.2	9.9	34.0
Minority Female	16.7	21.3	11.6	31.9	16.6
RACE					
White	49.0	52.7	48.2	58.2	49.4
Minority	51.0	47.3	51.8	41.8	50.6
TOTAL	100.0	100.0	100.0	100.0	100.0

SOURCE: Computed from 1990 U.S. Census (STF-2C Data Tape).

**Table 2-4. Rates of Homelessness for Selected Groups,
By Type of Site (Per 10,000)**

	Homeless Shelters	Shelters for Runaways	Visible on Street	Battered Women's Shelters	Total
AGE					
0-17	4.9	1.4	0.4	0.9	7.5
18-34	8.7	0.2	3.3	0.6	12.9
35+	6.7	0.2	1.9	0.2	8.8
GENDER					
Male	9.8	0.5	3.2	0.2	13.7
Female	3.9	0.4	0.8	0.7	5.8
RACE-GENDER					
White Male	6.6	0.3	2.3	0.3	9.3
White Female	2.4	0.3	0.6	0.5	3.7
Minority Male	21.7	1.2	5.8	0.8	29.5
Minority Female	9.9	0.9	1.6	2.2	14.6
RACE					
White	4.5	0.3	1.4	0.4	6.5
Minority	15.7	1.1	3.7	0.9	21.9
TOTAL	6.8	0.4	2.0	0.5	9.7

NOTES: Rates are computed based on total population in designated group, i.e. 7.5 rate for 0-17 year olds means that there are 7.5 homeless 0-17 year olds for each 10,000 persons of this same age group.
SOURCE: Computed from 1990 U.S. Census (STF-2C Data Tape).

The age breakdown of people who are currently homeless provides important clues as to their service needs. However, to understand the role of age in influencing vulnerability to homelessness, group specific population rates are more revealing. Table 2-4 presents such rates, specifically, the number of homeless persons in the designated subgroup who are homeless, out of each 10 thousand persons in the same subgroup in the overall population. These rates reveal that young adults, those in the 18 to 34 age group, have about a 50 percent greater likelihood of being homeless than children or older adults. Just about 13 out of each 10 thousand young adults are homeless, compared to 7.5 and 8.8 in the younger and older age groups. Urbanization clearly aggravates the vulnerability to homelessness, especially among adults as their rates grow by a factor of 6 for younger adults, and 7 for older adults, compared to a 4.3 increase for children, between the most rural and the most urbanized counties (see table 2-5).

One of the most pronounced characteristics of the contemporary homeless population is the over-representation of men: more than two-thirds of the homeless, or 68.8%, are males, in contrast to the 31.2% who are females (see table 2-3). This is almost identical to the Urban Study's 68.4%-31.6% male-female split.[60] It is, however, less than the 79.7% which Rossi calculated as an average of 37 homeless studies.[61]

The Census figures are supported by the findings from Rossi's 1986 Chicago study. While Rossi found over four-fifths (81.8%) of the street homeless to be males, and 70.4% of those in shelters,[62] the Census likewise found 78.9% of those on the streets and 69.9% of those in shelters to be men.

---

[60] Computed from, Martha Burt, Over The Edge, pp. 14-15.

[61] Peter Rossi, Down and Out in America, p. 118.

[62] Ibid., p. 118.

42

Table 2-5. Rates of Homelessness for Selected Groups, By Level of Urbanization (Per 10,000)

	RUR-AL	URBAN						
		50,000-99,999	100,000-249,999	250,000-499,999	500,000-999,999	1 M-2.5 M	2.5 M-5 M	5 M+
AGE								
0-17	3.2	5.9	6.3	6.7	6.1	6.0	8.1	13.7
18-34	4.1	8.7	9.1	10.6	10.6	14.7	14.7	24.4
35+	2.3	7.8	7.3	7.3	8.4	10.0	9.7	16.1
SEX								
Male	3.6	9.7	10.2	11.5	12.4	16.3	14.9	25.0
Female	2.3	5.7	4.9	4.6	4.7	4.9	5.7	11.5
RACE-SEX								
White Male	3.4	8.3	8.8	9.5	9.3	31.1	8.0	14.1
White Female	2.1	4.4	4.2	3.6	3.6	3.5	3.2	5.6
Minority Male	10.4	25.8	24.2	28.1	28.2	32.5	30.0	47.9
Minority Female	7.7	24.9	12.6	14.3	10.7	11.8	12.0	24.4
RACE								
White	2.7	6.3	6.4	6.5	6.4	8.2	5.6	9.8
Minority	9.1	25.2	18.4	21.2	19.1	21.9	20.6	35.8
TOTAL	2.9	7.7	7.5	8.0	8.4	10.5	10.2	18.0

NOTES: Rates are computed based on total population in designated group, i.e. 3.2 rate for 0-17 year olds under Rural areas means there are 7.5 homeless 0-17 year olds for each 10,0000 persons of this same age living in these areas.

SOURCE: Computed from 1990 U.S. Census (STF-2C Data Tape).

The group specific rates for males (see table 2-4) reveal that men, with a rate of 13.7, are almost two and half times as likely to be homeless than are women, who have a 5.8 rate. The disparity is most apparent with the street homeless, with a male-female split of 3.2 - 0.8, but still quite pronounced in the shelter population with its 9.8 - 3.9 differential. Just as is the case with adults, males are most dramatically impacted by the conditions of urban areas. In the most rural counties, men are about 1.6 times as likely to be homeless as women, whereas in the most urbanized areas, they are over twice (2.2) as vulnerable. Despite the effects of urbanization, the disparity between male and female rates are the lowest in the New England (1.7) and Mid-Atlantic States (2.0), and highest in the Western Mountain (2.8) and Pacific (2.7) states (see table 2-5).

The preponderance of males among the homeless represents a paradox, one which appears to contradict the well known trend in recent years towards the feminization of poverty. In 1990, among working age adults, 18 to 64, women had a 12.8% poverty rate, compared to 9.2% for men. This disparity is aggravated by the effects of age, as women over 65 have almost twice the 8.4% poverty rate of men in the same age group (15.8%). The structure of employment and retirement opportunities generally favor men, minimizing their overall poverty rates. However, when men fail to capitalize on these opportunities, their failures may be more acute due to the greater likelihood they will be viewed as the non-deserving poor. Women, in contrast, are more likely to be economically disenfranchised as reflected in their higher poverty rates, but when they are impoverished, they are more likely to be viewed as among the deserving poor and be considered eligible for a wider range of income maintenance and social welfare benefits than are men.

One of the most important demographic characteristics associated with a person's likelihood of becoming homeless is race. Just over half (50.6%) of the homeless are persons of color (see table 2-3). Some studies, such as the Urban Institute's, have placed this as high as 57%,[63] a finding which may reflect a slight

---

[63] Computed from Martha Burt, Over The Edge, p. 14.

tendency for there to be a greater proportion of non-whites in the most urban counties. This is very similar to the results of Rossi's review of 31 homeless studies in which he reported a mean of 45.8% backs and 11.8% Hispanic.[64] Many researchers still classify Hispanics as non-white, whereas the U.S. Census regards Hispanic status not as a racial but a cultural group, individuals of which may be either white or black. Another study of the clientele of the Robert Wood Johnson's health care program for the homeless in 16 cities found that an identical 51% were non-white.[65]

Rarely has minority status been identified in the literature as a condition which places people at risk of homelessness, and when it has, it has often been discounted through the observation that the inner cities, where homeless are most likely to be found, have higher proportions of minority populations. Yet, the group specific rates for minorities of color are highest, demonstrating their over- representation among the homeless. Minorities have a rate of homelessness (21.9 per 10,000) over three times that of whites (6.5). This disparity produces a moderate correlation of 0.49 between a counties' proportion of non-whites and its rate of homelessness. Urbanization appears to only moderately aggravate the effects of race, as a 3.4 differential between minority and white rates in the most rural areas grows to 3.7 cities over 2.5 million population. However, this is not a consistent trend in areas with moderate levels of urbanization. The ratio between the minority and white rates is greatest in the Mid-Atlantic (5.9), New England (5.1), East North Central (4.4), and West North Central states (4.6), and least in the Pacific states (1.8).

There is clearly a dramatic interaction between gender, race, and urbanization which collectively are associated with extreme rates of homelessness among minorities in the largest cities, especially among males. Almost one in every two hundred black males in cities over 5 million population are homeless (47.9 per

---

[64]   Peter Rossi, Down and Out in America, p. 123.

[65]   See Richard First, Dee Roth, and Bobbie D. Arewa, "Homelessness: Understanding the dimensions of the problem for minorities," Social Work 33 (2): pp. 120-24 (March-April 1988).

10,000), and about half as many black women (24.4). This contrasts with a moderate 14.1 rate for white males, and a more favorable 5.6 rate for white females. Prior to the 1980s, few studies noted many persons of color among the homeless. Thus, it is clear that racial minorities have emerged as a growing and key sub-group among the homeless. Understanding homelessness, thus, requires an appreciation of the growing impact of racism in the increasingly hierarchical structure of American society.

One other characteristic of homeless persons which needs to be noted here is marital status, a topic which will be elaborated on in Chapter 6 which examines the role of the family. Specifically, the homeless are overwhelmingly single adults, especially those with few family ties. Some of the most detailed data on marital status comes from the Urban Institute study which found that over four-fifths (82%) of homeless adults were single, another tenth (9%) were accompanied by other adults, and a final tenth, mostly women, had children with them. Only 11.6% of the 1,700 respondents were found to be currently married, with over a half (54%) never married, and the remaining third (34.3%) divorced, separated, or widowed. Only a quarter (25.3%) of those who have ever been married were married at the time of being interviewed.[66] Burt's overall finding that 88.4% of the homeless are currently unmarried is virtually identical with the result of Rossi's review of 26 studies which reported a mean of 88.5% currently unmarried.[67] It is clear from Burt's 54% never married figure that homeless individuals lack immediate family supports to begin with. It is, however, unclear what proportion of the 34.3% previously married experienced divorces, separations, or bereavements prior to or after the start of their first homeless episode. The possibility that homeless individuals are predominantly being recruited from the larger population of single person households is supported by a strong bivariate correlation of 0.59 ($\alpha < .001$) between the rate of homelessness in each of the nation's 3,141 counties and the proportion of its households which contain only

---

[66] Computed from, Martha Burt, Over The Edge, pp. 14-15.

[67] Peter Rossi, Down and Out in America, p. 129.

one person. Weaker but still significant correlations were found with the proportion of female headed households (r = 0.31) and the proportion of adults who were separated, widowed, or divorced (r = 0.28). The extent that the lack of primary family supports is a cause of homelessness or a symptom of other personal or economic problems will be explored in subsequent chapters. Here it will suffice to identify the subgroups involved and their apparent association with the size of an area's homeless population.

The over representation of young single people in the homeless population suggests that several possibilities involving the impact of general population shifts. One is that overall population growth has fueled the development of homelessness. A related hypothesis is that the aging of the baby boom generation, those born between 1945 and 1964, has created particularly intense competitive pressures on young adults, resulting in the development of current homeless populations. The other involves what has been referred to the epidemiological transition, which involves improving socioeconomic conditions, the resulting increase in average ages and the development of a larger population of older adults, and among other things, increased political pressures to shift resources and services to older adults.[68] Table 2-6 presents preliminary tests of these three possibilities in respect to the contribution of these trends to both poverty and homelessness. Between 1980 and 1990 the overall U.S. population grew by just about a tenth (9.8%). The extent of this growth was, however, not associated with overall levels of homelessness, and only negligibly with the specific shelter and street rates. The growth, however, was associated with a diminution of overall poverty levels, suggesting that the economic activity that is stimulated by such growth has had a beneficial impact.

---

[68] See S. Jay Olshansky and A. Brian Ault, "The fourth stage of the epidemiological transition: The age of delayed degenerative diseases," Milbank Quarterly, 64 (3), p. 355 (1986).

Table 2-6. The Impact of Population and Aging Trends on Individual Poverty and Homelessness: 1980-1990

| | In Millions | | % Change 1980-1990 | Pearson's r with: | | | | |
| | | | | Poverty Rate | | Homeless Rate | | |
	1980	1990		Individual	Extreme Individual	Total	Shelter	Street
POPULATION								
Total	226.5	248.7	9.8%	$-.24^c$	$-.12^c$	$-.02$	$-.07^b$	$.09^c$
Age 26-45 ('90) (Baby Boom)	62.7 (28%)	80.8 (32%)	28.8%	$-.23^c$	$-.08^c$	$.01$	$-.04^a$	$.10^c$
Age 65+	25.5 (11%)	31.2 (13%)	22.4%	$.20^c$	$-.31^c$	$-.20^c$	$-.21^c$	$-.13^c$
MEDIAN AGE	30.0	33.4	11.3	$.04^a$	$-.12^c$	$-.30^c$	$-.27^c$	$-.27^c$

NOTE: Pearson r's represent zero-order correlations between rates in 3,141 counties. All correlations are weighted using relative population size of county.

[a]. $\alpha < 0.05$

[b]. $\alpha < 0.01$

[c]. $\alpha < 0.0001$

The overall growth of the 25 to 44 age group--the baby boom in 1990--was a dramatic 28.8%. And, just as was the case with overall population growth, the emergence of the baby boom into the prime age range of the homeless population (mean age 36) had no effect on the overall homeless rates as would be expected (0.01), and a very small effect ($r = 0.10$) on the rate of street homeless. Furthermore, the aging of the baby boom generation served to diminish overall poverty levels.

Two areas of impact of the continuing epidemiological transition were examined. The growth of the over 65 population between 1980 and 1990 was calculated to be 22.4%, and instead of aggravating the rates of homelessness, it served to diminish them. But, in the case of poverty, the growth of the over 65 population has diminished the rate of extreme poverty--including that among the aged due to the indexing of social security benefits--but has also been associated with an overall increase in poverty, no doubt the percentage of persons just below the poverty line. Similarly, as median age has increased from 30.0 to 33.4, the overall aging of U.S. society has clearly been associated with lower, not higher rates of homelessness. This analysis suggests that although overall population growth and the aging of the baby boom generation have had little impact on the development of homelessness, that improving economic conditions for the increasing proportion of older adults is having a somewhat positive impact in diminishing levels of homelessness. The relatively low rates of homelessness among those over 35 (8.8 / 10,000), and extremely low levels among the over 65, is consistent with such an interpretation. Another explanation involves shifts of population as people age and the increasing segregation of socioeconomic and age groups.

Patterns of Homelessness

Much of the research on homeless persons has examined this population at one point in time, and thus, has tended to portray it in static terms, missing many of the complicated dynamics how people enter and exit the homeless condition. Nonetheless, there is substantial information on temporal patterns which can be inferred from cross-sectional studies, as well as from a few longitudinal and ethnographic studies. This section will, therefore, digress from the overall focus of this chapter to review what is known about what happens prior to the first homeless episode, the length and types of homelessness, and the 'careers' of homeless persons.

The individual who eventually becomes homeless typically experiences an extended period of unemployment and impoverishment. During this time he or she doubles up with friends and family and eventually exhausts his or her welcome, sometimes due to concomitant mental illness, substance abuse, or criminal involvements. For many others, however, extended unemployment is accompanied by a life in single room occupancy units, cheap hotels, or Y's. These arrangements

49

also eventually fail, either due to deepening impoverishment, disruptive behavior, or destruction of the properties due to renovation or arson.[69] An important exception to this pattern are women, along with their children, who are escaping dysfunctional or abusive marriages. Many of these women have not been indigent, and experience poverty and homelessness initially at the same time. These women often have little work experience or self-confidence, as well as no child care, and may be paralyzed in their efforts to respond to their new circumstances.[70]

A key question in homeless research has involved how long people typically are homeless: to what extent are we confronted with individuals requiring acute and other emergency services, versus those requiring a range of additional services and supports? Unfortunately this has been an issue for which the research has failed to produce a consistent picture, no doubt due to the variety of populations surveyed as well as the ways the questions are asked and data analyzed. One study which inquired about time since the first homeless episode revealed a mean of 4.1 years and a median of 0.8 years.[71] In contrast, Rossi's review of five studies placed the mean length of the current episode at 25.6 months. The mean, however, tends to be an inflated figure due to a small subgroup of individuals who are homeless for extended periods of time. The median, the most typical value, is more appropriate as it is not as influenced by a small minority of individuals with extreme values. In his own study of the homeless of Chicago, Rossi found that while the mean length was 21.9 months, the median was 7.6 months. This finding is more similar with that of his review of a larger collection of 13 studies in which he reported that 44.6% were homeless for 6 months or more, and 26.6%, one year or more (this would imply a median of just

---

[69] Rene I. Jahiel, Chapter 4, "Empirical studies of homeless populations in the 1980s," in Rene I. Jahiel, (ed.), Homelessness: A Prevention-oriented Approach (Baltimore: John Hopkins Press, 1992), p. 40.

[70] Kay Y. McChresney, "Homeless families: Four patterns of poverty," in Marjorie Robertson and Milton Greenblatt, (eds.), Homelessness: A National Perspective (New York: Plenum Books, 1992), p. 245.

[71] Westerfelt, "The ins and outs of homelessness," p. 112.

over 5 months).[72] Medians from other studies range between about one month in Minneapolis,[73] two months in Ohio,[74] to 74 weeks in Los Angeles.[75] The Urban Institute's multi-city research would place the median in the middle part of this range, as they found that fewer than one-fourth (24%) had been homeless for 3 months or less.[76]

These variations reflect not only methodological differences in the studies, but also differences in the populations and service systems involved. In his 1986 Chicago study, Rossi found that the homeless in shelters had generally been homeless less often than those on the streets, as only 9.4% had been homeless continuously in the previous five years, and 25.3% more than once during this period. In contrast, 13.4% of the street homeless had been homeless continuously, and 39.7% had more than one episode of homelessness.[77] A large scale survey of close to a thousand homeless persons in Ohio found substantial variations in length of episode based on both gender and race. While men were homeless for a median of 90 days, women were for 35 days. An even more dramatic disparity was found for whites and blacks in Ohio: while whites had a median episode of 90 days, blacks had been homeless for a median of 30 days.[78] Each of the above figures are not estimates of the length of an episode of homelessness, but of the length of the current episode up until the time of data collection. Each of the respondents will continue to be homeless, some for brief

---

[72] Peter Rossi, Down and Out in America, p. 95.

[73] Herb Westerfelt, "The ins and outs of homelessness," p. 112.

[74] Dee Roth, Beverly G. Toomey, and Richard J. First, Chapter 15, "Gender, racial, and age variations among the homeless," in Marjorie Robertson and Milton Greenblatt, (eds.), Homelessness: A National Perspective.

[75] Richard H. Ropers, The Invisible Homeless: A New Urban Ecology (New York: Human Sciences Press, 1988), p. 45.

[76] Computed from Martha Burt, Over The Edge, p. 18.

[77] Peter Rossi, Down and Out in America, p. 96.

[78] Richard First, Dee Roth, and Bobbie Arewa, "Homelessness: Understanding the dimension of the problem for minorities," pp. 120-24.

periods, some for extended periods. If it assumed that the overall homeless population has stabilized, and that incidence of new entries and exits is balanced and fairly evenly distributed over time, we can conclude that these estimates represent approximately half the actual length of a typical homeless episode. Thus, if it is estimated that 5 months is the median length of the current episode up to data collection, based on the reported range of findings in the research, the actual length of these episodes should be about 10 months. If homelessness was increasing, with more entries than exits (i.e. finding a home, institutionalization, or death) during the period of these studies, then the 10 month estimate would be on the low side, as the typical respondent would be less than half way through their episode when interviewed. And conversely, if respondents were finding homes faster than new people were losing them, then the typical respondent would be more than half way through their episode, and the estimate would error on the high side.

Both the demographics and the data on length of homeless episodes portray the homeless as a heterogeneous population consisting of a variety of subgroups, each with its distinctive needs. For this reason, considerable effort has been invested in defining typologies of the homeless, but with minimal agreement. Each of the proposed typologies are based on one or a combination of principles, most commonly, (i) sleeping arrangement, (ii) etiology, (iii) duration, (iv) service need, (v) a combination of the foregoing, or (vi) other special considerations. Those based on sleeping arrangement, duration, or some combination of these, have been the most widely used, whereas the others based on etiology or service needs require considerably greater information for their use.

A well known example of a typology based on sleeping arrangement was developed by Roth and his associates, based on the Ohio homeless study. Their initial version identified homeless sleeping in, (i) cars, abandoned buildings, or public facilities; (ii) shelters or missions specifically designed for the homeless; (iii) flop houses or cheap hotels; (iv) cheap hotels with longer term rates; and (v) limited or no shelter, including people who sleep on benches, under bridges, or in cardboard boxes.[79] This was later simplified to three groups, (i) street people, (ii) shelter people, including anyone who used a shelter in the previous 30 days; and, (iii) resource people, who use cheap motels, family, friends, etc.

Probably the next most commonly used typology is that based on duration, an example of which was advanced by Ropers: (i) long term homeless, no present residence, and homeless longer than 12 months; (ii) episodic homeless, those with no present residence, homeless less than 12 months, with at least one previous episode; and, (iii) transitional homeless, those with no present stable residence, less than 12 months, with no past episodes.[80]

Typologies based on etiology or need, though more difficult to use, have greater potential as an aid to service planning. A U.S. Department of Housing and Urban Affairs report included an etiological breakdown of the homeless between the following three groups: (i) chronically disabled; (ii) those experience personal crises; (iii) and those experiencing the effects of adverse economic conditions.[81] Finally, Redburn proposes that the homeless be grouped according to their primary service need: (i) shelter (21%); (ii) crisis care (21%); (iii) developmental services (27%); or, (iv) custodial services (31%).[82]

There are, in addition, more specialized efforts to categorize subgroups of the homeless, ones which highlight the diversity of needs of homeless persons who otherwise appear to be similar. An important subgroup are homeless families, a population which consists of (i) unemployed couples, who may or may not have children with them. These typically include men with marginal education and training who are particularly vulnerable to downturns in the business cycle; (ii) single mothers

[79] Mary E. Stefl, "The new homeless," in Richard D. Bingham, Roy E. Green, and Sammis B. White, (eds.), Homeless in Contemporary Society (Beverly Hills, CA: Sage, 1988), p. 46.

[80] Richard Ropers, The Invisible Homeless, p. 178.

[81] Mary E. Stefl, "The new homeless," in Bingham, Green and White, (eds.), Homeless in Contemporary Society, pp. 23-27.

[82] F. Stevens Redburn and Terry F. Buss, Responding to America's Homeless: Public Policy Alternatives (New York: Plenum Press, 1986), p. 102.

53

leaving relationships, ones who have previously been attached to an economically successful partner; (iii) Mothers on AFDC; (iv) and mothers who have been homeless teenagers. These women tend to be younger, often have only one child, and have had histories of abuse in their family of origin, resulting in foster care, and its breakdown in the adolescent years.[83]

In contrast, Snow and Andersen have proposed a detailed typology of individuals living on the street, one which includes subtypes which may be more specifically applicable to their Austin, Texas, sample. This was based on an ethnographic study which attempted to capture the ways homeless individuals view themselves and their peers, and thus utilizes some conventional, derogatory language: (i) The Recently Dislocated, who represented 19% of their sample, are those experiencing shock and anomie at finding themselves living on the streets, and these people, they note, gravitate toward local service agencies. (ii) The Straddlers, 33% of their sample, are "at a critical turning point in their lives, with one foot in the domiciled world of their past, with which they still identify and feel some continuity, and one foot planted in street life".[84] There are the Regular Straddlers, and the "Institutionally Adapted Straddlers" who have jobs working with the homeless that fall somewhere between day labor and steady work.[85]

Unlike the foregoing groups there are the outsiders who Snow and Andersen see as consisting of "Tramps", "Bums", and the Mentally Ill. These are all street people who are resigned to being outside the system, as "They often see themselves in terms of various street identities and not merely as individuals who are down on their luck...They are people for whom the past and the future have collapsed into the

---

[83] Kay McChresney, "Homeless families: Four patterns of poverty," in Robertson and Greenblatt, Homelessness: A National Perspective, p. 245.

[84] David A. Snow and Leon Andersen, Down on Their Luck: A Study of Homeless People (Berkeley: University of California Press, 1990), 52.

[85] Ibid., p. 52.

54

present".[86] Of the Outsiders, (iii) the Tramps (15% of sample) are highly migratory, moving often in a patterned manner, and who possess a strong sense of independence and self-control. Alcohol is fairly central to their lives. This group consists of Traditional Tramps, heirs to the hobo lifestyle; and the Hippie Tramps, heirs to the 1960s counter culture.

In contrast to the Tramps, (iv) the Bums (18% of sample) tend to be non-migratory and also are heavily reliant on alcohol consumption. They can be divided into the Traditional Bums—the classic skid row alcoholic, and Redneck Bums whose livelihood is based on a mixture of selling plasma and panhandling. (v) Finally, about a tenth of their sample fell into the category of the Mentally Ill, those who are severely psychiatrically impaired, have experienced past institutionalization, and are designated as being crazy by other homeless due to their typically bizarre behavior.

The most difficult dimension of the homeless experience for researchers to study has been the temporal. Just as we have limited understanding of the length of homeless episodes, we have even less information on the patterns that homeless careers assume. We do know some of the general outlines: "...recent research shows these people to be a mixture of chronic long-term and transitory homeless: in Chicago, 31% had been homeless less than 2 months, 25% for 2 or more years."[87] In the Robert Wood Johnson project, just over half (52%) were found to be episodically homeless; 29%, chronically homeless; and just under a fifth (19%) were recently homeless for the first time.[88] One of the more useful analyses of homeless career patterns was that proposed by Snow and Andersen who used the previously discussed typology as a basis for understanding common transitions that homeless individuals experience. By definition, each homeless persons begins as a Recently Dislocated person, some of whom immediately get off the street, while others join the

---

[86] Ibid., p. 58.

[87] James Wright, Address Unknown, pp. 72-73.

[88] Ibid., pp. 72-73.

ranks of the Straddlers. The Straddlers, who experience a gradual transition to "greater liminality", and if they fail to return to conventional housing, then become either the Institutionally Adapted Straddlers, or one of the Outsiders (Tramps, Bums, or Mentally Ill). Likewise, the Institutionally Adapted may either transition into conventional society, or become one of the Outsiders. Snow and Anderson make the point that there is considerable looping between these categories, quoting one of their subjects as saying, "My problem is not getting off the streets, its staying off of them."[89]

While Snow and Andersen do not specifically discuss the homeless in shelters, it would be assumed that many shelter residents consist of the Recently Dislocated, Straddlers, and Institutionally Adapted, and that considerable transitioning goes on between the shelter and street homeless, though the research has not produced consistent data on this question. Because of the small size of Snow and Andersen's 168 person sample, it was impossible for them to meaningfully quantify the relative frequency or generalizeability of many of the identified transitions.

Snow and Anderson, however, propose that of all the possible combinations of transitions between the different types of street homelessness, there are five which stand out: (i) Some individuals only experience homelessness as a Recently Dislocated person, and then return to conventional society; (ii) Others sink into a pattern of episodic homelessness; (iii) Another group becomes permanently embedded as Straddlers "in a liminal plateau, typically in an institutional niche outside conventional society"; (iv) Another career pattern becomes stuck in a pattern of chronic, unrelieved homelessness as an Outsider; (v) and a few, permanently managed to leave street life and return to conventional society after years on the street.[90]

These researchers hypothesize that street life among the homeless functions as a self-perpetuating system or culture which tends to maintain many homeless in this

---

[89] Snow and Anderson, Down on Their Luck, p. 276.

[90] Ibid., p. 277.

56

state. While disabilities, lack of human capital, material resources, and social margin play important roles for many in precipitating homelessness, street based ties with other homeless, as well as cognitive factors impede exits from street life. These cognitive factors include the inability to formulate concrete plans of action, fatalism regarding the homeless condition, the experience of double-binds (i.e. need for a residence to get a job and vice versa) and resulting despondent paralysis; increased identification with street life; and unfamiliarity and discomfort with conventional social life.[91]

Much of this analysis suggests that very different strategies may be required for the prevention of homelessness and for serving the currently homeless, and for work with the recent homeless, in contrast to long-term homeless. A similar point has been made by Westerfelt who conducted one of the only studies specifically on exits from homelessness and the reasons some have been able to accomplish this. He points out that the original causes of a persons' homelessness may not be the same as those which serve to entrap a person in homelessness, or enable them to return to housing.[92]

Westerfelt interviewed a sample of homeless persons and then re-interviewed them 6 months later. Despite the short period, three-quarters of the subjects had found places to live at least once.[93] Among those who did, the majority became homeless one more time in the same period, and 55% of these succeeded in becoming housed again. Between episodes, the average person in the study spent a mean of 59 (median of 42) days off the street. After the first exit from homelessness, 57% within six months returned to the street.[94] Predictors of successful exits included childhood placements, involvement in crime, and receipt of shelter from family in the 30 days prior to the study. In contrast, illness and receipt of shelter from friends were

---

[91] Ibid., p. 299.

[92] See Herb Westerfelt, "The ins and outs of homelessness".

[93] Ibid.

[94] Ibid., p. 121.

negatively related to these exits.[95]

Tests of the Demographic Model

The preliminary analyses presented so far in this chapter have suggested that urbanization, racial minority status, as well as gender, age, and transiency contribute to a propensity or risk for homelessness. This propensity develops for some into full-fledged homeless careers through a variety of paths which may be shaped by individual disabilities and the availability of economic, family, social service, and housing supports. The data reviewed so far has been of several types. In addition to a review of previous research findings, most of this data has typically involved an examination of the characteristics of homeless persons vis-a-vis' characteristics of all persons in the same locales. It has also included the association of characteristics of the general population with overall homeless rates. In most cases, these have been analyses which use descriptive bivariate statistics which associate pairs of variables, i.e. county transiency and homeless rates. While these analyses enable the development of a comprehensive profile of homeless populations and their associated environments, their value is heuristic when questions of causation are considered.

For this reason, this study has also used multivariate statistical techniques, specifically techniques of structural equation modeling (SEM). Structural equation modeling is a relatively recent approach, developed since the late-1970s, which permits the testing of a set of causal hypotheses, reflected in a path diagram which interrelates both observed and latent variables, while at the same time taking into account both random and systematic sources of error in the data. In addition, the approach permits testing hypotheses regarding two way, interactive relationships, as well as incorporating data which violates such assumptions in conventional analyses as normality, interval level data, or non-correlated random error.

The approach taken in this chapter as well as in subsequent chapters is incremental and developmental. Using previous research, as well as descriptive and

---

[95] Ibid., p. 150.

bivariate analyses, provisional and specialized models are constructed focusing on key predictors from each chapter. These are tested first by themselves, then with systematic error included, and finally, in conjunction with the preceding models to determine whether the predictors under consideration improve our ability to understand homelessness. In this chapter, only demographic variables indicative of the conditions so far reviewed are used, and these few variables apparently account for close to three-eighths (36.7%) of the variation in homeless rates throughout the 3,141 counties of the U.S. In subsequent chapters this model will be progressively tested by the inclusion of measures of personal disabilities, economic opportunities, family fragmentation, or housing affordability, each of which represent models which will reveal that part of this 36.7% of the variation, as well as parts of the so far unexplained variation, to be actually a function of other conditions yet to be considered. The characteristic of the county populations which is most closely associated with levels of homelessness is density, a proxy measure for urbanization. When the tendency of the Census Bureau to search more thoroughly in urban areas is taken into account, an initially very strong Beta coefficient of 0.69 drops to a moderately strong 0.43, accounting for about three-tenths of the variation in the rates (29.3%). Bivariate analyses initially suggested that the proportion of the population which is nonwhite or foreign born would be associated with the homeless rates ($r =$ 0.44, 0.45). However, the variation explained by these associations (19.8% & 20.2%) drop to almost negligible levels (0.7% & 3.9%) when both urbanization, the other demographic conditions, and systematic error are controlled for in the final SEM model reported in table 2-7 (also see appendix 2). We can, therefore, assume that the high proportions of minorities among the homeless represents the fact that there are high proportions of minorities in urban areas, and that it is population congestion and growth in these areas, rather than any inherent feature of these populations, which places them at such high risk. When such controls are used, we discover that the percentage of foreign born is actually negatively associated with the levels of homelessness.

59

Preliminary analyses also suggested that the extent of the epidemiological transition--involving the increasing proportion of persons aged 65 or over--was strongly associated with homelessness, but this was revealed to be spurious when the differential search efforts were controlled for. In fact, the direction of the relationship was reversed, revealing that such changes have a slight tendency to diminish homeless levels (β = -0.10). One may expect that the more older adults, the fewer social welfare supports to be available to younger adults who may then become homeless. However, the more older adults there are, the pool of younger adults *at risk* of homelessness is reduced. Furthermore, it may be that as older adults successfully lobby for improved social services and health care, this may improve the availability of institutional supports for other segments of the population as well.

The two other features of county populations most closely associated with homeless levels are the extent of growth from 1980 and 1990, and the proportion of baby boomers or those born between 1945 and 1964. For each standard unit in variation in the growth of the population, there was just about four-tenths of a standard unit ($\beta = 0.38$) increase in homelessness. This is consistent with findings of Burt's that high growth cities engendered the growth of homelessness. Not only do high rates of population growth contribute to congestion, but they appear to have an independent effect on homelessness, perhaps through the concomitant economic growth involving the development of service industries. Despite the fact that the median age of the homeless is in the early 30s, the proportion of Baby Boomers, aged 26 to 45 in 1990, was found to be negatively associated with the rates of homelessness (-0.26). It may be that many in this generation were approaching their prime years of economic productivity by 1990 and have more frequently moved to the suburban counties than younger adults.

Table 2-7. Effects of Demographic Conditions on Homeless Rates

Variables	Bivariate Correlations		Demographic Variables Only		Demographic & Measurement Error	
	r	Variation Explained	β	Variation Explained	β	Variation Explained
DEMOGRAPHIC CONDITIONS				62.4%		36.7%
Population Density (per Sq. Mile)	0.77	59.0%	0.69[c.]	50.8%	0.43[c.]	29.3%
% Population Nonwhite	0.44	19.8%	0.12[c.]	5.2%	0.02	0.7%
% Change, Age 65+, 1980-1990	-0.21	4.5%	0.53[c.]	3.5%	-0.10[c.]	1.9%
% Foreign Born	0.45	20.2%	0.04[a]	1.6%	-0.10[c.]	3.9%
% Population Growth, 1980-1990	-0.02	0.0%	0.53[c.]	0.9%	0.38[c.]	0.6%
% Population in 'Baby Boom' Generation (Birth dates--1945-1964)	0.01	0.0%	0.34[b]	0.3%	-0.26[b]	0.2%
SYSTEMATIC ERROR: Rate of Sites Enumerated	0.85	72.5%			0.63[c]	47.4%
TOTAL (R^2)				62.4%		84.1%

NOTES: See appendix 2 for goodness-of-fit statistics. Each model computed using weighted least squares and estimates of measurement error.

[a.] $\alpha > 0.05$
[b.] $\alpha > 0.01$
[c.] $\alpha > 0.001$

Perhaps one of the most significant patterns revealed through the testing of these models is that even when the greater search efforts in the cities are taken into account, urbanization remains the strongest predictor of levels of homelessness, though less so. The rate of sites enumerated is clearly the strongest predictor, supporting the adage that the more one looks, the more one finds. In addition, this rate accounts for almost half (47.4%) the variation in the homeless rates. When combined with the 36.7% of the variation explained collectively by the demographic conditions, the combined model explains about five-sixths (84.1%) of the variation in levels of homelessness. It should be emphasized that virtually all of the effect of demographic conditions originates from the levels of population density or urbanization, which represents 29.3% or four-fifths of the 36.7% explained by the demographic variables. Population growth and the proportion of minorities only slightly added to homelessness, whereas the proportion of foreign born, baby boomers, and older adults served to a very small extent to counteract these effects.

Both models--that with and without systematic error included-- substantially meet the criteria for statistical significance and fit. Figure 2-8 summarizes the overall goodness of fit of the two structural equation models computed. Both have unusually low chi-square figures which, along with six to seven remaining degrees of freedom, indicating that almost certainly ($p = 0.99$ & 1.00) the hypothesized pattern of correlation corresponds to the observed correlations. The superiority of the second model, which includes systematic error, over the first is based not only on the greater variation accounted for, but on the many substantive reasons for including systematic error in the model (see appendix 2). However, despite the high levels of variation accounted for, this model must be assumed to be incomplete, given all that has been observed, found, or conjectured concerning the personal disabilities, economic difficulties, lack of family and social supports, and problems of housing unaffordability faced by homeless individuals. It is to the topic of personal disabilities, which may or may not play a causative role in accounting for homelessness, to which we will now turn.

Chapter III
THE DISABILITY HYPOTHESIS

A n ongoing problem in the study of homelessness has been the question of whether the homeless condition is best explained by causes which are in some sense specific to the individual. These may include social disabilities such as inadequate education or lack of work experience, but more commonly, disabilities associated with serious mental illness, substance abuse, or physical illness. There are several versions of this approach. At one extreme are those who 'blame the victim' and propose that defects in character are central. For instance, some have gone so far as to propose that because many homeless people suffer from schizophrenia, and schizophrenia is believed to be genetically caused, homelessness must, therefore, be a genetically determined condition.[96] Similarly, others suggest that homelessness is essentially a psychological affliction--"a tendency to drift"--involving a fantasy of finding closeness, search for autonomy, and a way of denying dependence.[97] Most, however, take seriously the pervasiveness of disabilities among the homeless, but are reluctant to either blame the individual, suggest that little can be done, or minimize the role of underlying systemic causes such as poverty, unemployment, or unaffordable housing.

This chapter will review the research pertinent to individual-specific explanations of homelessness and test a few versions of the disability hypothesis: that

---

[96] D. Tomb, as cited by Richard H. Ropers, The Invisible Homeless: A New Urban Ecology (New York: Human Sciences Press, 1988), p 160.

[97] Herbert R. Lamb, "Deinstitutionalization ad The Homeless Mentally Ill," In H.R. Lamb, (ed.), The Homeless Mentally Ill: A Task Force Report of the American Psychiatric Association (Washington, D.C.: American Psychiatric Association).

low levels of education and high levels of self-reported disability in the general population predict rates of homelessness throughout the 3,141 counties of the United States. The data does, in fact, lend some support to this hypothesis, though it does so inconclusively. The body of research from local studies on characteristics of homeless individuals provides strong evidence, when taken as a whole, that homeless individuals suffer disproportionately from a wide range of afflictions, in particular, serious mental illness and substance abuse, as well as criminal involvements, and that there is accumulating evidence that these conditions, for the most part, predate individuals' homeless careers. The national statistical data also provide some support for this view. While bivariate and uncontrolled analysis suggests that education and disability are strongly associated with each other and with homelessness, when controls are introduced for demographic features of local populations, as well as the differential efforts in the enumeration process, this association is revealed to be more complex than the preliminary analyses would indicate. While low levels of education are clearly associated with high homeless rates, in at least some respects, high disability rates are paradoxically associated with low levels of homelessness, a topic which will be explored at the conclusion of this chapter.

Poor Education as a Social Disability

Most homeless individuals suffer from the effects of minimal education. Almost half (47.8%) have not completed high school, and this includes about a seventh (14.6%) who have gone no further than the 8th grade. Only about a fifth (21.3%) have any education beyond high school, including the one in 18 (5.7%) who has a bachelors degree or higher. These percentages represent weighted averages, derived from ten major studies during the late 1980s, representing close to 4,900 homeless individuals (see table 3-1).[98] One study of 1,700 subjects broke down educational levels by

---

[98]   Rene I. Jahiel, Chapter 4, "Empirical studies of homeless populations in the 1980s," in R.I. Ja hiel, (ed.), Homelessness: A Prevention-oriented Approach (Baltimore: John Hopkins Press, 19 92), pp. 42 & 44.

**Table 3-1. Summary of Findings on
Educational Levels of Homeless From Selected Studies**

Educational Level	# Studies	# Subjects	Weighted Percentage
Grades 0-8	7	2,811	14.6%
Grades 9-11	7	2,811	32.9%
Under Grade 12	10	4,913	47.8%
Grade 12 Only	9	4,838	31.2%
Grade 12 or Higher	10	4,913	52.2%
Over Grade 12	9	4,838	21.3%
Bachelor's or Higher	1	1,700	5.7%

SOURCE: Computed from data in Rene I. Jahiel, Chapter 4, "Empirical Studies of Homeless Populations in the 1980s," in R. I. Jahiel (Ed.), Homelessness: A Prevention Oriented Approach, (Baltimore: John Hopkins Press, 1992), pp. 42, 44; and, Martha Burt, Over the Edge, (New York: Russell Sage Foundation & Urban Institute Press), 1992, pp. 14-15.

gender, revealing that 57% of women with children completed high school, compared to the 37% of single women and 22% of women in other kinds of groups. The men, however, clustered more closely around the average with 50% of the single men and 49% of men in other groupings completing high school. An exception was the very small group of men with children, of whom only 8% had completed their high school education.[99]

These data indicate that the homeless are almost half as likely as the general population to have graduated from high school (25% versus 48%), and just over a third as likely to have either gone beyond high school (21% versus 57%), or completed a bachelor's degree (6% versus 18%) (see table 3-2). On one hand, we must assume that such a disproportionate representation of homeless among those

---

[99] Computed from Burt, Over The Edge, p. 15.

Table 3-2. Educational Levels of Homeless, Compared with Those of General Population, By Level of Homelessness

Educational Level	Homeless Population	General Population	General Population; County Homeless Rate		
			Low	Medium	High
Non-HS Graduate	48%	25%	24%	23%	27%
HS Graduate or Higher	52%	75%	76%	77%	73%
More than HS Graduate	21%	57%	56%	57%	58%
BA or Higher	6%	18%	21%	20%	15%
% Change HS Grads, 1980-1990		8%	7%	8%	11%
Number of Counties		3,141	1,047	1,049	1,044

SOURCE: Homeless Percentage—see note, Table 3-1; Other—Computed from 1990 Census, STF-3C Data Tape.

who do not even possess such a minimal qualification as the high school diploma must represent a significant handicap in the competition for employment. Yet, several studies have indicated that, when compared with other poor individuals, the homeless have a similar level of education.[100] Thus, while lack of education may be a better predictor for poverty, it is nonetheless a significant handicap which homeless individuals unsuccessfully face in the overall competition for employment. This is illustrated by the fact that homeless levels are highest in those counties which have a greater range of educational achievement in the general population, compared to those in which educational levels cluster closer to the national average (see three rightmost columns of table 3-2).

More indicative of the impact of higher education levels on homelessness is

---

[100]   Burt, Over The Edge, p. 15; Rossi Down and Out in America; Michael Sosin, Paul Colson, and Susan Grossman, Homelessness in Chicago: Poverty and Pathology, Social Institutions and Social Change (Chicago: School of Social Service Administration, University of Chicago, 1988).

the finding that in areas with high levels of homelessness there has been an 11% increase in the percentage of people completing high school between 1980 and 1990. In contrast, the increase has been only 8% overall, and 7% in the areas with the lowest homeless rates. One possibility is that the surge in high school graduation rates in the 1980s has served to squeeze those who do not graduate from high school out of the regular employment market. Thus, while education on the individual level clearly serves as a powerful antidote to poverty and homelessness, the improving educational levels are paradoxically stimulating homelessness. While the rate of non-high school graduates is apparently positively associated with homelessness (r = 0.39), for perhaps the very reasons suggested the rates of high school and college graduation are also associated with the homeless rates (r = 0.39 & 0.53). The available measures of education, unfortunately, do not address issues of quality, nor of the availability of post-graduate training opportunities, both which are critical issues for individuals at risk for eventual homelessness. These figures probably camouflage the magnitude of the role of education in the various causal pathways to both poverty and homelessness.

Marginal Employment Histories

A central outcome of the educational handicaps and disabilities of homeless individuals involves the inability to maintain employment, as it is has been estimated that a third of the homeless may be too disabled to work.[101] Nonetheless, a review of research concerning the work status and histories of the homeless reveals that while most homeless individuals have very sporadic work histories, the homeless have generally made concerted efforts to support themselves. Of those currently homeless, estimates of those working at a steady job range from 6% to 10%.[102] Of those few

---

[101] See Rossi, Down and Out in America, p. 24.

[102] Computed from Burt, Over The Edge, p. 18; Gary A. Morse and Robert J. Calsyn, Chapter 10, "Mental health and other human service needs of homeless people," in Robertson and Greenblatt, (eds.), Homelessness: A National Perspective, p. 122.

who are employed, it was found in one city that most worked as laborers (63.9%), about a quarter (25%) as service workers, and the remaining few as machine operatives (5.1%) or as professional or technical workers (2.8%).[103]

Homeless adults have been unemployed typically for two to three years. While Rossi reported that the homeless in Chicago had spent a median of 3.3 years unemployed, Morse reported a mean of just over 1.9 years in his St. Louis sample.[104] Just about a fourth of Rossi's Chicago sample reported working in the previous week, and two-fifths (38.9%) any time during the preceding month, leaving three-fifths (61.1%) who had not worked at all during this same period.[105] Almost three-quarters of these individuals worked in the semi-skilled or unskilled sectors of the economy, and of these about half (37.3%) had been laborers and a seventh (15.9%), newspaper sales people.[106] Similarly, Ropers found in a Los Angeles sample that 22.7% had been laborers; 26.6%, service workers; 15.6%, operatives; 14.8%, technicians or professionals; 10.2%, craftsmen; 7.8%, clerical workers; and, 1.6%, farm laborers.[107]

Despite the above picture of the sporadic and minimally skilled work histories of the homeless, only about a seventh (14.6%) were found to have never held a steady job.[108] It is, however, clear, as Rossi contends, that very few of the extremely poor or homeless have fallen into this position as a result of having lost a regular, moderately skilled position, that employment problems typically predate the loss of a single position. Piliavin, et al. found that the percentage of adult life spent working was a significant predictor of the persistence, and thus of overall levels of

---

[103] Ropers, The Invisible Homeless, p. 84.

[104] Rossi, Down and Out in America, p. 49; Morse and Calsyn, in Robertson and Greenblatt, (eds.), Homelessness: A National Perspective.

[105] Rossi, Down and Out in America, p. 135.

[106] Ibid., p. 136.

[107] Ropers, The Invisible Homeless.

[108] Burt, Over The Edge, p. 19.

homelessness.[109] It has been pointed out that the homeless "suffer from the psychosocial stress produced by their state of unemployment and lack of a home, and that the empirical evidence demonstrates that demoralization is a leading psychological affliction of the homeless.[110]

One particular type of work experience among homeless males which has been frequently noted is their Veteran's status. Most studies suggest that there is a similar or slightly higher proportion of Veterans among homeless men than in the larger population of men.[111] For instance, the Ohio survey of a thousand homeless individuals found that Veterans constituted two-fifths (39%) of the homeless male sample, compared with 36% for Ohio males.[112] This research has identified only a few differences between the Veterans and non-Veterans among homeless males. The Veterans tend to be older and better educated, and are more likely to be white and to have been married. However, they have higher rates of physical and psychiatric impairment, especially alcoholism.[113] One study found that the Veterans among the homeless also had a higher prevalence of substance abuse and psychiatric illness, including antisocial personality disorder.[114] It may be that subgroups of the homeless, such as Veterans who have not experienced the effects of as many of the demographic risk factors, tend to be more disabled, in this case, due to the traumatic experiences of combat and problems in reintegrating into civilian life.

---

[109] Rossi, Down and Out in America, p. 137.

[110] Ropers, The Invisible Homeless, p. 143.

[111] Dee Roth, Chapter 16, "Homeless veterans: Comparisons with other homeless men," in Robertson and Greenblatt, (eds.), Homelessness: A National Perspective, p. 213; Robert Rosenheck, Linda Frisman, and Linda Chung, "The proportion of homeless among veterans," American Journal of Public Health 84 (3), pp. 466-69 (1994).

[112] Roth, "Homeless veterans:...", in Robertson and Greenblatt, (eds.), Homelessness: A National Perspective.

[113] Ibid., p. 218.

[114] Rosenheck, Frisman, and Chung, "The proprotion of homeless among veterans".

Mental Illness

One of the images of the homeless which has captured public attention has been that of the lone, disheveled, street person who is actively hallucinating and cursing passer bys. This image has reinforced the notion of many that individuals become homeless primarily because of serious mental illness and the failures of the deinstitutionalization and community mental health movements. Most knowledgeable observers have, however, concluded that this theory can account for only a minority of those who become homeless, albeit an important minority.

There have been numerous attempts to generate data on this issue, most commonly through community surveys, some of which include retrospective questions pertinent to the sequence of events leading up to the loss of a home. Because most of this research has consisted of point-in-time surveys, it has been easy for critics of the mental illness version of the disability hypothesis to dismiss the high prevalence of mental illness among the homeless, pointing out that any one would develop such symptoms while attempting to survive without a home. Furthermore, the use of standardized mental illness inventories has often meant the use of instruments on populations for which they have not been tested for, and the use of questions which may not differentiate symptoms of mental illness from the survival strategies of the homeless.

Nonetheless, there is persuasive evidence that mental illness does play an important role in many of the pathways to the loss of one's home and in the perpetuation of this condition. This section will review this research, involving overall levels of mental illness, hospitalization rates, profiles of symptomatology, diagnostic studies, and finally, evidence of the time order of the development of mental illness and precursors in the personal histories of the homeless. Research on erall levels of serious or chronic mental illness among the homeless has produced estimates which range between 10%[115] and over 90%.[116] However, most estimates which have utilized any one or a combination of several methods have been usually in the 20% to 35% range. Rossi, for example, concluded that "Putting together the findings on depression and psychotic thinking, it appears that about 20 to 30 percent of the Chicago homeless either are deeply depressed or show signs of psychotic thinking."[117] In 1988, HUD surveyed a national probability sample of shelter managers who estimated that 34% of adult clients have problems of mental illness.[118] Similarly, a review of 17 studies by Wright concluded that 34.3% suffered from chronic mental illness, though had weighting for sample size been used in aggregating these results, the summary figure would be approximately 30%.[119]

It is, thus, clear from both formal research and service statistics that approximately a third of the homeless suffer from a serious mental illness. Few studies have sought to assess the severity of impairment of the homeless who have a mental illness. An important exception was the survey of the HCH providers conducted by Wright. Over half (51%) were found to have no obvious impairment of functioning, and about a sixth (16%), a slight impairment. In contrast, 18% were found to be moderately and 15% severely impaired, totaling 33%.[120] Similarly, Koegel developed a definition of chronic mental illness and with data collected using the Diagnostic Inventory Schedule (DIS), concluded that 28% of his sample met the criteria for a

---

[115] David A. Snow, S.G. Baker, and L. Erson, "The myth of pervasive mental illness among the homeless," Social Problems 33, pp. 301-17 (1986).

[116] Ellen Bassuk, "The homelessness problem," Scientific American 251 (1), pp. 40-45 (1984).

[117] Rossi, Down and Out in America, p. 155.

[118] U.S., Department of Housing and Urban Affairs. A Report to the Secretary on the Homeless & Emergency Shelters (Washington, D.C.: HUD Office of Policy Development and Research, Division of Policy Studies, 1989).

[119] Wright, Address Unknown, p. 154.

[120] Ibid., p. 105.

severe and chronic mental illness, and another 5%, "probable but unconfirmed."[121]

One of the most easily collected and commonly used indicators of mental illness is the history of mental hospitalization, in particular, the percentage of the homeless who have ever been hospitalized for mental illness. Table 3-3 presents several breakdowns of the results of 36 studies which elicited this information. This body of research collectively indicates that about a fifth (20%) of the homeless have been hospitalized in a psychiatric facility.[122] This is a weighted average that takes into account the relative sample size of each study, giving proportionately greater weight to studies with larger samples, ones which typically cover multiple sites. These figures will, therefore, be somewhat lower than that of other reviews which either do not aggregate the figures, or do so in an unweighted manner, as the larger samples typically generate hospitalization rates in the 15% to 18% range, compared with the smaller ones which result in rates in the 24% to 27% range. Most studies find that while close to a sixth (17%) of homeless men have been previously hospitalized, more than a fourth (27%) of the women have been. One study of the homeless in shelters in New York found that while higher rates of psychiatric hospitalization for women occurred in all age groups, an important exception involved women with children who generally had lower rates than men. The overall disparity between male and female rates also shows up in most subgroups of the studies, with the exception of the three Midwest studies which collectively found an equally high 30% level of hospitalization for both genders. Hospitalization rates, however, are rather unreliable indicators of levels of mental illness due to the wide disparity of admission practices, economic conditions, and popular acceptance of psychiatric treatment between areas.

---

[121] Paul Koegel and M. Dubrey Burnham, Chapter 7, "Problems in the assessment of mental illness among the homeless: An empirical approach," in Robertson and Greenblatt, (eds.), Homelessness: A National Perspective, p. 84.

[122] This is based on Table 5.1, Chapter 5, "The prevalence of mental disorder among homeless people," in Jahiel, (ed.), Homelessness: A Prevention-oriented Approach, pp. 60-64.

Table 3-3. Rates of Hospitalization of Homeless, Reported in 36 Studies, From 1980s

	Total		Men		Women	
	Percentage	#	Percentage	#	Percentage	#
STUDY YEAR						
Pre-1980	22%	1	--	--	--	--
1980-1983	24%	7	30%	3	--	--
1984-1987	20%	25	16%	10	27%	10
1988-1990	10%	3	--	--	--	--
TYPE OF SITE						
Shelter Only	18%	16	16%	8	28%	6
Mixed	23%	18	21%	5	24%	4
Street Only	21%	2	--	--	--	--
REGION						
Northeast	18%	12	15%	5	28%	4
Midwest	27%	10	30%	5	30%	3
South	30%	1	--	--	--	--
Mountain	11%	4	--	--	--	--
Pacific	24%	7	27%	2	24%	2
Other	19%	2	17%	1	19%	1
SAMPLE SIZE						
Under 250	24%	20	25%	8	33%	6
250-499	27%	6	--	--	--	--
500-999	18%	6	19%	2	22%	1
1,000-1,499	15%	1	13%	1	27%	1
1,500 & Over	18%	3	15%	2	27%	2
OVERALL	20%	36	17%	13	27%	10

NOTE: These percentages are averages of the findings of all studies exhibiting the designated characteristic. They are weighted by sample size.

SOURCE: Computed from Table 5.1, in Chapter 5, "The Prevalence of Mental Disorder among Homeless People," by Marjorie J. Robertson, in Rene I. Jahiel, (ed.), Homelessness: A Prevention-oriented Approach, (Baltimore: John Hopkins, 1992),

Patterns of psychiatric hospitalization among the homeless can be gleaned from the diverse breakdowns of the hospitalization rates provided in the various studies. Few of these elicited information on the specific number of hospitalizations of the homeless, however, those that did so found that the mean number of hospitalizations to be 3.7 in an Ohio study and 4.1 in a St. Louis study.[123] Typically, the highest rates of hospitalization came from surveys of those in psychiatric emergency rooms (97%), whereas the lowest rates are found in surveys conducted in shelters of homeless mothers and children (7%).[124] A particularly pertinent finding reveals that for the almost three-quarters (73.8%) of the homeless who have been hospitalized, the first admission preceded the initial homeless episode.[125] Another study found that about a half of the admissions of the homeless were referred by police, a quarter by other hospitals, and a sixth by the homeless person him or herself.[126] Once referred to a psychiatric facility, it is unclear whether the domiciled or undomiciled poor are more likely to be admitted. While one large Illinois study found that the homeless are more likely to be refused admission,[127] several studies have indicated the opposite pattern.[128] Fewer than a fifth (18%) of the homeless who had

---

[123] Beverly Toomey and Richard First, Homelessness in Ohio: A Study of People in Need, Franklin County Report Columbus, OH: Ohio Department of Mental Health, 1985), p. 25; Gary Morse and Robert Calsyn, Chapter 10, "Mental health and other human service needs of homeless people," in Robertson and Greenblatt, (eds.), Homelessness: A National Perspective, p. 121.

[124] Paula F. Eagle and Carol L.M. Caton, "Homelessness and mental illness," in Carol L.M. Caton, Homeless in America (New York: Oxford University Press, 1990), p. 61.

[125] Gary Morse and Robert Calsyn, "Mental health and other human service needs..." in Robertson and Greenblatt, (eds.), Homelessness: A National Perspective, p. 121.

[126] Lawrence Appleby and Prakash N. Desai, "Documenting the relationship between homelessness and psychiatric hospitalization," Hospital & Community Psychiatry 36 (7), pp. 732-37 (1985), p. 735.

[127] Ibid., p. 735.

[128] See Marjorie Robertson, Chapter 5, "The prevalence of mental disorder among homeless people," in Robertson and Greenblatt, (eds.), Homelessness: A National Perspective, p. 59.

been hospitalized had ever been in a state facility.[129] A particularly disheartening finding revealed that most all (80%) of those admitted while homeless in a Chicago facility also left homeless.[130]

Several researchers have gone beyond reliance on hospitalization levels and sought information on the frequency and types of symptoms of mental illness that the homeless experience. While this approach still falls short of a rigorous diagnostic assessment, it does provide valuable information on types of emotional distress and personality patterns that many homeless individuals must deal with.

The most common kind of symptomatology studied has been depression and suicidality. Depression has been most frequently assessed through the Center for Epidemiological Studies' Depression scale (CES-D). Whereas about a sixth (16%) of the adult population score above the cut-off of 9.4 on this scale which indicates a potential need for treatment, almost half (49.2%) of the homeless in one study scored at this level, including 47.9% of males and 52.0% of females, over three times the national average.[131] It is remarkable that over half of the homeless did not score above this cutoff.

Suicidality is common among the homeless. Depending on how their questions are framed, researchers have found that between a tenth and a quarter of the homeless have considered suicide. Rossi reported that the figure was about a tenth (10.7%) when the homeless are asked whether they thought about suicide in the last few weeks, while Robertson found that it was as high as a quarter (25%) when

---

[129] Richard C. Tessler and Deborah L. Dennis, A Synthesis of NIMH-funded Research Concerning Persons Who are Homeless and Mentally Ill (Amherst, MA: Social and Demographic Research Institute, University of Massachusetts, Feb. 9, 1989), p.29.

[130] Appleby and Desai, "Documenting the relationship...", p. 735.

[131] See Burt, Over The Edge, p. 21.

the person is asked about whether they have ever thought about suicide.[132] Findings on the percentage of the homeless who have attempted suicide range from 6.1% in Rossi's Chicago study[133] to around a fifth (20%) in two other studies.[134] In Rossi's study he found that while 6.1% had made one attempt, 4.9% had made 3 or more attempts.[135] Over half (51%) of those with a suicide attempt had no history of a major depressive episode in one study of the mentally ill homeless.[136] These figures document that the homeless are between 2 and 6 times more likely to attempt suicide than the U.S. adult population, a figure which averages 3%.[137]

Other studies have used general symptomatology scales. The Ohio study, for instance, has found that about a sixth of their sample had moderate or higher levels of Suspicion-Persecution-Hallucinations (15.6%) and Retardation-Lack of Emotion (15.3%); about a tenth, Speech Disorganization (10.6%) and Inappropriate Affect (10.5%); and close to a twelfth, Disorientation-Memory Impairment (8.8%) and Agitation-Excitement (8.4%).[138] Another project compared a sample of 100 homeless schizophrenic men with 100 never homeless schizophrenic men using the PANSS scale which measures positive and negative schizophrenic symptoms. This project concluded that the homeless sample scored significantly higher on the general

---

[132]   Robertson, Chapter 5, "The prevalence of mental disorder...", in Robertson and Greenblatt, (eds.), Homelessness: A National Perspective, p. 57.

[133]   Rossi, Down and Out in America, p. 151.

[134]   Burt, Over The Edge; Carol S. North, Elizabeth M. Smith, and Edward L. Spitznagel, "Violence and The Homeless: An epidemiological study of victimization and agreeson," Journal of Traumatic Stress 7 (1), pp. 95-110 (1994), p. 106.

[135]   Rossi, Down and Out in America, p. 151.

[136]   North, Smith, and Spitznagel, "Violence and the homeless...", p. 106.

[137]   Burt, Over The Edge, p. 21.

[138]   Richard First, Chapter 3, Draft Ohio Study, Feb.13, 1992; table 6.2.

psychopathology and positive symptom scales, involving the more bizarre and visible symptoms, but about the same on the negative scale involving the more subtle symptoms involving withdrawal, difficulties in abstract thinking, and ambivalence.[139] However, when subgroups of the medication compliant and non-substance abusers were compared, no differences were found on either scale, suggesting that the higher positive schizophrenic symptomatology of the homeless represents some combination of the greater lack of medication compliance and substance abuse among the homeless subjects.

Interpretation of this body of research is hampered by the diversity of instruments used, inadequate norms, as well as by well known biases which act to both exaggerate and minimize levels of mental illness. Practices which are believed to bias these studies towards higher rates of mental illness include sampling from shelters and other service populations, interpretation of symptoms of physical disease or malnutrition as indicative of mental illness, and use of point estimates which overstate characteristics of those with longer histories of homelessness. Examples of biases believed to operate in the opposite direction include self-selection of healthier people in samples at study sites, mental health assessments resulting from short-term observations, ignoring history, failure to provide multiple diagnoses, and overly broad definitions of homelessness which dilute prevalence estimates.[140]

A more important body of research to be considered here consists of studies which have sought to generate diagnostic profiles of the homeless. These tend to be more rigorous than the symptomatology profiles as they draw on more stringent and widely agreed upon criteria for diagnosing well known disorders, specifically, the

---

[139]   I.A. Opler, C.L. Caton, P. Shrout, B. Domingues, and F.I. Case, "Symptom profiles and homelessness in schizophrenia," Journal of Nervous & Mental Diseases 3, pp. 174-178 (March 1994.

[140]   Robertson, Chapter 5, "The prevalence of mental disorder...", in Robertson and Greenblatt, (eds.), Homelessness: A National Perspective, pp. 75-76.

diagnostic and statistical manual of the American Psychiatric Association. Data is typically collected through either a clinical interview or an instrument, most commonly, the Diagnostic Inventory Schedule (DIS), or occasionally, from a review of existing records. Table 3-4 aggregates the results of 9 such studies, with the summary percentages weighted by sample size. Among the approximately 1,000 subjects studied, over a quarter (26%) evidenced a personality disorder, about a sixth (16%) an affective condition, such as major depression; and a seventh (14%), schizophrenia--representing close to a half of the mentally ill homeless. While there is probably a minimal overlap between those with affective and schizophrenic conditions, most of this group no doubt overlaps with those with personality disorders. These data suggest that while those with personality conditions are moderately over represented among the homeless, those with affective and especially schizophrenic conditions are extremely over represented by factors of 2.7 and 15.6, respectively.[141]

The breakdown of mental health status of homeless individuals by gender suggests that the higher proportion of homeless women with histories of psychiatric hospitalization may very well reflect a much higher rate of personality disorders among the women, rather than affective or schizophrenic conditions. The personality diagnoses are known to have a lower level of reliability. Furthermore, the higher rates could be accounted for by the common critique of these diagnostic categories, especially the borderline personality disorder as they are disproportionately applied to women. Alternatively, it has been suggested that women with lower levels of pathology can more easily find housing, thus, leaving a residual group of highly disturbed women among the minority of the homeless who are women. Comparisons of homeless and non-homeless mentally ill women have generally found the major

---

[141] Based on overall totals for schizophrenia (14%) and affective conditions (16%) from table 4-4 and national prevalence estimates for schizophrenia (0.9%) and affective disorders (6.0%) from the ECA studies, summarized in, Ben Z. Locke and Darrel A. Regier, Chapter 1, "Prevalence and selcted mental disorders," in National Institute of Mental Health. Mental Health, United States, 1985. Taube, C.A., and Barrett, S.A., (eds.) DHHS Pub. No. (ADM) 86-1378. Washington, D.C.: Supt. of Docs., U.S. Govt. Print. Off., 1986.

Table 3-4. Summary of Diagnostic Studies of Homeless Individuals

TYPE OF STUDY	# Studies	Schizo-phrenia	Affective Conditions	Personality Disorders	Organic Disorders	Alcohol & Drug
METHOD						
Clinical Interview [5]		12%	16%	46%	--	43%
Diagnostic Inventory		9%	20%	18%	4%	32%
Existing Records [1]		34%	6%	7%	5%	25%
SAMPLING						
Census [4]		19%	7%	25%	5%	22%
Mixed [1]		1%	14%	26%	--	34%
Random [4]		12%	21%	27%	4%	42
TYPE OF SITE						
Shelter Only [6]		17%	12%	29%	6%	36%
Jail [1]		17%	21%	45%	--	38%
Shelter & Street Meal Programs [2]		10% (404)	20% (404)	19% (404)	3% (328)	32% (404)
GENDER OF SUBJECTS						
Over 94% Male [4]		10%	11%	24%	4%	42%
78-82% Male [3]		26%	30%	14%	5%	28%
100% Female [2]		10%	3%	58%	--	23%
OVERALL [9]		14%	16%	26%	4%	34%

NOTE: These percentages are averages of the findings of all studies exhibiting the designated characteristic. They are weighted by sample size. The figures in parentheses is the total number of subjects from the studies analyzed. The number of these studies is listed in brackets on the left.

SOURCE: This table is computed from Table 5.3, in Chapter 5, "The Prevalence of Mental Disorder among Homeless People," by Marjorie J. Robertson, in Rene I. Jahiel, (ed.), Homelessness: A Prevention-oriented Approach, (Baltimore: John Hopkins, 1992), pp. 70-71.

psychiatric diagnoses to be over represented, as well as post-traumatic stress disorder (PTSD). However, the occurrence of panic and generalized anxiety disorders in homeless women were found to be about the same as the larger population of women.[142]

The high prevalence of personality disorders among the homeless has been investigated at several sites. Fischer and Breakey concluded that,

> ...the full range of DSM-III personality disorders were represented, except the narcissistic personality disorder. The most frequently occurring, however, were the paranoid, schizoid, and antisocial types, each of which have the effect of interfering in some manner with a person's ability to form supportive and lasting personal relationships.[143]

Specifically, they found that 28% of the men and 22% of the women had disorders in the schizoid/schizotypal cluster. However, in a setting for homeless families the most common personality condition was the dependent personality disorder.[144]

Several more recent studies have highlighted the anti-social personality disorder, suggesting that between 17% and 25% of the homeless suffer from this condition. Two of these studies have attempted to adjust existing instruments to eliminate items which are biased against or otherwise inappropriate for the homeless in the diagnosis of antisocial personality disorder. While North, Smith, and Spitznagel concluded that there was a 25% rate with or without adjustments,[145] Koegel's

---

[142] See Elizabeth M. Smith, Carol S. North, and Edward L. Spitznagel, "Alcohol, drugs, and psychiatric comorbidity among homeless women: An epidemiological study," Journal of Clinical Psychiatry 4 (2), pp. 111-120 (June 1992).

[143] Pamela Fischer and William R. Breakey, "The epidemiology of alcohol, drug, and mental disorders among homeless persons," American Psychologist 46 (11), pp. 1115-28 (November 1991), p. 1124.

[144] Ellen Bassuk, L. Rubin, and L. Lauriat, "Characteristics of sheltered homeless families," American Journal of Public Health 76, pp. 1097-1101 (1986).

[145] Carol S. North and Elizabeth M. Smith, "A comparison of homeless men and women: Different populations, different needs," Community Mental Health Journal, 29 (5), pp. 423-441 (1993).

adjustments lowered his initial 25.2% current rate to 17.4%.[146] Other diagnoses investigated include mental retardation. In a group of 7 studies reviewed by Fischer and Breakey, up 6% of the homeless were reported to be retarded.[147]

Several other researchers have dispensed with the traditional diagnostic categories and attempted to define naturalistically their own categories using the statistical technique of cluster analysis with data from samples of mentally ill homeless individuals. Mowbray, Bybee, and Cohen, for instance, identified a cluster, representing over a third of their sample (35.2%) that fit the stereotype of the aggressive, psychotic, homeless person with skill deficits in many areas, and this group constituted about 10% of the homeless.[148] In contrast, Morse presents four subgroups of the homeless mentally ill, the first of which (53.2% of subjects) is average in most areas; the second (19.8%), evidencing high levels of alcoholic and other symptomatic behaviors, as well as pre-homeless imprisonment; the third (16.5%), characterized by mental health needs and interpersonal problems, having spent more time than the other groups in shelters; and finally, the fourth group (4.8%), distinguished by their relative strengths.[149] Most of this last group were females who had higher rates of employment and income and larger social networks than the other groups.

Breakdowns of the various indicators of mental illness by other demographic categories reveal few consistent, but several suggestive associations. In respect to race, most studies report little or no difference in mental disability between racial or

---

[146] Koegel and Burnham, Chapter 7, "Problems in the assessment of mental illness among the homeless," p. 88.

[147] Fischer and Breakey, "The epidemiology of alcohol, drug, and mental disorders among homeless persons," p. 1122.

[148] Carol Mowbray, Deborah Bybee, and Evan Cohen, "Describing the homeless mentally ill: Cluster analysis results," American Journal of Community Psychology, 21 (1), pp. 67-93 (April 1993).

[149] Morse and Calsyn, Chapter 10, "Mental health and other human service needs of homeless people," p. 125.

ethnic groups, however mental disability is measured.[150] An important exception is the Ohio study which revealed that in this state blacks had lower levels of hospitalization and psychiatric symptomatology, but more behavioral disturbance than did whites.[151] In a Chicago study, persons of color were found to have higher symptom and hospitalization rates than whites.[152] Three out of the four studies revealed higher rates of mental illness among younger homeless.[153] Contrary to popular opinion, there have been no consistent findings as to whether the street or sheltered homeless experience more mental illness.[154] In regard to the issue of mobility among the homeless, there are a few studies which suggest that the mentally ill tend to be the more mobile.[155]

Findings regarding whether the seriously mentally ill accumulate in the population of long-term homeless are equivocal, though they suggest that this may be so.[156] One important study indicated little or no difference in mental health status between the short- and long-term homeless;[157] and another found higher rates among the more recently homeless.[158] On the whole, there is evidence to suggest that women, Veterans, younger people, the more mobile, and the longer term homeless

---

[150] See Robertson, Chapter 5, in Robertson and Greenblatt, (eds.), Homelessness: A National Perspective, p. 73.

[151] First, Chapter 3, Draft of Ohio Study.

[152] Robertson, Chapter 5, in Robertson and Greenblatt, (eds.), Homelessness: A National Perspective, p. 73.

[153] Tessler and Dennis, A synthesis of NIMH-funded research concerning persons who are homeless and mentally ill, p. 73.

[154] Ibid., p. 72.

[155] Ibid., p. 73.

[156] Ibid., p. 76.

[157] M. Kahn, et al, "Psychopathology on the streets: Psychological assessment of the homeless," Professional Psychology: Research and Practice 18, pp. 580-86 (1987).

[158] E. Susser, E. Struening, and S. Conver, "Psychiatric problems in homeless men," Archives of General Psychiatry 46, pp. 845-50 (1989).

are more likely to be seriously mentally ill. However, each of these apparent associations no doubt mask disparate and unique pathways by which each of these groups experience social disintegration, as represented by their homelessness, mental disability, substance abuse, or criminal involvements.

The research considered in this section has often attempted to go beyond the mere description of significant associations to generate data which attempts to break out of the common chicken-and-egg causal conundrums which beset the interpretation of so much of this research. Most typically, these studies include a few questions on the time order of the various events in the lives of homeless individuals so as to elucidate what led to what. This data is retrospective in nature and subject to many sources of error and bias in the subjects' remembrance, an issue which is particularly pertinent to individuals who may be suffering from psychosis and the attendant problems of "reality testing". Ultimately, a body of longitudinal research will need to be developed to resolve these issues. However, this is an extremely difficult expensive methodology to use with a population with which it is so difficult to maintain contact for even six months or a year, let alone a lifetime. But until this is accomplished, all that can be done is to infer probable developmental pathways by synthesizing the often disparate findings of the existing research.

Probably the earliest hypothesized precursors to homelessness which have been investigated include traumatic events, such as physical or sexual abuse as a child, rape, or later combat experiences. A growing collection of studies has been documenting the remembrance of these events by the homeless mentally ill. Over two-fifths (41% men & 44% women) of the homeless mentally ill in one study have reported traumatic events in their earlier years such as assault or rape. Specifically, this study found that a sixth (16%) of the men and almost a third (30%) of the women experienced either physical or sexual abuse as a child.[159] Similarly, Weitzman and

---

[159] Carol S. North, Elizabeth M. Smith, and Edward L. Spitznagel, "Violence and the homeless: An epidemiological study of victimization and aggression," Journal of Traumatic Stress 7 (1), pp. 95-110 (Jan. 1994), p. 103.

Knickman compared the rates of trauma in the backgrounds of homeless and a matched non-homeless poor sample, and found that the homeless were 2.5 times more likely to have been sexually abused as children, 1.9 times more likely to be physically abused, and also, 1.9 times more likely to have been physically abused as an adult.[160] Likewise, it has been found that the homeless mentally ill were more likely than a matched group to have been criminally victimized as children.[161]

Other childhood difficulties have also been identified as precursors to the experience of the homeless mentally ill. One researcher interviewed the families of origin of 40 homeless individuals and described these families as, "unstable, isolated and isolating, violent, aggressive, and frequently alcoholic."[162] Such families of origin are often fragmented, with the subsequently created families described as riddled with spouse abuse and inadequate parenting, and also eventually failing.[163] One study noted a significant association between the symptoms of adult personality disorder among the homeless mentally ill and the number of childhood conduct disorder symptoms.[164] Another researcher reported that the homeless mentally ill were found to have a disproportionate number of runaway episodes in their youth.[165] Similarly, another study found that a majority of the men and a substantial proportion of women

---

[160] Beth C. Weitzman, James R. Knickman, and Marybeth Shinn, "Predictors of shelter use among low-income families: Psychiatric history, substance abuse, and victimization," American Journal of Public Health 82 (10), pp. 1547-50 (Nov. 1992), p. 1549.

[161] Les B. Whitbeck and Ronald L. Simons, "A comparison of adaptive strategies and patterns of victimization among homeless adolescents and adults," Violence and Victims 8 (2), pp. 1394-98 (Summer 1993).

[162] Fay E. Reilly, "Experience of family among homeless individuals," Issues in Mental Health Nursing 14 (4), pp. 309-21 (Oct.-Dec. 1993).

[163] Ibid., pp. 309-32.

[164] Carol S. North, Elizabeth M. Smith, Edward L. Spitznagal, "Is antisocial personality a valid diagnosis among the homeless?" American Journal of Psychiatry 21 (1), pp. 67-93 (April 1993).

[165] E. Susser, E. Struening, and S. Conver, "Psychiatric problems in homeless men," Archives of General Psychiatry 148, pp. 1026-30 (1991), p. 1026.

had a history of physically aggressive behaviors, often beginning in childhood.[166] Each of these indicators of family fragmentation is highlighted by the finding that over three-quarters (77%) of the homeless mentally ill did not live with both biological parents from birth through the age of 18, in contrast to the 65% of a matched never homeless sample.[167]

It is, therefore, not surprising that the homeless mentally ill have experienced unusually high levels of childhood placement. This includes placement in foster care,[168] as well as in group homes.[169] Specifically, it has been found that a tenth (10%) of men and a sixth (17%) of women among the homeless mentally ill had been placed in foster care before the age of 18, and 46% of these before the age of 10.[170] (See chapter 6 for further details on such findings.)

Another precursor in the lives of the mentally ill homeless involves minimal levels of educational achievement. It is, therefore, not unexpected that Burt found low educational attainment to be strongly related to later institutionalization. She concluded that, "Among those with neither mental hospitalization nor chemical dependency treatment, 31% had some post high school education compared with 18% or less for the other groups, and another 35% had high school diplomas."[171]

An important issue for disentangling the causal relationships between homelessness and serious mental illness is their relative periods of onset. While there are no definitive findings on this issue, the weight of evidence clearly suggests that

---

[166]   North, Smith, and Spitznagel, "Violence and the homeless...", p. 95.

[167]   Carol Caton, Patrick Shrout, Paula Eagle, Lewis Opler, Alan Felix, and Boanerges Dominguez, "Risk factors for homelessness among schizophrenic men: A case-control study," American Journal of Public Health 84 (2), pp. 265-70 (Feb. 1994), p. 267.

[168]   M.A. Winkleby, B. Rockhill, D. Jatulis, and S.P. Fortmann, "The medical origins of homelessness," American Journal of Public Health, 82, pp. 1394-98 (1992); Susser, Struening, and Conver, "Psychiatric problems in homeless men".

[169]   Ibid., p. 1026.

[170]   Winkleby, Jatulis, and Fortman, "The medical origins of homelessness," p. 1395.

[171]   Burt, Over The Edge, p. 25.

mental illness almost always predates the first homeless episode. The median age of onset of psychiatric disorder was found in one study to be 21 for the never homeless and 20 for the homeless. It has also been found that the never homeless were first hospitalized at a median age of 22, and the homeless at 21.[172] Likewise, Sosin found that in about 62% of the cases, initial homelessness followed the first hospitalization, occurring on average one year later.[173] However, the delay between first hospitalization and eventual homelessness may be a more extended period as most estimates of the mean age of initial homelessness place this around 30 or over. Using a large sample of mentally ill homeless individuals, North calculated the mean age at 30.7 for men and 26.5 for women.[174] In a different study, it was found that over two-thirds of the homeless who were depressed, became depressed prior to their first homeless episode, and in two-fifths (40.0%) of the cases, it preceded the first homeless episode by at least 5 years.[175] There is, therefore, strong evidence to suggest that in the large majority of cases, homelessness follows emotional disturbance, subsequent hospitalization, and a failure to cope with the evolving condition.

This period of unsuccessful coping, typically occurring in the 20s, involves a deteriorating work history, a failure to obtain needed treatments, and a crystallization of dysfunctional personality patterns. Those with a history of mental hospitalization among the homeless were found to be the least likely to have ever worked, as over a quarter (26%) in this group had never held a job.[176] Those who had been institutionalized among the homeless had been out of work for an average of 4 to 5

---

[172] Caton, et al., "Risk factors for homelessness...", p. 267.

[173] Sosin, Colson, and Grossman, Homelessness in Chicago.

[174] North, Smith, and Spitznagel, "An epidemiological study of victimization and aggression," p.101.

[175] Koegel and Burnham, "Problems in the assessment of mental illness among the homeless," p. 95.

[176] Burt, Over The Edge, p. 27.

years, most typically placing their last employment in their mid-20s, not long after their initial hospitalization.

It has been reported that the majority of men among the homeless mentally ill and a substantial proportion of the women had a history of physically aggressive behaviors. Aggressive adult behavior was found to be associated with substance abuse and major depression.[177] Specifically, it was found that 87% of the men and 82% of the women either engaged in aggressive behavior, such as mugging, starting fights, using weapons, assault, abusing a child, or property damage prior to their first year homeless. The frequency of these behaviors dropped to 51% for both men and women in the year after their first homeless episode.[178] Another researcher elaborated on the disability hypothesis as it pertains to serious mental illness:

> The disabling functional deficits of major mental illness appeared to be important contributing factors to homelessness. These deficits included disorganized thinking and actions, poor problem-solving skills, inability to mobilize oneself to seek help, depression and paranoia that prevented acceptance of help.[179]

It is, thus, understandable that the homeless were found to have used significantly fewer long-term therapists,[180] received less preventative health care,[181] used fewer prescription medication,[182] or had worse access to health insurance than

---

[177] North, Smith, and Spitznagel, "An epidemiological study of victimization and aggression," p. 95.

[178] Ibid., p. 105.

[179] Richard H. Lamb and Doris M. Lamb, "Factors contributing to homelessness among the chronically and severely mentally ill," Hospital & Community Psychiatry 41 (3), pp. 301-305 (March 1990).

[180] Caton, et al., "Risk factors for homelessness...", p. 268.

[181] Marilyn A. Winkleby, "Comparison of risk factors for ill health in a sample of homeless and nonhomeless poor," Public Health Reports 105 (4) (July-August, 1990), p. 404.

[182] Weitzman, Knickman, and Shinn, "Predictors of shelter use among low-income families...", pp. 1547-50.

matched non-homeless samples.[183]

Another study focused on the role of negative life events in the year prior to the initial homeless episode and found that the soon-to-be homeless experienced over three times as many negative events than the general population (4.5 vs. 1.4). Almost four-fifths (78.9%) confronted unemployment; about three-fifths (58.5%), loss of income; close to half (45.6%), debt; about a third, being fired from a job (35.9%), death of a friend (32.3%), and assault (28.7%).[184] It is, therefore, not surprising that when the homeless are asked global questions about the origins of their homelessness, they infrequently attribute it to mental illness. For example, in studies in both Boston and Los Angeles only 3% attributed the cause of the first episode of homelessness to emotional problems.[185] The immediate crises in the lives of the homeless detract both the homeless and concerned others from an understanding of a far more complex ongoing process of disintegration, one involving an interplay between personal and systemic conditions, and a breakdown in the interdependencies that most take for granted.

Alcohol and Drug Abuse

Alcoholism is about as prevalent among the homeless as serious mental illness. Most studies place the rate between 10% and 50%, usually in the 20% to 40% range. At the lower end is a review of six studies by Tessler, who placed the figure at 24%.[186] A review of 15 of studies by Rossi placed it at 32.7%[187] whereas Mulkern

---

[183] Winkleby, "Comparison of risk factors for ill health...", p. 404.

[184] Morse and Calsyn, Chapter 10, "Mental health and other human service needs of homeless people," in Robertson and Greenblatt, (eds.), Homelessness: A National Perspective, p. 121.

[185] R.K. Farr, P. Koegel, and A. Burnham, A Study of Homelessness and Mental Illness in the Skid Row Area of Los Angeles, (Los Angeles: Los Angeles County Department of Mental Health, 1986); R.K. Schutt, Boston's Homeless, 1986-1987: Change and Continuity. Report to the Long Island Shelter. (Boston: University of Massachusetts, 1988).

[186] Tessler and Dennis, A Synthesis of NIMH-funded Research... , p. 21.

[187] Rossi, Down and Out in America, p. 156.

and Spence's review and also Wright produced a 38% rate, with a range of 21 to 67%.[188] Several of these estimates are consistent with the finding that a third of the homeless (33.2%) have been in a detox unit for either alcoholism or drug abuse. Of the approximately third of the homeless who have problems of alcoholism, Rossi estimated that a third of those (10.1% total) are unable to work because of their alcoholism.[189]

The proportion of homeless with problems of alcoholism has probably declined because of the entry of various new groups into the homeless population in recent years, many of whom have few problems with alcoholism. Based on a review of studies in two periods, 1968 to 1972 and 1981 to 1984, Wright concluded that the proportion declined from 49% to 28% between these two periods.[190] Whatever the precise percentage, it is clear that with the overall rate of alcoholism in the U.S. population around 3 to 10 percent,[191] the homeless have between 3 and 10 times the national prevalence.

An examination of the demographics of those with problems of alcoholism among the homeless reveals several associations. It is perhaps significant that Wright observed that in both the HCH and a New York study the rate of problem drinking among the homeless was curvilinearly related with age, with both men and women. The rate is noticeably lower among the young and old.[192] The overall risk for homelessness is in a similar manner curvilinearly related with age (see table 2-4, chapter 2). In respect to race, differences between blacks and whites among the homeless are insubstantial. However, American Indians have a level of alcoholism

---

[188] V. Mulkern, V.J. Bradley, R. Spence, et al., Homeless Needs Assessment Study: Findings and Recommendations for the Massachusetts Department of Mental Health (Boston: Human Research Insitute, 1985); Wright ?

[189] Rossi, Down and Out in America, p. 156.

[190] Wright, Address Unknown, p. 96.

[191] Valiant, 1983.

[192] Wright, Address Unknown, p. 98.

(60%) which far exceeds the mean and is consistent with levels seen in many groups of non-homeless American Indians.[193]

Just as is the case in the overall U.S. population, men among the homeless have a considerably greater likelihood of suffering from alcoholism than do women. Wright placed the male-female ratio at about 3 times, with 47% of homeless men and 16% of homeless women having problems with alcoholism.[194]   In contrast, Burt placed the ratio at about 2.[195]   It has also been found that alcoholic men among the homeless tend to be singularly diagnosed, whereas the women evidence a wider range of problems such as mental illness.[196]   Despite the high proportion of never married persons among the homeless, those with alcohol problems are more likely to have been married and separated.[197]

The impact of education in the lives of alcoholic homeless persons is mixed. One study reported no difference in the level of educational preparation between alcohol and non-alcohol abusers among the homeless,[198]   whereas two other studies did. A report of Mulkern and Spence's,[199] as well as one of Corrigan and Anderson's[200] reported that those who abused alcohol were less likely to have graduated from high school, and to have fewer occupational skills than did those among the homeless who

---

[193]   Ibid., p. 98.

[194]   Ibid., p. 98.

[195]   Burt, Over The Edge, p. 109.

[196]   Fischer and Breakey, "The epidemiology of alcohol, drug, and mental disorders among homeless persons," p. 1116.

[197]   Brent B. Benda and Elizabeth D. Hutchison, "Homelessness and alcohol," in Belcher and DiBlasio, Helping the Homeless, p. 129.

[198]   B. Roth and J. Bean, "Alcohol problems and homelessness: Findings from the Ohio study," in F.D. Wittman, (ed.), The Homeless with Alcohol-related Problems (Rockville, MD: U.S. Department of Health and Human Services, 1985).

[199]   Mulkern, Bradley, Spence, et al., Homeless Needs Assessment Study..., p. 129.

[200]   E.M. Corrigan and S.C. Anderson, "Homeless alcoholic women on skid row," American Journal of Drug and Alcohol Abuse 10, pp. 535-49.

did not abuse alcohol. The well-known tendency for alcoholism to complicate and perpetuate the homeless condition is supported by the finding that those who abuse alcohol have been homeless for twice as long as the others.[201]

There has been only scant data reported pertinent to the question about the role alcoholism has in precipitating homelessness and the extent that it develops in response to homelessness. For instance, the longitudinal research of Cohen showed,

> ...that moderate and heavy alcohol consumption preceded by nearly a decade a man's permanent arrival on the Bowery... Marginal poverty and periodic unemployment created personal and family stressors which in turn produce increased exposure and desire for alcohol; increased alcohol consumption makes it more difficult to hold a job, as well as further exacerbating family strain.[202]

Another study found evidence that, for many of the homeless, problems of alcoholism and mental illness began in adolescence and continued into adulthood.[203] Similarly, it has been reported that alcoholics are more likely to have exhibited problem behavior as juveniles and to report dysfunctional families of origin.[204]

Others have focused on the consequences of alcoholism among the homeless. For example, "Alcohol abuse may be the single greatest risk factor for arrest among the homeless population."[205] It has also been reported that the homeless alcohol-dependent are between one and one-third to two times as likely to have criminal histories as those who are not alcoholics, however, the question about which is cause

---

[201] Roth and Bean, "Alcohol problems and homelessness...".

[202] Cohen and Sokolovsky, Chapter 5, "Alcoholism contributes to homelessness," in Orr, (ed.), The Homeless, p. 80.

[203] Benda and Hutchinson, "Homelessness and alcohol," in Belcher and DiBlasio, Helping the Homeless, p. 139.

[204] P.J. Fischer and W.R. Breakey, "The epidemiology of alcoholism in a homeless population: Findings from the Baltimore homeless study," Paper presented at the 16th Alcohol Epidemiology Symposium of the Kettil Bruum society for Social and Epidemiological Research on Alcohol, Budapest, Hungary, June 1990.

[205] Fischer and Breakey, "The epidemiology of alcohol, drug, and mental disorders among homeless persons," p. 1120.

and which is effect is unclear.[206]

Estimates for current drug abuse among the homeless range between 10% and 77%, with most falling within the 13% to 16% range.[207] The estimates vary considerably depending on the type of measure or the type of drug abuse used. Burt reports, for instance, of levels up to 10.1% for drug dependence among the homeless,[208] whereas estimates of the percentage who have ever had a drug abuse problem are around a half (48%) or higher (69.2%).[209]

In respect to type of drug, one study found that over four-fifths (80.4%) were found to abuse marijuana.[210] Almost as high is the finding that two-thirds of the homeless in New York shelters tested positive in urine tests for cocaine. However, cocaine use is generally believed to be unusually high in this city. This same report stated that little evidence was found for drugs other than cocaine, alcohol, and marijuana, despite the estimate that a third of homeless adults used crack regularly.[211]

Several of the drug abuse surveys have included data on the demographics of homeless drug abusers. Most studies have found higher rates among the street homeless (25%), compared with those in shelters (3%-20%).[212] It is also a fairly consistent finding that men are disproportionately represented among homeless drug

---

[206] Ibid., p. 1120.

[207] Wright, Address Unknown, p. 101; Dennis McCarthy, Milton Argeriou, and Robert Huebner, "Alcoholism, drug abuse, and the homeless," American Psychologist 46 (11), pp. 1139-48 (Nov. 1991); Tessler and Dennis, Synthesis of NIMH-funded Research..., p. 21.

[208] Burt, Over The Edge, p. 116.

[209] G. Vernex, et al, Review of California's Program for the Mentally Disabled (Santa Monca, CA: Rand Corporation, 1988); Koegel and Burnham, Chapter 7, "Problems in the assessment of mental illness among the homeless," in Robertson and Greenblatt, (eds.), Homelessness: A National Perspective, p. 84.

[210] Andrew Cuomo, The Way Home: A New Direction in Social Policy (New York: New York City Commission on the Homeless, 1992), p. c-2.

[211] Jencks, The Homeless, p. 43.

[212] Burt, Over The Edge, p. 116.

abusers. For example, Wright reported that 11% of males and 8% of females who used the Health Care for Homeless clinics currently abuse drugs other than alcohol.[213] One of the strongest correlates of drug abuse was found to be with age, and similar to alcoholism, this falls off in older adults.[214] Fewer than a third (29%) of homeless drug abusers report having received services in a residential treatment program.[215]

There is little evidence to suggest that a significant level of drug abuse among the homeless develops after the first homeless episode, but some which indicates that it may, on average, have developed many years prior to this time. Caton and Shrout report that the median age of onset of drug abuse was 18 for the never homeless, whereas it was only 16 for the homeless.[216] This would suggest that these individuals have managed to stave off the loss of a home for 10 to 15 years while they no doubt struggled with their addiction and attempted to develop or maintain home, employment, and social supports.

Physical Health Problems

It has been estimated that over a third (36.8%) of the homeless experience poor physical health, a level which is about twice the rate found in a national sample of U.S. adults.[217] Similarly, Burt found that 35% of her sample, and 31% of those who had never been institutionalized, perceived their health as fair or poor, compared with 20% of poor Americans, and 10% of the general U.S. population.[218] Another study found that between 25% and 40% reported that they had spent at least one day

---

[213] Wright, Address Unknown, p. 101.

[214] Ibid., p. 101.

[215] Ann Shlay and Peter Rossi, "Social science research and contemporary studies of homelessness," Annual Review of Sociology 18, pp. 129-160 (1992).

[216] Caton, et al., "Risk factors for homelessness...".

[217] Rossi, Down and Out in America, p. 89.

[218] Burt, Over The Edge, p. 28.

lying down during the previous month due to a health problem. Most of those reporting health problems also report that these problems preclude employment. A review of ten studies found that an average of 32.5% were reported too disabled to work.[219]

The most common health problems include high blood pressure (16.9%), arthritis (10.9%), and anemia (10.5%).[220] Tuberculosis has been found to be at least 25 times more prevalent in the homeless than in the general population. Similarly, sexual assault on women, 20 times as frequent; diseases of the extremities, such as chronically infested skin ulcers, 15 times as common; chronic lung disease, 6 times; neurological disorders, especially seizure disorders, 6 times; and other conditions that have been found to be at least 3 times more prevalent include nutritional disorders, tooth and mouth diseases, hepatic liver disorder, skin ailments, infestations such as lice, and trauma of all kinds.[221]

There is less to suggest that the health problems of the homeless have played a significant causal role in the development of the homeless condition. There is considerably more to indicate that such difficulties usually develop as a consequence of the abysmal living conditions of the homeless, and as secondary reactions to other disabilities. In recent surveys of homeless people, health problems were infrequently given as a reason for homelessness. They were mentioned as precipitating factors in just two surveys, by 4% and 7% of respondents.[222] Yet, some studies have reported that physical health problems are among the top ten precipitating causes of homelessness.[223] There is some evidence that health problems may play a role as

---

[219]   Rossi, Down and Out in America, p. 24.

[220]   Morse and Calsyn, Chapter 10, "Mental health and other human service needs of homeless people," p. 117.

[221]   Wright, Address Unknown, p. 111.

[222]   Jahiel, Chapter 11, "Health and health care of homeless people," in Robertson and Greenblatt, (eds), Homelessness: A National Perspective, p. 146.

[223]   J.D. Wright and E. Weber, Homelessness and Health (New York: McGraw-Hill, 1987).

predisposing factors, such as in a Boston survey where 7% of the respondents cited health as primary cause of their homelessness, and an additional 16% cited health difficulties as a basis for their unemployment.[224] In a 1986 study, a detailed case assessment and review questionnaire was used in 13 projects. The reviewers assessed the relative importance of 22 possible causes of homelessness in adults. Chronic physical disorder was scored as being without importance in 78% of the cases, minor importance 9%, and major importance in 10%, and most important in 3%.[225]

Criminal Involvements

A substantial proportion of the homeless have a history of arrest and incarceration. Although we did not know precisely how much of this has developed in response to the struggle to survive on the streets, and how much of it predates the homeless experience, there is a lot that is known. Overall, it has been estimated on the basis of a review of 15 surveys that rates of arrest or incarceration range from a fifth to two-thirds of the homeless.[226] Estimates of arrest rates, exclusive of incarceration, are generally in the upper part of this range. For example, in Los Angeles, close to two-thirds (64%) were found to have multiple arrests as adults.[227] In Detroit, those with arrest records were found to have an average of 5.3 prior arrests.[228] A more reliable measure of criminal activity is the level of incarceration. In another review of 16 studies, Rossi reported that the average percentage with

---

[224]   Mulkern, Bradley, Spence, et al., Homeless Needs Assessment Study.

[225]   Wright and Weber, Homelessness and Health, p. 146.

[226]   Fischer, Chapter 6, "Criminal behavior and victimization among homeless people," p. 90.

[227]   M. Robertson, R.H. Ropers, and R. Boyer, The Homeless of Los Angeles County: An Empirical Assessment (Los Angeles: University of California, School of Public Health, 1985), p. 91.

[228]   A. Solarz, "An examination of criminal behavior among the homeless," Paper presented at the annual meeting of the American Society of Criminology, San Diego, CA, Nov. 13-17, 1985.

prison experience was just over a fifth (21.3%), with jail experience, over a third (34.7%), and with either, over two-fifths (42.1%).[229] Thus, close to two-thirds of the homeless with multiple arrests have been held in a jail or served time in a prison because of these arrests.

Among the homeless who have been arrested or served time, men and young adults have been disproportionately represented. For example, of the 20.1% who have served time in a state or federal prison, close to three-fifths (59.9%) of homeless men fell into this category, while only 1.9% of homeless women did.[230] In contrast, a Baltimore study found that 88% of men and 54% of women who had been homeless longer than a year had been arrested, compared with 65% and 35% of those homeless for less than a year.[231] These figures are several times the rates for the general population, 22% for men and 6% for women, who have arrest histories.[232] While 57.4% of homeless arrestees in one study were aged 25 to 44, compared with 49.7% of arrestees in the general population; only 9.3% of the homeless arrestees fell in the 18 to 24 age group, compared to 41.1% of all arrestees. Similarly, 28.5% of the homeless arrested persons were between 45 and 64 compared with less than one percent (0.8%) of all those arrested.[233] This supports the notion that the homeless who become involved with criminal activity do so at a somewhat older age than the general population, more typically in their thirties than in their twenties, sometimes as a response to their homeless condition. It has also been found that homeless individuals with arrest records have lower levels of education, lower scores on IQ

[229] Rossi, Down and Out in America, p. 165.

[230] Burt, Over The Edge, pp. 22-23.

[231] P.J. Fischer, W.R. Breakey, and A. Ross, "Criminal activity among the homeless," Paper presented at the 88th annual meeting of the American Anthropological Association, Washington, D.C., Nov. 15-19, 1989.

[232] E. McGarrell and T. Flanagan, Sourcebook of Criminal Justice Statistics--1984 (Washington, D.C.: U.S. Department of Justice, Bureau of Justice Statistics, 1985).

[233] Fischer, Chapter 5, "The criminalization of the homeless in Baltimore," in Robertson and Greenblatt, (eds.), Homelessness: A National Perspective, p. 58.

tests, and greater signs of cognitive impairment than the homeless without such records.[234]

It has been reported that, "Fewer of the arrests of the homeless were made for serious or violent crimes, as defined in the Crime Index by the FBI." However, this is similarly true of non-homeless arrested persons, as close to two-fifths of both groups (39.8% and 38.8%). There are notable differences among the arrest patterns of whites and non-whites: whites have a higher than average rate of crimes against property (72.3% of homeless white arrests vs. 51.2% of overall white arrests), whereas non-whites have a disproportionate percentage of crimes against the person, 44.7% of non-white homeless arrests vs. 36.0% of total non-white arrests).[235] It has been noted that drug traffic is relatively rare among the homeless, except on a small scale.[236] Several have reported that most of the crimes of the homeless involve the struggle to survive and obtain necessities such as food and shelter:[237] "Where the offenses are reported, the results suggest that homeless people are most often arrested for relatively trivial and essentially victimless crimes arising more from the homeless condition than from deliberate criminal intent."[238] Similarly, around a fifth of a Detroit sample of shelter residents admitted to benefitting from some source of illegal income in the prior six months.[239] In a Baltimore study, 34% of men and 28% of the homeless women resorted to at least one means of illegally obtaining income, such as

---

[234] Fischer, Breakey, and Ross, "Criminal activity among the homeless," p. 94.

[235] Fischer, Chapter 5, "The criminalization of the homeless in Baltimore," in Robertson and Greenblatt, (eds.), Homelessness: A National Perspective, p. 59.

[236] Fischer, Chapter 6, "Criminal behavior and victimization among homeless people".

[237] Ibid., p. 103.

[238] Ibid., p. 103.

[239] Whitman, B. Graves, and P. Accardo, "Parents learning together: Training parenting skills for retarded adults," Social Work 34, pp. 431-34 (1989).

panhandling, stealing, selling drugs, or prostitution.[240] This picture is particularly true of homeless youth, who are reported to engage in illegal activities such as prostitution at alarming rates, compared with both non-homeless youth and homeless adults.[241]

Despite the evidence which suggests that much of the criminal activity of the homeless reflects a response to the homeless condition itself, there is also much to suggest that most of those homeless who are criminally involved have been so long before their first homeless episode. In one study, nearly two-fifths of homeless men and one-fifth of homeless women had first been arrested as juveniles.[242] Similarly, in a Detroit study, close to three-fifths of homeless shelter residents had first been arrested before the age of 21, with an average age at first adult arrest being 22.[243] In a Chicago survey, 7% were in jail just immediately prior to their current episode of homelessness.[244]

There are several views as to how criminal activity contributes to homelessness. One of the most common represents a version of the penal deinstitutionalization hypothesis. When asked about contributory causes to their homelessness, 14% of the men and 7% of the women mentioned discharge from jail.[245] Similarly, reports have frequently cited criminal activity as a pathway into homelessness, and that "People report having been released from correctional institutions directly to the streets with few resources with which to achieve

---

[240] Fischer, Chapter 6, "Criminal behavior and victimization among homeless people," p. 89.

[241] Ibid., p. 89.

[242] Fischer, Breakey, and Ross, "Criminal activity among the homeless," p. 91.

[243] Solarz, "An examination of criminal behavior among the homeless...".

[244] Belcher, 1989, cited in, Pamela J. Fischer, Chapter 5, "The criminalization of homelessness," in, Robertson and Greenblatt, (eds.), Homelessness: A National Perspective, p. 71.

[245] Ibid., p. 71.

reassimilation into society.[246] A St. Louis study that only about 22% of homeless respondents, or about a third of those with arrest records, reported that they had been arrested since becoming homeless.[247] But more generally, it has been hypothesized that, "It is likely that some habitual criminals accumulate in the homeless population through 'downward drift'."[248] It is, therefore, not surprising that the homeless are often victims of crime. One researcher reports that over a third (34%) have been victims of crime in the previous six months.[249]

Multiple Disabilities

The degree of overlap between the homeless with the various types of disabilities typically encountered is a critical issue for service planning, and one for which there is little hard data. If the overlap is high, with those with disabilities usually having multiple disabilities, then the need for linking multiple types of services become more important for this group, and a more modest approach involving crisis and financial assistance, and minimal services, can be used for those in the non-disabilities group. Whereas, if the overlap is minimal and the spread of disabilities throughout the homeless population is maximal, then a much more comprehensive strategy of services is indicated, but services which are less intensive and more specialized.

The portion of the homeless who have at least one or more disabilities, when this term is interpreted broadly, is probably in the 80% to 90% range, if for no other reason than the fact that over four-fifths (83%) have long-standing employment

---

[246] Fischer, Chapter 6, "Criminal behavior and victimization among homeless people," p. 105.

[247] G. Morse, et al., Homeless People in St. Louis: A Mental Health Program Evaluation Field Study & Follow-up Investigation (Jefferson City: Missouri Department of Mental Health, 1985).

[248] Fischer, Chapter 6, "Criminal behavior and victimization among homeless people," p. 103.

[249] Ropers, The Invisible Homeless, p. 166.

problems, the highest proportion found among any of the disability groups. It may be that the remainder do not report employment problems only because the severity of their other disabilities precludes any consideration of employment. Rossi found in his Chicago sample that all but 4% of the homeless reported one or more problems, lending credence to this explanation. A summary of the estimates of the prevalence of the various disabilities or problems would include the following: employment, 83%; education, 48%; criminal involvements, 42%; alcoholism, 35%; health, 35%; mental illness, 30%; and drug abuse, 15% . If these estimates are accurate, it would suggest that the typical homeless person is dealing with an average of 3 of the disabilities or problems reviewed. This represents slightly fewer problems than is implied by Rossi's conclusions, based on the subjective reports of his homeless sample, that, in addition to the 4% who reported no problems, another third (35%) had only 1 or 2 problems, and the remaining three-fifths (61%) had 3 or more problems, including a sixth (16%) who reported 5 to 7 disabilities or personal problems.[250]

There is probably significant overlap between the subgroups who abuse drugs and alcohol among the homeless. Most estimates of the combined percentage represented are just about the same as that of alcoholism by itself. This suggests that while most drug abusers also abuse alcohol, between a third and a half of the alcoholics also abuse drugs. This is consistent is Tessler and Dennis' estimate of 32% for the combination of drugs and alcohol.[251]   There does not appear to any clear consensus on the degree of overlap among mental illness and substance abuse. One reviewer reported that most studies found a lower rate of substance abuse among the mentally ill than the non-mentally ill homeless,[252] whereas Crystal, Ladner, and Towber reported that the mentally ill were only minimally more likely to have

---

[250]   Rossi, Down and Out in America, p. 177.

[251]   Tessler and Dennis, Synthesis of NIMH-funded Research , p. 21.

[252]   Ibid., p. 33.

substance abuse problems, including alcohol, than other homeless (43% v. 32%).[253] In several California counties the prevalence of dual diagnosis varied from 14% to 37% of the homeless. A weighted average of the findings from four of these studies[254] suggests that around 39% of the mentally ill, or 12% of the homeless, are also substance abusers. If this is so, then at least half of the homeless (53%) would be suffering from either mental illness, drug abuse, or alcoholism, or some combination. This is consistent with a HUD report which suggests an overlap of 10% to 20%, and that about half the shelter population suffered from at least one of these three interrelated conditions.[255] In contrast, Fischer and Breakey suggest that this figure ranges from one-half to three-fourths[256] and Wright, from one-half to two-thirds.[257]

In respect to the involvement of the mentally ill in criminal activities, a study in Los Angeles found that criminal activities were associated with previous hospitalization.[258] Another study supported this, and found that about a third (30%) of the mentally had current legal problems.[259] Similarly, 26% of drug abusers, and a smaller percentage of alcohol abusers (17%) were found to have current legal

---

[253] S. Crystal, S. Ladner, and R. Towber, "Multiple impairment patterns in the mentally ill homeless," International Journal of Mental Health 14 (4), pp. 61-73 (1986).

[254] See Tessler and Dennis, Synthesis of NIMH-funded Research..., p. 29.

[255] U.S., H.U.D, A Report to the Secreatary on the Homeless and Emergency Shelters, p. 4.

[256] Fischer and Breakey, "The epidemiology of alcohol, drug, and mental disorders among homeless persons," p. 1116.

[257] Wright, Address Unknown, p. 109.

[258] L. Gelbert, L.S. Linn, and B.D. Leake, "Mental health, alcohol, and drug use, and criminal hx among homeless adults," American Journal of Psychiatry 145, pp. 191-96 (1988), p. 194.

[259] Fischer, Chapter 6, "Criminal behavior and victimization among homeless people," p. 94.

problems.[260] Another indicator of the degree of overlap between these problems was the finding that almost half (46%) of mentally ill homeless individuals who also abuse alcohol had current legal problems, compared to less than a tenth (10%) of those with neither mental health or alcohol problems.[261]

Many of the popular theories of homelessness propose that it is only the particularly malignant combination of problems of serious mental illness with substance abuse, and possibly with other difficulties, that can explain why people become homeless. This is clearly simplistic, ignoring systemic causes, as well as the dynamic and interactive nature of the process of social disintegration involved. Yet, the well known tendency of multiple disabilities to aggravate and feed off of one another can not be dismissed. This is an idea which has taken many forms and goes back generations. For instance, in 1936, Sutherland and Locke proposed that low education, lack of job skills, and limited intelligence left individuals unable to compete for jobs.[262] It is implausible that with the moderate degrees of overlap found that there are an appreciable proportion of homeless who are free from personal disabilities, and perhaps no more than 20 to 30 percent--and possibly many fewer--who are suffering from merely employment, housing, or other economic difficulties, without the complications of poor physical or mental health, substance abuse, or criminal histories, or some combination.

Disabilities as a Cause of Homelessness

A Statistical Profile. Between 60% and 90% of the homeless have a significantly disabling condition, depending on whether educational and employment problems of the homeless are counted. Of these, at least a third may be too disabled

---

[260] Ibid., p. 94.

[261] R.K. Schutt and G.R. Garrett, Homeless in Boston in 1985: The View from Long Island (Boston: University of Massachusetts, 1986), p. 94.

[262] Edwin Sutherland and Harvey Locke, Twenty Thousand Homeless Men: A Study of Unemployed Men in the chicago Shelters (New York: Lipincott), cited by Westerfel, The Ins and Outs of Homelessness.

to engage in meaningful employment without substantial rehabilitation.[263] This compares with an overall rate of one in fifteen, or 7.0%, for those in the U.S. population who were reported in 1990 to be disabled due to mobility or self-care limitations. Five-eighths (63%) of these are reported to be unable to work. These are people who are reporting either for themselves or for a member of the household, and thus, these figures must be regarded as estimates, subject to both random and systematic error. The measure, in principle, includes physical, sensory, and mental disabilities.

The distribution of disabilities throughout the larger population only partly parallels those found in the population of homeless persons. While almost half (48.7%) of the U.S. population consists of males, less than two-fifths (38.3%) of the disabled with mobility or self-care limitations are male, representing a rate of disabilities of 5.5% for males. In contrast, the overall rate for females in 1990 is substantially higher at 8.4%. Yet, an overwhelming proportion of the homeless are men who have behavioral disabilities in the areas of substance abuse and criminal involvements, at levels higher than women, who have somewhat higher rates of mental illness. Whites in the United States also have a disproportionately small share of disabilities.[264] While the overall rate for severe work disabilities among whites is 4.1%, it is more than double for blacks, at 9.9%. The disparity between the rates for white males and black males is slightly greater at 4.3% vs. 10.3%, or a factor of 2.4 compared to a 3.2 differential among the homeless rates for these two groups. The discrepancy of disability rates between whites and blacks largely reflects an inverse correlation of disability rates with both education and income, a topic to which we will now turn.

The distribution of disabilities throughout the U.S. population is affected by a number of conditions, especially by levels of education and income, key indicators

---

[263] Rossi, Down and Out in America.

[264] Data on disability rates on racial groups is from, Cynthia Taeuber, Statistical Handbook on Women in America (Phoenix, AZ: Oryx Press, 1991), p. 224.

f social class. Many would like to consider all individuals equally at risk for disabilities no matter what their social standing. However, this is a myth that lingers on despite consistent findings on this issue[265]. Almost a quarter (23.4%) of those with the lowest levels of education, with less than 8 years of school, have a severe work disability, whereas this rate consistently drops as education increases, with only 1.3% of those with 16 or more years of school having a severe work disability (see figure 3-1). Similarly, those with less than a poverty level income have a severe work disability rate of 15.5%, compared with those with twice the poverty income who have a rate of only 2.4%.[266] As high as these rates are for the minimally educated and low-income, they are considerably less than the rates estimated for the homeless, which are at the least 32%, and for lesser degrees of disability, from 60% to 90%.

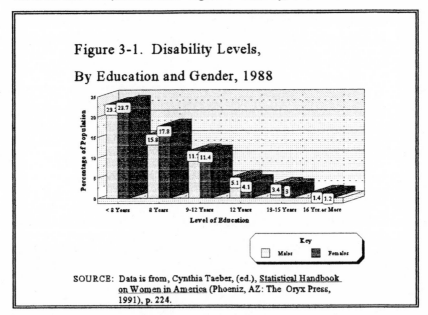

Figure 3-1. Disability Levels, By Education and Gender, 1988

SOURCE: Data is from, Cynthia Taeber, (ed.), Statistical Handbook on Women in America (Phoeniz, AZ: The Oryx Press, 1991), p. 224.

---

[265] See Christopher G. Hudson, "Socioeconomic status and mental illness: Implications the research for policy and practice" Journal of Sociology and Social Welfare, 15 (1), pp. 27-54; Leroy H. Pelton, "Child abuse and neglect: The myth of classlessness," American Journal of Orthopsychiatry 48 (4), pp. 608-17, (Oct. 1978).

[266] Taeuber, Statistical Handbook on Women in America, p. 224.

The proportion of the adult population who have graduated from high school throughout the 3,141 counties of the United States has an exceptionally strong correlation ($r = 0.79$) with the proportion of the county population with disabilities, potentially accounting for over three-fifths ($r^2 = 0.62$) of the variation. Without population weighting, or using alternative measures of education, the correlation continues to fall in the moderate to strong range. It should be emphasized that this is a bivariate correlation which does not take into account other potential causes.

It is an open question about the extent of the association between education and disability which can be accounted for by the impact of low education in placing individuals in dangerous or stressful work environments, or by the impact of pre-existing disabilities in interferring with the completion of high school. Figure 3-2 illustrates the relationship between rates of high school non-completion and disabilities on the county level, and indicates a fairly consistent and linear relationship, one which varies from 2% to over 20% disabled in those areas with the highest proportion of adults who have not graduated from high school. This county-level analysis is consistent with the individual level analysis of this relationship which is depicted in figure 3-1. For this reason, the measures of education and disability in this study are regarded as two indicators of a population's general capabilities and levels disabilities, broadly interpreted. It does not entail any assumptions as to the origins of these capabilities and disabilities, as we know they have diverse sources, involving social and educational opportunities, as well as the quality of family life and genetic factors, to mention a few.

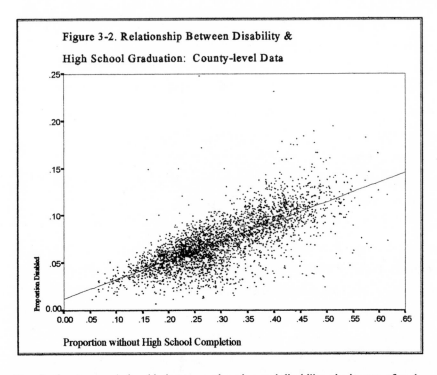

Figure 3-2. Relationship Between Disability & High School Graduation: County-level Data

Proportion without High School Completion

Despite the strong relationship between education and disability, the impact of each of these conditions on homeless rates is complex. Figure 3-3 breaks down homeless rates by the various combinations of low, medium, and high rates of disability and education, illustrating the homeless rates by the relative height of the bars. With one important exception, this chart suggests that just as homelessness increases with greater levels of disability, it is also higher in areas with significant levels of education, or diminishing levels of non-high school graduation. The average number of homeless persons per 10 thousand population increases from 7.7 in the counties with low levels of disability, to 8.1 in the medium-level areas, to 13.1 in the localities with the highest proportion of persons with disabilities.

With education, there appears to be a curvilinear relationship. While the rate of homelessness increases from 9.8 to 21.6 between the areas with low and medium of education, it then drops to 9.0 in the counties with highest levels of education.

Figure 3-3 shows us that this drop takes place completely within the strata of counties with the highest disability levels. There appears, therefore, to be an curvilinear interaction between education and disability in generating the highest levels of homelessness, 21.6 per 10 thousand, in those areas with high levels of disability and medium levels of education. One explanation is that 'education' actually represents the combined effect of at least two distinct and contrasting processes. On one hand, low levels of education directly contributes to homelessness as we know that most of the homeless originate from those with only a high school diploma or less. Thus, lack of education contributes to high levels of homelessness through creating a general vulnerability to economic disenfranchisement. On the other hand, the more people with college degrees, the more homeless. But in this case, we know that few homeless are being recruited from college graduates, so instead we are led to hypothesize that the relative numbers of these highly educated workers may make it extra difficult for those with low levels of education to successfully compete in the job market.

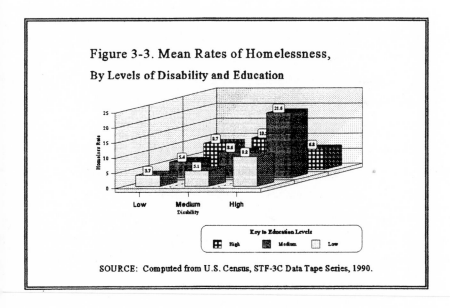

Figure 3-3. Mean Rates of Homelessness, By Levels of Disability and Education

SOURCE: Computed from U.S. Census, STF-3C Data Tape Series, 1990.

The combination of these two processes in creating higher levels of homelessness in those areas with intermediate levels of education clearly has its most virulent consequences when the proportion of persons with disabilities is high. These persons are much more likely to have low levels of education, to be particularly vulnerable to competitive pressures from college graduates and at the same time generally vulnerable to being recruited into the homeless population. In areas of low to medium rates of disability, there is a more consistent positive impact of education on homeless rates, and this suggests that competitive pressures of the college educated, rather than the general vulnerability of the uneducated, plays a more central role in generating local homeless populations if this theory is correct.

The theory reviewed above is supported by the regression of homeless rates on the various measures of education and disability using conventional multiple regression techniques which provide statistical controls for the various predictors. Table 3-5 summarizes these results and shows that while increasing levels of education apparently have an increasingly positive association with the homeless rates when the bivariate correlations are examined (column 1), all these correlations become moderately positive when statistical controls are introduced by this procedure. Thus, in areas with very low or very high levels of education, there is usually only one of the above reviewed processes generating homeless rates. At the intermediate levels, both processes can be expected to be at play, creating the highest levels of homelessness, especially when disability levels are high.

Likewise, the procedure demonstrates that a weak correlation ($r = 0.12$) between the disability and homeless rates actually masks a moderately positive correlation ($r = 0.41$) when education and the other indicators are controlled for. The greater impact of college graduation rates ($r = 0.53$) than high school ($r = 0.39$) or non-high school ($r = 0.39$) graduation rates suggests that competition rather than general vulnerability may be playing a more central role.

Table 3-5. Preliminary Regression of Rates of Homelessness, on Indicators of Education and Disability, Without Measurement Error Included (N=3,141)

	Zero-Order Correlation w/ Homeless Rate	Multiple Regression	
		Partial r	Standardized Coefficient
% Non-High School Graduates	-0.12	0.10	0.39[c]
% High School Graduates	0.18	0.12	0.39[c]
% College (BA) Graduates & Above	0.46	0.28	0.53[c]
% Change HS Graduates, '80-'90	-0.37	-0.27	-0.25[c]
% of 15+ Adult Civilian Noninstitutionalized Who are Disabled, with Mobility or Self-care limitations	0.12	0.27	0.41[c]
% of Disabled who are male	-0.22	-0.02	0.02
% of Disabled who are unable to work	-0.42	-0.01	-0.10

NOTES: This preliminary analysis uses ordinary least squares estimation, thus, values are expressed as base-10 logarithms to normalize distributions and are weighted by relative population sizes. Multiple R^2 = .41; F=317[c]

SOURCE: Computed from 1990 U.S. Census data, STF-3C Data Tape.

This analysis suggests that both education and disability levels can, in and of themselves, be used to explain about two-fifths of the variation in homeless levels (R^2 = 0.41). Although the proportion of the disabled who are males and unable to work does not contribute to this explanation, this model is consistent with the individual-level survey data which was reviewed earlier in this chapter. The model broadens our view of some of the dynamic interactions between education and disability, and highlights the dual roles education has in both supporting and complicating career survival among those who are disabled, and alerting us to the danger of half-way measures in the use of education as an anti-poverty strategy. The model leaves many questions unanswered as to the role of demographic, economic, and other systemic forces, as well as the uneven efforts of the Census Bureau in enumerating the homeless.

Structural Model. A further test of the disability hypothesis, as it has been framed in this chapter, was undertaken through the use of structural equation modeling to test the disability hypothesis by itself, and then with the inclusion of controls for the demographic conditions and measurement error investigated in the last chapter. In each case, these regressions differ from conventional multiple regression, not only in the fact that the WLS method is used, but also because estimates of measurement error are included in both the predictor and dependent variables. Although the disability indicators by themselves account for over a quarter (26.7%) of the variation in the homeless rates, when controls for the demographic variables are included, only 7.9% of the total variation is explained, and the power of the entire model is only slightly improved (4%). Model 2 (see table 3-6 and appendix 2) represents an only marginally better fit to the data than Model 1, which includes only the demographic and measurement indicators, mainly because of the smaller residuals or discrepancies between the observed and hypothesized correlations.

Each of the disability indicators have only marginal impact on the homeless rates. Although the disability-only model suggested that disability levels would be positively associated with homeless rates ($\beta = 0.27$), this relation not only disappears but becomes negative when demographic conditions are controlled for ($\beta = -0.09$). Indicators of behavioral disabilities--violent crime, suicides, and cocaine abuse--each make only a negligible contribution to the homeless rates, albeit at statistically significant levels because of the extremely large sample. Collectively these indicators of disabilities account for 6.2% of the variation, in contrast to the 1.7% accounted for by improving levels of education. The counties which have improved their high school graduation rates between 1980 and 1990 have tended to have slightly lower levels of homelessness ($\beta = -0.09$), again, a small effect but one which can be generalized with a high degree of confidence.

110

Table 3-6. Effects of Indicators of Disability on Homeless Rates

Variables	Demographic & Systematic Error Variation Explained	Disability Only β	Disability Only Variation Explained	Disability, Demographic, & Systematic Error β	Disability, Demographic, & Systematic Error Variation Explained
DISABILITY INDICATORS	--		26.7%		7.9%
Disability Rate	--	0.27^c	6.0%	-0.09^c	1.6%
Change in % Graduating from HS, 1980-1990	--	-0.28^c	6.6%	-0.09^c	1.7%
Rate of Violent Crime	--	0.00	0.1%	0.01^c	3.0%
Suicide Rate	--	-0.15^c	2.8%	-0.03^c	0.4%
Rate of Cocaine Abuse	--	0.29^c	11.2%	0.04^c	1.2%
DEMOGRAPHIC VARIABLES (See chapter 3)	36.7%	--	--	--	40.4%
MEASUREMENT ERROR	47.4%	--	--	--	40.5%
TOTAL MODEL (R^2)	84.1%		26.7%	--	88.8%

NOTES: See appendix 2 for goodness-of-fit statistics. Each model computed using weighted least squares and estimates of measurement error.

  [a] $\alpha > 0.05$
  [b] $\alpha > 0.01$
  [c] $\alpha > 0.001$

Thus, the hypothesis that extent of disabilities and low educational accomplishment would be positively associated with levels of homelessness was supported in an important respect. It was found that the more educational levels were improved, the lower were the homeless rates. However, the overall disability rates had the opposite impact as was expected, namely that high disability levels served to depress the levels of homelessness. Any one or a combination of several possible explanations may account for this counter-intuitive finding. We know that a substantial minority of homeless individuals move from county to county. It may be either that homeless individuals are likely to leave home counties which have particularly high levels of disability, or conversely, persons with disabilities avoid moving to urban areas where there may be more stringent competition for jobs and fewer informal supports.

Another possibility is that the measure of disability used is biased toward those traditional disabilities, such as blindness, physical incapacity, or developmental disabilities which are seen as the basis for entitlements for the 'deserving poor'. Individuals with such disabilities are more likely to be maintained by family or extended family, and thus, more likely to be reported as members of the household. In contrast, those with severe forms of substance abuse, mental illness, or criminality, are less likely to be considered as among the deserving poor and to be supported by their families or by formal social service or entitlement programs. These are, of course, the particular disabled persons who are most likely to show up among the ranks of the homeless. Thus, our measure of disability, is in part a measure also of the propensity of families to support the disabled, or at least certain subgroups among the disabled who are considered deserving. Thus, one would expect that the measure might be negatively associated with homeless levels: the more the disabled are included as members of the family household, the less likely they are to show up among those in shelters and on the streets.

The extent of measurement error, or the tendency of the Census to have made greater efforts to enumerate homeless in urban areas, so far can not be accounted for by the demographic and disability indicators, some of which were used by the Census Bureau to estimate where they would find more homeless persons and thus need to deploy more enumerators. With controls for both demographic and disability indicators included, the amount of variation accounted for by the differential search efforts drops only moderately, from 47.4% (see chapter 3) to 40.5%.

While there is support for the disability hypothesis, from both the existing research, as well as the preliminary analyses reported here, the specific nature of this relationship remains an open question. Clearly, the general disabilities inherent in low levels of education substantially contribute to homelessness as it is commonly known. The specific types of disability which an individual may eventually experience, whether it be serious mental illness, physical disability, mental retardation, or substance abuse, no doubt have very different implications for a person's likelihood of homelessness depending on the culpability for the homeless or disabled conditions which is attributed to the individual by significant others, as well as the institutional supports available. A more convincing test, therefore, will require inclusion of measures pertinent to other theories of homelessness, especially those involving economic opportunities, family, and social service supports, and it is to this task which we will now turn.

Chapter IV

THE ROLE OF ECONOMIC RESTRUCTURING

A central issue in debates concerning the homeless is whether declining employment opportunities for at risk populations have played a significant role in the genesis of homelessness, and if so, whether policies which emphasize job development, training, and placement can be expected to diminish the numbers of homeless persons. Both the data and popular opinion tend to be polarized on this issue. Many who explain homelessness by citing individual disabilities, or by other explanations such as family fragmentation, contend that those who are homeless have either not been part of the job market, or if they have, their extended unemployment is best explained by problems such as mental illness or substance abuse, rather than changes in the national economy. An example of the way many minimize the role of economic opportunity is exemplified by the statement, "In all probability, employment opportunities *have not increased substantially* [italics added] for homeless people because often they have unskilled or semi-skilled occupational backgrounds, limited work histories, and handicapping personal difficulties."[267] Others minimize individual disabilities, and argue that both the disabled and those without disabilities have been hurt by trends involving the globalization of economic activity, deindustrialization, and the development of the lower-tier of the service economy.

This chapter will, therefore, begin by reviewing some of the major trends involving the restructuring of an industrial to a post-industrial service economy. Because much of the data on these developments is essentially circumstantial in

---

[267] Morse, Chapter 1, "Causes of homelessness," in Robertson and Greenblatt, (eds.), Homelessness: A National Perspective, pp. 3-18.

respect to the creation of homelessness, the chapter will move to review data pertinent to the impact of these trends on at risk populations, and that relevant to their effects on the homeless themselves. It has been found that while some of the apparent or zero-order correlations of declining economic opportunities with homelessness turn out to be spurious, reflecting the role of urbanization, nonetheless, the inclusion of indicators of economic opportunity substantially improve our ability to understand variations in homelessness across the country, especially those involving the expansion of employment in the service sector of the economy.

Economic Restructuring

The economic restructuring of the U.S. as well as other Western economies in recent years has consisted primarily of three interlocking trends: globalization, deindustrialization, and servicetization. Globalization refers to the development of a world economy, interdependent trade relationships, a decline in trade barriers, and a resulting increased specialization among local national economies. Deindustralization is the specific decline of manufacturing, most typically due to its relocation to Lesser Developed Counties (LDCs) or to other parts of the United States, such as the Southwest. Servicetization, the development of a service economy, involves the proliferation of a range of services, from the least skilled to the most skilled professional occupations. Despite the fact that there is much to suggest that these represent three facets of a single trend, because the empirical evidence reveals that there is only a slight association between deindustrialization and the development of a service economy, these will be examined separately in this chapter for their relevance to the emergence of homelessness.

Globalization. The development of a world economy, with a dramatic expansion in the avenues of free trade, brings with it the opportunity for businesses to more easily locate capital, plants, and markets at locations which will generate maximum profits. For this reason, one of the central features of globalization is an increased international division of labor, typically, with developing nations assuming

116

a greater share of semi-skilled manufacturing and the developed nations, specializing in finance, development, high technologies, and other professional tasks. Also associated with the progressive globalization or integration of the world economy is the dissociation of the larger, transnational corporations from particular nations. Just as the ownership of these corporations is internationalized, so are their investments, manufacturing, and sales. While such diversification undercuts the role of national governments in regulation, greater interdependencies are created between nations, counter-acting isolationistic and nationalistic interests. Perhaps one of the more lucid descriptions of globalization is that of Shaikin's:

> The car was designed by the Japanese and its engine and transmission will also be built in Japan. The car itself will be assembled in Mexico and sold in the United States. What is important is not just the transfer of the labor-intensive parts of the vehicles production, but a worldwide division of labor from the point of design to the point of assembly, where ever both happen to be most convenient for the firm.[268]

Globalization, thus, means intensified international competition. To the degree this competition is unsuccessful, it has meant capital flight as businesses relocate to areas where wages and taxes are lower, and costly government regulations which force corporations to internalize social costs such as for pollution, are minimal. Globalization places considerable pressures on local and national governments to assume laissez-faire social policies. Its proponents argue that the resulting economic growth will more than compensate for the external costs of such reduced controls and services. Because of the inherently global nature of these changes, it has been rare that particular benefits or costs, such as increased homelessness, can be specifically attributed to these trends. For this reason, several authors are able to advance strong arguments linking globalization with homelessness, yet these remain essentially ideological.[269] For example, Barak would restructure the entire global economy to

---

[268]   Shaiken, 1987, quoted in Belcher and DiBlasio, Helping The Homeless, p. 152.

[269]   See Gregg Barak, Gimme Shelter: A Social History of Homelessness in Contemporary America (New York: Praeger, 1991); Belcher and DiBlasio, Helping The Homeless; Doug A. Timmer, D. Stanley Eitzen, and Kathryn D. Talley, Paths To Homelessness: Extreme Poverty and the Urban Housing Crisis (Boulder, CO: Westview, 1994); Ropers, The Invisible Homeless; Carolyn Adams, "Homelessness in the postindustrial city: Views from London and Philadelphia,"

fight homelessness as he sees, "by the end of the 1990s, if we stay the present course, the homeless population is estimated to grow as high as 20 million."[270] Similarly, Adams argues that, "Homelessness in the big cities of Europe and America is a product of their transition from industrial centers to postindustrial service cities."[271] Globalization, for the purposes of the analysis presented here, will be regarded as the context within which two somewhat better defined trends--deindustrialization and servicetization--will be considered, and it is to this subject which we will now turn.

Deindustrialization. The decline of manufacturing in the United States has been dramatic. In 1960, at the height of manufacturing, 28.2% of the work force was employed in industry,[272] whereas by 1990, this percentage had dropped to 15.1%, or by almost a half (see 4-1). While some of these jobs were undoubtedly lost due to improved worker efficiency and automation, most of the decline can be attributed to the relocation of industry in Mexico, the Caribbean, and the Far East.[273] The industries most affected have included steel, rubber, plastics, shoes, textiles, automobiles, and consumer electronics. In addition, jobs in the Midwest and Northeast industrial centers--the 'Rust Belt'--have been particularly severely impacted due to the internal relocation of industry from urban areas to suburbs, and especially to the 'Sun Belt' in the Southwest and Pacific coast.

While deindustrialization has progressed for at least 30 years, and in some areas, since the end of World War II, during the 1980s, the underlying movement of industry has been from the heartland or Midwest to the two coasts, including the Southeast, both of which enjoy maximum accessibility to global markets. In the mid-1980s it was reported that nearly 10 million Americans lost jobs to plant closures and

---

Urban Affairs Quarterly 21 (4), pp. 527-49 (June 1986); Kim Hopper, Ezra Susser, and Sarah Conover, "Economies of makeshift: Deindustrial-ization and homelessness in New York city," Urban Anthropology 14 (1-3), pp. 183-236 (1985).

[270] Alice S. Baum and Donald W. Burnes, A National in Denial: The Truth about Homelessness (Boulder, CO: Westeview Press, 1993).

[271] Adams, "Homelessness in the post-industrial city," p. 530.

[272] Blau, The Visible Poor, p. 42.

[273] Timmer, Eitzen, and Talley, Paths to Homelessness, pp. 86-87.

manufacturing layoffs. Close to 4.7 million of these were workers on the job for more than three years. Of those re-employed full time, less than half (44%) reported making less money.[274] However, such reports fail to mention new manufacturing jobs created elsewhere in the country which, in the 1980s, ameliorated many of the losses for the nation as a whole (but certainly not for the dislocated workers). Table 4-1 reveals that continuing losses of manufacturing jobs between 1980 and 1990 of 16.6% in the Northeast and 13.0% in the Midwest were almost offset by growth of manufacturing jobs of 7.6% in the South and 11.2% in the West, creating a net decline of 1.6% in the manufacturing sector throughout the 1980s, hardly enough to account for homelessness, especially the high rates in the Southwest and Pacific coasts. The losses in the Midwest and Northeast were disproportionately in the most urbanized counties, and this was especially so in the Midwest where the losses reached to over 20% in the most urbanized counties. In contrast, the greatest gains in the South and West were in counties which are between 1% and 50% urbanized. Average manufacturing earnings in the growth counties of the West and South--in the $30,000 to $35,000 range--were generally comparable to those in the parts of the rust belt which lost jobs, with the exception of urbanized counties of the Midwest where the mean salaries peak at around $39,000.

---

[274] New York Times, "Despite a 5-year upturn, 9.7 million jobs are lost," December 13, 1988, A12, cited by Timmer, Eitzen, and Talley, Paths to Homelessness.

**Table 4-1. Level and Change of Manufacturing Employment,
By Region and Urbanization, 1989**

Region, & Urbanization (& n)	Manufacturing Employment, % of Total	Change in Manufacturing Employment, '79-'89	Mean Manufacturing Earnings
NORTHEAST (632)	16.7	-16.6	$34,103
Low (261)	16.2	-11.7	$28,673
Medium (196)	17.8	-12.2	$33,746
High (175)	16.4	-18.7	$35,027
MIDWEST (754)	17.8	-13.0	$35,257
Low (614)	15.2	-2.3	$27,166
Medium (61)	18.0	-4.3	$35,832
High (79)	19.1	-20.1	$39,166
SOUTH (1095)	13.9	7.6	$32,185
Low (751)	16.9	1.8	$26,811
Medium (181)	15.4	15.7	$36,295
High (163)	11.9	8.3	$33,796
WEST (660)	12.5	11.2	$35,002
Low (53)	7.6	5.4	$30,774
Medium (26)	8.3	24.0	$33,459
High (121)	13.9	10.6	$35,910
TOTAL (3,141)	15.1	-1.6	$33,914

SOURCE: Computed from STF-3C data tapes, U.S. Bureau of the Census, 1989; means are weighted by the relative population size of the areas listed. Low Urbanization--Zero population urbanized; Medium--1-49% population urbanized; High--50%+ of population urbanized

Although deindustrialization represents a broad pattern of change, involving capital, technology, and labor, it is primarily measured through its impact on manufacturing employment. In addition, analyses of its impact have also considered the ripple effect of economic displacement. For instance, in a study of the layoff of 20 thousand steel workers in two counties of northeast Indiana in the early 1980s, it was found that an additional 10 thousand positions were lost in support services in the local economy.[275] These same studies, however, often fail to consider the reverse ripple effect involved in the creation of new jobs through the relocation of manufacturing to other areas of the U.S., or by the creation of new service sector business positions. Nonetheless, Burt points out that, "...during the 1980s industries with a history of paying relatively well have come to account for a smaller share of American jobs, while those that have historically been paid the least have grown most, both absolutely and a proportion of all private-sector jobs."[276] Many of the better paying jobs accessible to working class individuals have historically been in manufacturing, which shrank somewhat during the decade, and its average weekly pay barely kept up with inflation.[277]

Deindustrialization has represented a major restructuring of the U.S. economy, affecting at least four-ninths (44.9%) of the population (see table 4-2). This figure includes the combined population of all counties which have seen a 10% drop or more in their manufacturing employment during the 1980s. Over a quarter (28.1%) of the population in 1990 lived in counties where the manufacturing employment dropped or grew by no more than 10%. In addition, another quarter of the population (27.0%) lived in counties which saw continued industrialization, typically in suburban areas in the South and West. In some respects, these figures may overstate the impact of deindustrialization, as 10 million to perhaps as many as 20 million workers were impacted if the negative ripple effects are considered, considerably fewer than are represented by the 44.9% cited above. Nonetheless, ripple effects involving the social and psychological impacts of extended unemployment, as well as the replacement of many of these jobs with lower-paying service positions, no

---

[275] Ropers, The Invisible Homeless, p. 101.
[276] Burt, Over The Edge, p. 78.
[277] Ibid., p. 79.

doubt directly or indirectly impact on a majority of the population of counties which have been heavily reliant on manufacturing.

Table 4-2. The Relative Distribution of U.S. Population,
By Changes in Manufacturing and Service Sector Employment, '79-'89

Manufacturing Sector	Service Sector			
	DECLINING Under -.10	SAME -.10 to +.10	INCREASING Over .10	TOTAL
DECLINING: Under -.10	.5% (87)	1.3% (133)	43.1% (987)	44.9% (1,207)
SAME: -10 to +.10	.1% (17)	.6% (58)	27.3% (555)	28.1% (630)
INCREASING: Over .10	.2% (32)	.9% (90)	26.0% (698)	27.0% (820)
TOTAL	.8% (136)	2.8% (281)	96.4% (2,240)	100.0% (2,657)

NOTE: Figures in parentheses are numbers of counties included in group. Computed from data from U.S. Census, STF-3C data tape and U.S.A. Counties CD-ROM.

*   Calculations based on the 2,657 counties for which there was data available from both years on both variables. These counties represent 98.3% of the total U.S. population in 1990.

Servicetization. Deindustrialization is typically viewed as the decline of manufacturing employment and the replacement of many of these jobs with lower paid jobs in the service sector.[278] This view, however, oversimplifies the trend, obscuring the fact that growth in the service sector in the 1980s took place more so in areas of manufacturing growth than decline. The greatest areas of service growth were the South, at 76.2%, and West, at 60.1%, in contrast with the Northeast, at 52.9%, and Midwest, 42.6% (see table 4-3). In fact, because of the especially high growth rates in the South and West, there was a moderate positive correlation of 0.35 between growth in the 1980s in the manufacturing and service sectors of the economies (see

---

[278] See Blau, The Visible Poor.

table 4-4). Over the nation as a whole, the service sector represented just about one-fifth (19.9%) of all jobs in 1990, and this resulted from a 60.0% increase during the prior decade, more than offsetting the 1.6% decline in manufacturing employment.

Many of these newly created positions, however, have been in the lower-tier of the service sector, and have been jobs which have considerably fewer benefits and compensation than the lost manufacturing jobs. In fact, it has been reported that more than three-quarters of these positions were at the minimum wage level.[279] The service sector of the economy is a broad area, typically including "lower-order services" such as clerical, secretarial, custodial, restaurant, and retail services, as well as "higher-order services" such as finance, insurance, government, medicine, and education.[280] Reich has characterized the service economy as consisting of two escalators--a small one going up, composed of those few jobs in management and high technology that pay well, and a much larger one going down, representing the fate of the majority of workers who settle for retail, information processing, and other low-paying service positions.[281] This split between higher- and lower-order service economies has come to characterize divergent responses of various cities to globalization and deindustrialization. Some cities, such as New York, Chicago, Boston, Philadelphia, and Atlanta, have changed from centers of production to centers of higher-order services, intricately connected with the global economy, whereas other smaller cities, such as Buffalo, Cleveland, and Milwaukee have only succeeded in developing lower-order services.[282]

---

[279] U.S. Conference of Mayors, The Continuing Growth of Hunger, Homelessness and Poverty in America's Cities: 1987. A 26-City Survey (Washington, D.C.: Government Printing Office, 1987), p. 8.

[280] Timmer, Eitzen, and Talley, Paths to Homelessness, p. 25.

[281] Peter Dreir and Richard Applebaum, "Nobody home: The housing crisis meets the Nineties," Tikkun 5, pp. 15-18 (Sept.-Oct. 1990), cited by Timmer, Eitzen, and Talley, Paths to Homelessness.

[282] John D. Kasarda, "Urban change and minority opportunities," in Paul E. Peterson, (ed.), The New Urban Reality (Washington, D.C.: Brookings Institution, 1985), pp. 33-67.

**Table 4-3. Level and Change of Service Sector Employment,
By Region and Urbanization, 1989**

Region, & Urbanization (& n)	Service Employment, % of Total	Change in Service Employment, '79-'89	Mean Service Earnings
NORTHEAST (629)	24.0	52.9	$31,260
Low (258)	14.7	48.6	$26,683
Medium (196)	17.7	59.8	$27,824
High (175)	27.5	51.4	$33,056
MIDWEST (753)	18.9	42.6	$28,136
Low (613)	12.1	38.1	$26,529
Medium (61)	13.5	55.5	$25,831
High (79)	23.7	42.1	$29,483
SOUTH (1088)	17.8	76.2	$31,314
Low (744)	9.8	64.7	$31,577
Medium (181)	12.0	102.2	$34,741
High (163)	23.7	75.2	$34,241
WEST (651)	20.4	60.1	$34,427
Low (504)	13.0	50.7	$34,427
Medium (26)	13.6	65.9	$31,048
High (121)	22.5	61.0	$34,598
TOTAL (3,141)	19.9	60.0	$31,162

SOURCE: Computed from STF-3C data tapes, U.S. Bureau of the Census, 1989; means are
weighted by the relative population size of the areas listed. Low Urbanization--Zero
population urbanized; Medium--1-49% population urbanized; High--50%+ of population
urbanized.

Table 4-4. Zero-order Correlations Between
Indicators of Deindustrialization and Servicetization

Servicetization Indicators	Deindustrialization Indicators		
	Manufacturing Employment, % of Total, '89	Change in Manufacturing Employment '79-'89	Mean Manufacturing Earnings
Service Sector Employment as % of total, '89	.14 [c]	-.14 [c]	.09 [c]
Change in Service Sector Employment '79-'89	-.13 [c]	.35 [c]	.02
Mean Service Sector Earnings	-.03	-.00	.19 [c]

SOURCE: Computed from data from U.S. Census, STF3C Data Tape Series, 1990.
[c] $\alpha < 0.001$

Despite the range of positions generated by the service economy, there is much to suggest that the development of these positions has served as a whole to diminish the number of unskilled and semi-skilled jobs available. Blau argues that,

> Overseas and at home, the growth of the a service economy is closely associated with the need for a more educated work force. As education becomes ever more closely tied to the needs of the labor market, the corporate sector has expressed greater concern about the skills that applicants possess.[283]

In fact, an analysis of Census data for 1990 for the 3,141 U.S. counties reveals there is a substantial negative correlation of -0.48 between the percentage of positions in a county which are in the service sector and the percentage of low- and semi-skilled positions. This compares with a very weak negative correlation of -0.12 between manufacturing and low-skill employment. This no doubt greatly complicates the task of the laid off manufacturing employee to retrain for and successfully

---

[283] Blau, The Visible Poor, p. 43.

compete for one of the higher-order service jobs. The ripple effect of laid off manufacturing workers displacing those minimally qualified candidates for the lower-order service jobs from employment, thus, is no doubt considerable. In addition, unlike in the manufacturing sector where employers have traditionally assumed greater responsibilities for training long-term workers, the higher turnover rates in the service economy dampens the willingness of many employers to invest in any more than the most rudimentary training.

A particularly troublesome development in the service economy is that of contingent employment. In recent years there has been a proliferation in the use of temporaries, consultants, and other non-employee contractual relationships. As many corporations have slimmed their work forces, they have replaced these positions with temporary ones to provide enhanced flexibility and control on the part of the employer, and to minimize unemployment compensation, medical insurance, and other fringe benefits. This trend has been referred to as the "temping" of the work force. Between 1982 and 1992, contingent employment increased by almost 250%. By 1993, temporary employees represented a third (33%) of the work force.[284] Such arrangements no doubt permit employers to more efficiently identify and screen out employees with problems of mental illness, substance abuse, or criminal involvements, causing a concentration of such individuals among the ranks of the unemployed and homeless.

Unlike deindustrialization, servicetization has affected the entire country. Just about all of the U.S. population (96.4%) saw increases of 10% or more in the service sectors of their county's employment, while only 2.8% saw little change, and a scant .8% saw a decline of over 10% (see table 4-2). Close to half the population (43.1%) experienced declines in manufacturing and increases in service sector jobs--the type of deindustrialization / servicetization most commonly seen in the Northeastern and Midwestern urban counties. In contrast, over a quarter (26%) saw increases in both

---

[284] William McWirter, "The temping of America," Time, March 29, 1992, pp. 40-41; and Janice Castro, "The disposable workers," Time, March 29, 1992, pp. 43-47.

areas, and about one in two hundred (0.5%) saw declines in both areas in their counties of residence (see table 5-2).

Economic restructuring represents an array of trends which have consequences for a wide range of problems and social opportunities. The impact of deindustrialization and servicetization on the development of homelessness in the U.S., nonetheless, is believed by many to be a central and particularly acute human cost of these trends, whatever might be their long-range benefits. This view receives some support by an analysis of the correlation between these trends and homeless rates through most of the counties in the U.S., representing over 95% the population. Figure 4-1 depicts these relationships, for nine groups of counties, represented by each bar, by representing the homeless rate per 10,000 for each group of counties by the height of its bar. The figure reveals that just as homelessness increases as manufacturing declines, it also increases as service sector jobs *increase*. In fact, this second relationship is the most dramatic of the two, with rates of 2.3 per 10 thousand persons homeless in counties with declining service sector jobs, 3.9 in the counties with relatively small changes, and 10 in those with the increases over 10%. In contrast, relatively lower rates of homelessness, at 8.0 per 10 thousand population, are found in areas with growing manufacturing; while slightly higher levels (8.5) are found in areas of manufacturing stability, and the highest levels of homelessness (11.7) in areas with declining manufacturing. The most dramatic rate--11.7 homeless per 10 thousand--is found when services are growing and manufacturing is declining. When these rates are expressed as correlation coefficients, which take into account the specific values of each of the 2,868 counties for which there is available data on all three variables, a very strong 0.70 correlation is found linking increases in service sector jobs between 1980 and 1990 to levels of homelessness in 1990. However, no simple bivariate correlation is found with declines in manufacturing employment. A two-way analysis of variance of the data represented in figure 4-1 reveals that only services, not manufacturing or their interaction, contributes to homelessness, and this effect is highly significant at less than the 0.001 level. However, when urbanization is held constant as a co-variate, even the apparently strong impact of servicetization is no longer significant, suggesting that it may be masking a more specific type of servicetization which is an inseparable part of contemporary urbanization. Later in this chapter, we will report a more indepth exploration of these findings using techniques of multiple regression and structural equation modeling.

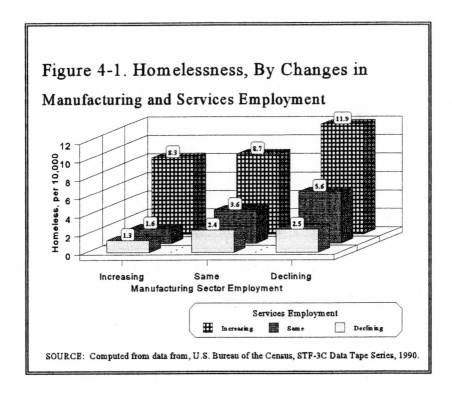

Figure 4-1. Homelessness, By Changes in Manufacturing and Services Employment

SOURCE: Computed from data from, U.S. Bureau of the Census, STF-3C Data Tape Series, 1990.

For some it may seem to be a counter-intuitive finding that increases in service sector jobs are associated with homelessness. After all, increased employment should reduce homelessness. However, what we are looking at are changes in the mix of jobs available, not in the total number. As noted earlier, many service jobs are characterized by instability, few benefits, and the increased use of temporary employees. In addition, educational requirements are higher and training opportunities fewer. But most important, servicetization is moderately associated with low-levels of unskilled and semi-skilled jobs, the kinds of positions with many at risk of homelessness, such as those with minimal levels of education, could be expected to find, if available. Thus, it would appear that the development of service economies and continued urbanization and gentrification in the major cities of the United States are inextricably intertwined, conditions which particularly impact on minorities, the minimally educated, and other populations at risk.

Origins of Economic Restructuring. While there is no consensus on the origins of deindustrialization, one of the most frequently cited antecedents is the economic experience of post-war Germany and Japan. These countries were forced to rebuild industry with a more modern infrastructure than present in the United States, because of the devastation they experienced during the war. The Marshall Plan, as well as Korean War expenditures in Japan provided important stimuli to the economic recovery of these countries. These same countries were also able to spend a considerably smaller portion of their GNPs on military preparedness, thus invest more in infra-structure.[285] While Germany and Japan were able by the mid-1970s to devote 25.8% and 35%, respectively, of their national outputs to capital investment, the U.S. was able to devote only 17.5%[286]. In addition, using cheaper labor and new technologies, countries such as South Korea, Taiwan, and Brazil soon followed the lead.[287]

In addition, a growing regulatory movement proved increasingly troublesome to business. Between 1964 and 1979, Congress passed 32 laws protecting consumers and workers, creating considerable costs for business.[288] In general, U.S. corporations faced declining profitability. After tax profits of domestic nonfinancial corporations fell from 10 percent in 1965 to less than 6 percent during the last half

---

[285] See Blau, The Visible Poor; and, Ropers, The Invisible Homeless.
[286] Blau, The Visible Poor.
[287] Ibid., p. 36.
[288] Ibid., p. 37.

of the 1970s.[289] The oil crisis of the early 1970s aggravated the problem of declining profitability and capital investment. Because of such developments, it has been pointed out that "getting more money into the hands of wealthy people has become a fundamental objective of business."[290] It has been proposed that sometime during the 1970s the national labor-business accord broke down. Business came to increasingly blame labor unions for many of its problems, thereby providing a pretext for abandoning the agreement, which had been in effect since World War II, in which labor would share in growing profits in exchange for its support and moderation of many of its demands.

Growing distrust between business and labor as well as a general drift to the right all set the stage for President Reagan's supply-side policies of the 1980s. These included the substantial tax cuts at this time which reduced the marginal effective corporate tax rates from 32% in 1980 to 18% in 1981.[291] These contributed to large federal budgetary deficits during the Reagan years which were easily financed through an influx of foreign investment. Finally, as the value of U.S. currency declined, the costs of exports increased and those of imports decreased, thus, further weakening industry, eroding its ability to sell its products abroad. By 1987, the trade deficit reached $159 billion, and manufacturing employed 19% of the labor force,[292] which continued to drop to 15.1% by 1990 (see table 4-1).

Other fiscal policies often cited as contributing to deindustrialization include intentional cyclical unemployment which Sawhill defines as, "a slowing of the economy with a resulting shortage of jobs--designed to discipline the inflation process." Specifically, she argues that periodically high unemployment rates result from governmental and Federal Reserve Board anti-inflationary policies in the 1970s and early 1980s, which led to an unemployment rate of over 10 percent in 1982.[293]

---

[289] Ibid., p. 38.
[290] Ibid., p. 92.
[291] Ibid., p. 40.
[292] Ibid., p. 42.
[293] I.V. Sawhill, "Rethinking employment policy," In Bawden and Skidmore, (eds.) Rethinking Employment Policy (Washington, D.C.: Urban Institute Press, 1989), p. 23.

Frequently government policy has been slanted in favor of higher unemployment because, "from the perspective of capital...inflation is less successful than unemployment as a strategy to maximize profits."[294] It has also been pointed out that during the 1980s the U.S. government made it possible for large corporations to easily switch to service employment by subsidizing the cost of such changes.[295]

Deindustrialization has been commonly attributed to the policies and practices of corporate executives (CEOs), especially those involving the management of corporate debt and acquisitions. Many liberal economists have charged that rather than develop new products which could effectively compete, CEOs became preoccupied with short-term profits.[296] For instance, between 1979 and 1982 corporations invested $170 billion to acquire new companies rather than to modernize old plants and equipment, and this figure just about doubled during the 1983 to 1984 period. The plethora of corporate takeovers and buy outs during the late 1980s placed considerable pressure on worker wages, especially since these were often financed with junk bonds with their exorbitant interest rates.[297] All this further reduced opportunities for genuine capital investment and improvements in efficiency. During the 1980s, U.S. corporations built up approximately $1.5 trillion in new debt to finance not only acquisitions and leveraged buy outs, but also the building of skyscrapers and office buildings. Such debt led to the use of bankruptcies by U.S. businesses in trouble, resulting in considerable layoffs, and eventual rehiring at lower rates.[298] The concentration of capital through mergers and acquisitions, in addition, tended to increase the power of corporations over their workers in other areas as well.[299] Much of the buying frenzy during the 1980s was fueled by the easy availability of capital. The deregulation of pension funds during the 1970s released

---

[294] Ibid., p. 23.
[295] Belcher and DiBlasio, Helping the Homeless, p.14.
[296] Ibid. p. 41.
[297] P. Kurgman, The Age of Diminished Expectations (Cambridge: MIT Press, 1990), pp. 153-68).
[298] Timmer, Eitzen, and Talley, Paths to Homelessness, p. 87-88.
[299] Ibid., p. 88.

131

enormous sums of money for investment in industry. In addition, many middle class individuals, reluctant to miss out on the opportunities of the 'roaring 80s', invested in the stock market, expecting a handsome rate of return.[300] The proliferation of mutual funds made such investments particularly easy and seemingly safe.

Finally, globalization and the resulting deindustrialization in Westernized nations has been fueled by continual developments in technology, especially microelectronics, computers, telecommunications, and automated production. Just as in agriculture in an earlier era, industrial automation, supported by computerization, has increased efficiency such that it now successfully competes with the cost of unionized labor, and increasing the attractiveness of non-unionized, cheap labor of the less developed countries (LDCs). Telecommunications, with a reduction of the 'information float', has further supported internationalization and the specialization of production, specifically, the disengagement of corporations from particular national markets. While most observers have minimized the role of technology in deindustrialization, its impact is becoming increasingly apparent to a variety of analysts.[301]

The Role of Labor. Labor has been cast as both the cause and the victim of deindustrialization. Especially in business, labor has been seen as excessive and inflexible in its demands, so much so, that disinvestment in the U.S. economy is considered good business. In 1980, no labor union signed a contract which included wage reductions. However, by 1982, close to half (44%) of the unionized work force had signed such contracts, and by 1984 at the height of recovery, a third (30%) of the work force agreed to such contracts.[302] The ability of the unions to resist these takebacks was undercut by the changing composition of the work force, as well as by the Reagan administration's efforts to weaken labor through deregulation and the

---

[300] Belcher and DiBlasio, Helping the Homeless, p. 8.

[301] Timmer, Eitzen, and Talley, Paths to Homelessness; Marjorie Hope and James Young, The Faces of Homelessness (Lexington, KY: Lexington Books, 1986); Belcher and DiBlasio, Helping the Homeless.

[302] Blau, The Invisible Poor, p. 40.

rulings of the National Labor Relations Board (NLRB) on collective bargaining. In addition, Piven and Cloward have pointed out that cuts in income maintenance programs during the 1980s created pressures on workers to accept lower wages than they would have when better income maintenance provisions existed.[303] One particularly insidious method used in some southern states was to implement right to work laws. These made union organizing difficult, and thus, they served to keep down wages and to attract business.[304]

At the same time that the power of rank and file workers was being systematically eroded, an increasing demand for professionals has been developing. Jahiel points out that, "A host of professionals or managers working as both employees or contractees have had increasing leverage within companies and their remuneration has tended to rise faster than that of low-income workers."[305] The skyrocketing salaries of CEOs effectively illustrates this trend.

The weakening of labor is also illustrated by the experience in recent years with the minimum wage. From 1968 through 1973 the minimum was $1.60. By 1981 it had risen in gradual increments to $3.35, just about keeping pace with inflation until 1979. It then leveled off at $3.35 until 1989. Thus, between 1980 and 1988, the minimum wage lost about 23% of its purchasing power.[306] Then in 1989 new legislation raised the minimum to $4.25 by 1991 in two steps.[307] The impact of the erosion of the minim um wage is exemplified by the finding that, "A full time year round worker earning the minimum wage during most of the 1960s and 1970s could have earned enough to raise a family of three to just above the poverty threshold. By

---

[303] Francis Piven and Robert Cloward, The New Class War (New York: Pantheon Books, 1985); See also: T.B. Edsall , "The Reagan legacy," In S. Blumenthal and T.B. Edsall, (eds.), The Reagan Legacy (New York: Pantheon Books, 1988), pp. 3-49.

[304] Belcher and DiBlasio, Helping the Homeless, p. 49.

[305] Rene' I. Jahiel, Chapter 18, "Homeless-making processes and the homeless-makers," in Jahiel, (eds.), Homelessness: A Prevention-oriented Approach, p. 284.

[306] Burt, Over The Edge, p. 73.

[307] Jahiel, "Homeless-making processes," in Jahiel, (ed.), Homelessness: A Prevention-oriented Approach, p. 245.

the mid-1980s this was no longer possible."[308]   It was also found that over a third (34.5%) of those households with people working at the minimum wage were living below the poverty line.[309] In addition, the depressed minimum wage has tended to depress income maintenance benefits, so as to uphold the principle of least eligibility, that welfare should never provide better benefits than what the lowest paid worker receives so as to maintain work incentive.

Just as the demand for unskilled labor has declined in recent decades, the casual labor markets in many urban areas have almost disappeared. These markets have historically been an important source of income for many groups of homeless, especially men living in Skid Row areas. As casual labor markets have evaporated, many the Skid Rows have been dispersed.[310] While the exporting of labor intensive industries, as well as developments in automation, have both contributed to the reduction of demand for unskilled labor, the breakdown of the corporate-labor accord should not be minimized. Edsall points out that since the Great Depression there has been an alliance of dependent poor people, workers, and the Democratic party, one which broke down in the 1970s as union leadership and the rank and file of labor increasingly dissociated themselves from the dependent poor, and as the Democratic party moved toward a more conservative position.[311] This breakdown, as well as increased international competition and technological developments, no doubt significantly weakened the ability of labor to maintain its position vis-a-vis' their employers. Those most acutely hurt by this are not only laid off industrial workers, but many of the minimally educated and other at risk populations that have been displaced or locked out of the expanding and unstable service economy. It is the impact on these groups to which we will now turn.

---

[308] Ralph E. Smith and Bruce Vavrichek, "The minimum wage: Its relation to incomes and poverty," Monthly Labor Review 110 (6), pp. 24-30 (1987), cited by Burt, Over The Edge.

[309] Burt, Over The Edge, p. 74.

[310] Rossi, Down and Out in America, p. 186.

[311] Edsall, "The Reagan Legacy," in Blumenthal and Edsall, (eds.), The Reagan Legacy, pp. 3-49.

Impact on At Risk Populations

Changes in the structure of economic opportunities in recent decades have had an unambiguous impact on both the population as a whole and a range of groups who are at risk of homelessness. These changes also originate from sources which go beyond economic restructuring, including the changing structure of the family and growing percentage of two-income households. The most dramatic impact of restructuring has been on the polarization of incomes and the shrinkage of the middle-class. It has been estimated by the Congressional Budget Office that between 1980 and 1990 the income of the poorest tenth of the U.S. households decreased by 8.6%, to an average of $4,695. At the top of the income range, families did considerably better. Those in the top fifth increased their income by 29.8%; the top 5% by 44.9%; and the richest 1%, by 75.3%, giving this group a mean annual income of $548,969.[312] The growth in inequality has been going on since the early 1970s, initially due mostly to increases at the top of the income range.[313]

Uneducated and Unskilled. In recent years the demand for unskilled workers has fallen faster than the supply of such workers. This, in turn, has resulted in falling wages, declining demand for casual labor, and also the falling minimum wage.[314] Young men, specifically those 25 to 34 with only a high school education, lost the most purchasing power (21%) between 1973 and 1986. Those aged 35 to 44 lost approximately 12% of their earning power during this same period, while high school graduates in the 45 to 55 age bracket lost 8%. This compares with college graduates of the same age who lost only 4%.[315] College women in the 35 to 44 age bracket gained the most, almost 38%.[316]

---

[312] Blau, The Visible Poor, p. 45.

[313] Burt, Over The Edge, p. 60, 69.

[314] Jencks, The Homeless, p. 53.

[315] Robert E. Litan, Robert Z. Lawrence, and Charles E. Schultze, Improving American living standards," Brookings Review 7 (1), p. 78 (1988/1989).

[316] Jahiel, "Homeless-making processes," in Jahiel, (ed.), Homelessness: A Prevention-oriented Approach, p. 245.

The less favorable experience of those with minimal levels of education can in part be attributed to a lesser likelihood of re-employment after periods of economic downturn. Those who had lost managerial or professional positions were 75% more likely to find new jobs. In contrast, those who were employed as operators and laborers in manufacturing were rehired in only 66% of the cases.[317] In general, the link between economic restructuring and the unfortunate experience of the minimally educated is not difficult to document. Shlay and Rossi summarize this experience:

> Because of economic restructuring, the loss of manufacturing employment, the rising skill level demanded in new jobs that pay well, and the increasing number of low wage jobs in the service sector, the metropolitan employment base is increasingly unable to provide jobs that pay enough to permit people with few skills to acquire and maintain tenure in permanent housing.[318]

Young People. One of the groups most affected by the decline in unskilled and semi-skilled entry-level positions have been young people. Earnings of workers under 35 declined between 1968 and 1984 to about 80% of the 1968 level, computed in constant dollars. In contrast, the wages of workers between 45 and 55 rose in the same period to 125% of their 1968 levels. Similar trends exist in the unemployment rates. At the beginning of this period, unemployment rates for young men below 35 were 5%, and then rose to a high of 15% in 1980, declining to 13% in 1984.[319]

Women and Single Parent Families. Despite increases in recent years in the personal incomes of women, traditional sources of economic support through marriage have declined.[320] This has resulted from both delayed formation of families, especially in the inner city with its shortage of marriageable males, out-of-wedlock births, as well as increases in the breakup of existing families. Rossi, building on the work of William J. Wilson, explains that

---

[317] F.E. Horvath, "The pulse of economic change: Displaced workers of 1981-1985," Monthly Labor Review 110, pp. 3-12.

[318] Shlay and Rossi, "Social science research and contemporary studies of homelessness," p. 147.

[319] Richard A. Easterlin, "The new age structure of poverty in America," Population and Development Review 13(2), pp. 195-208 (1987), cited by Rossi, Down and Out in America, p. 187.

[320] Jencks, Homelessness, p. 55.

...there is also an indirect effect on household formation that did affect the proportion of women with children who are married and thus contributed to what has been call the feminization of poverty...The abrupt rise in female-headed households from 1968 to 1984 in part reflects the uncertain economic fate of young men, who thereby become less attractive as mates, less willing to become household heads, and less able to fulfill the economic role of husband and father when marriage does take place.[321]

Perhaps the most problematic part of this trend has been the dramatic increase in teenage pregnancies. In 1969, only a sixth (16%) of all unmarried working-age women with very low incomes had a child. By 1979, the figure grew to 23%, and by 1989, it was 31% (see chapter 5).[322]

Single People. While there is clear evidence that single people have a higher than average risk for homelessness, there is little hard data to support the notion that economic restructuring is to blame for the rising proportion of single people. To the extent that unemployment contributes to delayed family formation and to family breakup, it can be assumed to contribute to the growing proportion of single person households. In fact, some of the data suggests that single and unrelated individuals who work represent 30.3% of poor workers. However, because many single people make good salaries, only 9.8% are poor, less than the national average.[323]

There have been several theories advanced as to the causes of changing family structures and the increase in single person households. Some have suggested that marriage has declined as women's improving job opportunities have made them more selective about the men they are willing to marry.[324] Or, poorly educated men may more frequently elect to be single because they do not want to marry unless they can enjoy the psychological benefits of being their family's sole breadwinner. In addition, changes in sexual norms may have also reduced the appeal of marriage.[325]

---

[321] Rossi, Down and Out in America, p. 187.

[322] Jencks, Homelessness, p. 55.

[323] Burt, Over The Edge , p. 73.

[324] Robert D. Mare and Christopher Winship, "Socioeconomic change and the decline of marriage for blacks and whites." In Christopher Jencks and Paul Peterson, (eds.), The Urban Underclass (Washington, D.C.: The Brookings Institution, 1991).

[325] Jencks, Homelessness, p. 57.

A related possibility is that the post-industrial service and information economy has created an enhanced demand for the skills which women have been socialized in. In the 19th and early 20th century there was little demand for the skills women typically possessed, and considerably more demand generated by the industrial revolution for traditionally socialized male skills. Changes in the post-industrial information and service oriented economy have served to draw many more women into employment, thus creating particularly severe competitive pressures on those males who have little education or training. As a greater proportion of women go to work as waitresses, lawyers, or doctors, their families require the purchase of more out of home services, whether they be from restaurants, day care centers, or lawyers, thus fueling the growth of the service economy. And as economic roles have no doubt changed faster than family and sexual roles, the increasing incongruence between work and home life contributes to problems of family fragmentation, especially among the poor and working classes, which in turn dramatically intensifies competition in both the job and housing markets. The second job becomes essential, just as do two housing units for a single delayed or broken family, thus contributing to unemployment and housing unaffordability, two key conditions hypothesized by many to lead to homelessness. Thus, single individuals and single parent families in many respects represent two sides of the same coin, each at risk of homelessness, and likewise, each having a domino effect on others with fewer skills and supports, placing them at even greater risk of homelessness.

Unemployed. At times of peak activity in deindustrialization, high and long-term unemployment has been one of the most visible impacts of economic restructuring. Between 1945 and 1975, the mean national unemployment rate hovered around 4.6%. By early 1984 it had more than doubled. This rise began in the mid-1970s and reached its zenith at 10.7% in November 1982, following the recessions between 1979 and 1982. This had been the highest unemployment rate since the Great Depression of the 1930s.[326] Much of this represented long-term

---

[326] Ropers, The Invisible Homeless, p. 103.

unemployment of men between the ages of 25 and 44. Those under 25 had higher rates of short-term unemployment, however, the proportion who went a full year without working was no higher in the late 1980s than the late 1960s.[327] By 1989, just about half (46%) of the unemployed found themselves in this condition because of job loss; 16%, because of leaving a job; 28%, resumption of job search; and 10% were no entrants to the job market. This pattern had been fairly stable since 1977, with the exception that the percentage of job leavers dipped to 8% in 1982 at the same time that re-entrants dipped to 22% and job losers peaked at 59%.[328] Official unemployment figures understate the magnitude of the problem as they leave out discouraged workers who have ceased to look for work. For instance, in June, 1984, when 8.13 million people were officially unemployed, an additional 1.2 million were considered to have stopped looking. Also, one should count the under-employed, an estimated 5.5 million who sought full-time employment but who work part-time involuntarily.[329]

Aggravating the unemployment effects of economic restructuring has been the decline in unemployment compensation. In 1975, the percentage of workers insured peaked at 76%, and since had declined to 32% by 1988.[330] This contraction can, in part, be attributed to tighter state eligibility requirements and changes brought about by the Reagan administration, as well as a severe curtailment of the federal component.[331]

While economic restructuring is the prevailing theory of the origins of high unemployment, high unemployment levels have also been attributed to changes in family structure:

---

[327] Jencks, Homelessness, p. 52.

[328] U.S., House of Representatives, Committee on Ways and Means, Overview of Entitlement Programs: The 1990 Green Book (Washington, D.C.: Government Printing Office, 1990).

[329] L. Belsie, "U.S. jobs tide rises, but many workers are still aground," Christain Science Monitor (Jan. 9, 1986), p. 9; cited in Ropers, The Invisible Homeless, p. 103.

[330] Jahiel, Chapter 18, "Homeless-making processes," in Jahiel, (eds.), Homelessness: A Prevention-oriented Approach, p. 284.

[331] Hope and Young, The Faces of Homelessness, pp. 212-13

...long-term joblessness increased because fewer men got married. According to this view, men work regularly at unrewarding jobs only if the people with whom they live depend on their earnings to make ends meet. Marriage rates declined precipitously during the 1970s and 1980s....making them choosier about the jobs they would take. In reality, however, long-term joblessness increased fastest among married men. This suggests--though it does not prove--that increased employment among wives may have made husbands choosier about jobs they would accept.[332]

Low Income Persons. Harrison and Bluestone report the finding that deindustrialization correlates one-to-one with increases in the size of the population earning low wages. For every 1% decrease in the number of manufacturing workers, there is an equivalent increase in the number of low-wage workers.[333] The Census Bureau has reported that 18.9% of full-time workers had low-wage jobs in 1979, a percentage which increased to 25.7% by 1992.[334] Many of those who held low-wage jobs can be officially classified as part of the poverty population. Burt points out that in 1987 about a third of all poor persons over 16 worked or looked for work for at least half the year and that about two-thirds of the working poor, who usually worked full-time, had earnings of less than $167 a week, hardly enough to rise above poverty.[335] Such poverty has become for many an integral part of life in the inner city as the percentage of low-income people living in the inner city has increased markedly from a low of 27% in 1959 to over 43% by 1985.[336]

Persons of Color. One of the most often cited impacts of deindustrialization has been its impact on minorities. In one study it was reported that between 1979 and 1983 a total of 11.5 million workers lost jobs because of plant closures or employment cutbacks. Close to half (42%) of the displaced workers hired back were

---

[332] Jencks, Homelessness, p. 52.

[333] Barry Bluestone and Bennett Harrison, "The growth of low-wage employment: 1963-86," American Economic Review 78 (5), pp. 124-28 (1988).

[334] Brian O'Reilly, "The job drought," Fortune (Aug. 24, 1992), pp. 62-74.

[335] Burt, Over The Edge, p. 73.

[336] U.S. Bureau of the Census, 1982, Characteristics of the Population Below Poverty Levels: 1980 (Washington, D.C.: CPS Reports); 1985, Money Income and Poverty Status of Families and Persons in the United States: 1985 (Washington, D.C.: CPS Reports.

black, compared with 52% of the Hispanics, and over 60% of the whites.[337] In general, young black men have had a declining rate of participation in the labor force. Unemployment for blacks has gone from 7.6% in 1969 to 30.4% in 1985, with an overall unemployment rate in central cities for black men, aged 16 to 64, at just over a half (51.2%) in 1988.[338] Mare and Winship suggest that this trend has been responsible for some of the decline in marriage rates among this group,[339] supporting Wilson's dislocation theory.[340] Blacks have historically been over-represented in manufacturing, as well as in the rustbelt urban areas. Thus, it would be entirely expected that they would be particularly affected by deindustrialization.

Combinations of Conditions. Those most acutely affected by economic restructuring are undoubtedly those 'in double jeopardy' by virtue of belonging simultaneously to two or several of the groups reviewed above. Sharp increases in those belonging to such groups between 1969, 1979, and 1989 suggests they have played a role in the emergence of homelessness in the 1980s. The percentage of household members between 21 and 64 rose from 5.3% to 9.9 % for men, but dropped from 41.2% to 26.9% for women. Men who were also married and had incomes below $2,500 represented 1.2% of household members in 1969, 1.5% in 1979, and 2.4% in 1989, whereas the percentage of women with the same characteristics started out at 2.6% in 1969, dipped to 2.3% in 1979, and peaked at 2.8% in 1989.[341] In general poor young people and unrelated individuals suffered the largest proportional income losses during the mid-1980s.[342]

Another perspective on the probable impact of economic restructuring on the prevalence of various at risk populations can be obtained by an examination of the

---

[337] Ropers, The Invisible Homeless, p. 101.

[338] Belcher and DiBlasio, Helping the Homeless , p. 152.

[339] Mare and Winship, "Socioeconomic change and the decline of marriage...". In Jencks and Peterson, (eds.), The Urban Underclass, p. 60.

[340] See William J. Wilson, The Truly Disadvantaged (Chicago: University of Chicago Press, 1967).

[341] Jencks, Homelessness, p. 51.

[342] Richard C. Michel, Economic Growth and Income Inequality Since the 1982 Recession (Washington, D.C.: Urban Institute, 1990), cited by Burt, Over The Edge, p. 59.

mean levels of these populations within counties with various levels of deindustrialization and servicetization, and these are presented in table 4-5. Differential levels show, at the least, the relative extent to which these populations at risk could be expected to be impacted on by these diverse conditions, but in themselves, do not demonstrate a casual relationship as there may have been high rates of a given population, i.e. single parent families, before any of these changes took place.

Differences in the presence of various at risk populations under conditions of decreasing, unchanging, and increasing industrialization are modest. Unemployment, extreme poverty, and rates of persons of color are clearly greater in areas of deindustrialization when the levels of servicetization are held constant. In addition, income change has clearly been the least under such conditions. In contrast, most of the groups have divergent levels under conditions of declining, stable, and growing However, the proportion of single parent families, nonwhites, and one person households are clearly greatest under increasing servicetization and declining manufacturing, though the pattern is not so clear cut when manufacturing employment is stable or increasing. In addition, the proportion of non-high school graduates and that of unskilled and semi-skilled jobs clearly varies according to levels of servicetization, with the lowest levels found in areas of high servicetization. This is consistent with the strong negative correlation between servicetization and

Table 4-5. Differential Rates of Populations At Risk of Homelessness, By Levels of Deindustrialization and Servicetization

Changes in Manufacturing Employment, '79-'89:	Declining: < -.10			Same: -.10 to +.10			Increasing: > +.10		
Changes in Service Sector Employment, '79-'89:	<-.10	-.10-+.10	> +.10	<-.10	-.10-+.10	> +.10	<-.10	-.10-+.10	> +.10
Unemployment Rate, 1989	8.2	7.4	5.7	8.0	7.1	5.1	6.6	6.7	5.0
Per Capita Income, 1990 ($1,000s)	11.5	12.8	16.5	12.0	12.2	17.0	11.8	12.2	17.0
Per Capita Income Change, '80-'90	69.9	68.9	77.7	73.3	71.7	80.5	71.6	75.1	83.1
Percentage under 0.5 Poverty Line	9.6	9.4	6.5	7.3	7.9	5.2	8.1	7.0	4.7
% Semi- & unskilled jobs	49.4	46.5	37.3	50.5	49.7	36.5	53.4	48.2	35.2
% Non-HS Graduates	34.4	30.7	25.6	34.7	32.8	24.2	33.9	30.3	22.3
% Non-white	19.9	21.9	22.1	16.6	17.3	19.7	18.1	17.5	16.2
% Female-headed Families	23.7	25.6	26.0	23.5	24.3	23.7	24.0	23.5	22.3
% One person Households	23.7	25.6	26.0	23.5	24.3	23.7	24.0	23.5	22.3

Source: Computed from U.S. Census, STF-1C, 3C, and U.S.A. Counties, 1990.

services, when manufacturing employment is held constant. The unemployment and extreme poverty rates are greatest when service employment has been declining. homelessness, and a moderate one between servicetization and low skilled employment, which were discussed previously. These findings reinforce the notion that the most problematic part of economic restructuring is not the loss of manufacturing employment but the highly competitive, unstable, and demanding nature of the new service jobs created, especially for those persons with minimal education and non-traditional disabilities, such as mental illness and substance abuse.

Employment Status of Homeless Persons

Most homeless individuals have had only a tenuous employment history. A group of 15 surveys from the late 1980s revealed their mean monthly income was only $174, ranging from $25 to $337 depending on the particular location. Median or most typical income was even lower, at $104 per month. Over four-fifths (81%) of these individuals were unemployed. Only about a fifth (20%) received income from their state's general assistance program; 10% from SSI; and 8% from the AFDC program.[343] Summarizing results from the Ohio study of one thousand homeless people, Redburn concludes that,

> Among the most striking findings of the Ohio survey is the lack of current income among the homeless, even when compared to other poor people. Not only are the homeless far less likely than the poor in general to be working; but fewer are looking for work. When unemployed, they are also less likely than others to be receiving some form of public assistance or other income support. In many cases also lacking support from family or friends, most will not be able to live on their own without first finding new sources of income.[344]

Nonetheless, most had previously worked, mostly in unskilled or semi-skilled jobs, such as selling newspapers, manual labor, restaurants, and the like (see Chapter 2). The mean time since the last job in Rossi's Chicago study was just about 4.5 years, while the median was just under 3.5 years (40 months), however almost one-fourth (22%) had been without employment for over a decade.[345] Reasons for the loss of the

---

[343] Shlay and Rossi, "Social science research and contemporary studies of homelessness," pp. 129-160.
  · [344] F. Stevens Redburn and F. Terry, _Responding to the Homeless: Public Policy Alternatives_ (New York: Praeger, 1986), pp. 52-53.
  [345] Rossi, _Down and Out in America._

last job include that the job was temporary, for 10.2%; that the respondent was fired or laid off, for 21.5%; drinking or drugs, 3.4%; poor mental health, 1.9%; or, went to prison or jail, 1.0%.[346] There is little evidence that a significant number had worked in manufacturing, and that most had held lower-level positions in the service sector of the economy. The single most important perceived barrier to new employment was the lack of high school graduation, for 40%; another third (30%) noted health problems interfering with work or daily functioning; close to a fifth (18%) mentioned their previous psychiatric hospitalization; and a ninth (11%), cited current probation or parole status.[347] For homeless persons with children, over a third (36.8%) mentioned child care responsibilities as a significant barrier, and a fifth (19.8%) said they had looked but could not find work.[348] Another study found that failure to find a job after migration to a new area was also a problem.[349] A multivariate analysis of a shelter sample in Maryland found that those homeless who were women, disabled, relatively less educated, previously in a mental hospital, relatively unhealthy, and who had not served in the military were most likely to be unemployed than other homeless people. No differences were found in respect to ethnicity, age, marital status, length of homelessness, food deprivation, or the use of alcohol.[350]

The Causal Connection

Tracing the specific role of changes in the economy and individual employment difficulties in the genesis of homelessness is hamstrung by the fact that such factors typically manifest years prior to the first homeless episode, and when

---

[346] Beverly Toomey and Richard First, Homelessness in Ohio: A Study of People in Need (Columbus, OH: Ohio Department of Mental Health, Feb. 1985).

[347] Jan L. Hagan, "Participants in a day program for the homeless: A survey of characteristics and service needs," Psychosocial Rehabilitation Journal 12 (4), pp. 29-37 (April 1989), p. 29.

[348] Richard First, Chapters 3 & 4, Final Report on Ohio Homeless Study (Columbus, OH: Ohio State University, Feb. 13, 1992).

[349] Jahiel, Chapter 18, "Homeless-making processes," in Jahiel, (ed.), Homelessness: A Prevention-oriented Approach, p. 282.

[350] Belcher and DiBlasio, Helping the Homeless, p. 26.

they do, disentangling them from the individual's history and large scale economic trends is formidable. Most surveys have only gone so far as to consider the homeless person's or knowledgeable observer's subjective assessments of the causative role of various conditions. Others have used only statistics on aggregated national trends or case studies on highly selective samples. A few studies have gone several steps further in attempting multivariate statistical analyses which permit isolating the relative effects of various hypothesized conditions from a range of confounding factors. These will now be reviewed as they clarify the role of economic trends and employment difficulties in the lives of the homeless.

National Trend Data. During the 1980s circumstantial evidence for a link between poverty and homelessness could be found in the simultaneous rise of homelessness in the early years of this decade and a sharp rise in the U.S. poverty rate.[351] Unemployment, which led to substantial numbers of home mortgage foreclosures, has been frequently cited as a cause of homelessness during this period. The Mortgage Bankers Association reported that 130 thousand Americans lost their homes due to foreclosure in 1982.[352] Palmer and Sawhill have estimated that recession and budget cuts contributed about equally to the increase in homelessness. During the Reagan administration, tighter income eligibility limits and sharper benefit offsets for earnings and other income eliminated an estimated 400 thousand to 500 thousand AFDC families and nearly a million potential food stamp beneficiaries from the rolls, and reduced benefits to others.[353] However, this apparent association with adverse economic conditions broke down as improvements in the economy in the later part of the decade failed to moderate the continuing increases in homelessness. Analyses of this kind can only be regarded as suggestive as they ignore the specific experience of individual states, cities, or counties.

---

[351] Redburn and Terry, Responding to the Homeless, p. 68.
[352] Carol L.M. Caton, Homeless in America (New York: Oxford University Press, 1990), p. 13.
[353] John L. Palmer and Isabel V. Sawhill, The Reagan Record (Cambridge, MA: Ballinger, 1984).

Subjective Reports. In 1985 the U.S. General Accounting Office reported on a survey of major Southwestern cities in which 6 out of 7 ranked unemployment as the single most important cause of homelessness, while all 10 cities included in the study cited unemployment as a major cause of homelessness.[354] In a similar survey of 26 cities by the U.S. Conference of Mayors, lack of affordable housing was cited as the leading cause of homelessness, and this was followed by unemployment and underemployment, substance abuse, mental illness, and domestic violence.[355]

Similarly, self-reports by homeless individuals usually cite economic difficulties. In the Ohio study economic factors were mentioned by over half (56.3%) of the respondents, whereas family problems were noted by another 17%.[356] Of specific relevance to economic restructuring was Belcher and DiBlasio's finding that a fifth (20%) of their subjects in Baltimore lost their former job as a result of their company's closing or moving, or because their temporary jobs ended.[357] In general, surveys of homeless people have shown retrospectively that loss of a job or failure to find a job was one of the most common factors cited as a cause of homelessness.[358] There have not been any studies which have succeeded in disentangling the relative contributions of various possible individual and structural factors in such job loss.

Case Studies. Several case studies have produced a rich descriptive narrative of some of the pathways through which large scale and individual economic difficulties may have generated impoverishment and homelessness, two of which stand out. Peterson and Weigand found that unemployment is sometimes the first step toward homelessness for many men. They interviewed men on skid row and found that the descent into extreme poverty began for many with the loss of a job, often

---

[354] U.S., General Accounting Office, (Washington, D.C.: Government Printing Office, 1985), p. 9.

[355] Kenneth Silverstein, "Homelessness commands attention," American City and County 109 (April 1994), p. 10.

[356] Toomey and First, Homelessness in Ohio, p. 18.

[357] Belcher and DiBlasio, Helping the Homeless, p. 31.

[358] Jahiel, Chapter 18, "Homeless-making processes," in Jahiel, (ed.), Homelessness: A Prevention-oriented Aprroach, p. 282.

through plant closures, other kinds of displacement, or temporary disability or illness. Most of the respondents had grown up "in relatively stable working classes or lower middle-class families and descended to the tramp life through a series of progressively less stable jobs.[359]

In a similar study about pathways to skid row, Cohen concluded that although it was not possible to identify any single pattern, several recurrent problems were identified in their subject's lives: (i) a disruptive early family life, (ii) low-skilled employment with relatively poor education; (iii) occupations that resulted in earlier exposures to the Bowery for briefer stays, such as merchant marines; (iv) a history of moderate to heavy alcohol consumption; (v) physical or psychological conditions which may have impaired work ability; and, (vi) psychological turmoil over the death of or separation from a spouse or girlfriend.[360]

Multivariate Studies. In several cases researchers have been able to employ multivariate statistical techniques to attempt to disentangle the role of economic conditions in the development or perpetuation of homelessness. Belcher and DiBlasio focused their study on understanding why some of the sheltered homeless in Baltimore were able to locate employment and others were less successful. They note that those employed were more likely to be male, without disabilities, and to be better educated than their unemployed counterparts. In addition, those successful at finding employment were more likely to seek out case advocacy services than the others.[361]

A similar study compared the success of a job training and placement program with homeless and similar but non-homeless individuals. It was based on the prediction that psychological resources and social supports would be positively associated with and would both make significant contributions to job procurement and sense of self-efficacy at follow-up. The study found that perceived social support

---

[359] Richard A. Peterson and Bruce Weigand, "Ordering disorderly work careers on skid row." In Richard L. Simpson and Ida H. Simpson, (eds.), Research in The Sociology of Work: Unemployment (Greenwich, CT: JAI Press, 1985).

[360] Carl I. Cohen and Jay Sokolovsky, Old Men of the Bowery: Strategies for Survival Among the Homeless (New York: The Guilford Press, 1989), p. 74.

[361] Belcher and DiBlasio, Helping the Homeless, p. 31.

may have been a particularly important element in the improvement of the participant's efficacy during the program. "Participants who felt they had an adequate level of available supportive resources may have had an enhanced capacity to deal with the challenges and stress of the employment training, subsequently allowing for more successful performance of tasks and ultimately greater confidence in job procurement capabilities."[362]

Several of the multivariate studies have relied on use of multi-city data, with homeless shelter rates being the focus of investigation. Elliott and Krivo used data from the 1980 Census as well as the 1984 HUD estimates of homelessness in selected metropolitan areas. They concluded that, "Last, both low-rent housing and total mental health expenditures have large and significantly negative effects, indicating that a lack of both low-cost housing and total mental health services are strongly related to higher homeless rates."[363] However, neither poverty nor unemployment have significant effects on homelessness, while the presence of unskilled jobs was related to increased rates of homelessness. Altogether, the various predictors accounted for just over half (51%) of the variation in the rates.[364]

A similar study using the same 1984 HUD data examined the more focused question of whether, controlling for other factors, cities with higher rents and unemployment rates have more homeless. In contrast, this study did find a significant correlation with unemployment rates, but unlike the previous study, these were expressed as logarithms, and included with them in the model was rent, AFDC, winter temperatures, average household size, and presence of rent control. However, this model only accounted for 38% of the variation in the HUD homeless rates.[365] It was

---

[362] Suzanne L. Wenzel, "The relationship of psychological resources and socials support to job procurement self-efficacy in the disadvantaged," Journal of Applied Social Psychology 23 (18), pp. 1471-97 (1993), p. 1488.

[363] Marta Elliott and Lauren J. Krivo, "Structural determinants of homelessness in the United States," Social Problems 38(1), pp. 113-131 (Feb. 1991), p. 124.

[364] Ibid., p. 124.

[365] Cecil Bohanon, "The economic correlates of homelessness in sixty cities," Social Science Quarterly 72 (4), pp. 817-21 (December 1991).

concluded that, "Although the ranks of the homeless may disproportionately contain those with profound personal and mental health problems, the evidence suggests that they would respond to general changes in the economic environment."[366]

No doubt the strongest of the multi-city shelter studies is that of Burt's, of the Urban Institute. In this study she sought to test the hypothesis that income, as influenced by unemployment and the structure of the job market, and housing availability together would best account for variations among rates of sheltered homeless in major U.S. cities.[367] She found that levels of employment, unemployment, and changes in manufacturing employment were all positively but weakly associated with homeless rates, after other non-economic variables were held constant, and these collectively accounted for just over half (50.1%) of the variation in homeless rates. In several subgroups of cities she also found that the proportion employed in the service sector was an important predictor. Probably the most critical non-economic variable was the proportion of one person households, also found in this study to be of critical importance[368]. While the study investigated a broad array of predictors, it unfortunately did not include either random or systematic error in the shelter estimates, or specifically test the theory using techniques of structural equation modeling.

Probably the only multivariate study which compared both urban and rural homeless rates examined variations in homeless rates from the 1990 Census using the 351 towns and cities in Massachusetts.[369] Despite the inclusion of employment and per capita income measures, these did not prove to add significantly to the model, and thus were dropped, as the demographic, housing, and services measures proved to account for approximately two-thirds (.67) of the shelter and street rates. The model then used to compute predicted true rates in each town, which were then validated

---

[366] Ibid., p. 823.

[367] Burt, Over The Edge, p. 7.

[368] Ibid., p.201.

[369] Christopher G. Hudson, "The homeless of Massachusetts: An analysis of the 1990 U.S. Census S-Night data," New England Journal of Public Policy 9 (1), pp. 79-100 (Spring/Summer 1993).

through comparison with independent studies and estimates.

On the whole, the few multivariate studies conducted have not produced consistent results, no doubt due to the range of measures and populations used. In instances in which similar measures or populations have been used, there have been some notable similarities. On the whole, these studies have found only a modest role for measures of employment and unemployment and the structure of the job market. The economic effects tend to disappear to the extent that controls are introduced for demographic, disability, and family variables, or when non-urban areas are included.

An Analysis of the Role of Economic Opportunity

Just as the foregoing review of research has shown a definite role of the changing mix of employment opportunities in the generation of homelessness, albeit inconclusively, the analysis presented here, likewise, demonstrates the impact of changing employment patterns. When a wide range of indicators of economic opportunity are analyzed by themselves, ignoring demographic, disability, and other hypotheses about the origins of homelessness, a substantial association is found, specifically with increasing service sector employment.

This preliminary analysis, which uses conventional OLS regression techniques (see table 4-6), reveals that the more generalized measures of employment and unemployment have very small or negligible associations with variations in homelessness throughout the 3,141 U.S. counties. Likewise, most indicators of earnings have negligible effects. One exception is per capita income--which had an initial 0.37 zero-order association with homelessness--dropped to 0.12 when the other economic opportunity indicators were controlled for. It should be pointed out that this is a positive association, indicating that the more economic activity, the more homelessness, and this is consistent with other studies which have found higher levels of homelessness in better off areas.

151

Table 4-6. Rates of Homelessness, Regressed on Indicators of Economic Opportunity (N=3,141)

	Zero-Order Correlation w/ Homeless Rate	Multiple Regression	
		Partial r	Standardized Coefficient
% Adults Employed, 1990	0.07[c]	-0.12[c]	-0.12[c]
% Change in Employment, '80-'90	0.00	0.14[c]	0.14[c]
% Unemployed, 1989	-0.07[c]	0.08[c]	0.08[c]
% Change in Unemployed, '79-'89	-0.07[c]	-0.05[b]	-0.05[b]
% Employed in Manufacturing, 1989	0.00	-0.10[c]	-0.10[c]
Change in % Employed in Manufacturing, '89/'79	-0.10[c]	0.02	0.02
% Employed in Service Sector, 1989	0.70[c]	0.69[c]	0.69[c]
Change in % Employed in Services, '89/'79	0.09[c]	-0.09[c]	-0.09[c]
Per Capita Income, 1988	0.37[c]	0.12[c]	0.12[c]
Change in Per Capita Income, '79-'89	0.07[c]	0.05[a]	0.05[a]
Mean Earnings in Manufacturing, 1988	0.04[a]	-0.01	0.01
Mean Earnings in Services, 1988	0.06[b]	0.04[c]	-0.04[c]
% Employed, in Semi- or unskilled jobs, 1990	-0.24[c]	0.25[c]	0.25[c]
Median Commute time to work (minutes), '90	0.34[c]	0.28[c]	0.28[a]

NOTES: Values are weighted by relative population sizes. Multiple $R^2 = .59$; SEE=8.5 ; F=325.87 [c]

SOURCE: Computed from 1990 U.S. Census data, STF-3C Data Tape and USA Counties, 1990

[a] $\alpha < 0.05$
[b] $\alpha < 0.01$
[c] $\alpha < 0.001$

Unquestionably, the strongest impact is the 0.69 correlation between the percentage of employment in the service sector and homeless rates, and this is virtually unchanged when all other indicators of economic opportunity are held constant (see columns 2 and 3). This is an unusually strong association, suggesting that there are some important features of service employment which are particularly unsuited for individuals who are at risk of becoming homeless.

Or alternatively, it may be that other unspecified types of employment are less often available in areas with high service employment. This is probably not manufacturing employment as there tends to be a positive (0.14), rather than negative association between these two types of employment. Rather, it may very well involve unskilled or semi-skilled positions, as there is a moderate -0.48 correlation between services and such low-skilled employment, reflecting the tendency for there to be relatively fewer low-skill jobs in areas of high service employment. However, the association between low-skill employment and homelessness, which is a -0.24, reverses to become 0.25 when the various other economic indicators are controlled for. While the initially negative zero-order correlation suggests that the more low-skill positions there are in a county, the less the rate of homelessness, the opposite is apparently closer to the truth. We do know that people holding low-skill positions tend to be one of the groups at risk of homelessness. Thus, it should come as no surprise that the more such individuals there are, the more become homeless. If this interpretation is correct, it would suggest that simply creating additional low-skilled positions, such as in newspaper sales, may not be as viable an intervention as would be providing longer-term training for skilled positions.

Service employment also tends to be associated (.08) with longer commute times, thus, we find a 0.28 association between mean commuting time and higher homeless rates. More distant employment, obviously means less accessible employment opportunities for the homeless who rarely have access to automobiles, and usually do not have the funds for public transport if it is available. Collectively, the economic indicators account for almost three-fifths (Adjusted R^2 = 0.59) of the variation in homeless rates. However, such an analysis is intended only to be a preliminary exploration of the data, and can not address questions about whether these effects may actually be reflecting or masking the role of other possible conditions, such as the demographic, disability, or methodological predictors, and it is to this topic we will now turn.

Structural Equation Model. Modeling the contribution of the indicators of economic opportunity contributes moderately to explaining why some counties have higher homeless levels than others. The inclusion of indicators of service sector employment, unemployment, the proportion employed in the services sector, and the proportion employed in low- or semi-skilled positions each significantly improves the overall ability of the model to account for the differential sizes of homeless populations. Although the economic indicators, as a group, only increases the explanatory power of the model from 88.8% to 92.6%, or by almost 4%, they explain away some of the effects of the demographic and disability indicators, accounting for just over a quarter (27.0%) of the total variation in the homeless rates, only slightly less than the demographic and measurement error indicators (see table 4-7).

Diverse combinations of economic indicators listed in Table 4-6 were tested. However, most of these indicators either added nothing to the overall fit of the model, or more typically, prevented the computer algorithms from converging on a stable, admissible, or otherwise optimal solution. The four economic variables finally selected accounted for just as high a level of variation as did the 14 indicators used in the preliminary regression (see table 4-6), although some of this is no doubt due to their disattenuation through the inclusion of measurement error for each of these variables.

Almost all of the effect of the economic indicators is accounted for by the impact of service employment, which accounted for 25.6%--or about 95%--of the 27.0% attributable to this group in the combined model. The results gained from using structural equation modeling, the reader may recall, paralleled what was found using descriptive and more conventional statistical techniques. Two way analysis of variance had revealed a strong impact of servicetization on the homeless rates, but this relation was dramatically reduced when urbanization was held constant as a covariate. In contrast, in the SEM models servicetization remains a potent force, even though the initial 56.7% of the variation explained in the economic-only model was reduced to 25.6% when the demographic and other variables are added in. Thus, while servicetization is partially masking a similar negative effect of urbanization on homelessness, the SEM analysis reported here demonstrates that it has a substantial independent effect on homeless levels. Since servicetization statistically can not be completely distinguished from urbanization, in part due to a moderate 0.40 correlation between the two variables, it would appear that the development of a service servicetization is partially masking a similar negative effect of urbanization on homelessness, the SEM analysis reported here demonstrates that it has a substantial independent effect on homeless levels. Since servicetization can not be completely distinguished from urbanization, in part due to a moderate 0.40 correlation between the two variables, it would appear that the development of a service economy is an integral, perhaps even a defining feature of contemporary urbanization, helping us to conceptually isolate a few of the key features of urbanization which have been so pathogenic. Hopper's theory that, "... the roots of the burgeoning homelessness problem in the US lie not in individual defects or disabilities of the homeless, but in the economic restructuring process of the city",[370] is clearly supported by the test of this model.

Although employment, unemployment, and low-skill jobs add significantly to the model, their explanatory power is very small, only accounting for about one percent or less of the variation in homelessness. The lower the employment, the higher the unemployment, and the more low-skilled positions there are, the higher the level of homelessness. These effects replicate what was found in the preliminary analysis, and by other researchers, but at lower levels. They illustrate that the most generalized measures of economic opportunity fail to illuminate much about the

---

[370] Hopper, Susser, and Conover, "Economies of makeshift", p. 183.

specific conditions acting on those at risk of homelessness, with the exception of servicetization. Although it may be expected that the potential availability of unskilled and low-skilled jobs may serve to diminish the number of homeless individuals, such availability may also be indicative of persons at risk of homelessness who find holding onto such jobs in active urban economies with high levels servicetization to be particularly difficult.

Table 4-7. Effects of Indicators of Economic Opportunity on Homeless Rates

Variables	Disability, Demographic, & Systematic Error	Economic Only		Economic, & Disability, Demographic, & Systematic Error	
	Variation Explained	β	Variation Explained	β	Variation Explained
ECONOMIC OPPORTUNITY	--	--	59.3%	--	27.0%
Total Employment, as % of workforce, 1990	--	-0.13[c]	0.8%	-0.01	0.1%
Unemployment rate, 1989	--	0.04[b]	0.3%	0.04[b]	0.2%
% of Jobs Low or Semi-skilled	--	0.06[c]	1.5%	0.05[c]	1.1%
Service jobs, as % of Total Employ., 1989	--	0.83[c]	56.7%	0.42[c]	25.6%
DISABILITY INDICATORS (See chapter 3)	7.9%	--	--	--	3.1%
DEMOGRAPHIC VARIABLES (See chapter 2)	40.4%	--	--	--	29.4%
MEASUREMENT ERROR	40.5%	--	--	--	33.2%
TOTAL MODEL (R^2)	88.8%		59.3%		92.6%

NOTES: See appendix 2 for goodness-of-fit statistics. Each model computed using weighted least squares and estimates of measurement error.
[a] $\alpha < 0.05$
[b] $\alpha < 0.01$
[c] $\alpha < 0.001$

Chapter V

PRIMARY SUPPORTS: FAMILY AND COMMUNITY

While only a minority of researchers propose that family fragmentation has played a central or even exclusive role in the genesis of homelessness,[371] many have identified family conditions as an intermediate means through which larger economic and demographic forces influence the lives of persons who eventually become homeless. Typically, family fragmentation is seen as exerting its influence either through the family of origin or the family of procreation of the adult homeless person. Lack of family support, early traumatization by physical or sexual abuse, and placement in foster care are regarded by many as setting the stage for the later disintegration of the homeless person's few social bonds. Alternatively, the lack of support or even victimization by the family of procreation is treated as a precipitant of the homeless condition. This chapter will review the substantial body of research conducted in recent years on the various facets of this question, as well as presenting the results of the analysis of the national database which shows that family fragmentation has only a modest effect on homelessness. This is an effect which undoubtedly masks the more powerful effects of urbanization, lack of education, and expansion of employment in the service sector of the economy.

Some authors have gone so far as to include the lack of social bonds in the

---

[371] See Bassuk, Lauriat, and Rubin, Homelessness: Critical Issues for Policy and Practice; McMurray, Chapter 4, "Family breakdown causes homelessness," in Orr, (ed.), The Homeless: Opposing Viewpoints.

157

definition of homelessness.[372] It has been suggested that to be homeless is to be without family or friends who can be relied on in times of crisis, an idea which goes back to a line of Robert Frost's: "Home is the place where, when you have to go there, they have to take you in." For this reason, Wright suggested that to be homeless, is to be without such bonds.[373] Other researchers, however, have treated the impact of family fragmentation more formally, within the context of the theory of social disaffiliation, as an instance of the breakdown of social ties. The theory of social disaffiliation can be traced back to the work of Nels Anderson who concluded that the hobo was, "...an individualistic person. Not even the actors and the artists can boast a higher proportion of egocentrics. They are the modern Ismaels who refuse to fit into the routine of conventional social life. Resenting every sort of social discipline, they have cut loose from organized society."[374]

It was Bahr and Caplow who formalized the notion of social disaffiliation as, "a faulty relationship between homeless people and society," one which could have various causes. They saw disaffiliation as the lack or weakening of ties to social institutions, and drawing from Merton's theory of anomie, suggested that one way people respond to the strains generated by the disjuncture between socially prescribed goals and available means for achieving them is by retreating.[375] This can result in: (i) loss of affiliation through external changes such as a death; (ii) deliberate withdrawal from social institutions; or (iii) lifelong isolation in response to inadequate childhood socialization. Bahr and Caplow tested their theory in New York in the 1960s through a comparison of homeless and non-homeless low-income men. This involved the use of 14 measures of lifetime and current affiliation, the results of which offered only limited support for their theory. Only 5 of their measures showed

---

[372] Pamela Fischer and W.R. Breakey, "Homelessness and mental health: An overview," International Journal of Mental Health 14 (4), pp. 6-41 (1985/1986).

[373] Wright, Address Unknown, p. 87.

[374] Nels Anderson, The Hobo: The Sociology of the Homeless Man (Chicago: University of Chicago Press, 1961, first published 1923), p. 23. Cited in Barak, Gimme Shelter.

[375] Bahr and Caplow, 1973, p. 55.

significant differences between the two groups, including frequency of contact with family in the past year and having close friends in the area. Furthermore, it was unclear whether the areas of weaker affiliation were the result of poverty and aging, or an independent, contributory cause to their homeless condition.[376]

Most researchers have eschewed developing or testing a theoretical model of the role of social and family conditions in the creation and or perpetuation of homelessness. More typically, theoretical considerations are confined to proposed typologies of social causes. Jahiel, for instance, proposes three homeless-making processes involving families: (i) Running away, by women and children, because of actual or threatened abuse, neglect, or incompatibility; (ii) being thrown away; (iii) Long-term processes, i.e. history of childhood in foster care. Jahiel is careful to suggest that social disaffiliation and family fragmentation is not routinely characteristic of the homeless, that these are processes which can play an important role at any of several stages in the development of homelessness, concluding that, "Homelessness is an unfortunate continuation of the displacement process that begins with the social and psychological disaffiliation from unemployment."[377]

Wright developed a similar notion that there is an important distinction between 'family leavers' and 'family rejects', the former being those who leave of their own accord.[378] In Rossi's Chicago survey, respondents were asked whether they would like to go back and live with their families of origin, and if so, whether they thought they would be welcome. Whereas most of the men said they would like to return but doubted that they would be taken in, most of the women reported they would be taken in, but did not want to go back, as most had fled from situations of domestic trauma and abuse.[379]

---

[376] Westerfelt, "The ins and outs of homelessness", pp. 54-55.

[377] Jahiel , p. 122

[378] Wright, Address Unknown, p. 90.

[379] Rossi, Down and Out in America.

Trends in Marriage and Family

Before the more pertinent research on the role of family fragmentation in the lives of homeless persons is reviewed, I will first discuss some of the major trends which are often cited in support of the notion that the disintegrating family is central to homelessness. Although the data on these trends is circumstantial, since it establishes no essential connection with the problem of homelessness, it nonetheless forms an important backdrop, defining the dimensions of family fragmentation. The most relevant trends include the decline in marriage rates, changing sexual mores, increasing rates of teenage pregnancy and single parent families, changes in divorces rates, and the resulting diminution in the size of the typical family and household.

Since the 1960s, marriage rates have declined precipitously. Whereas a fifth (20.3%) of men were unmarried in 1969, this percentage had almost doubled by 1989, to 36.9%. Similarly, close to a quarter (23.9%) of women were unmarried in 1969, and by 1989, their rate virtually equaled that of men, at 36.8%.[380] The only group which saw increasing rates of marriage were affluent men.[381] Declines in marriage among women have been reported to be due to the fact that they have come to marry later, divorce more often, or to remarry less frequently. In 1969, most women (91%) with extremely low personal incomes were married, however by 1989, this rate had dropped to 82%.[382]

Declines in marriage rates may be particularly pertinent to understanding the spread of homelessness among women and single parent families. There have been a range of explanations offered for the decline of marriage, such as increased labor participation rates of women, declining salaries of lower and middle-income men, or the growing disagreement about the proper division of labor between men and women. In addition, it has been proposed that relaxation in sexual mores may have reduced the appeal of marriage.[383] But more fundamentally, the development of a

---

[380] Jencks, Homelessness, p. 51.
[381] Ibid.
[382] Ibid., p. 55.
[383] Ibid., p. 57.

160

post-industrial information economy may have created a greater demand for the skills of women, straining traditional family roles, and thus, reducing the appeal of marriage. The role of women in supporting the war effort during World War II undoubtedly set the stage for the more permanent restructuring of roles during the post-war years.

One of the causes of declining marriage rates is the increasing incidence of divorce. Since the mid-1960s, the divorce rate has moved up dramatically, reaching a peak in 1981 with a slight decline since then. Just about half of marriages now terminate in divorce, however, this rate is inversely correlated to socioeconomic status: the lower the socioeconomic status, the higher the likelihood of divorce or separation.[384]

The increasing divorce rates have been attributed to anti-family policies, as well as the social and economic marginalization of teenagers, both of which create extraordinary pressures on family relationships and too often, their eventual breakdown.[385] Another cause may be the innovation of no-fault divorce laws in most (48) states. Weitzman, for example, states that in a sample of three thousand cases, divorce resulted in an immediate 73% drop in the standard of living of women and their children, while the former husbands involved saw a 42% increase in their's. No-fault divorce statutes are also likely to force the sale of the family home, giving the husband 50% of the proceeds, whereas prior to no-fault divorce, the house was more likely to be awarded to wife and children.[386]

Just as marriage rates have declined, out-of-wedlock births and the formation of single parent families have increased, especially among the extremely low income. In 1969, only a sixth (16%) of all unmarried working age women with extremely low incomes had a child. But by 1989, this had risen to almost a third (31%).[387] This

---

[384] Timmer, Eitzen, and Talley, Paths to Homelessness, p. 28.

[385] Ibid., p. 126.

[386] Lenore J. Weitzman, The Divorce Revolution (New York: Free Press, 1985).

[387] Jencks, Homelessness, p.55.

trend has been most evident among teenage black girls, as 41% are reported to have experienced at least one pregnancy by the age of 18.[388] Almost all (90%) of the births to black teens are to unmarried girls.[389] Virtually all (99.3%) of these teenagers decide to keep their babies.[390] Adolescent pregnancy may be a particularly problematic precursor to homelessness, both for the mothers, the families, and for the children once they grow up, as these young parents are economically and socially unprepared to care for their children. Wilson has proposed that it may be the economic marginality of young inner city males which generates declining marriage rates and increasing out-of-wedlock birth rates. But it may also be a general decline in the presense of two-parent family role models, along with hopes for economic independence. These no doubt undercut any incentive to postpone motherhood, which comes to be viewed as more practical in the household of the teenage girls' family of origin.

The decline in marriage, increase in divorce, and formation of single-parent families have all resulted in smaller family and household sizes. This is supported by the U.S. Census data which shows that the average household size fell from 2.76 members in 1980 to 2.63 in 1990.[391] Even as the population growth of the United States has been leveling off, there are more households because the size of the average household is shrinking.[392] These changes place increased demand on the housing market to supply multiple housing units when traditionally one unit would suffice. For this reason, it has only been in recent years that the number of rooms per unit has exceeded the number of people in the typical household. In addition, smaller household sizes require increased labor force participation, no doubt creating a downward pressure on wages. The proportion of children living within two parent

---

[388] Timmer, Eitzen, and Talley, Paths to Homelessness, p. 131.

[389] Ibid., p. 131.

[390] Janet M. Simons, Belva Finlay, and Alice Yang, The Adolescent and Young Adult Fact Book (Washington, D.C.: Children's Defense Fund, 1991).

[391] D. Stanley Eitzen and Maxine Baca Zinn, In Conflict and Order: Understanding Society (Boston: Allyn and Bacon, 1993), p. 451.

[392] Ibid., p. 451.

families declined from 85% in 1970 to 72% in 1991. And for black children, this percentage decreased from 68% in 1970 to 43% in 1991.[393]

Several of the indicators of family fragmentation which will be examined in this chapter are summarized in tables 5-1 and 5-2. These tables present mean levels for each of these indicators for the major regions of the United States and are broken down by level of urbanization. They indicate that, for most of these measures, levels of family fragmentation are fairly consistent across the United States. However, there is somewhat greater variation when urban and rural areas are compared. Just over four-fifths (82%) of Americans lived in a family unit in 1990, a percentage which was lowest in the West (80%) and highest in the South (83%), and which varied moreso between urban areas (80%) and rural (86% in South). The opposite pattern was found with family size, with the lowest levels (4.1) in the West and highest in the Midwest and South (3.%). In fact, there is a very strong negative correlation of -0.76 (r) between the proportion of persons living in families and the average family size when examined throughout the 3,141 counties. When a greater proportion of people are part of families, families tend to be smaller, and conversely, when families contain less of the population, they tend to be larger.

---

[393] U.S. Census data, reported in Rocky Mountain News, "57% of black children live with one parent," (July 21, 1992). Cited by Timmer, Eitzen, and Talley, Paths to Homelessness, p. 130

**Table 5-1. Indicators of Family Formation and Size,
By Region and Urbanization, 1990**

Region & Urbanization (& n)	Proportion of Persons in Families	Family Size	Mean Family Household Size	Mean Non-Family Household Size
NORTHEAST (629)	.81	3.9	3.0	1.10
Low (258)	.82	3.8	2.9	1.10
Medium (196)	.82	3.8	2.9	1.11
High (175)	.81	4.0	3.0	1.10
MIDWEST (753)	.82	3.8	2.9	1.10
Low (613)	.84	3.7	2.8	1.07
Medium (61)	.85	3.7	3.0	1.10
High (79)	.81	3.9	2.9	1.11
SOUTH (1088)	.83	3.8	2.9	1.09
Low (744)	.86	3.7	2.9	1.06
Medium (181)	.85	3.6	2.9	1.09
High (163)	.81	3.9	2.9	1.12
WEST (651)	.80	4.1	3.0	1.15
Low (504)	.83	3.9	2.9	1.12
Medium (26)	.82	3.9	2.9	1.14
High (121)	.80	4.1	3.1	1.16
TOTAL (3,141)	.82	3.9	2.9	1.11

SOURCE: Computed from STF-3C data tapes, U.S. Bureau of the Census, 1989; means are weighted by the relative population size of the areas listed. Low Urbanization--Zero population urbanized; Medium--1-49% population urbanized; High--50%+ of population urbanized.

Almost a quarter of the population (24%) lived in one person households in 1990, a rate which varied by no more than a few percentage points between regions or levels of urbanization. Likewise, almost a fifth (18%) of adults were either

**Table 5-2. Indicators of Family Fragmentation,
By Region and Urbanization, 1990**

Region & Urbanization (& n)	Proportion Persons in One Person Households	Proportion Adults Separated, Divorced, or Widowed	Proportion of Families Female Headed	Teenage Births
NORTHEAST (629)	.25	.18	.12	142
Low (258)	.24	.17	.09	153
Medium (196)	.23	.17	.10	133
High (175)	.26	.18	.14	143
MIDWEST (753)	.24	.18	.11	177
Low (613)	.24	.17	.08	160
Medium (61)	.21	.16	.09	163
High (79)	.26	.18	.13	190
SOUTH (1088)	.24	.18	.12	265
Low (744)	.22	.19	.12	281
Medium (181)	.21	.18	.11	265
High (163)	.26	.20	.13	257
WEST (651)	.23	.18	.11	229
Low (504)	.22	.18	.09	234
Medium (26)	.22	.18	.10	252
High (121)	.24	.18	.11	225
TOTAL (3,141)	.24	.18	.12	211

SOURCE: Computed from STF-3C data tapes, U.S. Bureau of the Census, 1989; means are weighted by the relative population size of the areas listed. Low Urbanization--Zero population urbanized; Medium--1-49% population urbanized; High--50%+ of population urbanized.

separated, widowed, or divorced in 1990, a rate which is remarkably consistent throughout the United States, with only slightly higher (18%-20%) levels in urban compared with rural areas (17%-19%). And similarly, the percentage of female-headed families is consistently in the 11% to 12% range throughout the country, and somewhat less (8%-12%) in rural areas than in urban areas (11-14%). But teenage pregnancies become considerably more prevalent the further west and south one goes: whereas the mean levels are 142 in the Northeast and 177 in the Midwest, they go up to 265 in the South and 229 in the West. The figures in table 5-2 reveal that this tends to be a rural problem more so, with the exception of the Midwest, where the rates are the highest in urban areas. In general, most of the indicators of family fragmentation suggest that levels are higher in most urban settings, though not consistently so, and that levels of family fragmentation may be greater in the western part of the nation.

Overall Findings and Their Interpretations

Many of the studies which have been conducted have not distinguished between the various kinds of family and social support, whether such support involves the family of origin, the current nuclear family, or friends. They have, thus, generated findings which are of an essentially general nature. This body of literature, nevertheless, tends to support the notion that the presence of perceived social support is an essential ingredient in the prevention and remediation of homelessness. After considering homeless persons' own assessments of the role of the family in their plight, I will review the evidence which supports or fails to support the social disaffiliation model.

Self-Reports of Family Causes. Perhaps the most comprehensive data set pertinent to homeless persons' self-assessments of causes for their conditions comes from the Ohio interview survey of 979 homeless persons in the late 1980s.[394] When asked about the reasons for their homelessness, only about an eighth (13.3%) cited family conflict and a twelfth (8.0%), family dissolution. In contrast, nearly half (48%) of the respondents mentioned economic reasons. When these figures are

---

[394] Dee Roth, Beverly G. Toomey, and Richard J. First, "Gender, racial, and age variations among homeless persons," in Robertson and Greenblatt, (eds.), Homelessness: A National Perspective, p. 207.

166

broken down by gender, race, and age, two patterns emerge. Whereas family conflict is cited more frequently by women (27.4%), blacks (16.8%), and the young (20.8%), family dissolution is more often mentioned by women (9.7%), whites (9.6%), and somewhat by the old (8.3%-8.5%).[395] Those respondents who lost contact with friends or relatives were also asked why they had not maintained these relationships. They typically stated that their friends or relatives would not help if contacted, that they did not live close by, or that the homeless person was ashamed of his or her condition. But it was unwillingness of others to help which was the reason most frequently given (33%) for not maintaining these relationships.[396]

In Support of Disaffiliation Model. Most of the general findings pertinent to the disaffiliation model originate from surveys of the homeless in which the respondents are typically asked to assess the level of support which they have received from family and friends as a whole. Earlier surveys tended to use single samples of homeless individuals, and thus whatever information was generated on family support was difficult to evaluate without some comparison group. In contrast, the more recent studies have often included a matched comparison group of housed but otherwise similar respondents, providing a stronger basis for interpreting the findings. Even in these studies crude matching procedures too often create groups of questionable comparability.

The single sample studies have revealed a sparsity of social supports reported by the homeless.[397] Rossi, for example, found that a third (33.3%) of the homeless

---

[395] Ibid., p. 207.

[396] F. Stevens Redburn and Terry F. Bus, Responding to America's Homeless: Public Policy Alternatives (New York: Praeger, 1986), p. 48.

[397] K. Hopper, E. Baxter, S. Cox, et al. One Year Later: The Homeless Poor in New York City (New York: Community Service Society, 1982); G. Morse and R.J. Calsyn, "Mentally disturbed homeless people in St. Louis: Needy, willing, but underserved," International Journal of Mental Health 14 (1986), pp. 74-94; P.J. Fischer and W.R. Breakey, "Homelessness and mental health: An overview," International Journal of Mental Health 14 (1986), pp. 6-41; S. P. Segal, J. Baumohl, and E. Johnson, "Falling through the cracks: Mental disorder and social margin in a young vagrant population," Social Problems 24 (1977), pp. 387-400; K.H. Dockett, Street Homeless People in the District of Columbia: Characteristics and Service Needs (Washington D.C.: University of the District of Columbia, 1989); R.K. Farr, P. Koegel, and A. Burnam, A Study of Homelessness and

in Chicago were socially isolated and not in contact with any relatives, spouse, or children, and that almost a quarter (23.7%) had contact with neither family nor friends.[398] He concluded that, "the strong impression left...is of persons who have extensive ties to neither relatives nor friends.[399]

Some of the single sample studies have included questions aimed at assessing concrete forms of support that the homeless receive from family and friends. The respondents in Rossi's Chicago study reported that an average of only 2.9% of their income was provided by family and friends, compared with 30.2% received from welfare, 29% from economic activity, and 21% from pensions and disability benefits.[400] Rossi reported that, "It appears from our Chicago data that the average life of tolerance and help [from family and friends] ...is about four years, the period that the homeless were without steady work before becoming homeless."[401] In contrast, in the Ohio study respondents were asked where they had spent the previous night and where they planned on spending the current night. Out of 868 respondents to the question, 98 (10.6%) spent their last night with family or friends, and 95 (8.4%) planned on the same for the current night. And of the 10.2% who planned on spending the night with family or friends, 8.4% did so the previous night.[402] On the whole, these studies reveal that although a substantial minority of the homeless--

---

Mental Illness in the Skid Row Area of Los Angeles (Los Angeles: County Department of Mental Health, 1986); K.Y. McChresney, Characteristics of the Residents of Two Inner-city Emergency Shelters for the Homeless (Los Angeles: University of Southern California, Social Science Research Institute, 1987); C.Mowbray, A. Solarz, S.V. Johnson, E. Philips-Smith, and C.J. Combs, Mental Health and Homelessness in Detroit: A Research Study (Lansing, MI: Michigan Department of Mental Health, 1986); P.H.Rossi, J.D. Wright, G.A. Fisher, and G. Willis, "The urban homeless: Estimating composition and size," Science (235), pp. 1336-41 (1987); A. Solarz and G.A. Bogat, "When social support fails: The homeless," Journal of Community Psychology 18, pp. 79-96 (1990); E.L. Bassuk, L. Rubin, and A. Lauriat, "Is homelessness a mental health problem?" American Journal of Psychiatry 141, pp. 1546-50 (1984); H.R. Lamb, "Deinstitutionalization and the homeless mentally ill," Hospital & Community Psychiatry 35, pp. 899-907 (1984); J. Leach and J. Wing, Helping Destitute Men (London: Tavistock, 1980).

[398] Rossi, Down and Out in America, p. 177.

[399] Ibid., p. 77.

[400] Ibid., p. 113.

[401] Ibid., p. 189.

[402] Redburn and Buss, Responding to America's Homeless , p. 41.

around a quarter or third--have lost all ties with family and friends, only a very small percentage--around a tenth or twentieth--receive any meaningful concrete assistance such as money or emergency lodging. The remaining majority of the homeless maintain sporadic contact and receive a modicum of moral support from family, whether parents, spouse, or children are involved.

In recent years about a half dozen studies of the homeless have been conducted which compared levels of social support among the homeless and similar housed groups. Each has used a different type of comparison group, and thus, while their results can not be aggregated, they are instructive nonetheless. One of the first of these involved patients recently discharged from a state mental hospital. These 132 people were followed for 6 months, and during this time, 47 became homeless (35.6%). Although the only statistically significant differences between the two groups involved gender and income, it was concluded that community support was less evident in the lives of the homeless subjects. In addition, it was concluded that the homeless subjects had less family involvement than the non-homeless.[403]

Two studies have focused on homeless women. Jackson and Borgers investigated whether a multi-dimensional model of disaffiliation that included the family of origin and current social supports could discriminate between a sample of 76 adult homeless and 74 adult non-homeless women.[404] It was found that coping scores were correlated with both the number of social supports and the respondent's satisfaction with their social support network, supporting their hypothesis that the disaffiliation model distinguishes between similar homeless and housed women. In a similar study, Bassuk and Rosenberg found that the support networks of homeless women were fragmented and included a greater proportion of men, while those of housed women included greater contact with mothers, other female relatives, as well

---

[403] John R. Belcher, "Moving into homelessness after psychiatric hospitalization," Journal of Social Service Research 14 (3-4), pp. 63 (1991).

[404] Anita G. Jackson-Wilson and Sherry Borgers, "Disaffiliation revisited: A comparison of homeless and nonhomeless women's perceptions of family of origin and social supports," Sex Roles 28 (7-8), pp. 361-377 (April 1993), p. 361.

as extended family living near by.[405] The one comparative study of homeless men also found that a smaller proportion of the homeless were in contact with family or friends, or had a confiding relationship.[406]

Bassuk and Rosenberg also compared 49 female-headed families with 81 similar families which were housed. While a third (34%) of the homeless families had daily contact with adult supports, two-thirds of the housed families had a similar level of support. In contrast, another third (34%) of the homeless had monthly or less frequent contact with such supports, the same could be said of only a fifteenth (7%) of the housed group.[407] On the whole, this group of studies reveals that the homeless do have decidedly fewer supports from family or friends, though the design of the studies do not permit conclusions about whether such a sparsity of support is a cause or consequence of the homeless condition, or the specific nature of the support which is provided--who it involves, the type of help provided.

Not Supportive of Disaffiliation. There have been considerably fewer studies which have failed to provide support to the notion that the homeless have weaker social supports than the non-homeless, and these include three which examined the issue with homeless adults; and two, with homeless families. The first of these actually produced results quite similar to those of the Ohio study and Rossi's Chicago study, however, they were interpreted as failing to support the idea that the homeless were disaffiliated. This exemplifies the difficulty with single sample studies, in this case, it is the proverbial problem of deciding whether the glass is half-full or half-empty. A study of the homeless in inner-city Los Angeles was interpreted as yielding "more indicators of meaningful social ties." Two-thirds of the respondents reported feeling attached to their families, almost three-quarters had contact with at least one relative during the past year. And for 64% of the respondents, the contact

---

    [405] Ellen L. Bassuk and Lynn Rosenberg, "Why does family homelessness occur? A case-control study," American Journal of Public Health 78 (7), pp. 783-788 (July 1988).

    [406] Fischer, Breakey, Anthony, and Kramer, "Mental health and social characteristics of the homeless", p. 519.

    [407] Bassuk and Rosenberg, "Why does family homelessness occur?", p. 785.

was at least once a month. Similar to Rossi's findings, it was reported that about one-fourth were estranged from their families, and 71% had contact with friends and family during the last year.[408] One other single sample study focused on adults in a temporary homeless shelter. These subjects were interviewed about their resources and specific types of support, as well as their subjective appraisals of this support. The researchers concluded that, "Few differences on social support variables were revealed between subgroups. The presence or absence of support is not the critical variable that prevents homelessness."[409] The one comparative study of homeless and housed adults found no significant difference between the groups. Sosin, Colson, and Grossman compared homeless and housed poor adults in Chicago in respect to the receipt of shelter and cash from friends and family. They found that once those living with family were excluded from the analysis, the difference in respect to receipt of food and shelter was no longer significant.[410] However, Westerfelt has appropriately questioned the logic of excluding those homeless residing with families when the receipt of shelter and food is being studied.[411]

In addition to the foregoing studies of adult individuals, two comparison group studies of homeless families have largely failed to support the disaffiliation hypothesis. Molnar et al., found no difference in the reported network size or the amount of support between 84 homeless and 76 housed families in New York.[412] Another study hypothesized that current social ties and housing support would reduce vulnerability to homelessness, and that either recent or early victimization or disruptions in social relationships would increase vulnerability. The researchers

---

[408] Farr, Koegel, and Burnham, "A study of homelessness and mental illness...", cited in Russell K. Schutt and Gerald R. Garrett, Responding to the Homeless: Policy and Practice (New York: Plenum Press, 1992).

[409] Andrea Solarz and Anne Bogat, "When social supports fails: The homeless," 18 (1), pp. 79-96 (Jan. 1990), p. 79.

[410] Sosin, Colson, and Grossman, Homelessness in Chicago.

[411] Westerfelt, "The ins and outs of homelessness".

[412] J. Molnar, W.R. Rath, T.P. Klein, C. Lowe, and A. Hartman, Ill Fares the Land: The Consequences of Homelessness and Chronic Poverty for Children and Families in New York City (New York: Bank Street College of Education, 1991).

specifically state that they did hypothesize that homelessness is caused by poor social ties, because "we believe that homelessness is primarily a consequence of poverty and a lack of affordable housing." [413] The study found little evidence that homeless families had a paucity of social supports. In fact, the homeless reported more members of their social networks than did housed families, and that they had seen both family and friends more recently. However, the mothers in families requesting shelter were more likely than housed mothers to report a variety of traumatic experiences "that suggest disruptions in social relationships in childhood and adulthood."[414] In sum, they found no evidence that homeless mothers are currently socially isolated.[415]

The foregoing studies represent a body of research which lends support to the notion that the homeless experience considerably fewer current supports from family and friends than extremely poor housed persons, but with a few exceptions. While the evidence for this conclusion is stronger for homeless individuals, at least some groups of homeless families clearly are exceptions, at least in respect to current levels of contact and network size. But because this body of research has usually failed to adequately operationalize the various sources and types of support, as well as to utilize longitudinal designs, many questions remain to be answered, a few of which will be addressed in the following sections on research which considered separately the various possible sources of support from family and friends.

Loss and Dysfunction in The Family of Origin

One of the most common types of family disorganization often considered as a precursor to homelessness involves the family of origin. This may involve either early dysfunction involving abuse or neglect, loss of a parent or placement in foster

---

[413] Marybeth Shinn, James R. Knickman, and Beth C. Weitzman, "Social relationships and vulnerability to becoming homeless among poor families," American Psychologist, pp. 1180-1187 (Nov. 1991), p. 1183.

[414] Ibid., p. 1185.

[415] Ibid., p. 1185.

care, or insufficient support by the family to the currently homeless adult child. Although most observers do not believe that either type of problem is central in the genesis of homelessness, most treat such conditions as either predisposing or aggravating causes with various levels of saliency.

Family Structure. The overwhelming majority of homeless persons (77%) have not had the opportunity to live with both biological parents from birth through 18, compared with 65% of a similar group of extremely poor but never homeless adults.[416] Accordingly, Wright concludes that about a tenth (10%) of the homeless were orphaned at birth or sometime early in childhood, "...which is to say they have been homeless in some sense from the day they were born."[417] This is supported by a review of the HPS studies which concluded that between 8% and 31% of the homeless respondents in these studies had no relatives.[418]

These results have been replicated with a variety of subgroups among the homeless. The correlation between loss of family in childhood and lifetime prevalence of homelessness was found to be especially strong in three samples of mental patients.[419] In addition, a higher proportion of homeless than housed mothers were themselves born into female-headed families.[420] Thus, while an overwhelming proportion of the homeless have experienced some important gap in the availability of family relationships during childhood, a substantial minority were raised in a single-parent family, and a smaller minority, perhaps around a tenth, did not live with their biological family at all.

---

[416] Carol Caton, Patrick E. Shrout, Paula F. Eagle, Lewis A. Opler, Alan Felix, and Boanerges Dominguez, "Risk factors for homelessness among schizophrenic men: A case-control study," American Journal of Public Health 84 (2), pp. 265-270 (1994), p. 267.

[417] Wright, Address Unknown, p. 87.

[418] Jahiel, Chapter 4, "Empirical studies of homeless populations in the 1980s," in Jahiel, (ed.), Homelessness: A Prevention-oriented Approach, p. 52.

[419] E. Susser, S.P. Lin, S.A. Conover, and E. Struening, "Childhood antecedents of homelessness in psychiatric patient." Presented at the meeting of the American Psychiatric Association, New York, May 1990.

[420] Bassuk and Rosenberg, "Why does family homelessness occur?", p. 78.

Early Family Dysfunction. It has been often implied, but rarely explicitly stated, that early family experiences lead to homelessness later in life.[421] Two key sources of strain on family systems are no doubt involved: (i) external stresses, due to outside events over which a family has no control, such as unemployment, disasters, etc., and (ii) internal stresses, generated by genetic, psychological, behavioral, or social forces that are carried over from one generation to the next.[422] Often the family of origin is believed to have been deficient in at least one of several areas, such as 'early training'[423] or providing a nurturing emotional environment.[424] One study of 40 homeless adults who were interviewed each for several hours using a semi-structured instrument concluded, "The families of origin were described as unstable, isolated, and isolating, violent, aggressive, and frequently alcoholic."[425] Another study compared 100 homeless mentally ill adults with a similar number of housed mentally ill adults, and concluded that the homeless subjects "experienced greater disorganization in family settings in childhood and less adequate family support, and fewer had a long term therapist."[426] A study of homeless mothers also concluded that its subjects, "experienced family disorganization in childhood." Two-thirds reported major family disruptions, such as separation, divorce, death of a parent, or out-of-home placement, and a third never knew her own father. A similar proportion reported abuse by a parent or another adult during childhood or

---

[421] Morse, Chapter 1, "Causes of homelessness," in Robertson and Greenblatt, (eds.), Homelessness: A National Perspective, p. 12.

[422] E. Carter and M. McGoldrick, (eds.), Family Life Cycle: A Framework for Family Therapy (New York: Gardner Press, 1980).

[423] M.A. Block, "A program for the homeless alcoholic," Quarterly Journal of Studies on Alcoholism 23 (4), pp. 644-49 (1962).

[424] S. Borg, "Homeless men: A clinical and social study with special reference to alcohol abuse," Acta Psychiatric Scand Suppl 276 (1978); Morse, Chapter 1, "Causes of homelessness," in Robertson and Greenblatt, (eds.), Homelessness: A National Perspective, pp. 3-17.

[425] Fay E. Reilly, "Experience of family among homeless individuals," Issues in Mental health Nursing 14 (4), pp. 309-21 (1993), p. 309.

[426] Caton, Shrout, Eagle, and Opler, "Risk factors for homelessness among schizophrenic men,", p. 265.

adolescence.[427]

In addition to some of the findings on general dysfunction, a range of studies have generated data on levels of physical and sexual abuse of the homeless as children. One study reported that about two-fifths (41%) of the homeless had experienced at least one violent physical or sexual assault during childhood.[428] For men, the most common (21% out of 41%) was physical assault.[429] In contrast, Wimbleby reports that only 13% of homeless men were physically abused prior to the age of 18 and that only about one in sixteen (6%) were sexually abused.[430] For women, the most frequent (21% out of 44%) form of abuse was sexual.[431] However, other estimates of sexual abuse of homeless women as children range from 9.9%[432] to 33%.[433] Two published estimates of physical abuse among homeless women as children range from 11.4% (compared with 6.5% in a similar housed sample)[434] and 28%.[435] Close to two-fifths of those reporting physical (38%) or sexual abuse (39%) had also been placed in foster care.[436]

In total, almost a tenth (9%) of all homeless are reported to have been sexually abused as children, and a seventh (14%), physically abused.[437] The one study which compared levels of abuse between homeless and similar but housed individuals found that the homeless generally had levels around twice that of the comparison

---

[427] Caton, Homeless in America, p. 35.

[428] North, Smith, and Spitznagel, "Violence and the homeless," p. 103.

[429] Ibid., p. 103.

[430] Marilyn A. Winkleby, Beverly Rockhill, Darius Jatulis, and Stephen P. Fortmann, "The medical origins of homelessness," American Journal of Public Health 82 (10), p. 1395 (1992).

[431] North, Smith, and Spitznagel, "Violence and the homeless,", p. 103.

[432] Shinn, Knickman, and Weitzman, "Social relationships and vulnerability to becoming homeless among poor families," p. 1185.

[433] Winkelby, Rockhill, Jatulis, and Fortmann, "The medical origins of homelessness", p. 1395.

[434] Shinn, Knickman, and Weitzman, "Social relationships and vulnerability to becoming homeless among poor families," p. 1185.

[435] Winkelby, Rockhill, Jatulis, and Fortmann, "The medical origins of homelessness," p. 1395.

[436] Ibid., 1396.

[437] Ibid., p. 1395.

group.[438] A range of other studies have generally replicated these findings, most often among homeless women.[439]

There is some controversy as to the relative influence of early versus recent domestic violence in the lives of homeless women. Whereas one study found that very few subjects who had been assaulted by their father or stepfather were later assaulted by a husband, common-law partner, or boyfriend,[440] another survey of homeless individuals in a community shelter concluded that domestic violence was a leading cause of their homelessness.[441] It may be that those who experienced abuse as children are a separate subgroup vis-a-vis those who experienced abuse as adults in their family of procreation. The various ways that abuse leads to homelessness range from the direct routes involving teenagers and women fleeing from violent homes to more indirect processes involving the abuse undermining personal functioning, perhaps through post-traumatic stress disorder (PTSD).

Another indicator of family dysfunction involves substance abuse or mental illness in its members, particularly parents, although the question of cause and effect remains unsettled (see chapter 3). Many authors have regarded family deficiency as a result of either parental pathology or marital separation.[442] In one sample of 900

---

[438] Shinn, Knickman, and Weitzman, "Social relationships and vulnerability to becoming homeless among poor families," p. 1185.

[439] Bassuk and Rosenberg, "Why does family homelessness occur?"; Margot Breton and Terry Bunston, "Physical and sexual violence in the live s of homeless women," Canadian Journal of Community Mental Health 11 (1), pp. 29-44 (1992); Angela Browne, "Family violence and homelessness: The relevance of trauma histries in the lives of homeless women," American Journal of Orthopsychiatry 63 (3), pp. 370-84 (July 1993); Lisa A. Goodman, "The prevalence of abuse among homeless and housed poor mothers: A compairson study," American Journal of Orthopsychiatry 61 (4), pp. 489-500 (Oct. 1991); J.L. Hagen, "Gender and homelessness," Social Work 32, pp. 312-16 (1987); and D. Wood, T.N. Valdez, T. Hayashi, and A. Shen, "Homeless and housed families in Los Angeles: A study comparing demographic, economic, and family function characteristics," American Journal of Public Health 80, pp. 1049-52 (1990).

[440] Breton and Bunston, "Physical and sexual violence in the lives of homeless women," p. 29.

[441] Hagen, "Gender and homelessness," pp. 312-316.

[442] Borg, "Homeless men..."; A.K. Jordan, "Homeless men and the community," Australian Journal of Social Issues 2 (3), pp. 27-33 (1965); L.L. Bachrach, "The homeless mentally ill and mental health services: An analytical review of the literature," Unpublished manuscript, 1984; Morse, Chapter 1, "Causes of homelessness," in Robertson and Greenblatt, (eds.), Homelessness: A National Perspective.

homeless individuals in St. Louis, it was found that a fourth had an alcoholic parent, and a third described some alcoholism in their family of origin. Similarly, a fifth reported drug abuse, and another fifth, mental illness on the part of their parents.[443] One study compared 90 homeless men with 20 comparison subjects and found that the homeless were more likely to describe their early family relationships as, "rejecting, emotionally impoverished, chaotic, and socially isolating."[444] It should, therefore, be no surprise that over a fifth (21.6%) of the homeless in one study had run away from home as a teenager for at least a week, compared with a third (6.5%) as many in a similar sub-sample of housed and poor persons.[445]

Foster Care and Childhood Placement. A review of eight studies, which utilized nine separate samples, revealed a mean rate of just over a quarter (26.0%, unweighted) of the homeless who had spent at least some time in foster care in childhood or adolescence, with a range of 9.9% to 43%.[446] The one study which broke these rates down by gender reported an overall rate of 11%, with 10% of the men and 17% of the women found to have been in foster care.[447] Three of these studies also included comparison groups of housed but extremely poor persons, and these revealed the homeless were on average 3.5 times as likely to have experienced foster care than similar groups of housed but extremely poor persons, a ratio which

---

[443] North, Smith, and Spitznagel, "Violence and the homeless," p. 101-103.

[444] Robert T. Zozus and Melvin Zax, "Perceptions of childhood: Exploring possible etiolgical factors in homelessness," Hospital & Community Psychiatry 42 (5), pp. 535-37 (1991), p. 535.

[445] Shinn, Knickman, and Weitzman, "Social relationships and vulnerability to becoming homeless," p. 1185.

[446] Richard Barth, "On their own: The experiences of youth after foster care," Child and Adolescent Social Work 7 (5), pp. 419-440 (Oct. 1990), p. 419; Joel Blau and Barbara Kleiman, Homeless Youth in the New York City Municipal Shelter System: The Project A.I.D. Final Report (New York: Human Resources Administration, 1985), p. 15; Goodman, "The prevalence of abuse among homeless and poor housed women,", p. 496; Piliavin, Sosin, and Westerfelt, "Conditions contributing to long-term homelessness," p. 22 ; Shinn, Knickman, and Weitzman, "Social relationships and vulnerability to becoming homeless," p. 1185; Ezra Susser, Elmer Streuning, and Sarah Conover, "Childhood experiences of homeless men," American Journal of Psychiatry 144, pp. 1599-1601 (1987); Westerfelt, "The ins and outs of homelessness," p. 111; Winkleby, Rockhill, Jatulis, and Fortmann, "The medical origins of homelessness".

[447] Winkleby Rockhill, Jatulis, and Fortmann, "The medical origins of homelessness."

varied from 2.0 to 4.5.[448] In contrast to foster care, Shinn, Knickman, and Weitzman found the homeless were only slightly more likely (10.2%) to have been placed in an institution or group home than in a foster home (9.9%) as a child.[449]

The impact of these experiences on the later careers of homeless persons, however, is unclear. On one hand, Piliavin and his colleagues found those who had experienced childhood placement to be more likely to be among the chronically homeless than those who had not.[450] On the other hand, Westerfelt found those who had experienced such placements were more likely to exit homelessness than those who had not. It may be that the long-term homeless are over-represented in the typical cross-sectional sample and that these individuals exhibit more entries and unsuccessful exits than those who had not been placed. But in either case, foster and institutional care no doubt weaken already troubled bonds with the family of origin, greatly complicating the person's later adaption to adult life and the ability to call on family resources in emergencies.

Contact with Family of Origin. It has been found that almost a ninth of the homeless (11.7%) do not have any living family members, and that two-fifths (40.4%) do not have any contact with their family of origin.[451] This is consistent with a review of the findings from the HPS studies which showed that between 20% and 40% had not seen a blood relative for more than a year.[452] Another review of 15 other studies found that the average proportion which had no contact with any family members was close to a third (32%).[453] At the other end of the spectrum of contact is the finding

---

[448] Sosin, Colson, and Grossman, Homelessness in Chicago; Goodman, "The prevalence of abuse among homeless and housed poor mothers," p. 496; Shinn, Knickman, and Weitzman, "Social relationshps and vulnerability to becoming homeless," p. 1185.

[449] Shinn, Knickman, and Weitzman, "Social relationships and vulnerability to becoming homeless", p. 1185.

[450] Irving Piliavin, Michael Sosin, and Herb Westerfelt, Conditions Contributing to Long-term Homelessness: An Exploratory Study IRP Discussion paper no. 853-87 (Madison, WI: University of Wisconsin, Institute for Research on Poverty, 1987).

[451] Rossi, Down and Out in America, p. 177.

[452] Jahiel, Chapter 4, "Empirical studies of homeless populations in the 1980s," in Jahiel, (ed.), Homelessness: A Prevention-oriented Approach, p. 42.

[453] Rossi, Down and Out in America, p. 170.

from the Ohio study that over two-fifths (42%) of the homeless have some form of weekly contact with relatives.[454]

Few studies break this contact down by type of family member. Those studies which do suggest that more of this contact is with siblings than parents. Rossi found in his Chicago sample that three-fifths (58%) of the homeless had living parents, and a majority of these (57%) lived in the area. While over two-thirds (70%) of the homeless were in contact with parents if these relatives lived nearby, overall, only a quarter (25%) of the homeless had contact with their parents.[455] This would be consistent with a finding from Boston in which close to a quarter (24%) of homeless mothers said they received support from their mother, and a tenth (10%), from their father. While the level of support from fathers was no different than a similar housed group of women, the percentage indicating support from their mothers was substantially less than the housed group (24% vs. 60%).[456] Contact with siblings, in contrast, was somewhat higher, at least in Chicago. While three-fourths (75%) of the homeless reported having siblings still alive, and close to a half (47%) having some living nearby, just over two-fifths (43%) of the total sample reported some contact with these family members.[457]

In contrast, Rossi reported that just over a quarter (28%) of his sample had contact with other relatives.[458] Higher levels of recent contact with relatives, however, have been reported in Minneapolis (65%).[459] Two-thirds (66%) of the Chicago sample reported having any living relatives, a figure which replicated a finding from a Baltimore study that 68.6% of the homeless had at least one relative.[460] Interpretation of data on levels of contact with family of origin and other relatives is

---

[454] Redburn and Buss, Responding to America's Homeless , p. 48.

[455] Rossi, Down and Out in America, p. 169.

[456] Bassuk and Rosenberg, "Why does family homelessness occur?", p. 785.

[457] Rossi, Down and Out in America, p. 169.

[458] Ibid., p. 169.

[459] Westerfelt, "The ins and outs of homelessness", p. 81.

[460] Pamela J. Fischer, Sam Shapiro, William Breakey, James Anthony, and Morton Kramer, "Mental health and social characteristics of the homeless: A survey of mission users," American Journal of Public Health 76 (5), pp. 519 (1986), p. 521.

ambiguous as wording of questions has sometimes been unclear in differentiating between the family of origin and the extended family.

Only a minority of the homeless (36%) reported that they could count on their relatives for material help, a level substantially higher than the actual frequency of support given.[461] Perhaps the finding which best exemplifies the views of the homeless toward the perceived likelihood of support from their families is that from the Chicago study.[462] Even though the about same proportion of the homeless want to live with relatives (38.3%) as do relatives who wish the homeless person would move in (35.9%), these two groups have minimal overlap: only a sixth (16.3%) of the homeless wish to live with relatives who they perceive would like the same. In contrast, two-fifths (39%) of the homeless do not want to live with relatives perceived to share the same aversion, and the remaining 44.7% represent situations in which either the homeless person or the relatives are reported not to be interested. One interview study of 80 sheltered homeless mothers found that some of the factors contributing to family homelessness included the size of the kin network and estrangement from the family of origin. A key conclusion of this study was that, "The availability of kin housing support is proposed as a selection factor in determining which of the families at risk will become homeless."[463]

Disengagement and Support from the Family of Procreation

More critical than support from the family of origin, is the homeless person's relationship with his or her family of procreation, if it exists. This family may include both his or her children and current or former spouse. Data on the structure of these families is particularly revealing, but also of significance are findings on the homeless person's own assessments of these relationships and on the actual levels and types of contacts, as well as type of assistance received.

---

[461] Redburn and Buss, Responding to America's Homeless, p. 48.

[462] Rossi, Down and Out in America, p. 171.

[463] Kay McChresney, "Absence of a family safety net for homeless families," Journal of Sociology and Social Welfare 19 (4), p. 55-72 (Dec. 1992).

Structure of Family of Procreation. One of the most salient characteristic of these families is their rarity as reflected by the low levels of marriage. In one of the largest multi-city surveys, it was found that about a eighth (12.6%) of the homeless are currently married and over half (54%) have never been married, despite the median age being in the mid-thirties.[464] Most of the difference between the foregoing figures represents the three out of ten (29.4%) who are divorced or separated, with the remainder (4.9%) consisting of the widowed.[465] The low levels of marriage are particularly dramatic among the majority group of male homeless persons. Among males, only 7% are currently married and 57% have never been married. In contrast, 9% of the females are currently married and 49% have never married. A Baltimore study compared homeless males with those of the general population and found none were currently married compared with almost half (48.4%) of the comparison group, and three-fifths (60.8%) never married, compared with just over a third of the non-homeless (34.6%).[466] Burt's findings are almost the same as what Rossi found in Chicago, where 6.9% were currently married, and 56.8%, never married,[467] as well as Wright's health care sample.[468] Only one in fifty (2%) of the homeless in one study were couples without children.[469]

Thus, the largest single group of homeless persons are single individuals. Over one third--35% of the single men and 39% of the single women--lived alone before their first episode of homelessness, compared with an overall figure of 14% for the adult population. These rates are even higher for those with a history of mental health and substance abuse treatment (43%) and with jail or prison experience (56%).[470] Many of those who were not living alone recently experienced a breakup

---

[464] Burt, Over The Edge, p.15.

[465] Ibid., p. 15.

[466] Fischer, Shapiro, Breakey, Anthony, and Kramer, "Mental health and social characteristics of the homeless," p. 521.

[467] Rossi, Down and Out in America, p. 129.

[468] Wright, Address Unknown.

[469] Burt, Over The Edge, p. 16.

[470] Ibid., p. 29.

181

of a significant relationship. In one study of homeless women, it was found that 16% had stopped living with a boyfriend, compared with 4.2% in a housed comparison group; and 15.5% were told to leave by parents, compared with 1.2% in the comparison group. However, the level of separation, divorce, and widowhood during the previous year was actually slightly less than the comparison group, 12.4% compared to 14.5%.[471]

Despite the low levels of marriage among the homeless, over half (54%) have had children.[472] Yet, only a tenth of the adults that Burt interviewed had children with them, and of these adults, almost all (90%) were women .[473] Only a small proportion (12%) of the women who had children with them also had their spouse with them, compared with just about a quarter (24%) of the men who had children accompanying them.

It is, thus, clear that the overwhelming majority of homeless persons have few spouse or children from whom they can draw support in their current circumstances. In addition, the low levels of family formation and high levels of family breakup among the homeless often play a role in the disintegration of their social supports.

Impact of Family Conflict and Dissolution. Despite the dramatic levels of family fragmentation among the homeless themselves, only one fifth (20%) of the homeless in the Ohio study cited family conflict as the major reason for their homelessness, and a tenth (10.3%), family dissolution.[474] However, family conflict was mentioned more often by women (28.1%) than men (21%); by whites (31.7%), than by blacks (20.4%) or Hispanics (17.4%). One study utilized multivariate methods to compare the relative saliency of current family support and earlier circumstances, and concluded, "...the logistic regression analysis revealed that poor (current) family support is a more important risk factor for homelessness than childhood ante-

---

[471] Shinn, Knickman, and Weitzman, "Social relationships and vulnerability to becoming homeless among poor families", p. 1185.

[472] Rossi, Down and Out in America, p. 131.

[473] Ibid., p. 14.

[474] First, Draft Report of Ohio Study , table 5.11.

182

cedents."[475]

Contact and Support Received. Homeless people receive only minimal levels of assistance from the families they do have. Yet, a clear majority (57.5%) revealed in the Ohio study that the main reason they came to their current county was to be with family or friends, compared with the 17.7% who came for work or the 8.4% who came for shelter.[476] In another study, 128 men in a New York city shelter were asked why they came to the shelter. Just under a third stated that they did so because they could not stay with their family.[477] This is consistent with the experience of the Chicago homeless, 31% of which report having a spouse or former spouse who were still alive, but only a third (35%) of these spouse remained in the area. Though, three-fifths (62%) of those who had a living spouse or former spouse retained some contact, less than a fifth (19%) of the total sample could claim to have such contact.[478] Similarly, just over a quarter (27%) of the women in a Boston study could claim to received any contact or support from a spouse or boyfriend.[479]

Despite the fact that close to half (47%) the homeless in Chicago are reported to have living children, fewer than two-thirds (64%) maintain any contact with them, a group which represents only three-tenths (30%) of the total population of adult homeless persons.[480] In sum, only a slight majority (54.8%) of the homeless have living relatives remaining from their family of procreation, and fewer than a third (32.8%) are in contact with at least one of these family members.[481]

The homeless person's assessment of the reliability of his or her family parallels the extent of such contact. The Ohio study asked its subjects about whether they had family they could count on, and somewhat over one-third (36%) indicated

---

[475] Caton, Shrout, Eagle, Opler, Felix, and Boanerges, "Risk factors for homelessness among schizophrenic men," p. 269.

[476] First, Draft Report of Ohio Study, table 5.8.

[477] New York Human Resources Administration, Chronic and Situational Dependency: Long-term Residents in a Shelter for Men (New York, May 1982), pp. ii, 9, 18, 22.

[478] Rossi, Down and Out in America, p. 172.

[479] Bassuk and Rosenberg, "Why does family homelessness occur?", p. 785.

[480] Rossi, Down and Out in America, p. 177.

[481] Ibid., p. 177.

that they did have such family. The proportions of men and women, and whites and minority members reporting this were essentially the same. However, the levels of perceived reliability (or availability) tends to drop off with age: while 42.7% of those from 18 to 29 reported their families were reliable, this dropped to 28.1% for those in their 40s, and 34.1%, for those 50 or over.[482] The overall 36% figure is fairly consistent with the proportion who stated in this same study that they had stayed with family the previous night: 36.5% of the men and 55.2% of the women. Results from this rural study were considerably greater than the urban Minneapolis samples of Westerfelt's who reported that 20% and 23% of his samples had stayed with family during the previous 30 days.[483] This same study found that over a fifth (21% & 22%) had received at least some cash assistance from their families in the last 30 days.[484] Also consistent with these findings is that of Stevens, et al.[485] He reported that, "Few people in our survey are helped by their families. Only 33% reported any kind of help at all, and only 23% would tell us the form of the help provided." In another, qualitative study of 40 homeless people, it was concluded that, "Created families had failed and had been riddled with spouse abuse and inadequate parenting."[486] However, in those instances when assistance is forthcoming, it was found to be related to the likelihood of exiting from the homeless condition.[487]

Isolation from Friends

The homeless report receiving a slightly higher level of support from friends than they do from family, but nonetheless experience significant isolation from peers. The level of such isolation found is less when interviewers use terms such as

---

[482] Roth, Toomey, and First, "Gender, racial, and age variations among homeless persons," in Robertson and Greenblatt, (eds.), Homelessness: A National Perspective, p. 207.

[483] Westerfelt, "The ins and outs of homelessness", p. 111.

[484] Ibid., p. 111.

[485] Stevens, Ann O'Brien, Les Brown, Paul Colson, and Karen Singer, When You Don't Have Anything: A Street Survey of Homeless People in Chicago (Chicago: Chicago Coalition for the Homeless, 1983).

[486] Reilly, "Experience of family among homeless individuals", p. 309.

[487] Westerfelt, "The ins and outs of homelessness," p. 111.

184

'associate' or 'hangout'. Such qualitative approaches to research have frequently revealed that many of the homeless have extensive peer relationships with other homeless persons.

Frequency of Contact. Most studies show that between 30% and 40% of the homeless report having no friends. While Rossi's review of 13 studies produced a mean of 36% who have no friends,[488] another review of the research placed the range at 25% to 45%,[489] with the highest figure found in Baltimore, where more than six times the percentage of homeless as similar housed men (7%) reported having no friends.[490] Just as a mean of 64% of the homeless report being in contact with friends, similar proportions report *recent* contact with friends: in Minneapolis, 72%; in Ohio, 55%; and in Chicago, 44%.[491] While the larger body of research suggests that close to two-thirds of the homeless are in contact with friends,[492] in Rossi's own Chicago study he found that almost half (48%) claimed to have *good* friends, most of whom (92%) the homeless were in contact with, representing an overall proportion of 44% of the homeless who are in contact with good friends.[493] While one study in Chicago reported that the homeless were in contact with a similar number of friends as a comparable housed group,[494] a study in Rochester found smaller networks and less frequent positive interactions with network members than housed men experiencing economic hardship.[495]

The Baltimore study conducted by Fischer provides another view about the number of friends the homeless have. Among the majority (54.9%) of the homeless

---

[488] Rossi, Down and Out in America, p.174.

[489] Jahiel, Chapter 4, "Empirical studies of homeless populations in the 1980s," in Jahiel, (ed.), Homelessness: A Prevention-oriented Approach, p. 52.

[490] W.R. Breakey, "Treating the homeless," Alcohol, Health and Research World 11, pp. 42-46 (1987).

[491] Westerfelt, "The ins and outs of homelessness", p. 81.

[492] Rossi, Down and Out in America, p. 174.

[493] Ibid., p. 174.

[494] Sosin, Colson, and Grossman, Homelessness in Chicago.

[495] H.J.M. Passero, M. Zax, and R.T. Zozus Jr., "Social network utilization as related to family hisotry among the homeless," Journal of Community Psychology 19, pp. 70-78 (1991).

who reported having at least one friend, the median number was 3.5.[496] Almost half of her sample (49.1%) reported having two or more friends, considerably fewer than the 87.1% of the comparison group who could say the same. But many of these friends are not considered confidants, as Fischer found that only a sixth (15.7%) claimed to have two or more confidants. This was just about a third of the level (44.5%) found in the comparison group of housed persons.[497] Those who do have friends, appear to have fairly regular contact with them. It was found that the average number of visits of homeless with friends during the last 30 days to be in the 16 to 18 range.[498]

Type of Assistance from Friends. Just as was the case with relationships with families, the perceived level of support from friends parallels the overall level of contact. Westerfelt found that between 55% and 66% of the homeless in Minneapolis reported being supported by friends during the past 30 days. This is, as expected, considerably higher than the levels of material support these same respondents report. Close to a quarter (23% & 24%) reported receiving food from friends during this same period, and a slightly smaller proportion, said they had received cash from their friends.[499] Because the friendship network of the homeless no doubt contain other homeless, it is not surprising that the levels of contact and assistance reported from friends would be slightly greater than that with their families.

Attitudes Towards Friends. About a half of homeless persons report having friends they can count or rely on. Like most survey questions, the levels depend not only on the specific locale, but also the way the questions are phrased. In Minneapolis, when the homeless as asked about whether they feel their friends care about them, between 54% and 66% answered in the affirmative, yet only about a third (33% & 34%) said they would be willing to ask these friends for help. This was

---

[496] Computed from grouped data, Fischer, Shapiro, Breakey, Anthony, and Kramer, "Mental health and social characteristics of the homeless", p. 521.

[497] Ibid., p. 521.

[498] Westerfelt, "The ins and outs of homelessness", p. 111.

[499] Ibid., p. 111.

despite the finding that around three-fifths (58% & 63%) said their friends would be willing to help.[500] In Chicago, fewer than half (48%) said they could "count on" their friends,[501] and in Ohio only two-fifths (41%) could say the same of their friends.[502] However, using the same study Redburn and Bus report that over half (55%) could count on their friends for "material help".[503] Two other studies confirm that the level of trust of the homeless in friends is less than that of matched housed groups.[504]

On the whole, approximately a third of the homeless report no friends and a majority of the remaining two-thirds--around 40% to 60% of the total--report having good friends or friends they can count on to some extent. It is clear that such reliance usually does not carry with it the expectation of significant material assistance, as probably only around a fifth of the total receive any such material help. When they do, such assistance represents a far smaller proportion of their total income, meeting even fewer of their needs. To what extent these relationships enable the homeless to remain in their current condition or empower them to reintegrate into the larger society is an open question.

A Test of the Impact of Family Fragmentation

This chapter has so far reviewed some of the major trends regarding the fragmentation of families, specific findings on the minimal levels of formation and substantial levels of dissolution in the families of homeless persons, as well as the marginal levels of support they provide. Yet the causal role of these trends in understanding the origins and dynamics of homelessness has not been established, as persuasive as they may be. We can not rule out the possibility that other trends involving urbanization, individual disabilities, or a restructuring economy have led to

---

[500] Ibid., p. 111.

[501] Rossi, Down and Out in America, p. 173.

[502] Roth, Toomey, and First, "Gender, racial, and age variations among homeless persons", p. 207.

[503] Redburn and Bus, Responding to America's Homeless, p. 48.

[504] Bassuk and Rosenberg, "Why does family homelessness occur?"; Wood, Valdez, Hayashi, and Shen, "Homeless and household families in Los Angeles".

187

both the breakdown of the family and to the expansion of the homeless population.

The zero-order correlations between key indicators of fragmentation and homelessness are also very suggestive of the impact of the family (see table 5-3). For instance, there is a substantial negative correlation between the proportion of a counties population which live in family households and the rate of homelessness (r = -0.57). Figure 5-1 portrays this same relationship along the horizontal axis, with the height of each bar indicating the average rate of homelessness for each group of counties. This figure shows that counties with the lowest levels of family formation have almost 6 times the level of homelessness as those with the highest. At the same time, those areas with the largest families have the highest levels of homelessness (r = 0.58), and as figure 5-1 illustrates, counties with the largest families have from 2 to

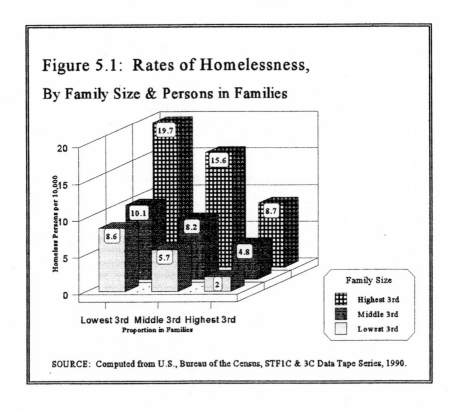

Figure 5.1: Rates of Homelessness, By Family Size & Persons in Families

SOURCE: Computed from U.S., Bureau of the Census, STF1C & 3C Data Tape Series, 1990.

over 4 times the homeless rates as those with the least. While family size is not a direct indicator of fragmentation, but of poorer economic circumstances, it is noteworthy that there is a -0.75 correlation between family size and extent of family formation, demonstrating that the higher the proportion of individuals who live as part of family units, the smaller these families tend to be.

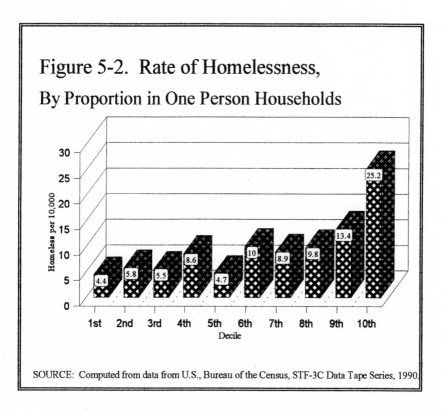

Figure 5-2. Rate of Homelessness, By Proportion in One Person Households

SOURCE: Computed from data from U.S., Bureau of the Census, STF-3C Data Tape Series, 1990.

More significant is the finding that there is also a substantial positive correlation (r = 0.59) between the proportion of adults living alone and the rate of homelessness. Figure 5-2 illustrates the extent of this relationship, showing that while the mean rate is 4.4 in the counties with the lowest rates of one person households, this rate increases by a factor of almost 6, to 25.2 in the counties with the highest levels of one person households. This finding replicates that of Burt, who found this rate to be one of the strongest affecting homeless rates in a substantial sample of major urban centers.[505] While there is evidence that single adults do develop more disabilities, and have greater employment difficulties, than the married,[506] it is unclear to what extent this relationship reflects these problems or the obviously weaker social supports such adults experience, or whether they are simply more numerous in tight housing markets. Certainly, smaller family sizes with more single households will tend to squeeze existing housing resources and drive up housing prices. Single person households are associated with the extent of separated, divorced, and widowed persons, as well as with female-headed households, two other indicators of family fragmentation. Thus, the extent of one person households in a county is simply another way of considering a fragmented family population, the other side of the coin being single parent households. Support for the family fragmentation hypothesis can also be found in the fact that there is a moderate correlation ($r = 0.31$) between the extent of female-headed households and homelessness. But, unexpectedly, there is a negative zero-order correlation of the percentage separated, widowed, or divorced, and homelessness ($r = -0.28$). This is due to the impact of non-family variables which are not controlled for in this analysis, as the direction of this relationship reverses itself only when structural equation modeling techniques are used in a generalized test of the hypotheses developed up until this point (see Figure 5-1, Table 5-4, and following discussion).

When homelessness is regressed collectively on the group of family indicators (table 5-3), over half of the variation in homelessness can be accounted for ($R^2 = 0.54$). The most important predictor in this model is the proportion of households which have one person (0.53), as well as the mean number of persons per household (0.47). Also important in this model are the percentage of persons in families (0.26).

[505] Burt, Over The Edge.

[506] See John Mirowsky and Catherine E. Ross, Social Causes of Psychological Distress (New York: Aldine de Gruyter, 1989), pp. 90-92.

190

**Table 5-3. Rates of Homelessness, Regressed on
Indicators of Family Structure and Fragmentation (N=3,141)**

	Zero-Order r Correlation w/ Homeless Rate	Multiple Regression	
		Partial r	Standardized Coefficient
Percent of Persons in Families	-0.57^c	0.08^c	0.26^c
Median Number Persons per Family	0.58	0.14^c	0.47^c
Median Size of Non-Family Households	-0.18^c	-0.07^c	-0.10^c
Percent of Persons in Family Households Nonrelatives	0.50^c	$0.26^{\text{ C}}$	$0.32^{\text{ b}}$
Percent of All Households One Person	0.59	0.28^c	0.53^c
Percent of Adults 15+ Separated, Widowed, Divorced	-0.28^c	-0.11	-0.20
Teenage Birthrate per 100,000, 1980	0.02^c	0.00	0.00
Percent of Households Female Headed	0.31^c	0.06^c	0.08^c
Median Size of Family Households	0.01^c	-0.09^c	-0.24^c
Percent of Aged in Family Households	-0.35^c	0.03	0.03

NOTES: Values are weighted by relative population sizes. Multiple R^2 = .54; SEE=9.1 ;
     F=369.3 [c]

SOURCE: Computed from 1990 U.S. Census data, STF-3C Data Tape and USA Counties,
     1990

    [a] $\alpha > 0.05$
    [b] $\alpha > 0.01$
    [c] $\alpha > 0.001$

Structural Equation Results. When indicators of family fragmentation are included in the model so far developed, along with economic, disability, and demographic variables, there is clear evidence that such fragmentation aggravates the homeless levels. Collectively, the indicators of fragmentation account for close to a quarter (23.0%) of variations in levels of homelessness (see table 5-4). In addition, two specific indicators--the proportion of persons in families and the percentage of adults who are separated, widowed, or divorced--do so in the direction expected. The more often people live in family units ($\beta = -0.21$) and the less often they are broken by separation, death, or divorce ($\beta = 0.20$), fewer people become homeless.

However, contrary to what was hypothesized and found in the preliminary analyses, the greater the preponderance of female households as well as one person households, fewer people tended to become homeless. The direction of these findings reversed when the economic, demographic, and disability indicators were controlled for, suggesting that the apparent detrimental effect on homelessness actually is camouflaging the effect of unfavorable economic and demographic conditions. With single parent families, it may be their poor economic circumstances whereas with one person households it may be their concentration in urban areas which makes them appear to be contributing to the ranks of the homeless. When such circumstances are controlled for, we find that areas with high rates generate fewer homeless persons than other areas.

Although the family indicators only improved the explanatory power of the overall model by 1.6% over the version (see chapter 5) which did not include the family variables, family conditions accounted for a substantial proportion of the effects from the economic and measurement error variables. The model reduced the explanatory power of the indicators of economic opportunity by a third, from 27.0% to 18.2%, and the measurement error variables, also by close to a third, from 33.2% to 23.7%. In contrast, indicators of individual disabilities became slightly more important when analyzed with controls for family conditions, their explanatory power increasing from 3.1% to 3.8%.

Table 5-4. Effects of Family Fragmentation on Homeless Rates

Variables	Economic, & Disability, Demographic & Systematic Error — Variation Explained	Family Only — β	Family Only — Variation Explained	Family & Prior Variables — β	Family & Prior Variables — Variation Explained
FAMILY FRAGMENTATION	--	--	50.0%	--	23.0%
Proportion of persons in families	--	-0.28^c	13.1%	-0.21^c	8.3%
% Adults separated, widowed, or divorced	--	-0.25^c	5.7%	0.20^c	3.8%
% Female Headed Households	--	0.27^c	6.7%	-0.12^c	2.5%
% One Person Households	--	0.50^c	24.3%	-0.21^c	8.5%
ECONOMIC OPPORTUNITY (See chapter 4)	27.0%	--	--	--	18.2%
DISABILITY INDICATORS (See chapter 3)	3.1%	--	--	--	3.8%
DEMOGRAPHIC VARIABLES (See chapter 2)	29.4%	--	--	--	25.5%
MEASUREMENT ERROR	33.2%	--	--	--	23.7%
TOTAL MODEL (R^2)	92.6%		50.0%		94.2%

NOTES: See appendix 2 for goodness-of-fit statistics. Each model computed using weighted least squares and estimates of measurement error.

a. $\alpha > 0.05$
b. $\alpha > 0.01$
c. $\alpha > 0.001$

This analysis supports the notion that current levels of family dissolution and lack of formation play independent roles in both the genesis and perpetuation of homelessness. It does not permit disentangling the effects of early versus recent family experiences, as well as the relative sparsity of friendship supports, in the lives of the homeless. But it does confirm that the extent that people reside in family units, and deal successfully with the loses inherent in separations, divorces, and premature deaths, plays an integral role in preventing episodes of homelessness, regardless of the concurrent effects of urbanization, individual disabilities, and economic restructuring. Whether secondary or institutional supports can compensate for the scarcity of family and friendship supports, and for the many other difficulties among the homeless, as well as as those who are at risk for homelessness, is a key question to which we will now turn.

Chapter VI

SECONDARY SUPPORTS:
INCOME MAINTENANCE AND HUMAN SERVICES

Several popular theories propose a central role for inadequate and declining benefits in the genesis and perpetuation of contemporary homelessness. Many commentators have, for instance, identified steady declines in income maintenance benefits since the early 1970s, as well as the neglect of the homeless by mainstream service providers, as pivotal. One version of this approach involves deinstitutionalization, or the notion that the dramatic declines in levels of psychiatric hospitalization, as well as the inadequate development of community mental health services, have led to the abandonment of the mentally ill and their having to fend for themselves on the streets. A competing account hypothesizes that an exclusive focus on the short-term emergency needs of the homeless, brought about by the efforts of the homeless advocacy movement, has led to a neglect of the substantial service needs of a highly disabled population of homeless persons, and thus has created a 'revolving door' syndrome in the utilization of many homeless persons of shelters and other services.

The positive possibilities of income maintenance and other services in eradicating homelessness will be explored in the final chapter. This chapter will instead attempt to disentangle the roles that different types of supports have played in the genesis and perpetuation of homelessness. In only a few types of situations can reasonable arguments be made that inadequate services actually *cause* people to become homeless. These situations usually involve a discontinuation of concrete financial or housing benefits, such as a termination of disability benefits, or an abrupt and unsupported discharge from a psychiatric or correctional institution. There are many other situations where inaccessible, inadequate, or untimely services *fail to prevent* people from either becoming homeless or successfully dealing with such a crisis, whether or not this is an official goal of the service. Thus, a far more modest role can be expected for mainstream outpatient mental health and social services in accounting for variations in levels of homelessness.

The complex role of services in both the problems and solutions that homeless persons face suggests that conventional correlational analyses may be inadequate to fully explicate their role. Most analyses assume a unidirectional and linear relationship between service utilization and outcome, typically indicated by the rate of homeless persons. And often, to many researcher's disappointment, this relationship turns out to be a positive one, meaning that the more benefits, or the more people receiving them, the more homeless there are. Such findings are then used to rationalize cutbacks in services, using the argument that services, such as shelters, simply encourage people to remain homeless.

Whether we are concerned with positive or negative associations of services with homeless rates, there are several major interpretations possible for such findings. A positive association could indeed indicate ineffective services. But perhaps more likely, it may indicate that services are being targeted to locations where many homeless persons are found, or that the homeless persons are being attracted to move close to the services. Alternatively, there may be an interactive clustering and interdependency of service providers and targeted recipients. A negative association, on the other hand, may indicate the effectiveness of services in reducing the number of persons in need. It may also provide evidence that the intended beneficiaries are avoiding service providers; or, even that the providers are avoiding mandated beneficiaries. Any combination of these or other processes may be operative in a particular field.

One theory considered in this chapter rests on a developmental understanding of service delivery. In the early stages in the development of a new type of service, such as homeless shelters, one will note several processes: an interactive clustering of recipients and providers, eventually to the point that providers become overwhelmed. Concurrently, providers are passing through their learning curve in mastering needed technologies and ways of identifying suitable clients to apply them to. Thus, services become increasingly effective, causing an initially positive relationship between indicators of services and recipients to become negative, to slope downward from left to right. Secondarily, there may be some creaming of motivated clients, and a mutual avoidance of providers and the most disturbed clients. If such a dynamic of increasing provider proficiency, creaming of capable clients, and eventual avoidance of clients with poor prognoses actually happens, one would expect a curvilinear relationship, one resembling an upward positive trajectory which then turns downward, becoming a negative association. Such a pattern may characterize both the pattern of service delivery with the population of those in need at a given point in time, as well as the aggregate pattern plotted over a long period of time. If the same relationship is assumed to be linear, then the researcher will find only the most prominent of the two parts of the more complex curvilinear relationship, if anything.

After reviewing what we know about the impact of each of several types of services on homeless rates, this chapter will report on several tests of the above hypotheses which use initially bivariate curvilinear regression analyses for a more focused view of particular relationships, and a broader structural analyses of the impact of multiple services on levels of homelessness.

The Impact of Reductions in Income Maintenance Benefits

It is now well-known that since the early 1970s there have been dramatic reductions in most income maintenance programs, especially AFDC and General Assistance. The likely impact of these reductions is characterized by Rossi who concluded that the, "Government creates homelessness and shelter dependency when it *provides too little money even to pay the rent*".[507] Blau amplifies this theme, contending that declining benefits are part of the larger problem of the declining 'social wage', which according to the Elizabethan poor law principle of least eligibility, must always be less than the lowest earned wage so as to maintain work incentive. Since the role of labor has progressively weakened in recent generations, and the minimal wage has stagnated, it is then of little surprise that income maintenance benefits should have been forced down during this same period. And of course, with the decline in the level and availability of such benefits, especially as they are provided to able-bodied 'undeserving' poor individuals, impaired by mental illness, substance abuse, or criminal involvements, increasing numbers of such individuals have become further marginalized.

Although one may expect most homeless individuals to be eligible for one kind of income benefit or another, less than a third (30.2%) receive any. A similar proportion obtain some income from economic activity (29%) or pensions and disability (21%), as well as other sources.[508] This is consistent with most other studies which report between 23% and 55% of the homeless receive at least one kind of income maintenance benefit. Of the homeless recipients of the Health Care for Homeless multi-city project who received welfare, about half received more than one type.[509] But perhaps most revealing is the finding that despite the fact that 34% of the homeless in Boston received welfare benefits, almost all of the homeless (86%) had sought such benefits in the preceding six months.[510] Even among those who receive benefits, the typical monthly check (a few hundred dollars) is so meager that it requires extraordinary skill to budget it so as to meet minimal survival needs with out

---

[507]   Peter Rossi, Down and Out in America, (Chicago: The University of Chicago Press, 1989), p. 108.

[508]   Ibid., p. 113.

[509]   James Wright, Address Unknown: The Homeless in America (New York: Aldine,1989), p. 126.

[510]   Tessler, Richard C. and Deborah L. Dennis, A Synthesis of NIMH-funded Research Concerning Persons who are Homeless and Mentally Ill, (Amherst, MA: Social and Demographic Research Institute, University of Massachusetts, Feb. 9, 1989), p. 37.

substantial supplementation.

The impact of the long-term declines in income maintenance benefits has been the subject of several analyses which have suggested that the rise of homelessness during the 1980s may have been one of the chief consequences of such reductions, though there is little to establish a definitive connection. For instance, one study concluded that,

> ...changes in means-tested programs added 2.9 million to the poverty population, changes in market income added 0.1 million, and changes in the social insurance programs [including social security] added roughly 0.9 million. Population growth and all other changes added an additional 3.0 million. In percentage terms, the largest contributing factor was the reduced effectiveness of means-tested welfare programs (38%), followed by population growth (33%), and changes in demographics (17%), and the reduced effectiveness of social insurance programs.[511]

It has also been found that the worst effects of the restructuring economy of that time involved the transfer of many of the hardships to the working poor. Social Security, Medicare, and unemployment insurance did, however, succeed in insulating many of the working and middle classes from destitution.[512] Nationwide, almost half million people (491,300) lost income maintenance benefits during the early 1980s, however, about two-fifths of these were reinstated upon appeal.[513] If one adds to this the cumulative effects of cuts in nutrition assistance, Medicaid, the elimination of the work-incentive program, as well as substantial cuts in family planning, one sees a government policy which places substantial numbers at risk of extreme poverty and homelessness.[514]

As easy as it is to juxtapose the cutbacks in assistance programs during the

---

[511] Martha Burt, Over The Edge (New York: Russell Sage Foundation, 1992), citing: U.S. House of Representatives, Committee on Ways and Means, Overview of Entitlement Programs: The 1990 Green Book, Washington, D.C.: Government Printing Office, 1990, pp. 1054.

[512] Peter Rossi, Down and Out in America, 1989, p. 108; cites David C. Schwartz, Richard C. Ferlauto, and Daniel N. Hoffman, A New Housing Policy for America, 1988.

[513] General Accounting Office, Homelessness: A Complex Problem and The Federal Response, GAO/HRD -85-40 April 9, 1985, p. 24.

[514] Doug A. Timmer, D. Stanley Eitzen, and Kathryn D. Talley, Paths to Homelessness: Extreme Poverty and the Urban Housing Crisis (Boulder, CO: Westview Press, 1994), p. 30.

early 1980s and the sudden rise of homeless persons, there is little hard data which establishes a definitive link between welfare cutbacks and homelessness. There are certainly many case studies.[515] However, in surveys which ask the homeless about causes of their predicament, only a few mention cutbacks in government programs. For instance, 2.8% of the respondents in the Ohio study cited cutbacks in government benefits as the primary reason for their homelessness.[516] In a correlational study which failed to support the hypothesis that exits from homelessness would be

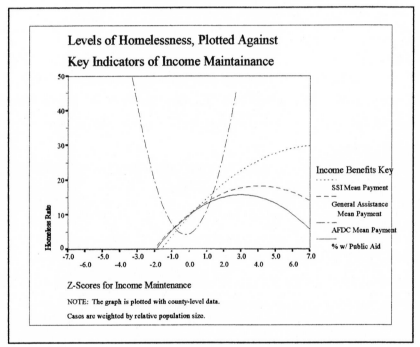

Figure 6-1

---

[515] Gary Morse and Robert Calsyn, "Mental health and other human service needs..." in R Robertson and Greenblatt, (eds.), Homelessness: A National Perspective, Chapter 1, p. 7.

[516] Dee Roth, Chapter 9, "Homelessness in Ohio: A statewide epidemiological study," Momeni, Homelessness in the U.S.: State Surveys, p.154.

positively associated with welfare receipt, it was concluded that the level of the actual benefits was probably too little to have a discernible impact.[517]

The overall correlation of aggregate indicators of public aid receipt with homeless rates does indeed suggest a curvilinear relationship as hypothesized. The lower arc in figure 6-1 illustrates a positive association of public aid benefits with homeless levels in areas with lower benefit levels, whereas the slope reverses and mildly declines above a certain threshold, indicating that the more generous the benefits, the fewer homeless persons are found relative to the population size. This association, however, accounts for only a small part ($R^2 = 0.057$) of the variation in homeless rates, and the negative slopes only occur at extremely high benefit levels. When the homeless rates are plotted against changes in transfer payments between 1980 and 1988, a fairly dramatic negative association indicates that the smaller the increase, the higher the homeless rate (figure 6-2). However, this association also accounts for only a small part ($R^2 = 0.07$) of variations in homeless rates. Other indicators of changes in income maintenance benefits reveal a similar pattern.

Some of the more meaningful analyses of the impact of income maintenance benefits focus on the effectiveness of particular programs, such as the Aid to Families with Dependent Children (AFDC) program. This program, established by the Social Security Act of 1935, is intended to provided cash payments for needy children who have been deprived of parental support or care because of the continuous absence of a parent from the home (85.2% of cases), or because of their incapacitation (3.2%), death (1.9%), or unemployment (7.4%).[518] But because most homeless persons are single, few qualify for AFDC.[519] Eight studies which examined this question resulted in a mean of 5.0% of the homeless who receive AFDC.[520] In respect to homeless

---

[517] Herb Westerfelt, "The ins and outs of homelessness: Exit patterns and predictions," Ph.D. Dissertation, The University of Wisconsin at Madison, 1990, p. 173.

[518] Martha Burt, Over the Edge, 1992, p. 83-84.

[519] James Wright, 1998, p. 121.

[520] Peter Rossi, Down and Out in America, 1989, p. 109.

women with children, one researcher concluded that only about a half were either receiving or applying for AFDC benefits.[521] This is similar to the results of an Urban Institute Study which noted that only 33% of eligible homeless families actually received AFDC.[522] Those who are enrolled in the program have received progressively smaller payments since the early 1970s, after adjusting for inflation. The median monthly AFDC benefit for a family of four declined 44% between 1970 and 1991, from $777 to $435.[523] Even when combined with food stamps, the average of $847 per month in 1972, dropped to $623 by 1991, a 27 percent decline.[524]

A range of problems in the implementation of the program have hurt the ability of many to take advantage of it. Until 1987, the lack of a fixed address was often used as criteria for denial of benefits. In many states, such as Massachusetts, many are reported to avoid the AFDC program for fear of losing their children, since the legal definition of child neglect is quite similar to the condition of homelessness:

> failure by a care taker either deliberately or through negligence or inability to take those actions necessary to provide a child with minimally adequate food, clothing, shelter, medical care, supervision, emotional stability, and growth or other essential care...Provided, however that such inability is not due solely to inadequate economic resources.

---

[521]   James Wright, Address Unknown, 1989, p. 120.

[522]   Martha Burt and Barbara Cohen, America's Homeless: Numbers, Characteristics, and the Programs that Serve Them (Washington, DC: Urban Institute Press, 1989.

[523]   Timmer, Eitzen, and Talley, Paths to Homelessness, 1994.

[524]   Jason DeParle, "Why marginal changes don't rescue the welfare state," New York Times (March 1 1992), E3.

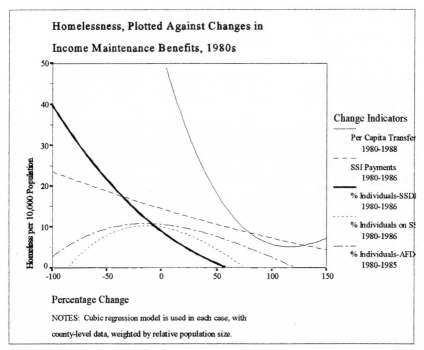

Figure 6-2

Despite attempts to reform the AFDC program in the late 1980s through the addition of job search, training, and work requirements, the extension of the unemployed parent option, and automated child support deductions from paychecksof absent fathers,[525] the program has continued to have only limited value to the homeless. The preliminary correlational analyses conducted as part of this project support this view, confirming a clear but modest impact. Mean payment levels, as illustrated in figure 6-1, suggest that strictly average levels are associated with the smallest homeless rates, although this relationship accounts for a small portion ($R^2 = 0.14$) of the variation in homeless rates. Figure 6-2 shows that when there have been declines in the proportion of the population receiving benefits, homelessness has been relatively low. Likewise, when there have been increases in this proportion,

---

[525] Joel Blau, <u>The Visible Poor</u>, 1992, p.53.

homelessness has also been low. One explanation may be that eligible homeless individuals are avoiding the less generous areas, and finding success in arranging housing in the more generous areas. However, the overall low proportion of homeless on AFDC suggest such any direct causal link could well turn out to be spurious.

Of the various benefit programs, General Assistance is the one of the most relevant to the homeless. These state and local programs, which tend to be the 'line of last defense', have relatively few restrictions,[526] and sometimes include single unattached working age individuals. However, only some states and localities actually offer these programs, and in recent years they have been dramatically reduced, not infrequently eliminated. In the late 1980s, about one in ten (10.0%) of the extremely poor, and one in sixteen (6%) of the general population received GA or similar payments.[527] A review of 20 surveys of homeless individuals revealed that almost a fifth (18.3%) of the homeless were on general assistance,[528] considerably more than the AFDC program. The level of benefits is particularly low, ranging from $80 in Missouri (or 16% of the poverty line) to $328 in Massachusetts in 1987.[529]

The recipients of general assistance are fairly similar to homeless individuals, with a few important exceptions. Homeless individuals are less socially integrated, with fewer receiving supports from family and relatives; they tend to be more disabled, with much higher levels of utilization of medical and psychiatric facilities; and have been unemployed for longer periods of time, 40 months versus 19 for domiciled GA recipients.[530]

Research on the role of general assistance benefits in accounting for variations in homeless populations has produced mixed results. Burt concluded that general

---

[526] James Wright, Address Unknown, 1989, p. 129.

[527] Peter Rossi, Down and Out in America, 1989, p. 111.

[528] Ibid., p.109.

[529] Martha Burt, Over the Edge, 1992.

[530] James Wright, Address Unknown, 1989, p. 85-86.

assistance programs "have only a limited ability to stave off homelessness. One third of all states do not have a GA program of any kind."[531] In her regression analyses of homeless rates in leading urban areas she found a positive correlation, which she interpreted as reflecting the migration of homeless persons to areas of greater benefits, "...Thus, program availability may create a self-fulfilling prophecy."[532] In contrast, Devine found a negative correlation which she interpreted as demonstrating that general assistance is associated with significant reductions in homelessness.[533] These mixed findings may simply reflect the two sides of the previously discussed curvilinear relationship, revealed also in the preliminary analyses done in this project. While changes in mean payment levels had little discernible correlation with homeless rates (see appendix 3, table A3-1), mean payment levels (see figure 6-1) have the expected positive relation at low levels, and negative relationship at higher benefit levels.

Another program which might be expected to minimize the number of homeless persons is the Supplemental Security Income Program (SSI) under the Social Security Act, which supplements state programs for individuals who are aged, blind, or disabled. A related program is Social Security Disability Insurance (SSDI) which provides support to those permanently and totally disabled, who have made the requisite payments into the Social Security system and, therefore, it is not available to persons with marginal work histories. Although SSI and SSDI payments have maintained their value since the early 1970s, as they have been indexed to the Consumer Price Index, the state supplements to the SSI payments have not, and in only 11 states do they exceed $50 per month.[534]

Despite the substantial levels of disability among homeless persons which have

---

[531] Martha Burt, Over the Edge, 1992 , p. 101.

[532] Ibid., p. 101.

[533] Doborah Judith Devine. 1988. "Homelessness and the social safety net." Doctoral dissertation. (Ann Arbor, MI: University Microfilms International, 1989), pp. 293-294.

[534] Martha Burt, Over the Edge, 1992, p.87.

been found by many researchers (see chapter 3), only a small proportion of the homeless receive either SSI or SSDI payments. Estimates of the percentage of the homeless who receive SSI range from 4%[535] to 6.8%.[536] Similarly, SSDI levels were reported to range from 4.2% in Chicago to 14.3% in Baltimore. Much of the surge in homelessness during the early 1980s has been attributed to the Reagan Administration's case monitoring and review procedures. These were reported to have resulted in the termination of SSDI benefits to approximately a half million people from disability roles,[537] a third of which may have been seriously mentally ill.[538] However, these cutbacks came to an end with the enactment of the 1984 Disability Benefits Reform Act. This act outlawed the termination of benefits unless improvements in a person's medical condition permitted employment.[539] It is, therefore, not surprising that there should be substantial increases in the proportion of psychiatrically disabled persons among the homeless during this period.

The results from this project's preliminary correlational analyses present a mixed picture. The level of SSI payments is largely positively correlated with homeless levels, accounting for almost 14% ($R^2 = 0.14$) of the variation in homeless levels (see figure 6-1). However, changes in SSI payments between 1980 and 1986 present an initial positive slope, which is followed by a negative correlation in those counties where there were increases (see figure 6-2). Again, such findings support the initial hypothesis that a given threshold must be reached before benefits, or positive changes in them over time, are associated with reductions in homelessness.

Several other income maintenance programs provide some income or benefits to homeless individuals, but the overall effectiveness of these have been hamstrung

---

[535]   Burt and Cohen, America's Homeless, 1989, p. 43.

[536]   Peter Rossi, Down and Out in America, 1989, p. 109.

[537]   Joel Blau, The Visible Poor, 1992, p. 56.

[538]   U.S. Conference of Mayors, "Homelessness in America's Cities: Ten Case Studies," June 1984).

[539]   Joel Blau, The Visible Poor, 1992, p. 56.

by restrictive eligibility criteria and declines in funding levels. Food stamps are not restricted to individuals on other welfare programs and are potentially open to persons with incomes up to 130% of the poverty level. Despite an allotment of $12.5 billion worth of food stamps in 1989 and some liberalization of rules in the late 1980s and early 1990s, "the net effects on program participation have been relatively small",[540] especially among the homeless. Without facilities for food preparation, food stamps will have limited impact on the ability of homeless individuals to support themselves.

One of the programs which illustrates the shrinking 'social wage' is unemployment insurance which has covered progressively fewer individuals in recent years, and particularly few homeless persons. Between 1971 and 1989 the percentage of unemployed insured has dropped from 52% to 33%.[541] In Rossi's study it was found that only 1.6% of the homeless were receiving unemployment insurance, and a study of men in Baltimore Shelters reported a rate of 0%, compared to 4.1% for a similar housed population of men.[542] It is well known that most of the homeless have either such marginal employment histories that they are not covered, or if they have been covered, they have long since used up their benefits due to problems of long-term unemployment.

One of the few programs that appears to be relatively effective in preventing homelessness is the Social Security Old Age and Survivors Insurance (OASI). These benefits have been indexed to inflation since the early 1970s and have resulted in a reduction of the poverty rate among the aged by almost a half. Perhaps for this reason the rates for homelessness among the aged are the lowest among all the age groups (see chapter 2). The most dramatic cutbacks of benefits in recent years have been

---

[540] Martha Burt, Over the Edge, 1992, pp. 91-93.

[541] Isaac Shapiro and Marion E. Nichols, Unprotected: Unemployment Insurance and Jobless Workers in 1988 (Washington, D.C.: Center on budget and Policy Priorities, 1989), p. 1-2.

[542] Fischer, Pamela J., Sam Shapiro, William R. Breakey, James C. Anthony, and Morton Kramer, "Mental Health and social characteristics of the homeless: A survey of mission users," American Journal of Public Health 76 (5), May 1986, p. 519.

those used by single adults, the unemployed, and the behaviorally disabled, and secondarily, single-parent families--all populations which have been increasingly seen among the homeless. Figures 6-1 and 6-2 illustrate the relative impact of several of these programs. The bottom three arcs illustrate the impact of SSI, General Assistance, and overall public aid levels, and support the hypothesis that at low levels there is a positive association and at higher levels, a negative association, indicating a favorable impact only when payment levels are above a given threshold. Perhaps because the payment levels for these programs are particularly low, this threshold--the uppermost point of the arc--is in each case several standard deviations above the mean for the program's payment level. However, with the more established and comprehensive AFDC program, lower homeless rates are associated with higher payments until those levels approach the mean, after which, above average payment levels are increasingly associated with higher homeless levels, perhaps due to the greater visibility of this program and the possibility that recipients move from areas with lower benefit levels. It needs to be pointed out that AFDC is also included as part of the aggregate public aid variable. Figure 6-2, in contrast, plots the relationship of *changes* in selected participation and benefit levels against the homeless rates. In virtually every case in which there have been increases, these increases have been associated with lower homeless rates, whereas in three of the five programs in which there have been declining benefits there have been relatively high homeless rates. It should be noted that the variation accounted for in the homeless rates by the levels and changes in income benefits account for a relatively small proportion of its variation.

Mental Health Services and Deinstitutionalization[543]

Deinstitutionalization refers primarily to the depopulation of inpatient psychiatric units and hospitals, most commonly state and county mental hospitals.

---

[543] Background parts of the following section have been adapted from: Christopher G. Hudson, Curtis B. Flory III, and Rose Marie Friedrich. Trends in Psychiatric Hospitalization and Long Term Care: A Plan for Ongoing Advocacy and Monitoring. (National Alliance for the Mentally ill, Hospital and Long Term Care Network, Feb. 1, 1995).

This depopulation typically occurs through both the shortening of hospital stays, often resulting in premature discharge, and the diversion of persons from admission to hospitals. Either of these practices may be appropriate or inappropriate in particular cases. Justification for early discharge or diversion from admission partly depends on the availability of treatment, rehabilitation, and support for severely mentally ill persons in the community. Thus, deinstitutionalization has also been equated with the development of community mental health services.

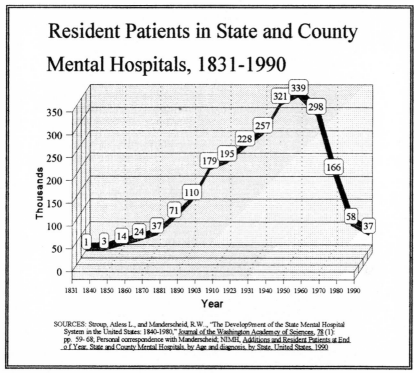

Resident Patients in State and County Mental Hospitals, 1831-1990

SOURCES: Stroup, Atless L., and Manderscheid, R.W.., "The Develop9ment of the State Mental Hospital System in the United States: 1840-1980," Journal of the Washington Academy of Sciences, 78 (1): pp. 59- 68; Personal correspondence with Manderscheid; NIMH, Additions and Resident Patients at End of Year, State and County Mental Hospitals, by Age and diagnosis, by State, United States, 1990

Figure 6-3

The depopulation of state hospitals has been possible because of a related but less well known trend, the 'transinstitutionalization', or transfer of care from public inpatient facilities to a variety of other institutions, whether or not appropriate.[544]

---

[544] See Brown, 1985.

These involve private psychiatric hospitals and units, general hospital medical units, nursing homes, prisons, and more recently, homeless shelters. These direct and indirect transfers, while less visible to the public, have represented a far more significant reality for the severely mentally ill than the literal depopulation of hospitals and transfer of care to the community. The aggregate impact of the declines in state and county hospital censuses, transfers to other institutions, and recent contractions in the private psychiatric sector has been referred to as *dis*-institutionalization, or a general contraction in the availability of psychiatric inpatient facilities.[545]

Hospital care for the severely mentally ill, thus, has become increasingly scarce in the United States (see figure 6-3). Throughout the first half of the Twentieth Century, the number of persons in state mental hospitals mushroomed from 144,653 to a peak of 558,922.[546] Many state hospitals by the 1950s were accurately depicted as snake pits, with hundreds of unclad persons warehoused in single wards, and with over 10,000 patients in some institutions. However, between 1955 and 1990, the average daily census of state and county hospitals, according to NIMH statistics, dropped to 92,059, by 83.5%.[547] In fact, by 1990 state and county hospitals were serving about the same proportion of Americans, 37.3 per 100,000, as they were in 1870--just after the Civil War--when the rate was 36.6.[548]

Figure 6-4 elaborates on these trends, and indicates that the bulk of this decline did not take place until the 1965 to 1975 period. In the first ten years, the depopulation of state and county hospitals was fairly moderate, and in some respects, non-existent. The middle line, "Total Residents", provides the most accurate overall

---

[545] Alice Baum and Donald Burnes, A Nation in Denial: The Truth about Homelessness (Boulder, CO: Westview Press, 1993), p. 165.

[546] A.L. Stroup, and R.W. Manderscheid. (1988, March). The development of the state mental hospital system in the United States: 1840-1980. Journal of the Washington Academy of Sciences, 78, , p. 64.

[547] U.S., National Institute of Mental Health (NIMH), Additions and Resident Patients at End of 1990, p .x.

[548] Stroup and Manderscheid, 1988, p. 60; U.S., National Institute of Mental Health (NIMH), Addition and Resident Patients at End of 1990.

indicator of the trend. This figure is a point in time count, and consists of all hospitalized persons whether admitted the day before or six years before. At the same time that discharges increased, diminishing the length of stay, readmissions and the recidivism rate increased, and this is reflected in the bottom, upward slopping line which depicts total admissions. The pre-existing patient population, as well as all new

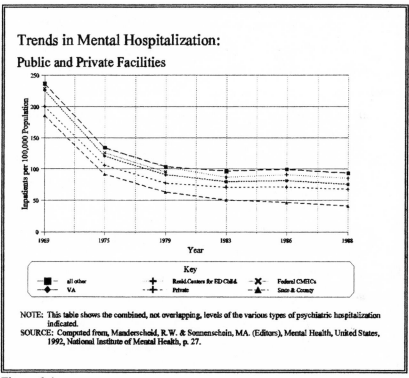

Figure 6-4

admissions, represent the total patient care episodes which continued to increase until the mid-1960s. This trend, however, obscures the declining number of people receiving inpatient services at a given time.

It has been suggested that deinstitutionalization is not something that we should be concerned about, as there has been dramatic growth in the availability of private psychiatric services. Indeed, private hospitalization had become more accessible due to both the enactment of Medicare and Medicaid in the mid-1960s, and the spread of private insurance. Figure 6-5, based on NIMH statistics, provides a more current and in depth look at the overall trends and illustrates the impact that private psychiatric hospitalization has had in only partially moderating the effect of depopulation of the state hospitals since the late 1960s on total hospital censuses. While the bottom line depicts state and county hospitalization levels, the top most line shows the combined hospitalizations levels, of all public and private psychiatric hospitals and units. Between 1969 and 1988, private psychiatric hospitalization (including both general hospital psychiatric units and private mental hospitals) increased their rate of care from 14.4 to 26.3 per 100,000. Despite the 83% growth, this was a dramatic increase in a very small number, not even coming close to filling the gap. In 1969, state and county hospitals provided for 77% of the rate of inpatient care, whereas by 1988 this declined to 44%. Yet, the absolute rate of care provided by all public and private institutions per 100,000 dropped from 237 to 93, or 61%. Kessler and Silbulkin rightly point out that these statistics leave out a skyrocketing increase in mentally ill persons placed on general medical units, arguing that deinstitutionalization is in some respects a myth due to such neglected statistics on private hospital care.[549] Yet, their statistics focus on episodes and thus overstate the extent that the private sector has compensated for the depopulation of state hospitals.

---

[549] C.A. Kiesler and A.E. Sibulkin. Mental Hospitalization: Myths and Facts About a National Crisis. (Beverly Hills: Sage, 1987).

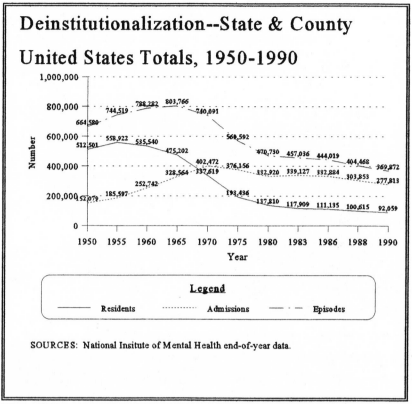

Deinstitutionalization--State & County
United States Totals, 1950-1990

Figure 6-5

The growing scarcity of both public and private hospital care is actually a much more serious problem than many suspect. The most recent statistics from the 1990 Census suggests that NIMH data may be understating the decline in the overall levels of psychiatric hospitalization in the United States. NIMH statistics on the total number of persons psychiatrically hospitalized shows that this population declined only slightly from 230,216 in 1979 to 227,863 in 1988, or a decline of 1.0%.[550] The Census

[550] U.S., Center for Mental Health Services and National Institute of Mental Health (NIMH). Mental Health, United States, 1992. Manderscheid, R.W. and Sonnenschein, M. A., eds. DHHS Pub. No. (SMA) 92-1942. Washington, D.C.: Supt. of Docs., U.S. Govt. Prin t. Off., 1992., 27, table 1.5.

Bureau, however, reports that while there was a total patient population of 245,029 in 1980, this number plummeted to 128,530 by 1990, or a 48.6% decline in 10 years (BOC, STF-1C, 1990). This represents a decline from 11.0 per 100,000 hospitalized in 1980, to 5.2 in 1990, or a drop of over one half (52.7%). This data also epitomizes the extreme degree of variation between states in their ability to provide hospital care. In 1990, hospitalization levels ranged from almost none (0.4) in Alaska, to 11.0 per 10,000 in New York, and 25.0 in the city of Washington, D.C. Only one state, Nebraska, saw an increase (15.5%), whereas every other state and Washington, D.C. experienced declines ranging from 5% to at least 89%. There is no evidence that such declines and variations in levels parallel changes in actual need. Thus, there is much to indicate a need for increased federal standards and financing to guarantee the needed services.

At the same time that hospital services have been disappearing, the development of outpatient and day programs for the severely mentally ill have also failed to compensate for the declines (see figure 6-6). Outpatient mental health services most typically consist of the provision of a range of intermittent, typically weekly or less frequent services, such as psychotherapy or medication monitoring, geared mostly to those with non-severe forms of mental illness, as well as those with adjustment reactions. The upper line on figure 6-6 shows that although the rate of persons receiving these services increased by 106% from 1969 to 1979, a period of much deinstitutionalization, in the next ten years the level only increased by 2.7%.

Many other community mental health services involve partial care or day programs, which consist of day hospital, day treatment, day care, social club, or rehabilitation programs in which patients or members participate in what is often a daily schedule of therapeutic, rehabilitative, occupational, or recreational activities. Figure 6-6 indicates that during the 1975-1988 period, the availability of day

214

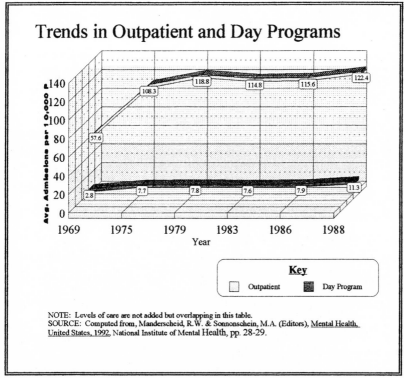

Figure 6-6

programs increased by 44.9%. This was, however, a large increase in a very small number. The disparity between the hospitalization and day program levels is epitomized by the fact that there are only 9.3% as many day program slots as inpatient beds. This figure understates the disparity since consumers typically use day programs for considerably longer periods than they do hospitals.

It is clear, therefore, that deinstitutionalization has continued full-throttle ahead. Declines in hospital censuses have been the most dramatic indicator, as overall levels have dropped by over a half during the 1980s. At the same time, there have only been slight increases in outpatient services and moderate increases in the pre-existing low levels of day program services. Residential services have reportedly increased, but are still at very inadequate levels. Similarly, funding for community

215

services has risen, but not nearly at the rate which would be needed or expected to compensate for the precipitous drops in the hospitalized population of persons with severe mental illness.

Deinstitutionalization clearly was not a unitary policy or planned development, but a result of a wide range of *de facto* forces, actions, and reactions of politicians, human service professionals, and the public.[551] Two of the first of these in the 1950s involved the introduction of psychotropic medications and the escalating costs of maintaining a state hospital system built in the nineteenth century. Psychotropic medications provided a means for discharging patients, and relieving the mounting financial pressure on the states. The medications used in the initial years, such as Thorazine, functioned mainly to control the more overt positive symptoms of psychosis, such as hallucinations or delusions. Because they did little to alter the more subtle yet equally debilitating symptoms of schizophrenia, such as social withdrawal or loose associations, they had limited utility in maintaining individuals in difficult community settings. However, recent developments in psychopharmacology, such as Clozaril, show much promise in altering some of the basic symptoms of schizophrenia and for successfully maintaining new subgroups of persons with severe mental illness outside of institutions.

Beginning also in the 1950s, new treatment philosophies were being introduced which emphasized short-term and community based treatments. Journalists such as Albert Deutsch and sociologists such as Erving Goffman and Thomas Scherz provided an additional rationale and sense of urgency for rescuing mental patients from the trappings of institutionalism and the snake-pit conditions in state hospitals, and discharging them into idealized communities.[552] The initial theorists rarely considered the range of community supports which were necessary to maintain severely mentally ill persons outside the hospital and some went so far as to

---

[551] See Alice Johnson, Out of Bedlam (Basic Books, 1990).

[552] Benson. (1980). "Labeling theory and community care of the mentally ill in California: The relationship of social theory and ideology to public policy", Human Organization, 39, 2.

216

acknowledge their earlier excesses.[553]

In the early 1960s, the introduction of the federal community mental health program and its associated rhetoric provided further rationale for the discharge of state mental patients. Many proponents of this program emphasized the preventative aspects of community mental health, effectively shifting the focus of this innovative program from the initial goal of caring for the severely mentally ill to addressing a wide range of mental needs of the 'worried well'. During these initial years, only a small fraction of the clients of community mental health centers were discharged state hospital patients. The interest of many professionals in working with motivated clients who keep office based appointments was no doubt, and continues to be, a major barrier to services for the seriously mentally ill. Also, complicating the discontinuity between the state hospitals and the community mental health system was the fact that the former is state funded, whereas the latter was federally funded and managed, and rarely did policy makers in these two systems talk with one another during this period.

The development of community mental health centers by the early 1970s resulted in coverage of less than half the nation, as many of the social programs of the 1960s saw major cuts in funding due to the impact of the Vietnam war and the shift of power to the Nixon administration. Yet, it was in the mid-1960s and early 1970s that the depopulation of state and county hospitals went full steam ahead (see figure 6-4).

In 1964 and 1965 the Medicaid and Medicare programs were introduced. These quickly led to the mushrooming of the nursing home industry over the next ten years, much of this due to the transfer of elderly psychiatric patients from state hospitals to nursing homes. By transferring these patients, state governments found a convenient means to transfer a significant part of the costs of care to the federal

---

[553] Andrew Scull, Decarceration: Community Treatment and the Deviant--A Radical View, Second Edition (New Brunswick, NJ: Rutgers University Press, 1984), p. 176.

217

government.[554] In 1972, the introduction of supplemental security income (SSI) also made it easier for severely mentally ill persons to be supported in the community by federal funds, and concurrent with this was the development of a board and care rooming house industry directed at mentally ill persons.

But perhaps what drove the stampede to depopulate state hospitals more than the financial incentives were a variety of new legal precedents in the late 1960s and early 1970s.[555] These took place in response to the many expose's of abuses of antiquated commitment laws originally promulgated in the nineteenth century. These laws usually gave sweeping powers to physicians and families to commit deviant individuals. The advocacy of civil libertarians led in the 1960s to a restriction of the criteria for psychiatric commitment in most states and to the requirement for imminent dangerousness. In addition, many procedural requirements were introduced which protected the rights of mental patients, but complicated the process of psychiatric commitment when needed.

Other important legal developments involved the requirement for treatment in the least restrictive environment necessary to achieve the purposes of the commitment. In the popular and professional press this has usually been abbreviated to the requirement for the least restrictive environment, with its proponents often forgetting to consider whether not a particular setting may be justifiable on clinical or humanitarian grounds. In 1972, the courts in Alabama mandated that civilly committed patients had a right to treatment, and so a financially strapped state government proceeded to discharge these patients rather than fulfill costly court

---

[554] See William Gronfein (1985). "Incentives and intentions in mental health policy: A comparison o f the Medcaid and community mental health programs". Journal of Health and Social Behavior, 26, 192-206; S.M.Rose (1979). "Deciphering deinstitutionalization: Complexities in policy and program analysis". The Milbank Quarterly, 57, 429-60.

[555] See Mary L. Durham and G. L. Pierce. (1986). "Legal intervention in civil commitment: The impact of broadened commitment criteria". The Annals, 484, 42-55.

mandates for inpatient treatment.[556]

The dangerousness criteria, the right to refuse treatment, the right to treatment, and the least restrictive environment, as well as the new due process and other procedural requirements, dramatically reduced state hospital populations. These decisions made it difficult to admit a patient, and if admitted, to keep the patient long enough for a favorable clinical outcome. Furthermore, the commitment criteria influenced the voluntary admission criteria, especially in state hospitals. The criteria for voluntary admission tends to reflect that for involuntary commitment. In many states, if a patient wants to voluntarily sign into a hospital, they must in principle meet the criteria for involuntary commitment.

Statistics on the rates of hospitalization in states with various levels of restrictiveness in their commitment laws and procedures dramatically reveal the impact of such legal developments. Table 6-1 suggests that these laws had their greatest impact on state and county hospitals. When overall indices are computed using a range of the above mentioned features, and mean rates of hospitalization are computed for the various subgroups of states, it becomes apparent that the more restrictive the psychiatric commitment laws--the more that they limit and complicate the possibility of involuntary hospitalization--the lower is the rate of hospitalization in state hospitals, and this is documented in the right column of table 6-1. The states with the most non-restrictive laws had state and county hospitalization rates three times that of the state with the most restrictive laws, with all others falling in between in respect to both the restrictiveness of their laws and their propensity to hospitalize mentally ill individuals.

---

[556]   Wyatt v. Stickney, 325 F. Supp. 781 (1971).

Table 6-1. Impact of Level of Restrictiveness of State Commitment Laws on Deinstitutionalization and Levels of Mental Hospitalization

Index of Restrictiveness of Commitment Laws	# States Hospitals	Deinstitution- alization, Rate, '55-'88 % Decline, '88	Total MH Hospital Rate, '88	State & County Rate
Non-restrictive	3	78	112	66
Mildly restrictive	5	79	102	46
Average level	15	79	116	48
Above average	10	82	98	37
Very restrictive	12	78	112	41
Extremely restrictive	1	94	108	22

SOURCE: Computed from, Dooley, J.A., Parry, J.W. (Editors), Involuntary Civil Commitment: A Manual for Lawyers and Judges, Commission on the Mentally Disabled, American Bar Association, 1988; pp. 90-121.

Thus, while the initial forces behind the deinstitutionalization movement--the introduction of psychotropic medications, the high costs of maintaining state hospitals, and the community mental health movement--each had an important role in initiating and even fueling the depopulation of state hospitals, they clearly were not the primary cause for the precipitous drops seen in the late 1960s and 1970s. The financial incentives for states to transfer the costs of care to the federal government and new legal precedents were perhaps the two most critical forces which caused a controlled trickle of patients from the hospitals to become a torrential dumping of long-term mentally ill persons into unprepared communities.

The most recent round of deinstitutionalization, that which began around the mid-1980s, has taken place both in the public and private mental health sectors. In the private sector, the driving force has been the spread of managed care and capitated payment plans which have served to dramatically limit the length of state in psychiatric hospitals and units, thus reducing the overall censuses. In addition, state mental health authorities have been aggressive in implementing group home and supported housing programs, as well as transferring psychiatric care to the private sector so as to circumvent HCFA requirements that Medicaid be used for mental health inpatient care only in institutions not classified as "Institutes of Mental Disorder" (IMDs) as is the case with state mental hospitals. By doing so, the states have continued to find ways of shifting costs to the federal government.

The Impact of Deinstitutionalization on the Homeless

During the early and middle 1980s, deinstitutionalization was one of the most often cited causes of homelessness. However, during the last five to ten years such an explanation has fallen into disfavor, in part due to the homeless advocacy movement which has emphasized the short-term emergency and concrete housing needs of the homeless, as well as the lack of a sufficient body of research to link the two trends. The research reported in this book supports the impression of many that declines in mental hospitalization have played a very small role, one which is barely detectable in a nation-wide analysis such as this. Before reporting on its specific findings in this regard, other pertinent research will be reviewed.

The record of previous mental health service utilization among the homeless is an important source of information on this issue. In a Boston sample of homeless persons, it was found that a quarter (25%) had previously sought mental health services,[557] or most all of the approximately 30% to 35% of the homeless which have a problem with mental illness. In contrast, fewer than half (68 out of 151, or 45%) of a sample of homeless in Philadelphia reported previous professional mental health care.[558]

It is not unexpected that the highest levels of prior care involve mental hospitalization. The reader may recall from chapter 3 that close to two-thirds of these (or 20% of total homeless) have been psychiatrically hospitalized one or more times

---

[557] Tessler and Dennis, A Synthesis of NIMH-Funded Research (1989), p. 37.

[558] General Accounting Office, Homelessness: A Complex Problem and The Federal Response (1985).

(see table 3-3). Among homeless mothers, the rate in one study was a modest 4.0%, but this was five times the level as a group of similar housed mothers.[559] Most studies report that only a small percentage of the homeless have received any outpatient mental health care, for instance, 8% in Los Angeles, and 12.2% in Ohio.[560] Even smaller numbers are reported to have ever used psychiatric medications. A study of homeless mothers found that the subjects were less than half (.4) times as likely to have used psychiatric medications as a similar group of housed mothers (3.1% versus 7.3%).[561] Thus, while most of the mentally ill homeless have been hospitalized at least once, very few of these individuals ever received traditional outpatient services. While evidence is not available on prior utilization of psychosocial rehabilitation and extended care, i.e. group homes, among the homeless, it is unlikely that a large proportion of the mentally ill homeless ever received such frequently recommended services.

The low rates of program participation among the homeless mentally ill would be particularly alarming if these programs had demonstrated consistent effectiveness in reintegrating the homeless into mainstream community life. But unfortunately, the record of the effectiveness of these programs is decidedly mixed. The few programs which have been evaluated tend to be demonstration programs, often funded by the National Institute of Mental Health. Case management is one type of program which has received some empirical support. For instance, Rife, et al, concluded from an evaluation of a case management program that after six months of the intervention, "clients perceived significant improvement in their global well-being, living situation,

[559] Weitzman, Beth C., James R. Knickman, and Marybeth Shinn, "Predictors of shelter use among low-income families: Psychiatric history, substance abuse, and victimization," American Journal of Public Health 82 (11), p. 1549.

[560] R.K. Farr, P. Koegel, and A. Burnham, A Study of Homelessness and Mental Illness in the Skid Row Area of Los Angeles, (Los Angeles: Los Angeles County Department of Mental Health, 1986); Toomey and First, Homelessness in Ohio: A Study of People in Need, Franklin County Report, p. 23.

[561] Weitzman, Knickman, and Shinn, "Predictors of shelter use...", p. 1549.

use of leisure time, finances, and physical health."[562] In another project, the combination of intensive case management with a drop-in and outpatient program was compared with two more traditional interventions and was partially supported.[563] So far, only a handful of evaluation studies have been completed, and these "have suggested that participation in specialized clinical programs can facilitate movement of the chronically mentally ill out of homelessness."[564] Analyses of program failures have generally shown that individuals, whose mental illness is associated with substance abuse or criminal involvements--a sizeable proportion of the mentally ill homeless--have been most likely to fail to benefit.

Another body of research has attempted to establish the extent of need for mental health services among the homeless, either by asking the homeless themselves about their preferences, or by surveying service providers. In one study, about a quarter (24%) of the homeless consider mental health care to be an unmet need, in contrast to almost two-thirds (64%) of the service providers.[565] When the homeless report service needs, they de-emphasize mental health, in favor of the more pressing concrete needs involving housing, income, and employment.[566] Yet, while many acknowledge a need for mental health services, a 60 day follow-up of homeless persons who were given mental health referrals revealed, found that less than a quarter (23%) successfully follow through. While over half (52%) accepted the

---

[562] J.C. Rife, R.J. First, R.W. Greenlee, L.D. Miller, M.A. Feichter. (Feb. 1991). "Case management with homeless mentally ill people". Health and Social Work. 16(1), p. 58-67.

[563] Gary A. Morse, Robert I. Calsyn, Gary Alvin, Betty Tempelhoff, and Ruth Smith, "Experimental comparison of the effects of three treatment programs for homeless mentally ill people," Hospital and Community Psychiatry, Oct. 1992, 43 (10), p. 10008.

[564] Catherine Leda and Robert Rosenheck. (Sept. 1992). "Mental health status and community adjustment after treatment on in a residential treatment program for homeless veterans," American Journal of Psychiatry 149(9), p. 1219.

[565] Tessler and Dennis, A Synthesis of NIMH-Funded Research (1989), p. 37.

[566] L. Gelberg and L.S. Linn. (May 1988). "Social and physical health of homeless adults previously treated for mental health problems". Hospital-and-Community-Psychiatry 39(5), pp. 510-16.; F.L.J. Ball and B.E. Havassy. (1984). "A survey of the problems and needs of homeless consumers of acute psychiatric services". Hospital and Community Psychiatry. 35(9), pp. 917-21.; Tessler and Dennis, A Synthesis of NIMH-funded Research. p. 37.

referral, but never received services, a quarter (24%) refused the referral outright.[567] Although professionals are more enthusiastic about mental health care than are the homeless, only a small proportion recommend inpatient psychiatric care for those homeless persons they work with, typically between 5%[568] to 7%[569] of them. More frequently professionals recommend outpatient care (21%), day treatment (10%), medication (7%), and case management (7%).[570] Other commentators have, in contrast, identified needs for more group homes[571] and vocational rehabilitation programs.[572]

Several researchers have attempted to identify the major barriers which prevent more of the mentally ill homeless from utilizing services. Unfortunately, none has adequately addressed the divergent views of professionals and the homeless about the need for 'soft' counseling services versus 'hard' concrete services involving housing or income. The U.S. Conference of Mayors, however, did identify several barriers to enhanced participation in income maintenance programs: eligibility requirements, application processes which were too long and complicated, lack of identification or supporting documentation, or lack of an address.[573] Barriers to community services, on the other hand, have been variously defined as including the

---

[567] G.N. Morse, C. Shields, C. Hanneke, R. Calsyn, G. Burger, and B. Nelson. Homeless People in St. Louis: A Mental Health Program Evaluation, Field Study, and Follow-Up Investigation. (Jefferson City: Missouri Dept. of Mental Health, 1985).

[568] Ohio Department of Mental Health, Homelessness in Ohio: A Study of People in Need (Columbus, Ohio, 1985).

[569] V. Mulkern, V.J. Bradley, R. Spence, et al., Homeless Needs Assessment Study: Findings and Recommendations for the Massachusetts Department of Mental Health (Boston: Human Research Insitute, 1985).

[570] Ibid.

[571] Gary Morse and Robert Calsyn, "Mental health and other human service needs..." in R Robertson and Greenblatt, (eds.), Homelessness: A National Perspective, Chapter 1.

[572] H.R. Lamb. (1984). "Deinstititionalization and the homeless mentally ill", Hospital & Community Psychiatry 35, pp. 899-907.

[573] The United State Conference of Mayors, Mentally Ill and Homeless: A 22-City Survey November 1991, pp. 44-45.

discharge of patients to unsupportive environments,[574] service fragmentation,[575] transience, burden to the community, inappropriate services, negative public attitudes, violence associated with street life, and in general, the chronicity of the condition of many of the homeless mentally ill.[576]

If deinstitutionalization is very broadly defined as encompassing the increasing inaccessibility to mental health services, then perhaps upwards of half of the homelessness of the 25% to 35% of the homeless who are mentally ill might be accounted for. Even with complete participation in community mental health programs, there is little evidence that any more than half would be successfully placed in the community. If deinstitutionalization is more narrowly defined to consist of the unavailability of psychiatric hospitalization, then a considerably smaller proportion of the homeless, perhaps 5% to 10%, would be adequately cared for. Yet, with adequate mental health services, the above 5% to 15% of the homeless represent tens of thousands of people who otherwise could expect to be reintegrated into community life.

Those who minimize the role of deinstitutionalization rightfully point out that much of what is recognized as deinsitutionalization occurred in the 1965-1975 period which preceded the skyrocketing of homelessness in the 1980s.[577] But they are wrong in entirely dismissing the connection, as it is known that overall level of psychiatric hospitalization fell by one half during the 1980s (see previous section).

A number of researchers have asked homeless persons about their reasons for being homeless. Typically, between 2%[578] and 7.8%[579] report that a psychiatric

---

[574] Ibid., p. 63.

[575] Morse and Calsyn, "Mental health and other human service needs...", Chapter 1, p. 9.

[576] S.P. Segal and J. Baumohl. (1980). "Engaging the disengaged: Proposals on madness and vagrancy". Social-Work. 25(5), pp. 358-65.

[577] Joel Blau, The Visible Poor, 1992, p. 85.

[578] James Wright, Address Unknown, 1989, p. 108.

[579] Thomas Hirschl and Jamshid A. Momeni, Chapter 8, "Homelessness in New York: A Demographic and Socioeconomic Analysis," in Jamshid A. Momeni (ed.). Homelessness in the

discharge played a pivotal role. For instance, in New York state the overall average was 4.5%, with considerably higher rates found in the major urban areas, and with single individuals.[580] Professional observers, likewise, often cite stringent admission criteria,[581] poor discharge policies,[582] shorter stays,[583] as well as inadequate community services as causes of homelessness,[584] often implying more powerful roles for these factors than the homeless themselves report.

Little data is available on how recent the discharges of those homeless individuals who had been hospitalized have been. In one study, 22% of the sample had been institutionalized, however, slightly fewer than half had been released five or more years before.[585] In contrast, 10% of shelter residents in New Jersey reported that they or a family member had been psychiatrically hospitalized within the past year,[586] or about half the overall 20% reporting any hospitalization (see table 3-3, Chapter 3). Of particular relevance is the propspective follow-up study discharges conducted by Belcher of a sample of 133 patients released from an urban state mental hospital. Belcher found that over a third (35.3%) were homeless for most of the first three months after discharge, with two-thirds of these becoming homeless in the first month after discharge. Of these, 21 or 15.8% were actually discharged homeless. He found that those who became homeless could be subdivided into two groups, one characterized by aimless wandering and decompensation, and the other by their vague

---

U.S.: State Surveys; p. 139.

[580] Ibid., p. 139.

[581] Ellen Baxter and Kim Hopper. Private Lives/Public (New York: Community Service Society, 1981).

[582] Morse and Calsyn, "Mental health and other human services needs...", Chapter 1.

[583] Ellen Bassuk. (1984). "The homelessness problem," Scientific American 251 (1), pp. 40-45.

[584] U.S. Conference of Mayors, Mentally Ill and Homeless, 1991, p. 17.

[585] Joel Blau, The Visible Poor, 1992, p. 86.

[586] Gerald Geoglio, Chapter 7, "Homelessness in New Jersey," in Jamshid Momeni. (ed.). Homelessness in the U.S.: State Surveys; p. 123.

and tenuous plans for the future.[587] The greater incidence of homelessness upon discharge can in part be attributed to increases in homelessness at admission, as one study of psychiatric admissions in a state facility in Chicago identified a consistent trend in this direction. Many of these patients left the hospital against medical advice, before plans could be worked out, and relatively few could be referred to long-term care facilities. The researchers concluded that "there appears to be a new groups of homeless mentally ill, characterized as 'urban nomads', who flee from structured settings.[588]

Almost all of the correlational studies have failed to identify any substantial effects of indicators of deinstitutionalization, or mental health services availability, on homeless rates, with one exception. Elliott and Krivo used data from the 1980 Census as well as the U.S. 1984 HUD study of homelessness in urban areas and regressed the estimated homeless shelter rates on mental health expenditures, residential mental health services, low-rent housing, economic indicators, as well as racial composition. They reported that their findings demonstrated that both the availability of residential services for the mentally ill and the economic conditions of areas have marked effects on homeless rates. "The strong effect of expenditures for residential mental health care supports the argument that community residential services for the mentally ill plays a key role in decreasing homelessness. However, overall spending does not have a significant impact.[589]

Preliminary correlational analyses by this author provide some support for the idea that deinstitutionalization has partly contributed to contemporary homelessness. Both the total level of hospitalization as well as declines in hospitalization between

---

[587] John Belcher and Beverly G. Toomey, "Relationship Between the Deinstitutionalization Model, Psychiatric Disability, and Homelessness," Health & Social Work 13 (2), Spring 1988.

[588] L. Appleby and P.N. Desai. (July 1985). "Documenting the relationship between homelessness and psychiatric hospitalization". Hospital and Community Psychiatry. 36(7), pp. 732-37.

[589] Marta Elliott and Lauren J. Krivo, "Structural determinants of homelessness in the United States," Social Problems 38 (1), Feb. 2991, p. 124.

1955 and 1990 are related in a curivilinear manner to homelessness: the greater the deinstitutionalization, the fewer homeless persons, but this is true at only below average levels (see figure 6-7). When deinstitutionalization, as measured by these two criteria are above average, they contribute *positively* to homelessness. While such a finding provides a basis for integrating the divergent opinions in the field by the hypothesis that when deinstitutionalization has been precipitous, or above average, it has resulted in dumping; otherwise, it has a beneficial effect in respect to the level of homelessness. In contrast, a community service, such as the CMHCs, have the opposite effect: only above a given thresh hold of coverage do they begin to reduce homelessness. These effects, however, only account for a small degree of variation in homeless levels, even when computed on a curvilinear basis. For instance, the strongest such association is between total inpatients in 1988 and the homeless rates and this account for only 20% ($R^2 = 0.20$) of the variation in the homeless rates

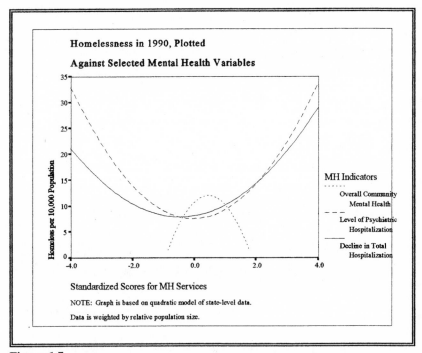

Figure 6-7

before any controls are introduced (see appendix 3, table A3-2).

Substance Abuse Programs

At the same time that community mental health systems were being flooded by discharges from state mental hospitals, in the 1965 to 1975 period, they were also inundated by large increases in substance abusers. In 1970, Congress decriminalized alcohol abuse through the enactment of the Comprehensive Alcohol Abuse and Alcoholism Act, also referred to as the Hughes Act, and in 1971, the Uniform Alcoholism and Intoxication Treatment Act was also passed. This legislation mandated the development of publically-funded detoxification centers and generally shifted alcoholics out of the criminal justice system.[590] The resurgence of homelessness among substance abusers has been attributed not only to the increases in the number of young adults as a result of the baby boom, but also to the inability of the service system to accommodate the decriminalization of persons suffering from alcoholism. In Michigan it was reported that almost a twelfth (8.6%) of substance abusers are homeless,[591] whereas it has been estimated that at least a quarter of the homeless (26.6%) suffer from alcoholism.[592] Despite the substantial prevalence of substance abuse among the homeless, one survey found that only a third (32%) of homeless shelters provided any substance abuse services, and those that did offered mostly AA meetings or referrals to services elsewhere.[593]

Similar to community mental health programs, substance abuse programs have a marginal record with homeless substance abusers. A large multi-site evaluation of programs in Michigan identified two subtypes of clients: those with mainly severe economic and employment problems, and those with multiple disabilities.

---

[590] Baum and Burnes, A Nation in Denial, 1993.

[591] Brian E. Mavis, Keith Humphreys, and Bertram E. Stoffelmayr, (Dec. 1993). "Treatment needs and outcomes of two subtypes of homeless persons who abuse substances," Hospital & Community Psychiatry, 44(12), p. 1187.

[592] Roth, Chapter 9, p. 160.

[593] Baum and Burnes, A Nation in Denial, 1993.

Unexpectedly, the evaluation found that "the reduction in problem severity from intake to follow-up was much greater for the multi-problem homeless than for the economic homeless clients, although the multi-problem clients at follow-up remained comparable to the problem levels of the housed clients at intake."[594] The researchers concluded that, "It is beyond the resources of most treatment agencies to completely rehabilitate multi-problem homeless substance abusers."[595] In an evaluation of a program for the homeless mentally ill, Caton, Wyatt, et al. observed that "It now appears that failure can be attributed to the ravages of substance abuse, high expressed emotion in the living environment, or an interaction of these two factors."[596]

Despite the known ravages of substance abuse among homeless persons, there is only slight evidence that the level of substance abuse programming has had a discernible impact. When county rates of homelessness are regressed against the rate of drug and alcohol program admissions for 1990, only 6% ($R^2 = 0.06$) the variation in homeless levels can be accounted for, without controls for other conditions (see appendix 3, table A3-3). This is a non-linear relationship which roughly assumes the parabolic shape discussed earlier: at low and average levels of programming, there are increasing levels of homelessness associated with increasing levels of services. Whereas at very high levels of admissions, a negative relation is found, suggesting that above a given threshold, greater levels of programming for substance abusers is associated with step declines in the level of homelessness (see middle line, figure 6-8).

[594] Mavis, Humphreys, and Stoffelmayr, 1993, pp. 1186-87.

[595] Ibid., p. 1187.

[596] Carol L.M. Caton, Richard J. Wyatt, Alan Felix, Feffrey Grunberg, and Boanerges Dominguez, (Nov. 1993). "Follow-up of chronically homeless mentally ill men," American Journal of Psychiatry 150, 11, p. 1641.

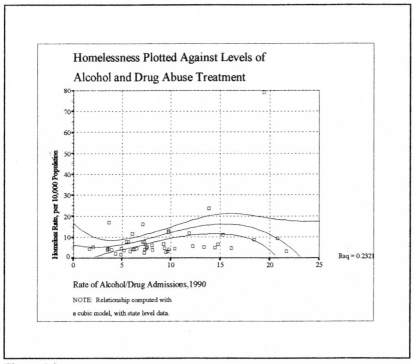

Figure 6-8

Other Mainstream Human Services

Other mainstream human services needed by homeless individuals include those provided through the medical, child welfare, educational, and criminal justice systems. In each case, substantial evidence can be found for service needs pertinent to each of these systems, and considerable anecdotal evidence about the difficulty of many homeless individuals in being effectively supported by these systems. Jahiel points out that,

> homeless people still face considerable barriers to the delivery of adequate health care. They have greater needs for health care than do the general or even the poverty populations. In addition, their needs are more complex because of the interaction among disease processes caused by homelessness, lack of financial resources, and the protective functions of a home, and diminished formal and

informal support networks.[597]

Of the various indicators of medical coverage, those which are most closely associated with rates of homelessness is the level of Medicaid coverage ($R^2 = 0.15$) and the availability of physicians ($R^2 = 0.32$). In Chapter 3, on The Disability Hypothesis, data was presented which indicated that the levels of educational attainment are strongly related with the prevalence of homelessness. It would, therefore, be expected that the adequacy of a county's educational systems would be associated with lower levels of homelessness. Two indicators of such adequacy, school spending per pupil and student-teacher ratios, were correlated with homeless rates, with both accounting for a modest but significant level of variation--9% ($R^2 = 0.09$) in the case of school spending, and 7% ($R^2 = 0.07$) in respect to the student-teacher ratio (see appendix 3, table A3-3). As a non-linear relationship, this was negatively correlated with homelessness at lower than average levels, and at very high levels; at intermediate levels, the more favorable the ratio, the higher the homeless rate.

The impact of mainstream human services on homeless rates, is thus fairly modest. Whether considered singularly or collectively, indicators of service availability or generosity typically account for a small to negligible proportion of the variation in homeless rates. These correlations are only slightly more favorable when the relationships are conceptualized as non-linear. However, the mixture of positive and negative effects becomes more interpretable, reflecting most typically positive correlations or detrimental impacts at low levels of service provisions, and negative or beneficial impacts when the level of service provision surpasses a given threshold, sometimes at an average level, but often at a considerable higher than average level. Evidence is especially scarce that declining or inadequate levels of service provision represents a significant cause of homelessness, except in the case of individuals being

---

[597] Rene' I. Jahiel, Chapter 11, "Health and Health Care of Homeless People," in Robertson and Greenblatt, (eds.). Homelessness: A National Perspective. (New York: Plenum Press), p. 133., p. 156).

discharged from institutions or discontinued from concrete income supports, in which case a definite but relatively small proportion of homelessness can be accounted for.

Theories Concerning the Effects of Services

There have been several theories advanced in the literature on homelessness about the role of services in the origins and perpetuation of homelessness. The most common involves either service inaccessibility and unavailability, as well as declines in such supports. Morse summarizes this theory as one involving, "Difficulty in gaining access to services also contributes to homelessness. Applying for disability benefits and seeking financial assistance are lengthy and complicated processes characterized by bureaucratic demand for details and documentation."[598] Studies have often shown that homeless persons often do not keep appointments and have difficulty in negotiating often arcane and geographically dispersed social services without considerable assistance.[599] Most typically, such problems are simplistically attributed to inadequate financial and political support for social services, without further consideration. Such analyses ignore not only the many structural conditions, involving demographic and economic trends, the social functions that the homeless have come to serve, and also limitations of current service technologies.

A variation of the theory of service inaccessibility, is that of service ineffectiveness. We know that there are many service models, while not panaceas, are capable of providing considerable help to many of the homeless, and these include intensive case management, transitional supported housing, and psychosocial and vocational rehabilitation. Yet, when the impact of model programs are counted along with all those of their cheap imitations which use similar rhetoric as the model programs, i.e. "intensive case management", but only provide a small fraction of the staffing and training levels, the moderately beneficial impacts of the model programs become so watered down so as to account for the almost negligible overall impacts

---

[598] Morse and Calsyn, "Mental health and other service needs...", Chapter 1, p.11.

[599] Baum and Burnes, A Nation in Denial, 1993, p. 75.

detected in this and similar studies. In one study it was found that a program for runaway youths had failed to place some youngsters successfully even after 35 attempts. Probably the more commonly cited reason for such ineffectiveness is the lack of any formal social service training on the part of staff in the agencies which service the most seriously disturbed, but this no doubt is only a small part of the picture.[600]

Another explanation for the ineffectiveness of many programs focuses on service philosophy and misplaced priorities. McKnight argues that mainstream human services often perpetuate homelessness because they: (i) emphasize deficiencies; (ii) divert funds from needed concrete supports; (iii) place social service providers in roles of authority, disempowering local citizens and consumers; and, (iv) in general, create an "environment of deficiency, resulting in dependency and negating the potential for positive effects that singular programs may offer.[601] In contrast, others suggest that too many concrete services are provided at the expense of rehabilitative services. These divergent positions suggest a failure by many programs to sufficiently individualize the services and supports which are provided.

In contrast to conservative theories which focus on individual disabilities and responsibility or liberal theories involving the unfulfilled promise of idealized services, there are those who view services as agents of "structural" economic and class interests. Piven and Cloward, in their classic work *Regulating the Poor*, argue that many of the human services are essentially devices of social control to maintain a class of indigent persons, as a pool of cheap labor ready for times of economic expansion, and otherwise, as a means for controlling their potential for disruption in times of economic scarcity.[602] Gregg Barak has specifically applied this theory to an

---

[600] Jan L. Hagen and E. Hutchison. (Oct. 1988). "Who's serving the homeless?" Social-Casework. 69(8), pp. 491-97.

[601] John McKnight. (1989). "Do no harm optionss that meet human needs," Social Policy 20(1), pp. 5-15.

[602] Francis Piven and Robert Cloward, Regulating the Poor: The Functions of Public Welfare. (New York: Random House, Vintage Books, 1972).

understanding of homelessness in his work, *Gimme Shelter*, concluding that,

> We must focus on examinations of homelessness on the forces underlying
> the dislocations occurring in the urban and rural environments. In other words,
> regardless of an individual's disability or special needs, the key to making sense
> out of his or her homelessness lies in the ability of our analyses to explain the
> distinctive structural arrangements in which homeless individuals occupy special
> niches.[603]

As a global theory about the confluence of demographic trends and economic class interests, the structural theory explains little of the ambivalent and contradictory stance Americans have taken toward the homeless, as one which encompasses both an obsession to rescue the innocents among the homeless, and to persecute those viewed as unworthy and indulgent. Several authors, such as Stern, and Hopper and Hamberg, have extended structural explanations and advanced a more specific disciplinary theory of the role of services in contemporary homelessness. Stern points out that, "After two decades of guilt and worry, the framing of the homeless issue served to reestablish the gift relationship of a bygone era".[604] It is a relationship which permits an atonement for guilt for individualistic striving, at the same time that the meager help given scarcely maintains many homeless into a revolving door syndrome, thus keeping alive an exhibit of the 'wages of failure', yet preventing it from getting out of hand. Hopper and Hamberg point out that "Containment of the deviant and discarded can not be allowed either to bankrupt the public fisc or to erase their image from the public consciousness. At the same time, the display of discredited ways of life cannot go so far as to contaminate the public spaces which play host to normal social intercourse."[605] If homeless persons do serve such functions, political and financial support for services for homeless persons would be circumscribed by the

---

[603] Gregg Barak, Gimme Shelter: A Social History of Homelessness in Contemporary America (New York: Praeger, 1989), p. 56.

[604] Mark Stern. (June 1984). "The emergence of homeless as a public problem," Social Service Review, p. 299.

[605] Kim Hopper and Jill Hamberg, The Making of America's Homeless: From Skid Row to New Poor, 1945-1984 (New York: Community Service Society, Dec. 1984).

continuing visibility of homeless persons on the streets: to the extent that homeless persons can be kept under control in shelters and other services, a stagnant equilibrium can be maintained, one which institutionalizes inadequate support for reintegrating the homeless into mainstream community life.

Another variation of the structural theory, one which also incorporates elements of the disciplinary version, is that advanced by Dear and Wolch who focus their analysis of homelessness on the "service-dependent ghettoes", sometimes referred to as psychiatric ghetto in the zone of transition in the inner city. They characterize these areas as reservoirs of potential clients resulting not only from the deinstitutionalization juggernaut, deindustrialized and stagnant economies with plentiful cheap housing, and also suburbanization. The influx of clients in these areas was fueled by the development of new services designed to care for them, which acted as catalysts in attracting further clients, becoming a self-reinforcing cycle.[606] By the late 1970s and early 1980s, "pressures to gentrify and redevelop the urban zone of dependence had begun to push mentally disabled and other service-dependent residents and their support facilities out".[607] They argue that the dismantling of the ghetto led to alternative treatment trends, including assignment to inappropriate services, homelessness, and a return to institutions.[608] While they emphasize structural forces, as well as the disciplinary and surveillance functions of mainstream social services, they also argue that the disruption of the dependency relationships, of the culture of poverty in the service ghettos, is what contributed to many people moving from extreme poverty into homelessness. Despite the range of social processes identified in their analysis, Dear and Wolch revert to the conservative recommendation for additional shelter and services as a short-term response with

---

[606] Michael J. Dear and Jennifer R. Wolch, Landscapes of Despair: From Deinstitutionalization to Homelessness, (Princeton, NJ: Princeton University Press, 1987), p. 9.

[607] Ibid., p. 172.

[608] Ibid., p. 252.

236

virtually no elaboration.[609]

Services Specific to Homeless Individuals

While mainstream human services have had only a modest impact on levels of homelessness, services developed specifically for the homeless have had only a slightly better record. In the last 15 years, the nation has seen the development of a new service system targeted at the homeless, consisting mostly of emergency shelters, and supplemented by food pantries and community kitchens, and occasional crisis counseling, transitional, and rehabilitative programs. Because the overriding focus of many of these private and local efforts has been on the provision of emergency services, these developments have been characterized as representing a policy of *de facto* shelterization, and of even, a return to the alm houses of the colonial period. In addition to charitable contributions, these programs have been funded primarily thorugh the Stewart B. McKinney Homeless Assistance Act, passed by Congress in 1987.[610]

Although some have argued that the shelter movement represents the implementation of a culture of poverty philosophy,[611] others see it as reflecting a minimization of problems of individual dysfunction, and as being based on an idealized view of the homeless as suffering from merely bad luck or simply economic problems, requiring only shelter and food.[612] During the 1980s Mitch Snyder and the Community for Creative Non-Violence, along with Robert Hayes and the National Coalition for the Homeless, created a national network of advocacy groups which claimed the right to shelter for the homeless. The issue was cast in terms of social justice rather than charity, and eventually many in the media accepted the paradigm

---

[609] Ibid., p. 256.

[610] Timmer, Eitzen, and Talley, Paths to Homelessness. 1994, p. 183.

[611] Ibid.

[612] Baum and Burnes, A Nation in Denial, 1993.

as presented.[613] In reality, both strands of thinking--charity and social justice-- inform the shelter movement, and neither has been allowed to entirely override the other or be fully implemented, as long as homeless individuals continued to be cast in the roles they are expected to perform.

According to the 1990 census approximately 80% of the homeless can be found in shelters. There is, however, ample reason to assume this proportion is considerably lower due to the greater problems of enumerating homeless individuals on street locations (see appendix 1). The Ohio survey, in contrast, found that 56.4% of the homeless used shelters,[614] whereas 40.2% had used them during the previous month.[615] The only other service so consistently used by homeless are community kitchens, as 60.8% of the homeless in this same study used them in the previous month.[616]

Despite the rapid expansion of shelters, there have been consistent reports of shortages in shelter services, especially in major urban areas. In Washington, DC, over two-thirds (68%) of people living on the streets had tried to get into shelters, however a majority of them had not been admitted either because they failed to meet admission standards or they did not request a place.[617]

Observers of the shelter system have generally emphasized the various negative functions that shelters fulfill. However a few have attempted to document the efficacy of model shelter programs, or to understand the range of services which are provided. In a St.Louis study, Alice Johnson developed a typology of the various constellations of service functions that shelters provide, whether a shelter is primarily involved in emergency, stabilization, or personal growth services. Shelters which

---

[613] Ibid.

[614] Beverly Toomey and Richard First, Homelessness in Ohio: A Study of People in Need, Franklin County Report. 1985.

[615] Richard First, Draft of Final Report, Ohio Rural Study, 2/13/92.

[616] Toomey and First, Homelessness in Ohio, p. 23.

[617] Baum and Burnes, A Nation in Denial, 1993, p. 76.

restrict their interventions to emergency management provided only basic services of food and shelter. Those which attempt to provide stabilization services additionally provided: transportation, laundry, showers, clothing, medical care, mental health services, entitlement assistance, referrals, recreation, dependency control, as well as advocacy. The most comprehensive programs, those premised on the goal of promoting personal growth, additionally provided case management, peer counseling, housing placement, work experience, and other types of individual assistance.[618] Unfortunately there is little data on the relative numbers of each type of shelter, the latter types no doubt being the exception, providing an even smaller fraction of the total available beds.

The less commendable functions which many believe shelters perform fall under several categories: warehousing, social control, tokenism and distraction, disincentives. Barak emphasizes warehousing, echoing the notions of Piven and Cloward: "Like the old vagrants who were warehoused for their cheap and hard labor, the new vagrants of today are warehoused in public and private shelters, and are busy providing ... inexpensive and hard labor ..."[619] In contrast, Hoch and Slayton contend that shelters serve to distract the public from the real causes of the homeless problem: "Building shelters, however, is like putting pots in the living room to catch dripping water without fixing the roof."[620] They are also critical of shelterization as it functions to provide a token response, which perpetually satisfies just enough public concern as to prevent the development of more enduring solutions. But probably the most common complaint about the policy involves negative incentives which are believed to be created, both for the homeless to remain homeless, for the potentially homeless person to become homeless, and for community caretakers to cease from caring for

---

[618] Alice Johnson, Out of Bedlam, 1990.

[619] Piven and Cloward, Regulating the Poor, p. 71.

[620] Charles Hoch and Robert Slayton, New Homeless and Old (Philadelphia: Temple University Press, 1990).

friends and relatives with particularly difficult economic and personal problems.[621] Linear correlational studies, not unexpectedly, show a strong positive correlation between the number of shelters and homeless persons.

Despite the view of many observers that the shelter movement has in many ways perpetuated homelessness, the homeless themselves have typically reported a more favorable view. In a survey by Rossi, almost three-quarters of the homeless agreed that "Shelters are the only places a person can get a decent place to sleep" (73.4%) and that "Shelters can really help homeless get on feet." (76.8%). Nonetheless, significant minorities were also concerned that "Shelters are dangerous because you can get robbed or beaten up" (46.6%), that there is not enough freedom (40.3%), or that there is too much emphasis on religion (23.3%).[622] It may be more instructive to explore with ex-homeless persons the various ways that shelters helped or hindered their reintegration.

Unfortunately, only marginal progress has been made in the development of longer term transitional and rehabilitative services, despite repeated calls for their use. Transitional services referr to such disparate activities as assistance with job search, support groups, employment placement and training, short-term assisted housing, mentoring, adult education, day care programs, and training in political organizing.[623] One of the major barriers has been the availability of treatment for alcohol and drug abuse, and especially for the dually-diagnosed (MI/SA). It has been suggested that such programs need to precede the provision of transitional services for the more disabled among the homeless, however, such treatment is beyond the resources of most homeless programs.[624]

---

[621] Christopher Jencks. (1994). The Homeless (Cambridge: Harvard University Press), p. 104-106; T. Maine. (1983). "New York City's lure to the homeless". Wall Street Journal. Sept. 12.; Michael H. Lang. Homelessness Amid Affluence: Structure and Paradox in the American Political Economy (New York: Praeger, 1989), p. 14.

[622] Peter Rossi, Down and Out in America, 1989.

[623] Baum and Burnes, A Nation in Denial, 1993, p. 81.

[624] Ibid.

The McKinney Act provides few funds for services, and in the fields of mental health and substance abuse the resources are limited to research and demonstration projects. Nonetheless, the overall association of funding levels with the level of homelessness is a negative one, accounting for 9% of the variation in homeless levels ($R^2 = 0.09$), suggesting that the funding may either result in lowered levels of homelessness, or conversely, is being misdirected to areas with few homeless persons. The relationship is, however, better explained on a curivilinear basis ($R^2 = 0.15$), assuming the familiar parabolic shape suggestive of the requirement for a minimal threshold of coverage for effectiveness to be found (see appendix 3, table A3-3)..

Multivariate and Structural Analyses

The analysis of the collective impact of income maintenance and services was conducted in three stages. In the first stage, the homeless rates were regressed on an extended group of indicators of service coverage using conventional multiple regression techniques (OLS). In the second stage, homelessness was regressed on a reduced group of service predictors, taking into account random measurement error using SEM techniques. In the final stage, these same service predictors were used to understand variations in homeless levels, but this time, controlling for the range of conditions considered up to this point, and these include the demographic, disability, economic, family, and systematic measurement error predictors.

The reduced group of service predictors similarly explains a substantial degree of variation in the homeless rates, about a third ($R^2 = 0.32$) (see table 6-3). This represents the combined effects of the rate of transfer payments ($\beta = 0.22$), mean SSI payments ($\beta = 0.27$), the level of McKinney funding ($\beta = -0.20$), and less so, the other variables. Because the impact of the transfer payments and SSI are *positive* it is necessary to hypothesize that either these programs are either ineffective, driving people to become homeless, or else, they are targeted to areas of greater need. This second interpretation is no doubt the more persuasive.

Table 6-2. Rates of Homelessness, Regressed on Indicators of Income Maintenance and Human Service Coverage (N=3,141)

	Zero-Order r Correlation w/ Homeless Rate	Multiple Regression	
		Partial r	Standardized Coefficient
INCOME MAINTENANCE			
AFDC--Mean Payment, 1980	0.05	-0.23[c]	-0.25[c]
General Assistance Mean Payment,	0.21	0.06	0.05[b]
SSI--Mean Payment, 1990	0.35	0.20[c]	0.22[c]
SSDI--Change in % Covered, 1980-	-0.24	0.02	0.02
OVERALL--% Households receiving	0.22	0.07[c]	0.07[c]
OVERALL--Change in total transfer	0.39	0.22[c]	0.24[c]
MENTAL HEALTH			
INPATIENT--Total Inpatients, 1988	0.27	0.18[c]	0.32[c]
INPATIENT--% Decline in state	0.04	0.16[c]	0.24[c]
COMMUNITY--Index of Community	0.12	0.03	0.03
QUALITY--Rated quality of state	0.05	-0.02	-0.02
SUBSTANCE ABUSE--Drug & alcohol	0.19	-0.01	-0.01
MEDICAL--Primary Care services	-0.12	0.01	0.01
EDUCATION--Per pupil school	0.29	0.03	0.04
SOCIAL SERVICES--Per capita social	0.23	0.24[c]	0.20
SERVICES SPECIFIC TO HOMELESS			
SHELTERS--% Homeless in shelters	-0.23	-0.16[c]	-0.14[c]
FUNDING--McKinney homeless	-0.30	-0.12[c]	-0.12[c]

NOTES: Values are weighted by relative population sizes. Multiple R^2 = .40; SEE=10.3; F=130.8 [c]

SOURCE: Computed from 1990 U.S. Census data, STF-3C Data Tape and USA Counties, 1990

The services-only model proves far inferior to the combination of all the previous models in understanding homelessness, accounting for only 32.0% versus 94.2% of the variation in the homeless rates. However, when all 30 variables are used to control for the differing environmental conditions in the various counties we see a slightly improved model, accounting for most all (95%) of the variation in the homeless levels. It reveals that almost all the initial 32% effect of the services variables turn out to be spurious, leaving only a fifth of this effect, or 6.3%, which can not be accounted for by taking into account the various other theories considered. Conversely, only a small degree of the effect of the economic, demographic, and measurement error variables are explained away by the available services. With controls for services, the disability and family indicators each had a slightly greater impact than previously revealed.

Of the 6.3% of the variation in homeless levels accounted for by the services variables, most of this originates from the level of Medicaid funding (2.4%), McKinney support for homeless programs (1.4%), and total transfer payments per capita (1.1%). Among these variables, only the McKinney effect is a negative one, suggesting that targeted services will service to reduce homeless rates ($\beta=-0.32$), even after considering that they are partly distributed based on anticipated numbers of homeless persons.

This chapter has explored many of the negative and a few of the positive effects of both mainstream and specially targeted income and human service programs on the homeless. It has found that many of the positive effects are hardly discernible when examined through the lens of a broad national statistical study such as this. Clearly, small areas of effectiveness which can be found in the exceptional programs are camouflaged and washed out by the effects of their targeting at the overwhelming need, as well as by their ineffectiveness or non-responsiveness to the acute needs of the homeless. Some of this ineffectiveness may be serving larger societal functions assigned to the homeless, characterized by some as a basis of social discipline, an

Table 6-3. Effect of Selected Secondary Supports on Homeless Rates

Variables	Family & Prior Variables — Variation Explained	Services Only — β	Services Only — Variation Explained	Secondary Services & Prior Variables — β	Secondary Services & Prior Variables — Variation Explained
SECONDARY SUPPORTS	--	--	32.0%	—	6.3%
Mean payment SSI, 1986	--	0.22ᶜ	7.8%	-0.04ᵃ	0.8%
Transfer payments per capita, 1988	--	0.27ᶜ	11.0%	0.05	1.1%
% Households w/ public assistance, 1989	--	0.05ᵇ	1.1%	0.01	0.1%
Overall rate psychiatric hospitalization, 1990	--	0.12ᶜ	3.4%	0.02	0.3%
Rate of Primary Care medical care	--	0.06ᶜ	0.5%	-0.09ᶜ	0.3%
Medicaid per capita, 1986	--	0.06	2.1%	3.59ᵇ	2.4%
McKinney support /homeless person, 1989	--	-0.20ᶜ	6.2%	-0.32ᶜ	1.4%
FAMILY FRAGMENTATION (See chapter 5)	23.0%	--	—	—	24.9%
ECONOMIC OPPORTUNITY (See chapter 4)	18.2%	--	--	--	16.9%
DISABILITY INDICATORS (See chapter 3)	3.8%	--	—	—	4.4%
DEMOGRAPHIC VARIABLES (See chapter 2)	25.5%	--	--	--	22.0%
MEASUREMENT ERROR	23.7%	--	--	--	20.6%
TOTAL MODEL (R^2)	94.2%	--	32.0%	—	95.0%

NOTES: See appendix 2 for goodness-of-fit statistics. Each model computed using weighted least squares and estimates of measurement error.

[a] $\alpha > 0.05$

[b] $\alpha > 0.01$

[c] $\alpha > 0.00$

exhibit which reminds all about the consequences of laziness and immorality. But despite the scant evidence of service effectiveness in minimizing homeless populations, this analysis has also demonstrated that at least targeted programs, such as the McKinney Program for the Homeless, can have an independent effect, over and above the improving economic conditions, in minimizing the numbers of persons without a home.

What has not been considered in this analysis--inaccessible or unaffordable housing--will now be examined. This will permit us to obtain some understanding of whether homelessness represents simply a scarcity of affordable housing, or also a confluence of personal and societal conditions which impact a person's ability to access available housing.

Chapter VII
HOUSING UNAFFORDABILITY:
SYMPTOM OR CAUSE?

Since homelessness is most specifically defined by the absence of a domicile, it is only natural that questions about the housing market should be central in debates on homelessness. At one extreme is the position of some advocates such as Robert Hayes who proclaimed homelessness to be primarily a problem of unavailable and unaffordable "housing, housing, and housing".[625] At the other extreme are the many who rarely mention housing in their analyses, or if they do, emphasize the inability of the homeless to take advantage of existing housing opportunities, due to either economic difficulties or personal disabilities. A more popular and intermediate position, though an oversimplified one, is that of the "musical chairs perspective" on homelessness[626] which focuses on an unfavorable ratio of available low-income units to low-income individuals. Certainly there exists individuals and families who would not be homeless if it were not for a combination of random misfortune, such as a layoff, with an increasingly unaffordable housing market, especially in the major urban areas. Likewise, there are many who, because of their lack of education, disabilities, and lack of other supports, have so little income and other resources that any housing, however cheap, is unaffordable. The either/or issue of housing unaffordability as a

---

[625] Quoted in, David A. Rochefort and Roger W. Cobb, "Framing and claiming the homelessness problem," New England Journal of Public Policy 8 (1), pp. 55.

[626] Caton, C.; Shinn, Marybeth and Colleen Gillespie. (Feb. 1994). "The roles of changing housing and poverty in the origins of homelessness. Journal of Social Issues 46 (4), pp. 157-74.

cause or symptom of homelessness, is better reframed as a question of how characteristics of local housing markets--housing availability and affordability-- interact with the economic and non-economic resources of particular subgroups, as well as the nature of the forces which are depressing the incomes of those at the bottom of the socioeconomic scale.

Just as with the theories reviewed in the preceding chapters, we can use housing conditions to account for much of the variation in homelessness only if we ignore competing theories of homelessness. However, the analysis to be presented in this chapter demonstrates that we can *much better* explain homelessness if we take the range of theories into consideration. When we do this, we find that housing conditions still account for a significant, but far more modest proportion of the variation in the homeless rates (14.1%).

The Low-Income Housing Shortage

There is a range of indicators of the availability and affordability of housing, especially in so far as low-income persons are concerned. They include overall figures involving the availability of rental units and vacancy rates, as well as specific indices of affordability for low-income individuals (see table 7-1). The typical county has slightly over a third (35.7%) of its housing units as rental units, however, perhaps because of the large range--from 12% to a 100%--this aggregate figure has an unusually strong 0.66 positive zero-order correlation with the rate of homeless persons: the homeless clearly either come from or gravitate to areas with relatively higher levels of rental housing.

Some of the main indicators of housing availability include vacancy rates. In 1990 close to a tenth (9.4%) of all housing units were vacant, and only a slightly smaller proportion (8.4%) of rental units were vacant, more than enough-- theoretically--to house all homeless persons. The existence of small negative correlations between vacancy rates and homeless levels suggests that either people are less likely to become homeless in such areas, or that if they do, they can more quickly find replacement housing. However, the picture become less clear when more

Table 7-1. Zero-order Correlations of Homelessness, with Selected Indicators of Housing Availability and Affordability

Subgroup of Homeless Population	Housing Availability					Affordability	
	Percentage Housing Rental	Overall Vacancy Rate	Rental Vacancy Rate	0-1 Room Rental Vacancy Rate	Available Rooms per Homeless Person	Mean Ratio Rent-Income Families < $10,000	% 0-1 Room Units Under $250
AGE							
0-17	0.54	-0.24	-0.16	-0.24	0.26	0.14	-0.30
18-34	0.67	-0.24	-0.14	-0.35	0.32	0.21	0.35
35+	0.61	-0.19	-0.01	-0.29	0.24	0.15	0.29
GENDER							
Male	0.65	-0.22	-0.10	-0.33	0.27	0.19	-0.33
Female	0.64	-0.24	-0.17	-0.31	0.31	0.15	-0.31
RACE							
White	0.44	-0.18	-0.09	-0.30	0.15	0.19	-0.30
Minority	0.67	-0.22	-0.12	-0.30	0.33	0.14	-0.29
OVERALL	0.66	-0.23	-0.13	-0.23	0.29	0.18	-0.34

NOTES: Correlations are computed using rate, per 10,000, of overall county population who fall
into the designated subgroup, i.e. persons over 35 of age. All correlations are significant
at the 0.000 level or better.
SOURCE: Computed from 1990 U.S. Census (STF-1C and 3C Data Tapes).

specific indicators of availability are considered. For instance, one index--available
rental rooms per homeless person--reveals that for each homeless person as officially
enumerated in 1990, there were an average of 140 rooms for rent, or anywhere
between 5 and 6,317 rooms per homeless person, depending on the county. This

index is, unexpectedly, positively associated with rates of homelessness at the 0.29 level, indicating people either become homeless in areas with many vacant rooms, perhaps leaving some of these rooms vacant, or are attracted to these areas, but are unsuccessful in renting these units.

A key to understanding such disparate experiences of the homeless is no doubt the affordability of the available units. A range of studies have documented the high proportions of income which low-income persons are forced to spend on housing. For instance, the American Housing Survey of 1989 revealed that 56% of all poor renter households pay at least half of their income on housing.[627] Other data from the same time showed that about a half (47%) of households below the poverty line spent more than 70% of their incomes for housing.[628] The situation is particularly acute in metropolitan areas, where 84% of low-income home owners spent at least 30% of their income on housing.[629] A particularly vulnerable subpopulation are single parents which spent 81% of its income on housing in 1987, up from 46% in 1974.[630]

Indeed, among households with less than $10,000 income, the average rent to income ratio is 56.9%, far greater than the 30% standard promoted by the Federal government[631] for housing affordability. Even though there is only a weak 0.18 correlation between low-income housing unaffordability and homelessness--because of considerable variation around the predominate pattern--figures 7-1 and 7-2 document the sharp slope or impact of this basic relationship, throughout the various regions of the United States, as well as in areas with various levels of urbanization.

---

[627]   Foster, Carol D., Alison Landes, and Nancy R. Jacobs (eds.). (1993), Homeless in America: How Could it Happen Here? Wylie, Texas: Information Plus, p. 18.

[628]   Timmer, Doug A., D. Stanley Eitzen, Kathrynm K. Talley. (1994). Paths to Homelessness: Extreme Poverty and The Urban Crisis. Boulder, CO: Westerview Press, citing DeParle, Jason. "Poor are increasingly facing a tough choice on housing." New York Times (Dec. 12, 1991), A1, A13..

[629]   Foster, et al, p. 30.

[630]   Apgar, William C. and H. James Brown. (1989). The State of the Nation's Housing: 1988 Cambridge: The Joint Center for Housing Studies of Harvard University.

[631]   Foster, 1993, p. 25.

So, although the association is not "strong" in the sense that we have the ability to consistently predict homeless rates from unaffordability levels, it is very strong in the sense that dramatically higher homeless rates are found in areas with rent to income ratios above the 45% level than in affordable areas of 30% or smaller rent to income ratios, where homelessness is about a tenth of what it is on average across the nation.

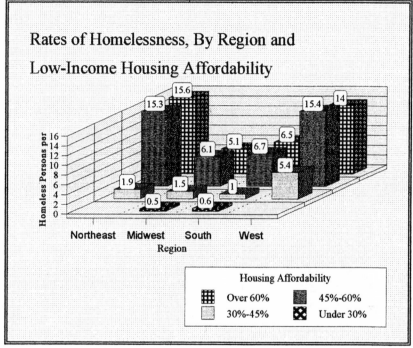

Figure 7-1

Similarly, if we consider the percentage of 0 to 1 bedroom units which rented for less than $250 a month in 1990, we find that almost a third (31.1%) fall into this category, ranging from none to 100% throughout U.S. counties. The higher the percentage, the lower the homeless rates. This represents an association of -0.34 which falls in the low to moderate range, again reinforcing the unaffordability hypothesis that it is not so much the availability of housing, but its cost to low-income persons. But, as Rossi pointed out, "To be sure, there is no way any housing market dominated by private providers can offer housing at an 'affordable price' for those who have close to zero income."[632]

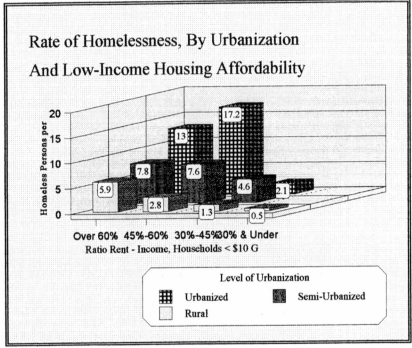

Figure 7-2

Some of the hypotheses about the impact of housing availability and affordability on homelessness involve the idea that it is not so much the absolute level, but rather increases in the prevalence of such conditions which would best explain contemporary homelessness. Extensive data on housing trends are cited in the literature to support these hypotheses, only some of which will be reviewed here. Just as overall levels of housing availability have been increasing, the availability of low-

---

[632] Rossi, Peter H. (1989). Down and Out in America: The Origins of Homelessness Chicago: The University of Chicago Press, p. 181.

income housing--really, an indicator of housing affordability--has been decreasing. The U.S. Housing Inventory reveals that between 1970 and 1980 the overall number of housing units grew from 68 to 87 million, and that renter occupied units grew from 24 to 29 million units.[633] However, during the 1980s there was a loss of anywhere between 1.1 and 2.5 million low-income units, depending on the particular indicator and years examined.[634] Jencks, however, suggests that the bulk of the loss of low-income units occurred in the 1970s.[635]

A comparison between 1980 and 1990 figures casts some doubt on the magnitude of the decline. After adjusting for inflation, Census data indicate that there was a overall 9.5% increase in the total availability of units renting for $250 or less in 1990 dollars. But an examination of aggregate means, even at two points in time, is inadequate to do much other than to suggest a relationship. A far stronger means involves examining patterns of variation and their correlation with homeless rates. Such an analysis does indeed support the notion that the increasing unavailability of low income units, or unaffordability, is associated with homeless rates. The solid line in figure 7-3 reveals that the greater the decline in units renting at $250 or lower, the lower the homeless rates. Despite the strength of this relationship in respect to its slope, it is a fairly weak relationship in respect to its predictability ($r = 0.12$) because of considerable variation from the basic pattern as epitomized by the plotted best fitting line.

A slightly better proxy for affordability than low-income availability consists of the changing level of rents. Reports suggest that while rents in real dollars remained fairly constant during the 1970s they began to rise in the 1980s.[636] In the 13 years between 1974 and 1987 it has been reported that the median housing costs

---

[633] Foster, p. 31.

[634] Burt, Martha R. (1992). Over the Edge. New York: Russell Sage Foundation, p. 40; Foster, 1993, p. 17; Jencks, Christopher. (1994). The Homeless. Cambridge: Harvard University Press, p. 64.

[635] Jencks--bulk of low-income housing reductions in 70s

[636] Jencks, 1994, p. 69.

for all renters rose by 16% in constant dollars. However, median rents for poverty level households rose at over twice that level, at 36%.[637] The growing levels of housing unaffordability have been well documented in the literature on homelessness. During the 1970s and 1980s average rents tripled, while mean incomes only doubled.[638] Dolbeare points out that in 1970, there were 5.8 million available rentals for 5.3 million households (figured at 30% income); however, by 1991 there were 2.8 million units for 8.0 million low-income households.[639] Similarly, Jencks points out that in 1973 there were 87,000 more cheap rooms than very poor tenants, and by 1981 the difference was just slightly less at 84,000, but after 1985 very poor tenants became more numerous than very cheap rooms.[640]

According to Census data, the median gross rent was $473 in 1990, up by only 2.1% in 1990 dollars from ten years earlier. However, this is a figure which masks substantial levels of variability. It is the pattern of these variations, specifically, variations above the mean, which need to be examined vis-a-vis' homeless rates. Just as was the case with low-income availability, figure 7-3 shows that the greater the increase in rents, the higher the homeless rates. And again, while the slope of this relationship is substantial, variations from the basic pattern are considerable, and for this reason the correlation is a weak one of only .08. Both declines in availability and the increasing costs of housing between 1980 and 1990 are, thus, weakly but meaningfully associated with the 1990 homeless rates.

---

[637]   Shinn and Gillespie, 1994, p. 509.

[638]   Barak, Gregg. (1991). Gimme Shleter: A Social History of Homelessness in Contemporary America. New York: Praeger, p. 70.

[639]   Dolbeare, C. N. (1991). Out of Reach: Why Everyday People Can't Find Affordable Housing, Second Edition. Washington, DC: Low Income Housing Information Service, p. 7, cited in Shinn and Gillespie, 1994.

[640]   Jencks, 1994, p. 67.

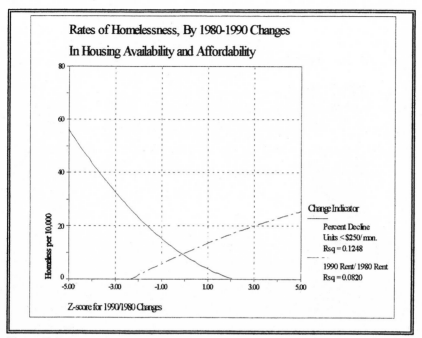

Figure 7-3.

Since most homeless persons are single, never married individuals, the diminishing availability of single room occupancy (SRO) units has often been proposed as an explanation for homelessness. Blau, for instance, points out that while "Public housing may be in short supply ... single room occupancy hotels have almost disappeared."[641] Estimates of the drop in SRO units during the 1980s vary from 60,000[642] to a million or more,[643] depending on the definition, data sources, and exact period examined. According to the 1990 Census, the rate of board and care--a variation of the SRO concept--was 5.1, with a range of none to 174 throughout the

---

[641] Blau, Joel. (1992). The Visible Poor: Homelessness in the United States New York: Oxford Press, p. 75.

[642] Jencks, 1994, p. 63-64.

[643] Reamer, Frederic. (Jan. 1989). "The affordable housing crisis and social work" Social Work 1989; Foster, 1993; Burt, 1992, p. 33.

range of U.S. counties, clearly only enough for a fraction of the homeless. Figure 7-4 depicts the strong positive association of board and care rates with levels of homelessness, and simultaneously, with levels of urbanization. Rates of homelessness are just about three times the level in areas with high levels of board and care, compared with those with the lowest levels, regardless of the level of urbanization. Just as may be the case with shelters, there very well may be a clustering of board and care facilities with homeless individuals, each attracted to areas with the other, although often even the low rents are prohibitedly expensive for most of the homeless. Jencks has calculated that a room in a cage hotel in 1958 required on average 12 to 20 hours work a month; by 1992, the room, if available, required typically 40 hours work a month.[644]

Causes of the Affordability Crisis

There is little consensus about the origins of the increasing unaffordability of low-income housing, especially as it is found in the major urban areas. Prevailing theories include the declining influence of labor and the resulting low level of the minimum wage; federal withdrawal from public housing programs; urban renewal and gentrification; the development of a service economy; decreased construction, centralization of the housing market, family fragmentation, changing tax regulations, and rent control.

Economic explanations alternatively focus on declining wages, especially for persons at the lower ends of the income distribution,[645] inflation, and the servicetization of the urban economy. Burt, for instance, points out that efforts to control inflation during the 1980s kept interest rates high for much of this decade, diminishing construction.[646] Inflation in housing prices during this period was particularly problematic, as the median cost of a single family dwelling was $62,000

---

[644] Jencks, 1994, p. .

[645] Shinn & Gillespie, 1994, p. 511.

[646] Burt, 1992, p. 52.

in 1980, but rose to $104,000, by 1993[647] Inflation in housing prices has often been attributed to decreased construction. In 1985 the GAO reported on a survey of 66 cities by the U.S. Conference of Mayors which found that the most often cited reason for a diminishing supply of low-income housing was decreased construction.[648]

The experience of the market for single-family dwellings has historically set the pace for the rental market. The inability of higher income renters to buy exerts an upward pressure on rents.[649] Alternatively, it has been pointed out that, at least in the major urban areas, the rent squeeze is caused by the concentration or monopolization of ownership of rental housing. In New York, for instance, 5% of all landlords control over half of the rental housing.[650] Even if such monopolization is not the cause of high rents, it introduces a rigidity and unresponsiveness in these markets to changing conditions.

Perhaps one of the most hidden causes of the housing crisis has been the fragmentation of the family. Single and divorced individuals, as well as single parent families all drive the number of individuals per unit down, placing considerable strains in many areas on the rental housing market. Burt points out that more households formed in the 1970s than would be expected from population growth, with both owners and renters opting for smaller households. In 1970 there were 23.6 million rental units containing 64.3 million persons, or 2.73 per unit; but between 1970 and 1980, the number of units grew by 21.4% while the total number of persons living in them went up by only 1.2%, causing the average to drop to 2.28 per unit.[651] Clearly, as more persons postpone marriage, or terminate it, a higher proportion of the population will be occupying two units who previously would have occupied only one

---

[647] Timmer, 1994, p. 18.

[648] U.S., General Accounting Office. (April 9, 1985). Homelessness: A Complex Problem and the Federal Response (GAO/HRD-85-40), p. 25, table 2.

[649] Burt, 1992, p. 39.

[650] Timmer, 1994, p. 19.

[651] Downs, 1983, p. 22-23.

unit. Similarly, as new technologies permit more disabled and older adults to remain at home, additional demands are placed on the housing market.

Probably the most often cited reason for the affordability crisis involves urban renewal, gentrification, and the speculation of slum lords.[652] The servicetization of the urban economy as well as decreased construction have both served to increase the market for rehabilitating existing structures, ones which formerly housed the indigent, sometimes as SROs and cage hotels. It has been estimated that during the 1980s over 735,000 households were displaced due to slum clearance[653] The effect was to force more people into fewer housing units and to raise the prevailing cost of a rental unit.[654] In marginal areas, often adjacent to gentrified neighborhoods, the behavior of speculators reduces available low-income housing further. Some will attempt to recoup their investment by 'milking' and abandoning properties. Others will 'warehouse' properties, not filling vacancies, and moth balling buildings until upscale neighborhoods expand and drive up prices. In either case the speculators have little incentive to maintain these buildings as they are often purchased as tax write-offs. Finally, a proportion of these properties, due to neglect, are at risk of fire; or because of greed, arson, in either case permanently removing them from the rental market.[655]

Speculation of slum lords is not new, but the financial incentives created by new tax regulations as well as banking practices, have clearly exacerbated the problem. For instance, the Tax Reform Act of 1986 effectively minimized the incentives to invest in low-cost housing. This resulted from the reduction of the maximum tax rate, lengthened depreciation periods, reduced availability of accelerated depreciation; the elimination of the unearned tax benefits for high income passive

---

[652] Piven and Cloward, 1987.

[653] Piven and Cloward, 1987.

[654] Belcher, John R. and Frederick A. DiBlasio. (1990). Helping the Homeless: Where do we go from here? Lexington: Lexington Books.

[655] Shinn & Gillespie, 1994, p. 508; Timmer, 1994, p. 21; Foster, et al, 1993, p. 17.

investors in housing tax shelters; and the elimination of special treatment of capital gains and tax exempt status for industrial development bonds.[656] Redlining by banks dramatically inflames the deterioration of inner-city neighborhoods, especially those with significant minority populations.[657]

Hoch and Slayton argue that stereotypes held both by the public and by social scientists also fueled some of the more lethal parts of the urban renewal crisis. They point out that, "The mis-perception of the [SRO] hotels as breeding grounds for social disease continues to legitimize public policies designed to remove and replace the hotels."[658] The destruction of these hotels has continued to be justified by analysts, developers, and public officials who deplore the lack of affordable housing, yet dismiss the demolition of these resources as simply the removal of substandard blight.[659]

Another frequently cited cause of the affordability crisis is the withdrawal of the federal government from support for public housing, especially during the Reagan Administration.[660] New appropriations for public housing dropped from 32.1 billion in 1981 to 6 billion by 1989.[661] At the same time total federal housing starts dropped from 183,000 to 20,000.[662] While new additions to the rental housing stock from federal sources averaged 160,000 per year during the 1970 to 1981 period, the level declined to 67,000 per year in the 1982 to 1989 period, a decline of 66 percent.[663]

---

[656] Burt, 1992, p. 53.

[657] Belcher & DiBlasio, 1990, p. 88.

[658] Hoch, Charles, and Robert A. Slayton. (1989). New Homeless and Old: Community and The Skid Row Hotel Philadelphia: Temple University Press, p. 9.

[659] Ibid., p. 198.

[660] Timmer, 1994, p. 22; American Heritage Foundation. Backgrounder. (1989). "America's Homeless: Victims of Rent Control", Jan. 12, 1989.

[661] Blau, 1992; p. 71.

[662] Appelbaum, Richard. (May/June 1989). "The affordability gap." Social Science and Modern Society 26 (4), p. 7.

[663] Burt, 1992, p. 32-33.

Despite such dramatic declines some question this trend, suggesting that most indicators cited involve authorizations which entail a substantial lead time before new units are actually constructed. Burt, for instance, argues that "In fact, federal subsidies reached more households and a larger proportion of the poverty population in 1989 than in 1981.[664] She points out that probably more significant has been changes in laws which affect the profitability of low-rent housing, such as tax treatments for investments and factors affecting interest rates.[665]

Just as the federal government has been withdrawing from support of public housing, it has become more involved in programs which emphasize market mechanisms. The prime example is the Section 8 housing program which uses housing vouchers that move with the tenant, and that can be used in a wide range of privately developed and owned housing.[666] Despite the successes of the program, a major problem involves the difficulty of certificate holders in actually locating housing in the private market. One study of the program found that an average of one-third of all certificates were returned unused by participants. In some urban areas with low vacancy rates, as many as 40% of all certificates were returned unused.[667]

There are also considerable waiting lists and difficult bureaucratic procedures which prospective Section 8 tenants must contend with. These tend to screen out homeless individuals as well as those with various behavioral disabilities. One study of homeless mentally ill clients in a case management program compared those who successfully secured certificates with those who did not. The main difference was the level of psychopathology, specifically, the non-receivers had significantly higher levels of schizophrenia than the receivers. While clients had a mean application time of 5.7 months, those with schizophrenia had to engage in significantly longer application

---

[664] Ibid., p. 49.

[665] Ibid., p. 51.

[666] Becher & DilBlasio, 1990, p. 92.

[667] Kennedy and Finkel, 1987, cited by Mulroy and Lane, p. 59.

efforts.[668]

Although the level of Section 8 vouchers and certificates has a slightly positive zero-order association with housing affordability, perhaps reflecting some targeting of the program at areas with expensive housing, when control for other explanations are introduced, the picture reverses. The more certificates and vouchers, the more affordable housing becomes, however the effect is only a small one (Partial r = -0.26; β = -0.06). An analysis of the correlation of the level of program vouchers and certificates also presents a mixed picture. Figure 7-5 indicates that the overall

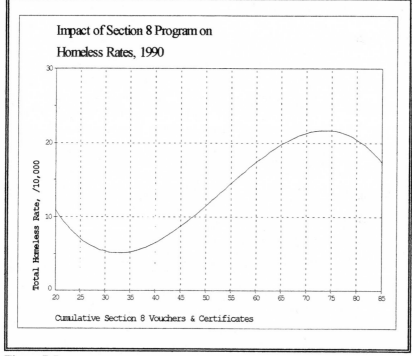

Figure 7-5.

[668] Dixon, Lisa, Patrick Meyers, and Anthony Lehman. (Dec. 1994). "Clinical and treatment correlates to Section 8 Certificates for homeless mentally ill persons". Hospital and Community Psychiatry 45 (12), p. 1196.

relationship is a positive one ($R^2 = 0.13$), suggesting that the program may be targeted at areas with high levels of homelessness, or alternatively but less plausibly, creates homelessness. However, in areas with unusually low and high levels of coverage, the relationship becomes negative, suggesting a reduction of the rate of homelessness after a threshold of about 75 certificates/vouchers is passed.

Finally, one school of thought suggests that it is local government controls, especially exclusionary zoning and rent control laws, which have served to cause the price of housing to become increasingly unaffordable. Vissing has pointed out that strict enforcement of building and fire codes has resulted in the closing of many previously occupied buildings,[669] just as Mulroy and Lane have documented how communities use legal zoning regulations to prevent the development of low-cost housing, through minimum lot sizes, maximum density rules, large 'setback requirements', parking restrictions, and the prohibition of multifamily developments. All these tend to be devices used to maintain a not-in-my-backyard (NIMBY) stance of many neighborhoods.[670]

One of the most controversial theories is that rent control eliminates the incentives for developers to build, causing the price of housing to skyrocket. Rent control is used in only a few parts of the United States. In total it covers about 10% or 2.8 million rental units in parts of six states: California, Connecticut, Maryland, Massachusetts, New Jersey, New York, and Washington, DC.[671] A 1991 HUD review of the literature points out that most analysts have concluded that rent control transfers income and wealth from landlords and tenants, accelerating the deterioration of housing stock, mainly because the landlord is forced to reduce maintenance expenditures in order to maximize his or her investment return. The reduced rate of

---

[669] Vissing, Yvonne M. (1996). Out of Sight, Out of Mind Lexington: University of Kentucky.

[670] Mulroy and Lane, p. 56.

[671] U.S., Department of Housing and Urban Development. (Sept. 1991). Report to Congress on Rent Control.

return, in turn, has created an impetus for condominium conversions.[672] The report concludes that rent control is an inefficient income transfer as substantial numbers of low-income families receive no benefit because their units are not rent controlled. In contrast, a significant minority of high-income families live in controlled units and receive disproportionately large benefits.[673] In addition, prospective tenants have an incentive to pay "key money" for better quality housing than that available for the controlled rent alone because the low cost of housing leads the tenant to want better housing than could be occupied at the uncontrolled level of rent.[674]

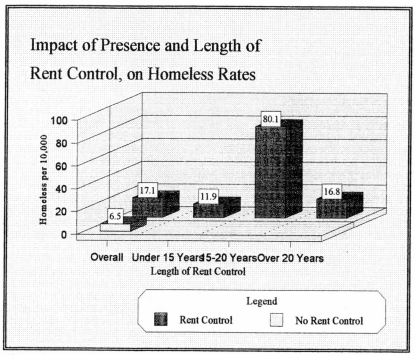

Figure 7-6.

---

[672] Ibid.

[673] Ibid.

[674] Ibid., p. 10.

An examination of the relationship of rent control with homeless levels reveals an apparent association, as presented in figure 7-6. Counties which have at least some rent control have almost three times the rate of homelessness as those which do not (17.1 vs. 6.5). Among those which have rent control, the impact of length of existence f rent control on homeless rates is less consistent. Those with rent control that is less than 15 years old have homeless rates of 16.8, versus 80.1 in those with rent control which is 15 to 20 years old, and 11.9, for counties where it is over 20 years old, such as New York County.

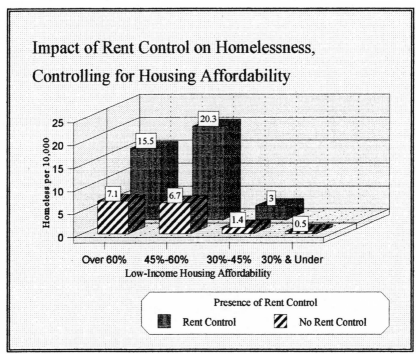

Figure 7-7.

It has been suggested that the apparent association between rent control and homelessness is actually a reflection of the greater pre-existing unaffordability of areas which decide to institute rent control to deal with the problem.[675] Figure 7-7 depicts the relationship of rent control and homelessness, controlling for the affordability of low-income housing. It clearly shows that increasing housing unaffordability--up to the 45% to 60% level--is associated with high rates of homelessness in *both* areas with and without rent control. However, it is at especially high levels in rent controlled counties. Thus, housing unaffordability does not explain away the impact of rent control, but rather, apparently interacts with it in a cumulative manner to exacerbate the problem of homelessness. Such data is only useful for examining relationships between very small numbers of variables; the problem of assessing the impact of rent control ultimately requires control for multiple variables, a task which will be pursued in the following section.

It is clear that housing unaffordability is a function of multiple conditions, some of which depress incomes and others impact on various components or determinants of housing prices. Table 7-2 presents summary statistics on the collective impact of several of the conditions so far discussed on housing affordability of families with incomes under $10,000. The most dramatic impact revealed by this analysis is that of rent control. Although the existence of rent control is strongly associated with housing unaffordability ($\beta = 0.88$), its length of existence is associated with affordability, suggesting that while rent control may arise in response to housing unaffordability, after several years, rent control may tend to diminish the problem ($\beta = -0.85$). The second most powerful set of conditions involve poverty and extreme poverty, which no doubt impact primarily on the income side of the affordability equation. In areas of high general poverty, housing for the poor is relatively affordable ($\beta = -0.57$), perhaps reflecting the depressed housing prices in many poor rural areas, especially in the South. However, when extreme poverty--the percentage of persons under 50% of the poverty line--is high, even the low-income housing market becomes inadequate, as there is a strong association of extreme poverty with

---

[675]   Blau, 1992, p. 70.

housing unaffordability ($\beta = 0.57$). In such areas of extreme poverty, there is perhaps no way that rents can be depressed sufficiently to be relatively affordable for persons having such nominal incomes, without significant public assistance.

Table 7-2. Regression of Mean Rent to Income Ratio for Families Under $10,000 Income, on Selected Predictors

Predictor	Zero-order Correlation	Part Correlation	Partial Correlation	Regression Coefficient	Stand-- ardized Regression Coefficient
Percentage in same house, 1985-1990	-0.61	-0.25	-0.36	-0.23	-0.33
Percentage employed with no or semi-skilled jobs	-0.53	-0.18	-0.27	-22.31	-0.31
Change in income, 1980-1990	0.06	-0.12	-0.19	-11.14	-0.15
Rate of Violent Crime	0.42	0.13	0.21	0.00	0.18
Percentage of those employed working in the service sector	0.24	-0.05	-0.07	-3.77	-0.06
Individual Poverty Rate	-0.17	-0.13	-0.20	-55.95	-0.57
Rate of persons in extreme poverty (< 50%of poverty line)	-0.04	0.14	0.21	110.16	0.57
Rent Control (1-Yes; 0-No)	0.23	0.19	0.27	14.11	0.88
Length of Rent Control (Years)	0.13	-0.20	-0.29	-0.97	-0.85
Total Section 8 Certificates & Vouchers	0.11	-0.04	-0.26	-0.04	-0.06

NOTES: Ordinary least squares regression used. $R^2 = 0.57$ (F=365.36; p = 0.0000; df, residual = 2703). All coefficients have a significant T at least the 0.001 level.

Also associated with housing affordability are the percentage of persons who remain the in same house after 5 years ($\beta = -0.33$), a high percentage of people employed in no or semi-skilled positions ($\beta = -0.31$), increases in income between 1980 and 1990 ($\beta = -0.15$), low rates of violent crime ($\beta = 0.18$), and the percentage of those working in the service sector ($\beta = -0.06$).

266

In addition, the more Section 8 certificates and vouchers provided in a given county, the more affordable housing becomes for the low-income, but the effect is only slight, no doubt because of the limited size of the program relative to the targeted population (β = -0.06).[676]

The Reported Housing Experience and History of Homeless Persons

Surveys of homeless people provide an alternative view of the role of housing conditions in the lives of the respondents, one which supplements and in some respects supports the results of structural analyses. A large survey of homeless persons in rural parts of Ohio asked its respondents about the major reason for their homelessness. Although family conflict was the most frequently cited reason (37.3%), almost a third (31.6%) of the subjects mentioned eviction or problems in paying rent as the major reason for their homeless condition, over three times as many as who mentioned unemployment (9.7%).[677]

Only a few surveys have included questions about respondent's housing history--critical information for establishing a link between the homeless and various possible housing conditions. One study of homeless families in rural areas asked about the most recent housing history of its subjects, inquiring about where the previous night was spent. About two-fifths (40.9%) reported family, a fifth (19.4%) mentioned friends. Close to a quarter (23.5%) have spent the previous night in a shelter or mission, whereas only 8.9% could afford a cheap hotel or motel.[678] In contrast, a study of the homeless in downtown Los Angeles, found that about a third of those in soup kitchen lines was renting a room in an SRO.[679]

---

[676] Indicators of family fragmentation did not contribute sufficiently to be included in the final equation computed. Data was not available on other explanations discussed, such as gentrification, redlining, and exclusionary zoning.

[677] First, Richard. (2/13/1992), Report on Ohio Study, chapter 7, table 7.2.

[678] Ibid., table 7-2.

[679] Rossi, 1989, p.184, citing Farr, Koegle, and Burnham, 1986.

267

Wright and Devine asked their literally homeless subjects about the distribution of locations used during the prior 60 days, revealing that the most frequently used location, accounting for about a quarter (24.1%) of the average subject's days was spent at "someone else's place". While the second most important location consisted of the street or outdoors, accounting for a seventh or 13.7%, of the last 60 days of these subjects, almost equally frequent were apartments and houses (10.5%) and parent's homes (10.3%). Crack houses (5.7%) and jails and prisons (4.3%) were considerably more frequented locations than the subject own residence (1.5%) or someone else's (0.5%) Single Room Occupancy unit, rental, or boarding houses (0.1%), transitional homes (0.2%), or group homes (0.0%).[680] It is apparent that more comprehensive longer term histories must be obtained in order to gain an accurate view of the subject's pre-homeless housing experience. Such recent histories, though informative, reveal a mixture of homeless and pre-homeless experiences at a rather late stage in the career of the homeless person to-be.

A study of homeless older adults in Chicago is one of the few which provides any kind of longer term view of the housing history of individuals who, at some point, have been homeless. Almost three-quarters (72%) of this sample had usually lived alone, and four-fifths had a history of residential instability (80%) or evictions (83%).[681] The findings on the recent residential history of these same individuals was not dissimilar to Wright and Devine's findings from their New Orleans sample: the last known living arrangement of a fifth (22%) of the ever homeless consisted of their own apartment and a similar proportion (22%), nursing homes. Only 2% had lived in an SRO and an equal number in assisted housing. In contrast, 12% had last been in shelters or on the streets, and 27% had living arrangements which were

---

[680] Percentages computed from Wright, James D. and Joel Devine. (July 1995). "Housing dynamics of the homeless: Implications for a count". American Journal of Orthopsychiatry 65(3), p. 326.

[681] Keigher, Sharon, and Sadelle Greenblatt. (1992). "Housing emergencies and the etiology of homelessness among the urban elderly". The Gerontologist 32(4), p. 464.

unknown.[682]

Data on the mobility of homeless individuals, especially during their prehomeless lives, is scarce. One study of the mentally ill homeless found that out of 102 patients with two or more hospitalizations over the course of a year, over a quarter or 27 had two or more changes of residence.[683] A lesser rate of mobility has been reported among single mothers, one which is reflected by the finding that three quarters of these mothers move at least once by the third year after the breakup of their marriage, typically for the purpose of reducing housing cost.[684]

Once individuals become homeless, it has been proposed that there may be three major patterns of mobility: (i) movement in and out of homelessness; (ii) diurnal or seasonal movement within defined geographic areas; and, (iii) migration characterized by "seemingly unbounded movement over wide geographic areas.".[685] Sosin, Piliavin, and Westerfel reported that few people in their single sample were able to successfully extricate themselves from homelessness without government assistance in paying rent.[686]

It is, thus, clear that the residential history of homeless individuals consists of substantial instability and mobility, one which gradually deteriorates from isolated life in efficiencies into an admixture of renting, doubling up with friends and family, staying in shelters or outdoors, and very scarce use of either SROs, boarding houses, and institutional or assisted housing facilities. Many questions remain as to the specific types of rentals which homeless individuals formerly occupied, as well as the mix of reasons for the termination and transfer to alternative arrangements. An alternative

---

[682] Ibid., p. 464.

[683] Appleby, L. and P. Desai. (1987). "Residential instability: A perspective on system imbalence," American Journal of Orthopsychiatry. 57, pp. 515-24.

[684] Mulroy, Elizabeth and Terry S. Lane, "Housing affordability, stress and single mothers: Pathways to homelessness," Journal of Sociology and Social Welfare, p. 57.

[685] Bachrach, Leona. (1987). "geographic mobility and the homeless mentally ill," Hospital and Community Psychiatry, 38, pp. 27-28.

[686] Sosin, M., Piliavin, I., and Westerfelt, H. (1990). "Toward a longitudinal analysis of homelessness," Journal of Social Issues 46(4), pp. 157-74.

perspective on the housing experience of the homeless is suggested by the results of a survey of 170 shelters residents in which the respondents were asked about their housing preferences. Two-thirds (67%) indicated they preferred living alone, typically, in efficiency apartments. A fourth (25%) said they would like a place which included some kind of supervision, such as a group home, board and care, or assisted housing, while only a fifth (19%) indicated they preferred to share an apartment.[687] It is clear that a significant proportion of the homeless come from situations involving social isolation--often efficiencies or studio apartments--with most preferring a housing arrangement which would maintain such a stance, though a significant minority would like to find some alternative.

Multivariate Analyses of the Impact of Housing on Homelessness

Several researchers have attempted to understand variations in levels of homelessness based on housing conditions as well as other features of the environment. All such analyses, with the exception of this author's, have been conducted using selected subsamples of cities as their units of analysis, typically using the 1984 HUD estimates, or in the case of Burt, her own tallies of the number of sheltered homeless.

A common finding of these studies is that vacancy rates are negatively correlated with levels of homelessness. This was found by Elliot & Krivo,[688] Burt,[689] and Tucker,[690] and Hudson,[691] with coefficients ranging between -0.04 (Hudson) and

---

[687] Neubauer, Ruth. (May 1993). "Housing preferences of homeless men and women in a shelter population," Hospital and Community Psychiatry 44, 5, pp.492-4.

[688] Elliot, Marta, and Lauren J. Krivo. (1991). "Structural determinants of homelessness in the United States," Social Problems. 38(1),a, pp. 113-31.

[689] Burt, 1992.

[690] Tucker, William, "Where do the homeless come from?" National Review, Sept. 25, 1987, p. 35.

[691] Hudson, Christopher G. (Spring/Summer 1993). "The homeless of Massachusetts: An analysis of the 1990 U.S. Census S-Night Data," New England Journal of Public Policy, 9(1), pp. 79-100.

-0.39 (Tucker). Other indicators of housing availability used include median rent, the percentage of rental units with rents of $150 or under, the percentage of units which are rental, as well as the ratio of available rental rooms to homeless persons. Some of these, such as the rooms to homeless ratio, have generated mixed findings. In the author's own earlier research on the towns and cities of Massachusetts, this condition was negatively associated with levels of homelessness, but in the national study being reported here, this predictor ceases to be significant when a full range of predictors are used. In general, Burt's summary of her research in 1992, is valid for much of the multivariate research conducted by others:

> Certain housing variables were strongly associated with homelessness, including the shortage of affordable housing and tighter rental housing markets. These effects were diminished when the model also included more antecedent variables reflecting components of affordability. Most analyses pointed to inadequate household income as the most important reason why housing became less affordable.[692]

Rent control has also been included as a predictor in several multivariate analyses, most notably by William Tucker. Tucker examined variations in homelessness in a select sample of cities, using the HUD 1984 estimates, as well as a small group of other predictors, including mean temperature, poverty, unemployment, and vacancy rates. He found that rent control was the single most powerful predictor of homelessness, accounting for 27 percent of the variation in urban rates. When rent control was used in the same equation as vacancy rates, the effect of the vacancy rates disappeared.[693] These findings have been interpreted to indicate that rent control closes the door to housing development: "If General Motors had to negotiate with every little planning and zoning board before it could sell cars around the country; America undoubtedly would be suffering a car shortage as well."[694]

Tucker's research has been severely criticized because of the non-random

---

[692] Burt, 1992, p. 218.

[693] Backgrounder, 1989.

[694] Ibid., p.8-9.

selection of cities, exclusion of housing affordability as a predictor and other possible determinants. A few of these problems were corrected in a follow-up analysis of the data by Edgard Olsen, but still using data on only 35 cities from the HUD estimates. This study found a substantial, but statistically insignificant effect.[695] None of the replications have attempted to go beyond using the questionable HUD guestimates on a truly national sample, using a full range of predictors, or more appropriate statistical techniques which do not assume multivariate normality. Samples of the major urban areas undoubtedly magnify the overall impact of urban-based rent control measures. Conversely, in national samples, the impact of the few areas with rent control will be appreciably diluted, and thus less easily detected.

Structural Analysis

When housing predictors alone are used to analyze variations in homeless levels across the country, almost three-fifths ($R^2 = 0.59$) of the variation in these levels can be accounted for (see table 7-3). But when other theories are taken into account, and indicators of disabilities, economic opportunities, family and social supports, as well as systematic measurement error are also considered, a much improved model results ($R^2 = 0.965$). But even with this model, indicators of housing availability and affordability still account for a substantial 14.1% of the variation in the homeless levels. The drop from 59.1% to 14.1% explained by the housing predictors no doubt reflects the removal of the effect of many housing conditions in mirroring the impact of social and economic conditions which is possible when these conditions are explicitly included in the model.

The single most important feature of the local housing market for the homeless is its affordability. Close to half of the impact of the housing variables (or 6.4% of the total) involves the combined effects of the level of affordability in 1990 (5.2%) along with changes in affordability since 1980 (1.2%) (see figure 7-8).

---

[695] HUD, 1991, p. 31.

However, the single most important indicator of affordability--median gross rent in 1990, accounting for 3.8% of total variation--had a negative association (-0.36) with homeless levels: the higher the rent, the fewer the homeless. Since it is unbelievable that increasing rents will ameliorate homelessness, a more plausible interpretation of this result would be that homeless people to some extent originate from and gravitate

Table 7-3. Effect of Extended Group of Housing Predictors on Homeless Rates

Variables	Housing Variables Only		Housing & All Others	
	β	Variation Explained	β	Variation Explained
HOUSING--TOTAL		**59.1%**		**14.1%**
Housing Availability		**27.4%**		**5.1%**
% Occupied Units rented	0.44[b]	17.4%	0.15[b]	4.0%
Vacancy rate, all units	-0.05	0.3%	--	--
Vacancy rate, rented units	0.00	0.0%	--	--
0-1 Bedroom units	-0.21[b]	3.5%	--	--
Vacancy rate, 0-1 bedrm.	0.10[b]	1.4%	-0.04[a]	0.4%
Rate, Board & Care	0.17[b]	3.8%	0.05[b]	0.7%
Vacant rooms for rent/person	-0.06[a]	0.4%	--	--
Rooms for rent/homeless	-0.07	0.8%	--	--
Crowding		**9.4%**		**0.0%**
Median # persons/room	0.25[b]	4.4%	--	--
Persons/household	-0.36[b]	4.8%	--	--
Affordability		**14.8%**		**5.2%**
Median gross rent, 1990	0.07[a]	1.1%	-0.36[c]	3.8%
% households <%10,000 paying >35% rent	-0.51[b]	5.3%	--	--

Table continued on next page

273

Variables	Housing Variables Only		Housing & All Others	
	β	Variation Explained	β	Variation Explained
Gross rent/household income, households <%10,000	0.44[b]	4.7%	--	--
Vacancy rate, 0-1rm.units <$250	0.17[b]	3.6%	-0.1[b]	1.4%
% 0-1 units under $250/month	-0.01	0.1%	--	--
Changes, 1980-1990		**0.8%**		**1.2%**
1990/1980 gross rent, (1990 $s)	0.04	0.6%	0.11[b]	1.2%
% Decline, units under $250 rent	-0.01	0.2%	--	--
Federal Support		**0.1%**		**1.5%**
Total cumulative Section 8 Certificates & Vouchers	0.00	0.1%	-0.11[b]	1.5%
Local Regulation		**6.3%**		**1.1%**
Presense of rent control	0.23[b]	5.2%	0.08[a]	1.1%
Length of rent control	-0.09[b]	1.1%	--	--
TOTAL		**59.1%**		

to low-rent districts. If the second interpretation is correct, then increasing rents only serve to transfer the problems of the homeless to less well-to-do counties. In contrast, the more vacancies there are in inexpensive units costing less than $250 a month, the fewer homeless there are. This more specific measure of low-income affordability does suggest that increasing the supply of affordable units will have an impact on minimizing the numbers of homeless. The third most important indicator of affordability is the extent that rents remained the same or did not increase from 1980 to 1990. The extent that they rose positively accounts for 1.2 percent of the total variation in homeless rates. Although homeless persons tend to avoid areas of generally expensive rentals, their presense is to a lesser extent associated with areas with low vacancy rates in low-income housing, as well as increasing rents. Thus, it may very well be that high vacancy rates in low-income units and stable rents play a causative role in minimizing the extent that people become or remain homeless.

The absolute level of availability of potential housing for the homeless was found in preliminary analyses to be critically important, but to the extent that more comprehensive models are formulated and tested, these conditions become considerably less important, but still salient. In the total model, indicators of availability collectively account for 5.1% of the variation in homeless levels, most of this consisting of the impact of the preponderance of rentals over private ownership arrangements (4.0%). Homeless persons not only originate in areas characterized by many rentals, but tend to remain or gravitate to these areas; the extent of the former or the latter remains unknown.

It may very well be that the rental housing market is inherently unstable and provides far fewer buffers for low-income and other persons who are otherwise at risk of homelessness. Nonetheless, rental housing is certainly more accessible for these same persons. Similarly, the presence of board and care facilities is associated with the presence of homeless persons. Whether such resources are being established in response to the presence of homeless persons, or homeless persons are attracted to such resources is again unknown. Nevertheless, the most plausible hypothesis remains that there is an interactive clustering of indigent persons and low-cost housing and other resources demanded by this population.

The third most important component of housing conditions for homeless persons involves the availability of Section 8 certificates and vouchers: the more such resources, the fewer the homeless there are (-0.11). This impact, however, only accounts for 1.5% of the variation in homeless levels. This modest effect no doubt reflects both the small size of the Section 8 program relative to the numbers of homeless and other persons in need and also the difficulty of homeless persons in accessing these resources without special help, such as that available from intensive case managers. But even with such caveats, this analysis supports the notion that the program does have a small but clearly beneficial effect on homelessness.

The final characteristics of the housing market which were considered in these modeling efforts were the presence and length of rent control. The notion that rent control aggravates the problem of homelessness, by diminishing the affordability of housing, is again supported. Unlike the suggestion of the preliminary analyses, the length of time that rent control has been around did not have a significant positive or negative impact, but the presence of rent control had a slight impact (0.08), accounting for only 1.1% in the total variation in homeless rates. Since rent control only covers a relatively small proportion of the 3,141 counties, it is not unexpected that the impact would be as modest as it is. It should be noted here that, unlike Tucker's analyses, housing affordability was controlled for in this model.

Clearly, housing availability and affordability remain important determinants of homeless levels. However, these are much less critical than would appear to be the case if we were to consider only the most concrete and recent events in the lives of homeless persons, such as evictions. When we also consider the impact of race, urbanization, economic opportunities, as well as the fragmentation of the family, and to a lesser extent, pre-existing disabilities of and services available to at-risk persons, we find that housing conditions can not effectively constitute the primary focus of any theory which purports to account for the origins or dynamics of contemporary homelessness. In aggregate housing conditions only improve the explanatory power of our model by about one percent, although they do reveal some of the effects of the other hypothesized conditions to be spurious (see table 7-4). Certainly, the "musical chairs" theory involving the balance between income and affordable housing is a useful one as far as it goes, especially since indicators of housing affordability and availability account for about a seventh of the variation in the size of homeless populations. But it is oversimplified, failing to account for the many demographic, personal, and economic forces diminishing either the income or affordable homes for at risk persons, a few of which have been reviewed in this and in previous chapters.

Table 7-4. Effect of Reduced Group of Housing Conditions on Homelessness

Variables	Services & Prior Variables	Housing Only		Total Model, Including Housing	
	Variation Explained	β	Variation Explained	β	Variation Explained
HOUSING CONDITIONS	--	--	55.0%	--	14.1%
% of occupied housing units rented	--	0.63[c]	39.3%	0.15[b]	4.0%
Est. vacancy rate, 0-1 bedrm units under $250	--	0.03[a]	1.1%	-0.10[c]	1.4%
Median gross rent, 1990	--	-0.03	0.7%	-0.36[c]	3.8%
Change in median gross rent, '80-'90	--	0.03	0.8%	0.11[b]	1.2%
Rate of Board and Care facilities	--	0.17[c]	6.0%	0.05[b]	0.7%
Vacancy rate for 0-1 bedrm. Apt.	--	0.10[c]	2.2%	-0.04[a]	0.4%
Total cumulative rate of Section 8 Certificates & Vouchers	--	-0.01	0.3%	-0.11[c]	1.5%
Rent control laws (1--Yes/0--No)	--	0.13[c]	4.7%	0.08[a]	1.1%
EXTREME POVERTY: % < 50% Poverty Line	--	--	--	0.12[a]	0.9%
SECONDARY SUPPORTS: Income Maintenance & Services (See chapter 6)	6.3%	--	--	--	5.7%
PRIMARY SUPPORTS: Family (See chapter 5)	24.9%	--	--	--	28.2%
ECONOMIC OPPORTUNITY (See chapter 4)	16.9%	--	--	--	13.5%
DISABILITY INDICATORS (See chapter 3)	4.4%	--	--	--	3.5%
DEMOGRAPHIC VARIABLES (See chapter 2)	22.0%	--	--	--	15.3%
MEASUREMENT ERROR	20.6%	--	--	--	15.3%
TOTAL MODEL (R^2)	95.0%	--	55.0%	--	96.5%

NOTES: See appendix 2 for goodness-of-fit statistics. Each model computed using weighted least squares and estimates of measurement error.

   [a] $\alpha > 0.05$
   [b] $\alpha > 0.01$
   [c] $\alpha > 0.001$

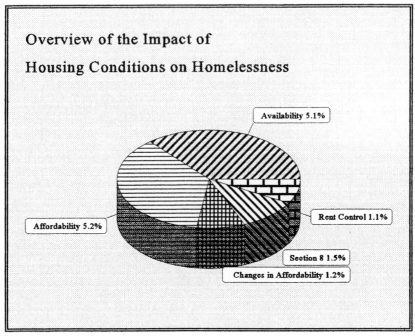

Figure 7-8.

Chapter VIII

AN INTERDEPENDENCY MODEL OF HOMELESSNESS

A central theme throughout this book has been that contemporary homelessness is a result of a breakdown in critical interdependencies between individuals and their social environments. In the exploration of demographic conditions, it was found that minorities, males, and young adults have been particularly vulnerable to the effects of urbanization. Personal limitations, especially lack of education and behavioral disabilities, were then found in Chapter 3 to play important roles in vulnerability not only to urbanization, but in particular, to the growth of the service economy which is so often found in the major urban areas. Some evidence was also found that family fragmentation, declines in income and social supports, and housing unaffordability aggravate these conditions, contributing to the observed variations in homelessness. However, in the foregoing chapters, each of these theories were, for the most part, considered individually and incrementally. When this is done, support for each can almost always be found. This chapter will take up the more difficult task of considering this range of the conditions simultaneously, so as to specifically assess the statistical support for them when each of the other explanations is taken into account.

Two models are presented in this chapter, a detailed model for explanatory purposes, and a simplified one for estimation and prediction. The explanatory model incorporated the maximum range of predictors possible so as to assess the evidence for the relative contributions of each of the explanations of homelessness. The second or prediction model, in contrast, is a parsimonious model, with only four predictors, so as to facilitate its use with easily updated information to estimate current and future levels of homelessness, and the probable impact of alterations in key programs to eradicate homelessness. The explanatory model provides clear support for the role of each of the hypothesized conditions, more so for the role of demographic, economic, family, and housing conditions, and considerably less so for the role of disability and income and human service supports. In contrast, the prediction model reveals that it is primarily the combination of urbanization with the expansion of the service economy, especially in areas where there has been less than average funding for homeless programs, that most effectively predicts high rates of homelessness. After a review of the methodologies used, each of these models will be presented, as well as the results of tests and projections made on the basis of the final, prediction model. These will then both be used to assess the status of the originally hypothesized conceptual model of homelessness from chapter 1, the Social Interdependency Model.

Review of Methodologies

In both statistical models presented here, techniques of structural equation modeling were used. These involve methods of addressing problems of non-normality of the data, both random and systematic error, correlated error terms, and problems in testing an overall system of equations, especially when it has been derived through an exploratory process. The U.S.Census data utilized in this study, such as the homeless rates themselves, significantly deviate from the traditional bell-shaped pattern or normal distribution which standard multivariate techniques such as multiple regression assume. For this reason, a procedure has been used which is referred to as the generally weighted least squares estimation algorithm, one which Browne demonstrated to be the best "asymptotically distribution free" estimation method.[696]

Traditional regression studies assume that the variables are measured without error. When such an assumption is made with predictor variables, the correlation

---

[696] Karl G. Jöreskog and Dag Sörbom. (undated). LISREL8 User's Reference Guide (Chicago: Scientific Software International). Cites: M.W. Brown. (1984). "Asymptotically distribution-free methods for the analysis of covariance structures," British Journal of Mathematical and Statistical Psychology, 37, 62-83.

estimates are typically downward biased, as the ignored error camouflages the underlying relationship. For this reason, modest error estimates are used, based on what is known of the methodologies employed and the intrinsic difficulties of measuring these variables. These estimates are inherently arbitrary, thus, with key estimates, i.e. with the homeless rates, a sensitivity analysis was conducted by recomputing the model with several divergent error estimates. The homeless random error estimate made little difference to the model fit indices as long as it was below the 15% level. In traditional regression analysis, such tests for the assumed zero error can not be done (see table 8-1).

The reader may recall that systematic error is also included in the various models computed in this study. The primary measure of such error involves the extent of the search or enumeration efforts that the Census Bureau conducted during their S-Night undertaking. The key indicator of such efforts is the number of locations to which enumerators were deployed, per 10,000 persons. This is based on the hypothesis that the more the Census Bureau looked, the more they found. This notion has substantial support, both from the bivariate analyses, as well as from the multivariate analyses (see appendix 1). Although bivariate analyses support the notion of a linear positive relationship, common sense suggests that this can only be true up to a point: the more one looks, the more one finds, until one finds all that there is to find. It has, therefore, been hypothesized that there is also a curvilinear relationship, with a declining slope, until a 'saturation point' is reached. This saturation point happens when there is sufficient search--staffing or sites--to locate virtually all homeless persons. Above this level, additional search efforts will typically fail to yield additional homeless persons. An exploration of the data initially revealed no such point; if anything, it suggested that the best fitting curvilinear relationship was exponential, with an increasing slope. However, when six of the 3,141 counties with the most extreme scores were excluded as outliers, a slope, as depicted in Figure 8-1, was identified. This provided a better fitting account of the observed points than a

Table 8-1. Regression Coefficients for Predictors of Explanatory Model

Predictor	Error Assumed	Standardized Coefficient	'Import -ance'	Variance Explained
SYSTEMATIC ERROR: Rate Sites Enumerated	1%	0.48[b]	4.8%	15.3%
DEMOGRAPHIC PREDICTORS				
Population Density	1%	0.32[b]	1.3%	9.3%
% Population Nonwhite	2%	0.21	0.5%	3.7%
% Foreign Born	2%	-0.03	0.7%	0.5%
% Change 65+, '80-'90	2%	-0.14[a]	1.8%	1.1%
% Population Growth, '80-'90	2%	0.69[a]	1.0%	0.5%
% Pop. in Baby Boom ('45-64)	1%	-0.51[a]	1.0%	0.1%
DISABILITY PREDICTORS				
% Disabled, w/ mobility & self-care limitations	4%	-0.01	0.6%	0.1%
% Change HS Grads, '80-'90	2%	-0.03	2.4%	0.3%
Rate of Violent Crimes	5%	-0.13[b]	1.3%	1.6%
Suicide Rate	5%	-0.16[b]	2.2%	1.1%
Hard core cocaine users Per 1,000 pop.	10%	-0.03	0.1%	0.4%
ECONOMIC PREDICTORS				
Employed as % of population	2%	0.09[b]	2.7%	0.2%
Civilian unemployment rate, 1989	2%	0.08[b]	2.0%	0.2%
% Employed un- or semi-skilled	2%	-0.15[b]	2.4%	1.4%
% Employed in services, 1989	2%	0.41[b]	5.9%	11.7%
FAMILY SUPPORT PREDICTORS				
% of persons in families	2%	-0.17[b]	10.6%	3.9%
% adults aged 15+ separated, widowed, divorced	2%	0.49[b]	12.9%	5.4%
% Households headed by female	2%	-0.52[b]	7.9%	6.3%

Predictor	Error Assumed	Standardized Coefficient	'Import -ance'	Variance Explained
% Households with only one person	2%	-0.53[b]	9.4%	12.6%
INSTITUTIONAL SUPPORT PREDICTORS				
Mean payment SSI, 1986	2%	-0.03	1.6%	0.4%
Transfer payments per capita, '88	2%	0.05	0.2%	0.8%
% Households w/ public assistance, 1989	2%	-0.03	0.2%	0.3%
Overall rate psych. hospitalization, 1990	2%	0.00	0.4%	0.0%
Rate of Primary Care medical care	2%	0.07[b]	0.5%	0.2%
Medicaid per capita, 1986		0.23[b]	1.4%	3.2%
McKinney support /homeless person, 1989	2%	-0.07[b]	0.5%	0.8%
HOUSING PREDICTORS				
% occupied housing units rented	2%	0.15[b]	2.8%	4.0%
Est. vacancy rate, 0-1 bedrm units under $250	2%	-0.10[b]	0.7%	1.4%
Median gross rent, 1990	2%	-0.36[b]	1.0%	3.8%
Change median gross rent, '80-'90	2%	0.11[b]	6.2%	1.2%
Rate of Board and Care facilities	2%	0.05 [b]	4.7%	0.7%
Vacancy rate for 0-1 bedrm. apartments	2%	-0.04[b]	0.3%	0.4%
Total cumulative rate of Section 8 Certificates & Vouchers	2%	-0.12[b]	0.4%	1.5%
Rent control laws (1--Yes/0--No)	2%	0.08[a]	1.6%	1.1%
EXTREME POVERY: % Under .5 Poverty Line	2%	0.12[a]	0.6%	0.9%

NOTES: See appendix B for sources of variables. χ^2, with 36 df, is 6.9, with p=1.00, indicating that the model and observed covariance matrices come from the same population. The attenuated R^2 for the rate of homelessness is 0.97.

[a]. $\alpha < 0.05$

[b]. $\alpha < 0.01$

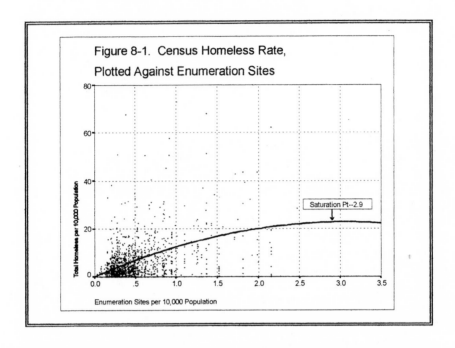

Figure 8-1. Census Homeless Rate, Plotted Against Enumeration Sites

linear relationship. Similar slopes were computed with subgroups of counties with varying levels of population density, with only minor differences in their shape or saturation points. The saturation point, that point at the apex of the curve when the slope or increase in observed homeless becomes zero, was then determined by solving the regression equation for enumeration sites when the deriviative (or slope) is set to zero. The regression coefficients were calculated using the generally weighted least squares (WLS) estimation algorithm as implemented in the LISREL program. The result of this calculation, 2.9 sites per 10,000, can be visually confirmed by inspecting figure 8-1.

The usefulness of such a saturation point becomes apparent when one considers that this 2.9 saturation point can then be entered into the computed multivariate model to produce an estimate of the number of homeless persons who would have been enumerated had the Census Bureau sent enumerators to an average of at least this many sites.[697]

Testing of the final model consisted of several phases. In the first phase, overall indices of goodness-of-fit were examined, as well as the resulting pattern of residuals. In structural equation modeling an examination of residuals refers to an examination of the differences between the sample co-variances and those implied by one's model. If there are only few differences, one assumes that the model is congruent with the data. The second stage involved the computation of model estimates for each of the 3,141 counties, and a comparison of the model and observed homeless rates; this was only possible through using the Extended LISREL Model, involving the computation of intercepts for the latent variables. These more traditional residuals were inspected not only through the conversion to z-scores, but also through statistical breakdown by the categories of region and level of urbanization, as well as a mapping of the data. Finally, revised model estimates of homeless rates for each of the 3,141 counties were calculated with the 2.9 site rate entered for each county which had fewer than this many sites visited, so as to calculate a value for the rate of literal homelessness in each county, after the observed effects of systematic undercounting were statistically removed. These results were then aggregated to various county, state, and national levels to enable comparisons with independent surveys and estimates for these areas. These results will be presented in table 8-2.

---

[697]   The equation for this is as follows, using SPSS syntax:

if (siterate lt 2.9)homadj=((.3782*empser89)+(.0600*(density*.01))-(.1023*(mckinhom*.0001))
    +(.0439*2.9)+.0043)*100.
if (siterate ge 2.9)homadj=((.3782*empser89)+(.0600*(density*.01))-(.1023*(mckinhom*.0001))
    +(.0439*siterate)+.0043)*100.

The terms, .01, .0001, and 100, modifying density, mckinhom, and the overall equation, are rescaling factors to correct for changes of scale used by the structural equation program. The intercept is the .0043 figure. KEY: siterate -- Rate of enumeration sites S-Night/per 10,000 population; homadj--Homeless rate per 10,000, 1990, adjusted for earch effort; empser89-- Proportion employment in services sector, 1989; density--1990 population density: Mckinhom-- McKinney expenditures

The Explanatory Model

This model supports the notion that the combination of urbanization and racial minority status has placed significant populations at risk of homelessness, and that this risk has been most dramatically aggravated by the shift to a service-based economy, family breakup, and housing unavailability (see figure 8-2). It also reveals that personal disabilities and institutional supports for troubled individuals have played a relatively minor role. The proportion of variation in home-less levels explained by each of these groups of variables is depicted in figure 8-3. These conditions, as a whole, account for virtually all of the variation in observed homeless rates ($R^2 = 0.96$). It should be noted that this 96% figure incorporates modest estimates of random measurement error; without this, the variables would account for approximately 80% of the variation. The model as a whole fits the data extraordinarily well, as there is virtually a 100% probability that the computed and the model implied co-variances come from the same population, despite considerable opportunities for model disconfirmation ($\chi^2 = 6.9$; df = 36; p = 1.00).

The demographic risk factors, as a group, account for almost a seventh (15.3%) of the variation in homeless rates, however, most of this (9.3%) is due to population density, a key indicator of urbanization. The impact of urbanization is clearly not only a reflection of the greater search efforts in urban areas, as this was also included in the model, explaining an identical level of variation in the rates (15.3%) in the expected direction. The proportion of the population which is non-white independently contributed another 3.7% of the variation, and in both cases the relationship is a positive one indicating that as population density and the non-white population increases, levels of homelessness increase. It is clear that racial minority status clearly places many individuals at risk, especially in urban areas, and this was shown through a comparison of differential rates in appendix 1. The percentage of foreign born, growth of the older adult population, general population growth, and the presense of a large baby boom cohort each contributed only to a nominal extent

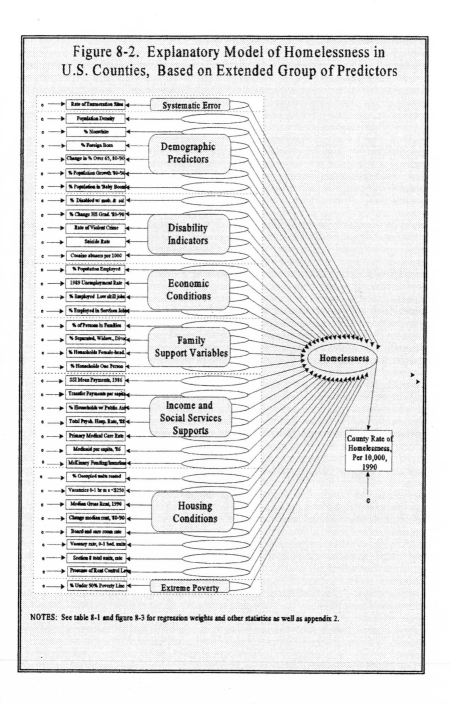

Figure 8-2. Explanatory Model of Homelessness in U.S. Counties, Based on Extended Group of Predictors

NOTES: See table 8-1 and figure 8-3 for regression weights and other statistics as well as appendix 2.

in understanding homelessness.

The disability hypothesis is at best only nominally supported by this analysis, despite the significant individual-level research and preliminary analyses which lend support to the theory. Collectively, the disability indicators account for only 3.5% of the variation in homeless rates. However, each of these has a marginally negative relationship with the homeless rates. The only two which are significant involve societal violence (suicide rate, β = -0.16; and violent crime rate, β = -0.13) and have an unexpected negative relationship with the homeless rates. It is, thus, clear that given the weakness of these relationships and the fact that differential environmental conditions have been controlled for, i.e. urbanization, that virtually no meaningful interpretation can be attached to the marginal impact of such conditions.

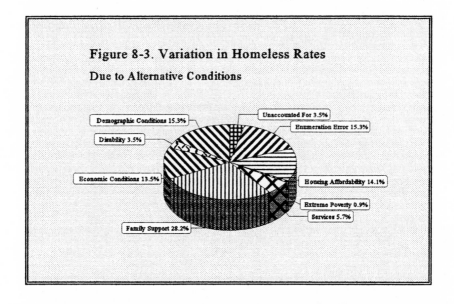

Figure 8-3. Variation in Homeless Rates
Due to Alternative Conditions

Demographic Conditions 15.3%
Disability 3.5%
Economic Conditions 13.5%
Family Support 28.2%
Unaccounted For 3.5%
Enumeration Error 15.3%
Housing Affordability 14.1%
Extreme Poverty 0.9%
Services 5.7%

Indicators of economic conditions account for about an eighth (13.5%) of the homeless rates. Virtually all of this (11.7%) is attributable to the impact of employment in the service sector, and a negligible level attributable to either overall employment levels (as a percent of population) or unemployment rates. However, the presense of un- or semi-skilled jobs was found to depress the homeless rates $(\beta = -0.15)$, accounting for only 1.4% of the variation in levels of homelessness. The strong impact of service sector jobs may be a reflection of the educational requirements of many of these positions, the high level of employment instability and "temping" in this sector, or, relatively high rates of psychiatric problems among this population.

Although family support indicators account for a substantial level of variation (28.2%) in homeless rates, interpretation of this impact is clouded by the fact that two of the indicators have unexpectedly strong positive negative relationships with homelessness, contrary to the preliminary bivariate analyses. Perhaps the most substantial impact is that of the cohort of persons who are separated, widowed, or divorced, accounting for 5.4% of the variation: the larger this population, the more homeless persons. Similarly, the more that people reside in family units, the fewer homeless, and this accounts for another 3.9% of the variation in homeless rates. Earlier, the percent of households headed by females and the percent of one person households were found to have a strong positive association with homeless rates, but in this model, the direction is reversed. Partial correlation analyses revealed that this reversal is not a result of the statistical controls for any other single variable Rather, it reflects the fact that when several or all other conditions are held constant, single people are actually less likely to be homeless, perhaps because of the greater economic resources available to single adults who have no dependents.

Indicators of the adequacy of the income maintenance and human service safety nets account for only about an eighteenth (5.7%) of the variation in homeless rates. Although most of the indicators have minor positive relationships with the homeless rates, such as the Medicaid rates, this fact no doubt reflects the targeting of these services to homeless persons and the insufficient levels of such mainstream services for meaningful effects to be detected. They also camouflage non-linear relationships between services and the impact on an indigent population such as the homeless (see chapter 6).

Table 8-2. Comparison of Census, Independent, and Model Estimates of Homeless Populations in Selected Jurisdictions

Jurisdiction	Census Count	Independent Estimate	Adjusted Model Estimate	Year	Type of Study
COUNTIES					
California counties[1] (Alameda, Orange, Yolo)	4,144	1,601-1,730	8,162	1987	Community Survey
Los Angeles County[2]	12,631	38,420-68,670	20,659	1990	Community Survey
Ohio rural counties (n=21)[3]	177	919	1,575	1990	Community Survey
Tennessee counties (n =7)[4] (urban and semi-rural)	2,119	2,597	4,675	1985-1989	Community Surveys
STATES					
Colorado[5]	3,114	5,500	6,279		Estimate
Florida[6]	10,900	2,200	25,690		Aggregation of Estimates
Illinois[7]	9,272	29,216	22,950	1989	
Massachusetts[8]	6,207	10,000	13,400	1990	Administrative Statistics
Oregon[9]	4,069	10,000	5,184	1987	
Tennessee[10]	2,451	3,203	8,210	1986	
Texas[11]	10,520	41,833	29,306	1985	Aggregation of Estimates
Utah[12]	1,250	1,700	3,191	1985	Key Informants Survey
Virginia[13]	3,161	64,592	11,186	1986	
Washington[14]	5,634	6,000	8,379	1987	

Jurisdiction	Census Count	Independent Estimate	Adjusted Model Estimate	Year	Type of Study
NATION	240,140		478,993		
Burt, M.[14]		500,000-600,000		1987	Aggregation of Local Surveys
Jencks, C.[15]		324,000		1994	
National Alliance to End Homelessness[16]		735,000		1988	Reanalysis of 84' HUD Study
U.S. HUD[17]		500,000 -600,000		1988	Rassessment of 1984 Study

NOTE: Whenever a range was given in the state and county estimates, the mid-point was used. The above are counts of persons in both shelters and in street locations.

SOURCES:
1   Burnam, M. A. Estimation of the number of homeless and mentally ill persons in three California counties. In, Tauber, C. (ed.). Conference Proceedings for Enumerating Homeless Persons: Methods and Data Needs. U.S. Bureau of theCensus, March 1991.
2   Shelter Partnership, Inc., The number of homeless people in Los Angeles City and County, July 1990 to June 1991, May 1992.
3   First, Richard. Draft report of NIMH Ohio rural study. Table 3.2.
4   Lee, Barrett, Homelessness in Tennessee, p. 181, in Momeni, J. (ed.). Homelessness in The United States.
5. Comprehensive Homeless Assistance Plan, 1987, cited in Momeni, J. (ed.) Homelessness in The United States.
6   Kovisto, in Momeni, J. (ed.). In, Momeni, J. (ed.). Homelessness in The United States, p. 63.
7   Timmer & Knotterus. In, Momeni, J. (ed.). Homelessness in The United States. p. 55.
8   Executive Office of Human Services, Commonwealth of Massachusetts. (1990). Compre-hensive Homeless Assistance Plan, Winter 1991-1992.
9   Banzer, 1987. Cites U.S. Conference of Mayors, 1986a. In Momeni, J. (ed.). Homelessness in the United States.
10 This projection for the state is less than that for the subset of counties since a number of counties had negative projections. Lee, Barrett, Homelessness in Tennessee, in Momeni, J. (ed.). Homelessness in The United States
11 Baker, S.G. and D.A. Snow. Homelessness in Texas: Estimates of Population Size and Demographic Composition. In, Momeni, J. (ed.). Homelessness in the United States.
12 Maurin, J. and L.S. Russell. 1987. Homelessness in Utah: Utah Homeless Survey Final Report. Salt Lake City Utah: The Task For Force for Appropriate Treatment of the Homeless Mentally Ill (Unpublished Report).
13 Bromlesy, B.B., D. M. Johnson, D. Hartman, and A. L. Ruffin. Homelessness in Virginia: Dimensions of the Problem and the Public Reaction. In, Momeni, J. (ed.). Homelessness in the United States.
14 Burt, M. R. Developing the estimate of 500,000-600,000 homeless people in the United States in 1987. In, Tauber, C., (eds.). Conference Proceedings for Enumeration Homeless Persons: Methods and Data Needs. Bureau of the Census. March 1991.
15 Jencks, Christopher, The Homeless, Cambridge: Harvard University Press, 1994.
16 National Alliance to End Homelessness, cited in Institute of Medicine. (1988). Homelessness, Health, and Human Needs, Washington DC: Academic Press, pp. 3-4.
17 Robert, P. (March 1, 1988). Data are elusive on the homeless. New York Times.

McKinney funding, which is specifically directed to the homeless, did have a small negative correlation, suggesting that it had an impact in reducing the rate of homelessness.

Finally, indicators of housing availability and affordability collectively accounted for about a seventh (14.1%) of the variation in homeless levels. The largest impact, the percent of occupied units rented, accounted for about 4.0% of the variation in rates, but probably reflected merely the greater propensity of homeless to gravitate to affordable areas with more rentals versus privately owned homes. It is also in these areas that the ratio of housing costs to income is greatest, reflecting conditions of unaffordability. Unexpectedly, the higher the median gross rent, the fewer the homeless. Similarly, this may very well reflect the tendency of homeless individuals to gravitate to areas with relatively low rents. In contrast, there is the finding that vacancy rates for small units, those with 0-1 bedrooms, especially those charging under $250 a month, tend to reduce the homeless rates. In these specific areas, at risk individuals may be better able to fend off homelessness, and homeless individuals may be able to find rentable units. Finally, the argument that rent control causes housing costs to skyrocket, leading to homelessness, finds some nominal support here, as the presence of rent control laws is positively associated with

homeless rates, accounting for just over one percent (1.1%) of the variation in homeless rates throughout the nation. Such a nominal effect is not unexpected, considering the very small proportion of counties which have any such laws, or any towns or cities with rent control.

The Prediction Model

One of the final steps in model development is the trimming of all variables which do not add meaningfully to the model. What resulted from this process is a dramatically reduced model which consisted of only three predictor variables--density, service sector employment, and McKinney funding--and one methodological variable, rate of sites enumerated, which accounted for almost 80% of the variation ($R^2 =$

0.799) of the homeless rates. This is a model which incorporated not only the systematic error, as represented by rate of sites, but also random error, and in addition, it used information regarding the means of each of the variables so as to enable the computation of figures referred to as intercepts, which are required for any

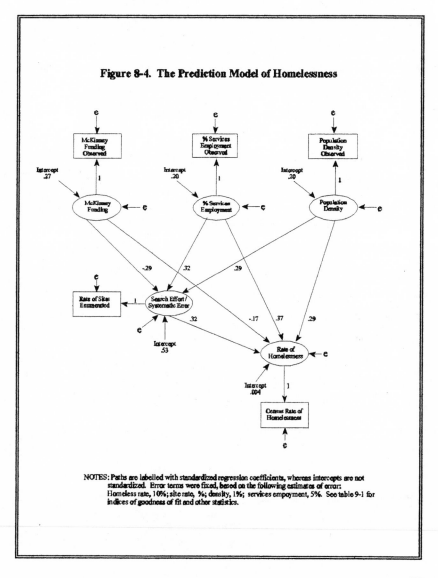

Figure 8-4. The Prediction Model of Homelessness

NOTES: Paths are labelled with standardized regression coefficients, whereas intercepts are not standardized. Error terms were fixed, based on the following estimates of error: Homeless rate, 10%; site rate, 9%; density, 1%; services empoyment, 5%. See table 9-1 for indices of goodness of fit and other statistics.

projections from the model. Although the model does not account for as much of the variation in the homeless rates (80% versus 97%) as the expanded model, the greater parsimony of the model makes it considerably more feasible to use with updated information to estimate or project new rates, as well as reducing the 'noise' which results from minor uninterpretable correlations which happen as a result of random measurement or sampling error. The disadvantage of the prediction model is that the more generalized variables and correlations do not permit as in depth a view of forces leading to homelessness. For this reason, both models are being presented in this chapter. This final, prediction model was developed by selecting the most important predictors, based on the previous analysis, and then by further reducing them one at a time until all remaining predictors and specified relationships were significant. And at that point repeated efforts were made to add variables at alternative points, but none of the other variables in the expanded model improved the model. What is presented here is the strongest model which could be identified after such a lengthy process of variable elimination and respecification.

Figure 8-4 presents the conceptual structure of the resulting model. It is based not only on the premise that each of the variables is an imperfect representation of a latent variable it is intended to measure, but also that systematic error--the differential search effort--both influences which is eventually found, and in turn, is influenced by the demographic and economic conditions of the various parts of the nation. Differential search efforts, in and of themselves, are insufficient to conclude systematic error since the Census Bureau may have had good reason to believe more homeless people would be found at given locations, and thus, justified in assigning more sites and staff to certain locales. For that reason, it was assumed necessary to control for some of the same kinds of conditions, such as urbanization or history of homeless programs, that the Census Bureau would have had data on and possibly used in assigning staff.[698] Thus, paths were tested for each of the predictors to the

---

[698] Inquiries were made of the Census Bureau about the basis for these decisions, but the researcher was informed that this information could not be released except through a lengthy

search effort variables, and each of these was confirmed to be important. Whether or urbanization or other similar variables were intentionally used by the Census Bureau is immaterial; these variables would be expected to be correlated with variables used by the Census Bureau. Controls for such conditions do indeed "explain" some of the differential search efforts, however, their effects are not explained away, as the correlation with the results of the Census are reduced, but not eliminated. In addition, tests were made for the possibility of a two-way relationship between the homeless and the enumeration rates, and though significant, in the end it only served to weaken the model. This was based on the premise that informal and preliminary reports on the actual levels of homelessness served to influence the search effort, for example, through the preliminary survey. [699]

In the prediction model, the single most critical predictor variable was the proportion of the county's population employed in the services sector, and this accounted for over a quarter (25.5%) of the variation in the homeless rates; for each standard unit of change in percentage of services employment, there was about two-fifths (0.37) unit change in the homeless rate. Why services employment would be so deleterious for the problem of homelessness is unclear, but since services positions usually require at least a high school diploma, and whether professional or semi-skilled, contact with the public, it is clear that persons with little education and behavioral disabilities will be especially affected. Likewise, according to Census Bureau surveys these positions are disproportionately filled through temporary-- 'temping'--means. The resulting instability and competitiveness for marginal employment possibilities, no doubt, represent particularly detrimental conditions for those with marginal educational preparation, a group marked by substantial levels of disability. In addition, those employed in the services sector have themselves a

---

Freedom of Information request, similar to the manner in which data had previously been obtained on the survey regarding the site enumeration process.

[699] This possibility was also tested through preliminary correlations with the rate of governmental response to the preliminary survey, and while the bivariate analyses indicated an effect, it quickly disappears when multivariate controls are used.

somewhat higher than average level of mental disability.[700]

That population density, a key indicator of urbanization, should be the second most important predictor, accounting for almost a fifth (18.2%) of the variation in the homeless rates, should come as no surprise. Much of the public's experience of the homeless comes from the streets of major cities such as New York, Washington, DC, and Los Angeles. For each standard unit change in population density, there was almost a third (0.29) unit change in the level of homelessness. It can now be said with some confidence that the much higher rates of homelessness found in urban areas are not merely a reflection of the nominal search efforts in rural areas. Indeed, part of the differential rates and the resulting correlation are explained away through such statistical controls, but not entirely. Thus, it is clear that something about the most highly urbanized areas directly contributes to homelessness. The preliminary analyses suggested that minorities, young adults, men, and single people are most at risk, especially those with minimal education and family ties. Whether it is the increasing stratification, anomie, or economic competitiveness, it is apparent that many from these groups become singled out and ultimately extruded from whatever communities they might have initially been connected with. A missing ingredient, for which it has not been possible to statistically model, may be cultural changes which take place above a given population density threshold, ones which emphasize independence, meritocracy, 'survival of the fittest', and the traditional distinction between the deserving and undeserving poor.

Together urbanization and servicetization account for over more than two-fifths (43.7%) of the variation in homeless rates, suggesting that this combination of conditions is particularly dangerous for the populations identified earlier--minorities, men, young adults, uneducated, and single people. The one variable in the model for which it is possible to impact on is the level of McKinney funding, and this accounted for just over a tenth (10.4%) of the variations in homelessness in the predicted

---

[700] This is based on preliminary findings from the author's analysis of epidemological data from the 1989 National Health Interview Survey (Mental Health Supplement).

direction: For each standard unit increase in funding, there was a decrease of about a sixth in a standard unit of the rate of homelessness. Unfortunately, it is is not possible to identify which of the many McKinney programs has made the most difference, but it is no doubt the continued support for transitional programs to move homeless from shelters, as well as adaptations in mainstream programs, which may be making a difference.

Finally, it should be noted that just over a quarter (25.7%) of the variation in homeless rates can be accounted for by the simple fact that the Census Bureau looked harder some places than others, even after the rational component of this differential search effort is taken into account. And specifically, the model supports the conclusion that the Census Bureau looked a lot less in non-dense, rural areas than the data would support. A lot of these were areas for which the Bureau did not get a response back from their preliminary planning survey, or for which the responding officials did not know of any likely sites for enumeration. In future efforts, considerably more care will be needed in these preliminary planning efforts to base the deployment of enumerators on statistical studies such as this one, with provisions for substantial variations from the predicted levels. A majority of the problems identified in the S-Night enumeration ultimately boil down to the problem of too many sites and homeless persons for too few enumerators.

Model Fit and Testing

The prediction model also fits the data well, explaining about 80% of the variation in the observed homeless rates, and 75% in the actual or latent levels. Of ten indices of goodness of fit, only one suggests a lack of fit, and that is the χ^2 probability level of 0.000, indicating a very high probability that the actual sample and the covariance matrices implied by the model do not come from the same population.[701] The model was also cross-validated using the ECVI index which

---

[701] However, it is generally agreed that such probability levels are only appropriate for samples up to 300 to 500, and that beyond this level, true models will often be inappropriately

permits a comparison of the ability of two similar models to pass the split-half cross validation test, and this was found to be 0.02, smaller than that of the two prior models for which this index could be computed (see appendix 2, table A2-2).

An examination of residuals permits identifying particular areas where the model fits or fails to fit the data. The first type of residual examined were those representing the differences between the actual covariances between the various variables and the covariances implied by the model, some of which are set to zero. An average of this is reflected by the standardized root mean square residual which is only 0.068, well within acceptable limits. The median was 0.0091, with the residuals ranging from -0.005 to 0.172.

Perhaps a more important type of residual involves the differences between the actual value predicted for each county for the homeless rate, and the observed Census rate figure. While a positive residual indicates a prediction which is too high, a negative one reflects a low prediction. When these are converted into standardized residuals, they can be broken down and mapped. While over four-fifths (83.4%) of the counties had predictions which were plus or minus 0.5 standard units from their actual values, over half (56.5%) were within 0.25 standard units, but only a ninth (11.5%) were within 0.05 units. Figure 8-5 plots these residuals on a map of the United States, and this indicates that the model was high in the North Central area, as well as the South Atlantic, it was low in New England, East South Central, and the Pacific regions. On the whole, the model over-predicted in the least urbanized areas, and under predicted the rates in the most urbanized areas, suggesting that the differential between these areas may not be as great as suspected (see table 8-3). It is, thus, clear that the computed model produces estimates which approximately reproduce the observed rates, but not without considerable variation.

---

rejected. This interpretation is supported by the fact that most of the other indices, such as the AGFI, partly correct for sample size, and in doing, so clearly support the acceptance of the model. Alternatively, the same model was tested, as recommended by L. Hayduk, with a sample size specified as 200, and this resulted in a highly significant (p<.05) probability level for the χ^2.

Table 8-3. WLS Regression Coefficients and Goodness of Fit Indices for The Prediction 0Model

Predictor	Unstandardized		Standardized		
	Direct	Indirect	Direct	Indirect	Total
Population Density	0.06	0.02	0.29	0.09	0.38
Percentage Employment in Services	0.38	0.10	0.38	0.10	0.48
McKinney Funding	-0.10	-0.06	-0.17	-0.09	-0.26
Rate of Enumeration Sites per 10,000	0.04	---	0.32	---	0.32

INDICES OF GOODNESS OF FIT	
χ^2, with 3 degrees of freedom	26.0; p = 0.000
Root mean square error of approximation (RMSEA)	0.062
Expected Cross Validation Index (ECVI, Saturated Model: 0.00955; Independence Model: 7.107)	0.020
Standardized Root Mean Square Residual	0.068
Goodness of Fit (GFI)	0.988
Adjusted Goodness of Fit (AGFI)	0.910
Parsimony GFI (PGFI)	0.132
Stability Index (SI)	0.002
Comparative Fit Index (CFI)	0.999
R^2 for Rate of Homelessness	0.800

NOTES: All direct and indirect effects are highly significant, below the .01 level.

How much of this variation is error on the part of the model, the observed rates, or some combination is unknown.

A final test of the model involved a comparison of rates from the model--after enumeration error is adjusted for--with the results of independently conducted estimates and studies from the same period. Instead of using the observed rate of enumerators, the adjusted estimates are based on the assumption that had the Census

299

Bureau deployed enumerators to sufficient sites such that there would be no evidence of enumeration error, they would have obtained accurate counts. This level, the reader may recall, is a type of saturation point where additional search efforts would not make any difference in the results, and was computed from the data to be 2.9 sites for each 10,000 persons. Estimates from entering the 2.9 figure into the model and recomputing the predicted rates are summarized in table 8-4, in the column "Adjusted Model Estimate". A comparison of the independent and adjusted model rates suggests considerable variation, but nonetheless confirms that impression given by the residuals. When subnational areas are considered, there is considerable variation characterized by over-prediction in the rural areas and under-prediction in the urban areas. The last part of table 8-4 compares national estimates with those generated by the model. With the exception of the Census Bureau's 240 thousand figure, all the other figures range from 324 to 735 thousand, around the 479 thousand predicted by the model, adjusted for enumeration error.

This research, thus, supports and strengthens previous estimates of approximately a half million persons who are literally homeless during the 1990 period. It should be noted that each of the independent studies and estimates was based on different definitions of homelessness and methodologies, and for this reason alone there would be considerable variation around any actual rate as this study has attempted to estimate. Figure 8-6 presents the adjusted model estimates of homeless rates for 1990 on a map of the United States. In contrast to Figure 8-4, the map indicates a considerably greater spread of homeless persons throughout the nation, but still with major concentrations in the Northeast, Florida, and Pacific areas of the nation. Just as there are considerably fewer areas with extremely high rates, there are only a few scattered counties with rates in the 3 to 7 per 10,000 level, and none below this. The vast majority of counties are split between the 7-12 and 12-16 homeless rate categories.

Table 8-4. Comparison of Census, Model, and Adjusted Model Rates of Homelessness, By Region and Urbanization (per 10,000 Population)

	N	1990			1995	
		Census Rate	Model Rate	Adj.Model Rate	Projected Rate	Homeless Population
REGION						
New England	67	10.2	9.2	18.7	12.8	16,919
Middle Atlantic	150	16.9	16.7	25.5	23.3	87,418
East North Central	437	5.7	7.7	17.8	12.8	53,581
West North Central	618	5.3	6.7	17.6	13.7	24,108
South Atlantic	591	7.4	8.4	18.6	14.4	62,675
East South Central	364	4.4	3.9	14.9	9.9	15,094
West South Central	470	5.9	5.7	16.3	13.2	35,256
Mountain	281	9.5	9.3	18.8	15.4	21,000
Pacific	163	16.0	13.3	20.4	17.1	67,029
URBANIZATION						
0%	2,486	2.8	3.2	14.2	10.1	58,988
1-19%	116	4.4	3.1	14.1	10.0	8,663
20-39%	114	6.0	5.6	16.1	11.8	17,970
40-59%	140	7.6	6.3	16.9	12.9	29,647
60-79%	127	8.4	8.9	19.0	15.2	52,509
80-99%	109	11.1	11.7	20.6	16.9	129,849
100%	49	24.7	23.8	30.1	26.8	85,453
NATION	3,141	9.7	9.7	19.3	15.4	383,079

Standardized Residuals of
Predicted & Actual Rates

	Over .5	(127)
	.25 - .50	(230)
	.05 - .25	(512)
	-.05 - .05	(360)
	-.25 - .25	(902)
	-.50 - -.25	(583)
	Under -.5	(427)

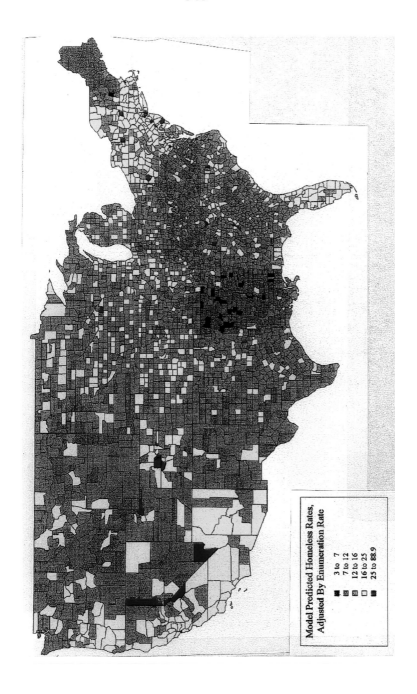

Model Predicted Homeless Rates,
Adjusted By Enumeration Rate

3 to 7
7 to 12
12 to 16
16 to 25
25 to 88.9

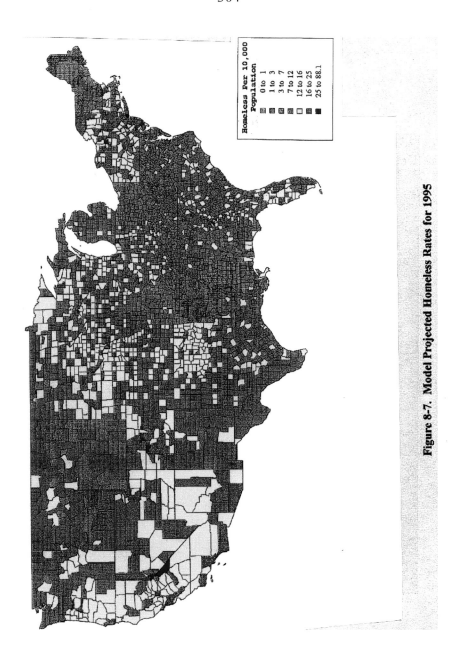

Figure 8-7. Model Projected Homeless Rates for 1995

1995 Model Projections

One of the advantages of modeling social problems such as homelessness is that updated estimates can be obtained by entering current data, and recomputing the predicted values from the model. For this reason, updated population estimates were obtained for each county for 1995. In addition, projections of services employment were computed, based on 1979 and 1989 data, and although 1995 McKinney expenditure amounts were not available for each state, a total was available. State estimates for the proportion for 1995 were based on 1992 and 1993 data, applied to the 1995 total. Finally, the 2.9 site enumeration rate was also used as a correction for the inadequate enumeration efforts made by the Census Bureau in most areas of the nation. While population and services employment continued to rise during this five year period, they did so only nominally, thus their effect would not be expected to be dramatic. At the same time, there were dramatic increases in McKinney Funding, from a total of approximately $581 million in 1989 to $1.495 billion in 1995,[702] a 157% increase; thus, clear declines in homelessness might be expected during this period.

In fact, the model projects 383,079 homeless persons in 1995, a decline of 20% in the five years, from 479,993 in 1990. This decline echoes that estimated by Jenck for the 1987/1988 to 1990 period, from 402,000 to 324,000, also about 20%,[703] as well as an analysis of 1987 to 1992 shelter data in Massachusetts. Figure 8-7 maps these new rates, suggesting a spreading out of the levels of homelessness throughout the nation. This impression is supported by a breakdown of the rates in table 8-4, which indicates that the most urbanized areas have a 26.8 rate, compared with 10.1 in the completely rural areas, or by a factor of 2.7, considerably less than the 8.8 in the actual S-Night rates. Still, the highest rates are found in the Middle Atlantic

---

[702]   The 1995 total was provided by phone, by the Interagency Council for the Homeless, whereas the 1989 figure represents one fourth of the 1987/1991 total from, Interagency Council for the Homeless, "Federal Progress Toward Ending Homelessness," Sept. 1992, p.38.

[703]   Jencks, Christopher. The Homeless, p. 17.

(23.3) (including Washington, D.C.) and the Pacific regions (17.1), and the lowest in the East South Central (9.9) region, including Louisiana, Mississppii. Although there was an average of a 20% decline in the number of homeless persons during the five year period, there was considerably variation throughout the nation and this is reflected in figure 8-8 which maps these changes. Those states with the smallest declines include New York, New Jersey, Minnesota, Oklahoma, and South Carolina, while those with the most dramatic declines, of over 35%, include northern New England, Michigan and Ohio, the South East Central area, and the northern Pacific and Mountain states.[704]

The Interdependency Model Revisited

In the first chapter, it was hypothesized that the most critical interdependency pertinent to homelessness involved the fit between the capabilities of an area's workforce and the structure of available economic opportunities. Only limited support was found for this hypothesis. In the explanatory model, statistically significant roles were found for both indicators of capabilities and disabilities, as well as indicators of economic opportunities. However, in the preliminary analyses, a minimal impact was found for the ratio of number of non-high school graduates and the availability of low- and semi-skilled jobs. In the final model, none of the disability indicators could be retained, whereas servicetization, an indicator of type of economic opportunity, proved to play a major role. Rather than disability, other conditions play a much more important role, such as urbanization, racial minority status, family supports, to mention a few. While there is little evidence that the major disabilities characteristic of many homeless persons are primarily a result of the homeless experience, with the exception of some medical and minor legal problems, they are more likely the result of the pre-homeless, probably adolescent and young adult, careers of persons for

---

[704] Given the strong impact of McKinney expenditures, which are used as a state-level rate variable and assigned equally to all counties within each state, the 1995 rates, especially the change levels clearly evidence state variations in contrast to intra-state county variations.

306

whom the aforementioned demographic, economic, and family conditions intermingle. Certainly, there is some level of preexisting disability which originates earlier in childhood or before which contributes to the later careers of a small minority of the homeless, and this is supported by the nominal correlations found between these indicators and homelessness.

Unexpectedly, indicators of employment and unemployment were found to have almost no impact, and this is similar to findings from previous correlational studies. What was found was that high services employment, as well as few unskilled or semi-skilled positions, contributed almost all the economic impact on homelessness. The impact of few low-skill positions is easily interpretable, given the marginal educational and work histories that homeless persons are known to have. However, this impact was very weak. Services jobs, most often found in urban areas, appear to have had multiply damaging impacts on homeless levels, possibly through their educational requirements, lack of employment stability, requirement for interpersonal skills for interacting with the public, and possibly even, relatively higher rates of mental illness among this population.

Contrary to previous speculation on the part of this researcher and others, de-industrialization proved to have had only a nominal impact on homeless levels. This is possibly due to the ability of many displaced workers to take lower paying services positions--often in very different locales--thereby, compromising the careers of new less skilled workers with a high school degree or less.

Some, but not all, of the demographic conditions which were hypothesized in chapter 1 to aggravate the network of critically interdependent relationships were found to be salient. Urbanization and racial minority status have no doubt been the most influential risk factors. Some evidence in preliminary analyses was found to support the notion that being male and a young adult also places individuals at slightly higher risk. However, this could not be confirmed in the multivariate analyses. It was hypothesized by both this researcher and others that the presense of large baby boom cohorts would have had an adverse impact on homeless levels, but if any relationship can be said to exist, it is in the opposite direction. Furthermore, it was hypothesized that in areas with relatively larger populations of older adults, indicating the advancing "epidemiological transition", homelessness would be increased due to a diversion of resources to the elderly population, away from young adults. Again, there is no support for this hypothesis in the current data, especially since it was found that larger elderly populations are instead associated with reduced homelessness, perhaps due to the relatively reduced number of younger people at risk for homelessness. The only other demographic condition found to aggravate the risk of homelessness is population growth, but only to a nominal degree.

Although in the preliminary analyses the proportion of one person households and those headed by females were found to be strongly associated with homeless levels, this apparent impact not only dissappears but is reversed when a full set of statistical controls are used. There are many reasons to expect such a positive relationship, such as the fewer social supports available to these groups, as well as the stress put on the housing market through reduced per unit occupancy. One possible explanation for the negative relationship found is that there may be more opportunities for doubling up among single individuals and single parent families than in areas with many two parent families. Nonetheless, family fragmentation as reflected by the rate of divorced, separated, or widowed persons was found to be associated with the homeless levels. A family breakup, when combined with marginal educational and career preparation, especially among minorities in major urban areas with an unstable and competitive services economy, may be one of the events precipitating eventual homelessness.

Given the minimal impact of rates personal disabilities in the general population on levels of homelessness, it is not unexpected that institutional supports and services directed at disabled populations would also have a minimal impact. It was also found that part of the marginal contribution of services to reducing homelessness is, in part, a reflection of the linear model which was used in the multivariate analyses. It was found in bivariate analyses of the impact of single service indicators on homelessness that non-linear models better described these relationships, also producing more interpretable findings (see chapter 6). Specifically, they revealed that often at low levels of service provision the relationship is often positive--indicating an attraction of service providers and recipients, creating areas of pronounced need--whereas when service provision reaches a given threshold, the relationship often becomes statistically negative, indicating that the services may be taking effect in reducing the number of persons with the designated problem (and perhaps also some "creaming"). In any case, incorporating non-linear relationships such as these into multivariate statistical models is often not possible as the number and complexity of variables quickly multiplies to unmanageable levels, as was the case in these efforts.

The analysis of the national data clearly supports the popular notion that both housing affordability and availability are important in explaining contemporary homelessness, but not nearly to the extent that many advocates would have us believe. Difficulties in accessing housing is one of the final, aggravating causes to homelessness for many, but it is a reality which is most pertinent to those who simultaneously lack the economic capabilities to generate income, as well as sufficient family and institutional supports. For this reason, much--but not all--of the apparent association of indicators of housing market conditions with homelessness dissappears when economic, primary, and secondary social supports are controlled for.

In summary, the results of the modeling efforts have only partially supported the Social Interdependency Model presented in chapter 1. It has largely confirmed that all major components of the model clearly have a direct impact in accounting for variations in homeless levels, and that collectively, they substantially account for these variations. However, in the case of indicators of disability and institutional supports, the impact is modest.

The exact structure of these relationships remains elusive, as the hypothesized flow of influences from the demographic, to the disability and economic conditions, and finally, as modified by family, institutional, and housing supports, could not be confirmed or disconfirmed. The model advanced in chapter 1 remains a highly simplified conceptual model, support for which was not forthcoming from the available data. Nonetheless, the lack of confirmation for such a conceptually satisfying structural model does not preclude either a detailed explanatory model, which simply compares the relative strength of the various predictors in accounting for levels of homelessness, or a simplied predictive model, which highlights only the most powerful forces and has some usefulness in estimating levels of homelessness.

Chapter IX
STRATEGIES FOR ENDING HOMELESSNESS

In the first chapter it was pointed out that homelessness involves more than the lack of a physical domicile, but also the lack of sufficient community ties to assure that a physical residence will constitute a home. If this is true, then any plan for ending homelessness must provide for the growth and preservation of the interdependent social and economic relationships which constitute a network of community ties. The plan will need to effectively and simultaneously confront the emergency and other service needs of those who currently are homeless, at the same time as it supports those who are at risk of expulsion from their homes and communities. In addition, it should be a strategy which is politically and economically feasible, consistent with Americans' sense of independence and work ethic, as well as our incremental and often decentralized approach to policy-making.

Since the early 1980s, a substantial literature has accumulated on homelessness, and in the first part of this chapter, the highlights of these recommended strategies and programs will be reviewed. Unfortunately, consideration of strategy is too often tacked on to articles or books as concluding afterthoughts, with few workable strategies or programs recommended and almost no meaningful specification. Or else, those more radically inclined recommend everything 'and the kitchen sink', expecting their readers to go away inspired to rebuild American society. Nonetheless, the literature does contain a range of workable ideas which I will attempt to build on in the second half of the chapter with my own recommendations.

The plan which I will advance in the latter part of this chapter is a social development strategy, one based on the interdependency model, and this involves the concerted linkage of competency-building and community-building interventions, of

311

targeted linkages of emergency responses to the homeless with the introduction of broader social insurance and mutual support initiatives designed for incremental universalization. The focus of the emergency response would be shifted from the homeless shelter to community lodges--somewhat like New York's Fountain House for the seriously mentally ill--and these would be carefully linked through the basic three stage--but multipath--service model to actual job, housing, income, and other ongoing community supports.

A Review of Current and Proposed Strategies

After reviewing the current shelter-based service system for homeless persons, this section will consider a range of broader, often long-term recommendations regarding such diverse areas as education, jobs, income maintenance, housing, and direct services. Finally, it will examine specific types of linkages, as well as legal, political, and administrative strategies for implementing them.

Current System. The current system emerged out of a broad-based local, often private and sectarian, response to the plight of the homeless during the 1980s. This consisted of a proliferation of emergency shelters, soup kitchens, and related concrete services. By 1988 there were 5,400 shelters, with an estimated 180,000 beds out of 275,000 available being slept in on a typical night.[705] The Reagan Administration assumed a minimalist, hands-off stance toward the glaring spectacle of homelessness, preferring a modest coordinative role in helping federal and local agencies to work sensibly together. The primary response was the Stewart B. McKinney Homeless Assistance Act, signed into law on July 22, 1987 (P.L. 100-77), and then reauthorized in November 1988 (P.L. 100-718). The effect of this bill was to establish the Interagency Council on Homeless to coordinate, monitor, and improve the federal response. The Department of Housing and Urban Development serves as the lead agency of a 15-agency council. Part of the initiative also establishes an

---

[705]   Gregg Barak.   (1991). Gimme Shelter: A Social History of Homelessness in Contemporary America New York: Praeger.

emergency Food and Shelter Program, with both national and local boards (P.L. 100-6). A range of grant and demonstration programs are authorized for emergency shelters, primary health services, mental health services, education of homeless children, and job training. In addition the food stamp program was improved.[706] In total, the act contains 17 subprograms, roughly corresponding to each of the member federal agencies.[707]

While the bulk of the McKinney Program's resources have gone into emergency services, some of the funds have been spent on programs aimed at inducing mainstream social, health, mental health services to adapt their services to the needs of homeless individuals. These are typically isolated demonstration programs, for instance, the stationing of mental health case managers in shelters, for which there is scant hard evidence of effectiveness. Nonetheless, the results of the analysis presented in this book and summarized in chapter 8, suggests that the extent of assistance to states from the program has an impact in minimizing the relative size of homeless populations, something that can not be said for most mainstream service programs. In short, while the McKinney program largely preserves and supports the current shelter-based emergency response to the homeless, it has also sought to broaden this response to include some transitional services.

Positions on Sheltering. Commentators on homelessness typically take either of two stances toward the current shelter-based system. A scant few argue that shelters should be improved. While Peter Rossi recommends that financial support for existing shelters should be maintained and improved,[708] Kozol emphasizes the need to offer decent and humane family shelters.[709] Others such as Mulroy and Lane and Baxter and Hopper qualify their recommendations for improving shelters with the

---

[706] Albert Gore. (August 1990). "Public Policy and the Homeless," American Psychologist, 45.

[707] Barak. Gimme Shelter.

[708] Peter Rossi. Down and Out in America, p. 181-211.

[709] Jonathan Kozol. (1988). Rachel and Her Children, New York: Fawcett Columbine.

suggestion that more services typically need to be made available to the residents.[710] Those who have argued that many homeless are merely down on their luck and lacking a home merely because of an eviction or layoff have promoted the right-to-shelter and other similar emergency responses.[711] Many commentators prefer not to consider the abysmal shelter conditions, pointing that the current system is merely a 'three hots and a cot' approach.[712] Instead they argue that we need to de-emphasize emergency measures,[713] or more to the point, that shelters as they currently exist contribute to the problem of homelessness.[714] Others who have pointed out the pernicious effects of shelters in maintaining the condition of homelessness include both conservatives such as Kondratis and liberals such as Barak. It is clear that the vast majority of shelters do not have the personnel, financial, and administrative supports to substantially and effectively move to a service-based model. In some respects, the ideology as well as the economic interests in sheltering may be antithetical to providing or linking with the longer term services needed to lift many persons out of homelessness.

Long-term Responses--General. The final success of any strategy may be a function of changes in public attitudes toward the homeless. Several commentators have pointed out the disciplinary functions that homeless persons serve in reminding many of the results of the failure of the work ethic.[715] While a conservative such as

---

[710] Elisabeth Mulroy and Terry Lane. (1993). "Housing affordability, stress and single mothers: Pathways to homelessness," Journal of Sociology and Social Welfare, 3, pp. 29-34; Ellen Baxter and Kim Hopper. (July 1982). "The New Mendicancy: Homeless in New York City", American Journal of Orthopsychiatry, 52(3), p. 406.

[711] See Whiteman. (Dec. 14, 1988). The Heritage Foundation, Rethinking Policy on Homelessness: A Conference Sponsored by the Heritage Foundation and The American Spectator.

[712] Ibid.

[713] Joel Blau. (1992). The Visible Poor, New York: Oxford University.

[714] Christopher Jencks. (1994). The Homeless, Cambridge: Harvard, "Reversing the Trend".

[715] Kim Hopper. (Fall 1983). "Homelessness: Reducing the Distance", New England Journal of Human Services iii (4), pp. 30-47; Mark Stern. (June 1984). "The emergence of the homeless as a public problem," Social Service Review, pp. 291-301.

Tucker rightfully links societal attitudes with oppressive land use policies--"If we are going to make room for each other in a more crowded America, we are all going to have to be a little more tolerant of each other's presence."[716]--other conservatives express their insights more sentimentally: the "homeless need love and acceptance, and a family."[717] Reducing stigma, no doubt, is critical. However, considering the many disciplinary functions homeless persons are recruited into serving, I would argue that transformed attitudes will more likely be a result of concrete interventions aimed at competency and community building than a strategy in and of itself for ending homelessness.

Many analysts insightfully identify key principles for designing a strategy for ending homelessness, but too often fail to embody them in specific programmatic recommendations. Westerfelt points out that preventing the first spell of homelessness should be a priority, yet the field has shown remarkably little imagination in assisting at-risk populations. In his sweeping recommendations, Blau cogently argues that "the homeless need what everyone else needs: housing, wages, and benefits sufficient to support themselves and accessible social services."[718] Similarly, Tessler and Dennis point out that the "Homeless give greater priority to material needs--housing, employment, and benefits, over mental health services."[719] Giving priority to material needs should not, however, mean neglect of various social and psychological needs. Less obvious is the need pointed out by Belcher and Toomey for a more structured environment for many homeless individuals,[720] as well as the finding from one study

---

[716] William Tucker. (1990). The Excluded Americans: Homelessness and Housing Policies Washington DC: Regnery Gateway, p. 349.

[717] See Steinbruck. (1988). Heritage Foundation.

[718] Blau. The Visible Poor, p. 180.

[719] Richard C. Tessler and Deborah L. Dennis. (Feb. 9, 1989). A synthesis of NIMH-funded research concerning persons who are homeless and mentally ill, Social and Demographic Research Insitute, U. of Mass., Amherst, MA 01003.

[720] John Belcher and Beverly G. Toomey. (Spring 1988). "Relationship between the deinstitutionalization model, psychaitric disability, and homelessness," Health and Social Work, 134 (2).

which showed lack of companionship to be the most commonly perceived need among homeless respondents.[721] Thus, programs which provide not only material support, but also appropriate structure and social support will most likely be effective in engaging their participants.

Other proposed principles for programming for the homeless include the obvious need for physical accessibility;[722] the need to base programs on consumer perception of need, as well as on what is known about the root causes of homelessness. Finally, the need for tailored, individualized interventions can not be over-emphasized,[723] especially when it comes to the delicate balance between providing concrete supports, establishing and maintaining contact, and linking persons with required service systems.[724]

Community-Building Strategies. Few commentators have considered the possibilities of community building as an intervention, even as a long-term response to homelessness. When they have, its meaning has wavered from improving neighborhood conditions, to developing self-help community organizations, or to upgrading existing secondary, institutional services. For problems of rural homelessness, Vissing argues for local responses involving diverse concerned parties coming together, creating community organizations, and systematically planning for the elimination of homelessness in their communities.[725] In contrast, Dear and Wolch, who are more concerned about the homeless who are found in the 'psychiatric ghettos'

---

[721] Lillisn Gelberg and Larence S. Linn. (May 1988). "Social and physical health of homeless adults previously treated for mental health problems," Hospital and Community Psychiatry, 39(5), p. 516.

[722] Whitman. (1988). Heritage Foundation.

[723] Mulroy and Lane, "Housing affordability..."; Kay Young McChresney. (1992). "Homeless Families: Four Patterns of Poverty," Chapter 19, p. 245 in Marjorie J. Robertson and Milton Greenblatt (eds.)(1992). Homelessness - A National Perspective, New York: Plenum Press.

[724] Richard J. First, Dee Roth, Bobbie Darden Arewa. (March-April 1988). "Homelessness: Understanding the Dimensions of the Problem for Minorities," Social Work, p. 124.

[725] Yvonne Vissing. (1996). Out of Sight, Out of Mind Lexington: U. of Kentucky Press.

of the major urban areas, recommend the development of "service hubs" in these areas: "Perhaps the best example of a potential service hub is the suburban shopping mall, with its extensive range of services and often good transportation links."[726] The proposal is reminiscent of the multi-service centers of the 1960s, and does little to address the range of cultural, organizational, and political barriers to service delivery. Rather it is over reliant on assuring geographic accessibility, which is usually not the main problem in the urban areas they are most concerned about. Beyond the urgent need for assuring the cultural, political, and physical infrastructures for communities, much of community-building must occur home-by-home, the essential building blocks of communities.

Educational Strategies. Despite the marginal education of most homeless persons, only a few analysts argue for educationally-oriented interventions. Belcher and DiBlasio are an exception, arguing for a range of programs including those which remedy unequal funding between school districts, increase access to summer programs, keep student-teacher ratios small, as well as detecting and preventing learning disabilities and other problems early.[727] Others who have sought to redirect existing education and training programs to the homeless include McChresney, as well as Vice President Gore.[728] For many, education reform appears to be a daunting, if not overwhelming task, with little immediate relevance to the homeless, but this is the case only when we consider the abstractions involved, rather than actual individuals and opportunities concerned.

Economic Strategies. Unlike educational strategies which seek to increase the *ability* of individuals to generate incomes, economic strategies often attempt this

---

[726] Michael J. Dear and Jennifer R. Wolch. (1990). "The homeless mentally ill should not be institutionalized," chapter 3.8, p. 144 in Lisa Orr, (ed.) (1990). The Homeless: Opposing Viewpoints (San Diego: Greenhaven), p. 74.

[727] John R. Belcher and Frederick A. DiBlasio. (1990). Helping the Homeless: Where Do We Go from Here? Lexington Books, p. 63.

[728] See Kay McChresney. (1992). "Homeless Families..."; Albert Gore. (1990). "Public policy and the homeless".

same goal through more direct means, either by increasing wages or by generating new jobs. In addition, economic strategies also include those which seek to alter the distribution of incomes, either through changes in the tax code or through income maintenance programs, to be discussed in a later section. A wide range of commentators, such as Blau, Burt, Belcher and DiBlasio, Hopper, all stress increasing incomes, but have only a few specific recommendations for doing so. Most notable is Blau's call for a raise in the minimum wage.[729] Most advocate additional employment and training programs,[730] and a few go so far as to call for full employment policies.[731] Recommendations for strategies of job creation range from increasing manufacturing jobs,[732] reducing the work week, using employment programs to develop the infrastructure,[733] improving worker conditions, including minimum wage,[734] and organizing day labor markets under public auspices to be used for enhancing the physical condition of communities.[735] This final recommendation of Rossi's is meant to be directed specifically to homeless individuals, who would be provided vouchers for hotels and restaurants for a half or full days work as they are capable.

Some commentators use the problem of homelessness to argue for a major

---

[729] Joel Blau. The Visible Poor. Martha Burt. (1992). Over the Edge New Yortk: Sage; Belcher & DiBlasio, Helping The Homeless; Kim Hopper, Ellen Baxter, Stuart Cox, Laurence Klein. (June 1982). One Year Later: the Homeless Poor in New York City, 1982. Community Service Society.

[730] Hopper, Baxter, Cox, and Klein. (June 1982). One Year Later...; Kay McChresney. (1992). "Homeless Families..."; Albert Gore. (1990). "Public policy and the homeless"; Burt, Over The Edge, p. 222; Marta Elliot and Lauren J. Krivo. (Feb. 1991). "Structural determinaants of homelessness in the United States," Social Problems, 38(1); Doug A. Timmer, et al, Paths to Homelessness, p. 180.

[731] George Thorman. (1988). Homeless Families, Springfield, IL: Charles C. Thomas; Blau, The Visible Poor, p. 182.

[732] Belcher & DiBlasio, Helping the Homeless.

[733] Timmer, et al., p. 177.

[734] Ibid., p. 176.

[735] Rossi, Down and Out in America, p. 181-211.

overall of the tax system, making it more progressive.[736] However, most advance delimited recommendations for revising the tax code to make it more difficult for U.S. corporations to relocate abroad,[737] easier to relocate to the central city,[738] and in general too expensive to engage in leveraged buyouts, corporate takeovers and mergers, rewarding those which invest in new equipment and work training.[739]

Income Maintenance Strategies. Although most analysts urge improvements in income maintenance benefits, only a few offer specific ideas about how this might best be accomplished. Several recommend restoring benefit levels to the 1970s levels,[740] whereas others also emphasize the broadening of eligibility criteria to include more individuals[741] and unemployed couples.[742] Some argue for an integrated, guaranteed national income or negative income tax,[743] and others urge that benefits more often be provided through vouchers for rent and food,[744] or for aid to families who support destitute and disabled members.[745] Probably the only way that it will be possible to develop an integrated income maintenance system, i.e. an negative income tax, that eliminates incentives for not working, is to initially target the benefits to the first two years of poverty, with exceptions for the disabled and the retired, after which cash benefits would be replaced with vouchers for necessities such as housing and food.

---

[736] Blau. The Visible Poor.

[737] Timmer, et al, 178; Belcher and DiBlasio, 1990.

[738] Belcher & DiBlasio.

[739] Ibid.

[740] Rossi, Down and Out in America; Jencks. The Homeless, p. 109.

[741] Burt, Over The Edge.

[742] McChresney, "Homeless families...".

[743] Thorman. "Homeless families; Blau. The Visible Poor, p. 183.

[744] Jencks. The Homeless.

[745] Rossi. Down and Out in America.

Service Models and Strategies. Occasionally scholars and advocates concerned with homelessness have promoted identifiable service models, or overall packaged approaches to organizing service delivery. Most of these are variations of the same three-stage model: While Hopper, Baxter, and Klein, drawing on ideas of Skano, divide shelter needs into three tiers--Tier 1, Basic Emergency Shelter; Tier II, Transitional accommodations; and Tier III, Long-term, supportive residences,[746] Kaufman advances a "continuum of services" model consisting of three phases: Phase 1, Emergency response; Phase 2, Transitional Phase; and Phase 3, Stabilization, i.e. supported housing.[747] Johnson builds on this model in her analysis of the range of shelters with both minimal and more comprehensive services, dividing them into three levels, each containing the preceding one: Level 1, Basic services; Level 2, Stabilization, including transportation, laundry, showers, medical and mental health care, referrals, entitlement assistance, and advocacy; and Level 3, Personal Growth, which also includes: case management, peer counseling, day care, life skills, employment counseling.[748] Several homeless advocates have argued for service models which combine the provision of concrete services with various behavioral health services, most commonly those involving mental health. Breakey, for instance, proposes that outreach, case management, direct clinical services, and housing constitute the essential elements of a service system for the mentally ill homeless.[749] Similarly, the American Psychiatric Association recommended a comprehensive integrated system of care for this same population, which would include: basic food and shelter provisions; supervised community housing; adequate comprehensive and

---

[746] Sakano, D. (Nov. 19, 1981). Testimony given at New York State Assembly Hearings, "Homeless New Yorkers: The Forgotten Among Us." cited in Hopper, Baxter, and Klein.

[747] Nancy Kaufman. (1986). "Homelessness: A Comprehensive Policy Approach". In Housing the Homeless. Jon Erickson and Charlemes Wilhelm (eds.). New Brunswick, NJ: Rutgers University Press.

[748] Alice Kay Kessler Johnson. (August 1990). Homeless Shelter Services in St. Louis. Dissertation, Washington University.

[749] William R. Breakey. (1991/1992). "Mental health services for homeless people," chapter 8, p. 101. in Robertson and Greenblatt, pp. 105-106.

accessible psychiatric and rehabilitation services and outreach; medical assessment and care; crisis services, such as medication and crisis housing; a system of coordination; general social services; and ongoing asylum. In addition, the group recommended the loosening of psychiatric commitment criteria to facilitate hospitalization when required.[750] Several studies have compared the effectiveness of more comprehensive case management systems--typically those which include community residences, day treatment programs, and intensive case management, with more traditional programs offering minimal services such as outpatient treatment or medication monitoring. These have typically found the former to be more effective in respect to a wide range of measures, including symptomatology, days homeless, and social functioning levels.[751] In another study, such community care was found to be substantially lower than that of hospital care for the less disabled patients, but greater than that of hospitalization for the most disabled.[752] It is clear that individuals who experience multiple disabilities usually require multiple and simultaneous services and supports, and thus, the extent to which these can be creatively packaged together, to complement rather than compete with one another, may be critical for their success.

Rather than arguing for particular service 'models', most analysts are content to advocate for individual services which they are particularly familiar with. Although few emphasize preventative services,[753] several authors promote early intervention services such as crisis intervention, outreach, and drop-in centers for the homeless. Perhaps one of the most promising modalities for crisis intervention and outreach is

---

[750] U.S., General Accounting Office. (April 9, 1985). Homelessness: A Complex Problem and The Federal Response.

[751] Karen Wletman, Lori Poveromo, Ralp Nofi. (May 1988). "Impact of community-based psychosocial treatment on clients' level of functioning," Hospital and Community Psychiatry, 39(5), p. 550; Gary A. Morse and Robert J. Calsyn. (1990). "Mental health and other human service needs of homeless people," chapter 10, p. 117 in Robertson and Greenblatt, 1992.

[752] Hafner, H. and Heiden, W. (1989). "Effectiveness and cost of community care for schizoprehenic patients", Hospital and Community Psychiatry, 40(1), p. 59.

[753] Belcher and DiBlasio. Helping the Homeless, p. 20.

that involving the mobile outreach van.[754] Significant numbers of seriously disabled individuals who avoid traditional clinical services can often be reached through low-demand settings such as drop-in centers and social clubs which address both basic concrete and social needs.[755] Such programs range in quality from smoking parlors with no attached services, to sophisticated self-help communities such as New York Fountain House which provide not only a range of services, but most important, develop a sense of competence and community among their members. The more successful programs of this kind which have a rehabilitation focus are often referred to as club houses, but sometimes suffer from insufficient linkages with formal professional services.

Examples of frequently needed transitional services include day treatment programs, conventional clinical services, residential treatment, and hospitalization. Only some of these programs have comprehensive rehabilitation components, most likely to be found in day programs, residential treatment, and sometimes, in intermediate term hospitalization. But even with intensive rehabilitation, many of these programs fail as transitional services, either because they provide inadequate discharge planning and follow-up, or because there are insufficient community supports available to their graduates. Those clients most likely to fail are typically those with multiple diagnoses, typically serious mental illness and substance abuse, and who have few community ties left. Many of these individuals require long-term residential or inpatient rehabilitation or sustaining care. One study found that as many as a fifth (21%) of the homeless were assessed as needing psychiatric hospitalization,[756] though in most areas, realistic estimates vary between 5% and

[754] Belcher & DiBlasio; Gelberg & Linn, p. 516; Slagg, 1994, p. 1140.

[755] Lawrence Appleby and Prakash N. Desai. (July 1985). "Documenting the relationship between homelessness and psychiatric hospitalization," Hospital and Community Psychiatry, 36 (7), p. 737; Tessler and Dennis; Belcher & DiBlasio; Whiteman. (1988). Heritage Foundation; Gary A. Morse and Robert J. Calsyn, "Mental health and other human service needs of homeless people," chapter 10, p. 117 in Robertson and Greenblatt.

[756] Nancy Butler Slagg, et al. (Nov. 1994). "A profile of clients served by a mobile outreach program for homeless mentally ill persons," Hospital and Community Psychiatry, 45 (11).p

15%.

Probably the most underserved subgroup of the homeless are substance abusers, both because of their denial and resistance to treatment, and the pervasive view that these people are among the most undeserving of the homeless. Few treatment agencies are equipped to offer comprehensive rehabilitative services to multiproblem homeless substance abusers.[757] Yet, model programs do exist, including ones in Minneapolis and Philadelphia, the cost of which range from $22,000 to $31,000 per year, per resident.[758] Even with the best programs there are substantial relapse rates, however Valliant suggests that we should develop the same attitude toward assisting the alcohol abuser that we use with other chronic diseases--even when we can not cure, we can provide the cure that provides the possibility of amelioration.[759]

While it is clear that the most pervasive entry point into existing services is at the emergency level, none of these models take into account the fact that the path from the homeless emergency to reintegration into the community will vary considerably for the various subgroups of homeless individuals, and that for some pervasive disabilities will preclude complete reintegration. Thus, for one person their path through the three tiers of reintegration--emergency response, stabilization, personal growth--may involve outpatient services and regular housing, for another person it may require intensive inpatient rehabilitation, followed by a day program, and an ongoing group home arrangement. Sloss points out that, "Until our approach to the crisis of homelessness moves from a shelter model of care to a home model, the destructive subculture of homelessness will not be eradicated and homeless people

---

1139.

[757] Brian Mavis, Keith Humphreys, and Bertram E. Stoffelmayr. (Dec. 1993). "Treatment needs and outcomes of two subtypes of homeless persons who are substance abusers," Hospital and Community Psychiatry, 44, (12), pp. 1185, in Mavis, Huymphreys, and Staffelmayr.

[758] Alice S. Baum and Donald W. Burnes. (1993). A Nation in Denial, Boulder, CO: Westview Press, p. 182.

[759] See Shandler and Shelpley, 1987.

will continue to live without stability and dignity." Through a Three-tier/Multipath model, it will be possible to systematically develop homes, and not merely residences, for as many homeless as feasible.

Housing Strategies. Since the defining feature of homelessness is the lack of a domicile, it should come as no surprise that the most widely promoted solutions involve directly impacting on housing affordability. Three goals typically underlie these recommendations: (i) the establishment of the right to housing;[760] (ii) increasing the variety of housing options available;[761] and most commonly, (iii) increasing the availability of low-income housing.[762] These goals are typically pursued primarily through either court action, the stimulation of housing construction, changes in zoning and other housing regulations, or the provision of housing subsidies.

Only a few analysts, such as Burt[763] and Blau,[764] recognize the need to stimulate new housing construction, as well as converting and rehabilitating existing units. This strategy is based on the premise that as more middle incomes units are made available at reasonable costs, even for purchase, then a reverse 'musical chairs' phenomenon will make additional units available to lower-income renters. It assumes that there is an overall shortage of units, however, this appears to be the case in only selected major metropolitan areas.

Proponents of reforms in zoning regulation often share the interest in stimulating new home construction, but they pin the problem on overly stringent regulations which prevent or discourage the building of low-income, multi-family rental units. One California builder eloquently described the situation:

---

[760] Michael H. Lang. (1989). Homelessness Amid Affluence: Structure and Paradox in the American Political Economy. New York: Praeger.

[761] Tessler & Dennis; Steinbruck, (1988). Heritage Foundation.

[762] Blau, The Visible Poor; Thorman, Homeless Families; Heritage Foundation; Elliot and Krivo, "Structural determinants..."; Janet M. Fitchen. (1992). "On the edge of homelessness: Rural poverty and housing insecurity," Rural Sociology, 57(2), pp. 173-193.

[763] Burt, Over The Edge, p. 221.

[764] Blau, The Visible Poor.

The artificial scarcity of buildable land is the biggest driving factor behind spiralling home costs...Constraints on density are a three to five times greater factor in driving up home costs than is the permit process. Its the old law of supply and demand at work. And the planners have drastically limited the supply of land with low-density zoning.[765]

City planners are accountable to the electorate, many of whom seek to preserve a sense of rural isolation in the midst of suburban sprawl. This often arises out of a Not-in-My-Back-Yard (NIMBY) stance towards people who are markedly different, effectively excluding low-income individuals from many suburbs, and concentrating them in the inner city and, to a lesser extent, in outlying rural areas. A range of analysts have promoted changes in such regulations, but to little avail due to the highly decentralized nature of town and city zoning regulations.[766] Some localities such as Orange County, California, have implemented linked development schemes where developers are asked to set aside 10% to 25% of units in their developments for low-income persons, in return for density bonuses, cost financing, or tax advantages.[767] Others have recommended that municipalities that exclude apartments or multi-family homes should compensate property owners and support the construction of multi-family housing in other communities as part of a 'fair share' formula.[768] Other forms of housing regulation have been more controversial, in particular, rent control which while seeking to preserve low-income housing, is seen by some as having the opposite effect, due mainly to the suppression of incentives for developers to build new units. Many conservatives such as Tucker argue for its elimination, whereas liberals, such as Belcher and DiBlasio recommend additional commissions be set up to control rents. What is needed are programs to attack the causes of tight housing markets, such as restrictive zoning regulations and the fragmentation of the family, which would then permit the phasing out of rent control

---

[765] Bob Reeder, quoted by Josepth Mehrten. (1990). "A national housing policy would harm the homeless," chapter 4.2, p. 156 in Lisa Orr.

[766] Mulroy & Lane. (1993); Vissing. (1996); Thorman. (1988); Tucker. (1990).

[767] Thorman. (1988).

[768] Tucker. (1990).

which, although it probably is not the primary cause of high rents, appears to aggravate the problem of unaffordability.

Clearly, the most commonly recommended housing strategy involves increasing the availability of vouchers or certificates for low-income renters, such as is provided through the Department of Housing and Urban Affair's Section 8 program.[769] While some recommend that such vouchers should be an entitlement, others argue that they should be targeted at only the very poorest individuals.[770] Others recommend adaptations of the current program, to make it easier for homeless to access these certificates,[771] to target younger unattached individuals,[772] or to make it possible for Section 8 certificates to also be used for housing purchase rather than rental only. Until more universal income support mechanisms are developed, there will be a continuing need for Section 8-like programs which can efficiently target housing assistance to low-income individuals. However, it is clear that considerable adaptations in this program will be needed to reach a sizeable proportion of the homeless.

A range of other housing strategies have been promoted which deserve mention. One involves the idea of providing supports to families who take friends and relatives in. While Shinn, Knickman, and Weitzman promote this approach,[773] Burt urges against it.[774] While it may not be wise for such supports to start immediately upon doubling up, making it easier for some evictions to take place, financial and

---

[769] Burt, Over The Edge; Hopper; Rossi, Down and Out in America; Beirne, Kenneth. (1990). "The government should not do more for the homeless," chapter 3.2, p. 100 in Lisa Orr; Gore, "Public policy..."; Tucker. (1990); Mulroy and Lane; Fitchen. (1992); Vissing. (1996); Belcher & DiBlasio; U.S. Conference of Mayors. (Nov. 1991). Mentally Ill and Homeless: A 22 City Survey.

[770] Burt, Over The Edge.

[771] Rossi, Down and Out in America.

[772] Ibid.

[773] Marybeth Shinn, James R. Knickman, and Beth C. Weitzman. (Nov. 1991). "Social relationships and vulnerability to becoming homeless among poor families," American Psychologist, p. 1180.

[774] Burt, Over The Edge.

services supports probably should begin with families who have been doubled up 2 to 3 months, so as to extend this period, and provide the necessary time and services for working out more permanent housing.

Many recommendations involve the need for the federal government to assume a strong role in assuming fair local housing laws and housing initiatives which do not unduly discriminate against low-income individuals. For example, the Heritage Foundation[775] recommends that the federal government should not permit local governments to undertake any urban redevelopment efforts with federal funds, such as those available through the Urban Development Action Grant Program, that substantially diminish low-income housing. Except for those who recommend more assisted housing and single residency occupancy (SROs) options, most housing strategies promoted do little to address the needs of that substantial subgroup of perhaps 20% to 40% of the homeless who are unable to manage traditional apartment rentals.

Linkages. The fragmentation of current supports and service for the homeless has been an ongoing problem, and this has involved either an unnecessary duplication of some services for which there is funding, as well as major gaps in services to those homeless with multiple disabilities and who do not neatly fall into the conventional service categories. Many analysts have urged the need for either a general integration of services and supports[776] or for the development of particular linkages, such as between services and housing or services and employment. However, few good ideas for accomplishing either of these goals have been forthcoming. Part of the problem involves a tension between the need for targeted services to the homeless--which has often meant unprofessional staff concerned mostly with emergency provisions, or on the other hand, the adaptation of mainstream and professional services. However, the

---

[775] The Heritage Foundation. (May 6, 1985). "A Strategy for Helping America's Homeless," The Backgrounder.

[776] Whitman. (1988). Heritage Foundation; Dattalo and Benda. (1991), p. 113; Tessler and Dennis; Thorman. (1988); Gelberg and Linn.

homeless are often not top priority when they must compete with more motivated and established client populations that are of greater interest to many professionals uncomfortable with outreach. There clearly needs to be a strong base of targeted services for the homeless, however, once such a base is established there is no reason that there should not be some shared programming with mainstream mental health, health, and social service providers.

There are three areas of linkage between concrete supports and services which are most typically identified as needed: housing and services; employment and housing; and criminal justice and services. The most commonly identified need involves linking housing options with services, either through the traditional group home option or supported housing, where services are provided but not by on-site staff. Clearly both of these housing models are needed, and it would be a mistake to attempt to support the most disabled among the homeless through supported housing, rather than group homes with at least some on-site staff.

Fitchen points out that a major problem is the lack of a spatial correlation in the distribution of low-cost housing vis-a-vis' employment opportunities, in particular, in rural areas.[777] Thus, it is clear that low-income housing construction and rental support programs need to be more effectively targeted to areas of expanding business, as well as providing relocation expenses for workers to take advantage of such employment and housing opportunities.

Finally, there is also a need to strengthen the linkage between services and the criminal justice system, not only by providing services in the context of existing jails and prisons, but also by effective diversionary programs to link homeless individuals with service providers as an alternative to incarceration or other punitive interventions. Fischer argues that, "Providing police with adequate training in mental health might reduce inappropriate arrests and help engage the homeless mentally ill

---

[777] Fitchen. (1992). "On the edge of homelessness...".

in treatment programs."[778]

Others focus instead on simply integrating existing service providers, or more specifically, mental health providers.[779] One suggested alternative is to centralize mental health care for the seriously mentally ill on either the federal level[780] or on the municipal level.[781] Both of these proposals ignore the historically central role that state mental health authorities have played in this field, and the considerable progress they have made in recent years in upgrading their service offerings.[782] It is clear as Shore and Cohen point out that, "A central authority with administrative, fiscal, and clinical responsibility for the chronically ill throughout [the city] can provide a full range of services and can ensure continuity of care,"[783] but who and how might best accomplish this must be considered as a function of the particular state and city involved.

Organizing Strategies. While most analysts are content to recommend one or several generic policies, such as improving the quality of shelters or increasing Section 8 vouchers, only a few have ventured to recommend political or other process strategies for implementing such policies. Vissing, for instance, urges greater efforts at grass-roots organizing in rural areas through the creation of local task forces, however Blau emphasizes extending coalitions between existing groups concerned with homelessness and the increasing income inequalities, the two classic strategies

---

[778] Pamela J. Fischer, (Jan. 1988). "Criminal activity among the homeless: A study of arrests in Baltimore," Hospital and Community Psychiatry, 39, (1), p. 51.

[779] Federal Progress Toward Ending Homelessness. (Sept. 1992). The 1991/1992 Annual Report of the Interagency Council on the Homeless, Washington DC; Tessler and Dennis; Miles F. Shore and Martin D. Cohen. (1992). "Homelessness and the Chronically Mentally Ill," Chapter 6, p. 67 in Robertson and Greenblatt, p. 74-75.

[780] Belcher and DiBlasio. Helping the Homeless.

[781] Shore and Cohen, pp. 74-75.

[782] Christopher G. Hudson, Jeffrey Salloway, and Yvonne Vissing. (1992). "The impact of state administrative practices on community mental health," Journal of Mental Health Administration and Policy, 19 (6), pp. 417-36.

[783] Shore and Cohen, "Homelessness and the chronically mentally ill ..."

in community organizing.[784] While Vissing is right to emphasize fresh grassroots efforts in rural areas, in urban areas a greater priority should be on enhancing the linkages between existing advocacy and related groups. Wright and Weber advise that the objects of such efforts should not be local welfare offices, but instead state legislatures which set the basic policies guiding these programs.[785] However, these efforts should not ignore the rule-making processes which state administrative agencies usually control, and although these go on independently of state legislatures, they often have more substantial impact than many of the general statutes promulgated by state legislatures.

Fabricant attempts to integrate several of these strategies in his recommended approach to organizing, which begins with case advocacy and stabilization, then moves on to class advocacy, and finally broader inter-coalition organizing efforts.[786] Case advocacy, when integrated with services directed toward stabilization, indeed is an excellent foundation for not only reintegrating homeless individuals into the mainstream community, but also for identifying and building policy or class advocacy initiatives. The linkages between case advocacy and policy advocacy is a delicate one which need to be nurtured through both professionals and agencies which are committed to learning from, systematically documenting, and building on the experience of individual homeless persons and their advocates.

Other commentators instead stress changing public attitudes toward the homeless as the essential foundation for needed changes. Ropers, for example, recommends that the President should declare homelessness a national emergency,[787]

---

[784] Vissing. (1996). Out of Sight, Out of Mind.

[785] James D. Wright and Eleanor Weber. (Aug. 1988). "Determinants of benefit-program participation among the urban homeless: results from a 16-city study," Evaluation Review, 12(4), p. 39.

[786] Michael Fabricant. (Fall 1986). "Creating survival services," Administration in Social Work, 10(3), p. 71.

[787] Richard H. Ropers. (1988). The Invisible Homeless: A New Urban Ecology, Human Sciences Press, p. 212.

noting that, "One of the first things that needs to be done is to correct public perceptions of the nature of the homeless population."[788] Ropers also stresses the use of legal strategies as a part of case advocacy, in particular, the establishment of the right to shelter, and in general, defining homelessness as a human rights issue. Both Ropers as well as Fabricant and Epstein review such efforts, mainly those in Los Angeles and New York, each concluding that despite the successes of the strategy, "the underlying conditions of homelessness can at best only be partially addressed by legal advocacy",[789] that the approach can not be regarded as a panacea. This reflects the experience of others in the mental health field where, although litigation has been successful in right-to-treatment cases, too often such cases backfire as the courts are ill-equipped to manage comprehensive changes in complex service systems without the willing cooperation of many other parties.

Still others look toward national efforts to end homelessness. Timmer and his colleagues urge a reversal of the federal and state abandonment of the major urban centers, through the use of a 'Marshall Plan' for rebuilding the cities.[790] This would include monies for the construction of new public housing, maintenance and rehabilitation of existing public housing, and "encouragement of not-for-profit, community based housing production, ownership, and management."[791] Timmer also urges the formation of regional governments, to force cities and suburbs to share income.[792] Others such as Lang reject this kind of strategy, warning that, "What we do not need is a Marshall Plan or another War-on-Poverty since both these approaches entail a return to flawed federal funding, locally implemented policies of

---

[788] Ibid., p. 211.

[789] Michael Fabricant and Irwin Epstein, "Legal and welfare rights advocacy: Complementary approaches in organizing on behalf of the homeless", Urban Review.

[790] Timmer, et al, Paths to Homelessness.

[791] Ibid., p. 182.

[792] Ibid., p. 178.

the past."[793] Instead, Lang urges a "commitment to a national policy of guaranteed social, economic, and civil rights and the implementation of those governmental programs necessary to secure their delivery."[794] While it is easy to advocate for comprehensive national policies, what is not so easy is to find specific means of introducing innocuous initiatives, which would then be allowed to incrementally grow into broad-based social insurance programs as new economic resources are generated and political support is nurtured. One such example would be the indexing of the minimum wage so that over perhaps five or ten years it would grow into a living wage, and form a basis for improving the income maintenance system. Such ideas might be the result of the work of a Council of Social Policy Advisors which would be in a position to make otherwise politically controversial recommendations. The recommendation for such a national council is an excellent one,[795] one which might initially be organized as a subcommittee of the Council of Economic Advisors, and later become more independent as it demonstrates its efficacy. While more decisive federal leadership is clearly needed if progress is to be made in respect to homelessness, this should not be interpreted to mean that the federal government should deliver all services or dictate all policies. Rather, it should set clear minimum standards, provide critical financial support to states and cities, and when ever the motivation and capabilities are present in lower levels of government, support the devolution of programmatic planning to states and cities to assure maximum creativity and responsiveness to local needs and conditions.

A Linked Social Development Strategy

What emerges out of the research reported here, as well as many other studies conducted in recent years, is a beginning understanding of the complex interdependencies which involve dysfunctional interactions between urbanization, poor

---

[793] Lang. (1989), p. 199.

[794] Ibid., p. 199.

[795] Ibid.

educational preparation, servicetization, the fragmentation of the family, and largely inadequate responses on the part of income maintenance, human service, and housing support systems. Given this understanding, I would argue for a social development strategy to confront contemporary homelessness and its related problems, one which is based on an interdependency perspective. This would consist of multiple and targeted linkages between reconfigured emergency and transitional services, supported by social insurance initiatives which, though initially circumscribed, would be designed for incremental expansion to more universal coverage.

The competency-building component of the strategy would have several key features. It would alter the entry point for most homeless to the emergency system, from the system of shelters to a system of community lodges. These lodges, in turn, would route homeless to any of a broadened array of housing and service options, which could include some of the better existing shelters and agencies. But most importantly, this would represent a change of control of emergency supports and of the flow of homeless persons through the system. The diversification of options would necessarily mean a greater emphasis on transitional and rehabilitative options, including medium and even longer-term residential and inpatient rehabilitation for those among the homeless with substantial and multiple disabilities. This competency-building component would, thus, seek the expanded use of the three-phase model discussed earlier--emergency, transitional, and growth services--but with explicit provisions for multiple paths traversing these three phases, for major subgroups of homeless persons who require unique services, such as runaways, women with children, or single adults who are mentally ill substance abusers. In this respect, the recommended approach to competency-building is a Three Phase/Multipath Model. The community-building component would emphasize targeted educational, jobs and training, and other programs linked to documented opportunities, as well as development of renters insurance, supports for doubled-up families, and indexed wage and income maintenance benefits. A third critical component is a revamped application of the notion of linkage building, involving the transformation of dysfunctional interdependencies which maintain the *status quo* into synergistic inter-dependencies--referred to as linkages--which bring existing opportunities and needs together under new sets of conditions and rules, such that they dynamically support one another. Linkage-building would be supported by two major initiatives involving the development of microlinkages and metalinkages. Microlinkages involve the linkage of specific individual needs and skills with social opportunities, such as through the sequencing of services, with job training, with existing jobs, sometimes involving relocation services. In contrast, the development of metalinkages consists of the linkage of the multiple systems of control or linkage which currently exist but often work at cross purposes. For example, case managers concerned with linking individuals to resources would be more effectively linked with systems of agency and policy coordination through the systematic aggregation of individualized service plans, which currently is rarely done. Both micro- and meta-linkage strategies require the development of large-scale internet-based computerized information systems.

This recommended social development strategy is premised on several understandings. It is assumed that contemporary homelessness is symptomatic not merely of a particular administration's policies or a specific recession, but instead represents the long-term social costs of the globalization of economic activities, of the expansion of the information and service economy, and of the inability of educational, human service, and housing support systems to respond to the needs of those who are being systematically excluded from this 'new world order'. Thus, an enduring institutionalized or social development response is required, rather than one which assumes the crisis is passing. The recommended strategy is also based on the notion that there are substantial unused resources, whether these involve jobs, housing, services, or other supports, and that creative and large-scale investments are needed in internet-based, user-friendly databases. Such systems would provide the key tools for linking the needs and skills of homeless and other persons with specific social and economic opportunities. The strategy is also based on the notion that as a complex system, there are no single points of intervention which can be exclusively focused on, such as has been done with the shelters. Rather, it is essential to simultaneously develop the competencies of homeless persons--whether these involve vocational or interpersonal skills--and the social opportunities, with which these would be specifically linked through the micro- and meta-linkages mentioned. It recognizes that considerably more planning is needed, not only top-down, but in each operative program or agency in the system so as to preclude the phenomenon of service providers working at cross purposes with one another, preventing the flow of homeless persons from emergency, through transitional, and growth-oriented services.

Competency-Building Component. The envisioned service system would have the threefold purpose of engaging homeless persons in receiving assistance, providing basic emergency supports, and developing the personal and vocational competencies they require for effective linkage with community opportunities, whether existing or newly developed. In each community the Three Phase/Multipath Model would be configured to local conditions, and in each case it would involve at least one or several community lodges tied to other traditional emergency services, and to a contracted system of concrete transitional service and housing options. Many of these components already exist in some communities. However, many new housing, rehabilitative, transitional services would typically need to be developed. Along with new service development, a critical change is that of the control, and this would involve boards for each community lodge and its associated catchment area that include representative homeless persons, service providers, and other concerned citizens and governmental representatives. Finally, in some urban communities specialized case management units would be required for that small subgroup of the homeless, perhaps 5% to 10%, who require either psychiatric in- or outpatient commitment, guardianship, or other protective legal measures. It would be critical that such control functions not be assigned to the community lodges, which would be purely of a voluntary drop-in nature, or even to most transitional or rehabilitative service programs, for otherwise the delicate relationship and trust between the vast majority of homeless persons and their service providers and supports would be substantially undermined.

The community lodges would provide three levels of services and supports to their patrons. (i) On the first level would be basic drop-in supports which ask little of the patron, such as setting up appointments or even registering. These would include a lounge for rest, telephone, hygiene facilities, and meal programs. Storage lockers and safes for personal belongings would also be available. Bulletin boards would include information of interest to the homeless. Larger urban lodges would probably require multiple lounges for specialized groups, such as women and children or smokers. Such basic amenities would no doubt attract many homeless persons, and if additional services were not provided for, such lounges would no doubt see serious abuses. As a lodge, the centers would provide temporary respite and serve as way stations to both emergency supports and transitional social services.

(ii) The second level of service provision in the lodges would involve the availability of case advocates who would provide referrals and vouchers for various nearby housing options, and if needed, transportation in one or several vans to these facilities. These would involve shelters only as a last resort, but more often hotels, family foster care arrangements, or any number of more normalized emergency, transitional, or ongoing housing options. In addition, these case advocates would be available to provide basic emergency counseling, and make service referrals, either internally or externally. This second level of service provision would require of the homeless patron some registration and the selection of a case advocate, who would develop in the initial week of the relationship an individualized service plan. As a case advocate, the staff member would provide generic services, as well as referrals, on a purely voluntary basis, although some minimum level of contact would be required for the homeless person to receive vouchers and referrals to housing resources. Included in this second tier of service delivery would be provisions for health, mental health, vocational, legal and other mainstream service providers to come in during designated hours, perhaps one or two days a week, to provide more specialized services. A rule of thumb for the lodges in contracting with agencies for such workers is that the agency workers must agree to provide certain minimum services, over and above assessment and referral, as too often such assignments constitute merely provisions for creaming the most desirable clients, and leaving the most disabled once again 'assessed' but without help. Another important inhouse service would involve support groups, some generic, and some specialized for particular populations or tasks. At the same time, the case advocates would attempt to engage their patrons in an ongoing working relationship for securing the needed supports, services, employment, or training that they require.

Finally, (iii) the third tier of services in the lodges would involve specific arrangements with external housing authorities, counseling agencies, vocational services, hospitals, and day programs, which would be used to refer homeless patrons to, once they had developed a trusting relationship with the lodge staff. Many of these administrative arrangements would involve the provision of the homeless persons with a voucher or certificate so as to provide some clout to assure successful referrals. Some of these links would be made through the visiting workers from community agencies, other times, the lodge van would take the patron for a preliminary visit. Finally, an important service of some larger urban lodges would be day labor work pools, similar to what Rossi has recommended, which would operate out of the lodges, in collaboration with local employers. Priority would be given to private employers, but community service projects would also be considered.

Many of the homeless may initially become engaged in working in the lodge, serving meals, greeting new guests, serving on the board or committees, and in these ways develop not only some new skills, but a sense of belonging. It would be expected that the lodge would come to represent a supportive community for many of its patrons, and to the extent that this can be accomplished, the homeless would have a powerful base for locating feasible re-entry points into the larger community.

It is proposed that the lodges would be delegated an important coordinative role in managing the system of services and supports for homeless persons. For instance, many of the McKinney as well as local homeless funds could be funneled through these lodges to various shelters, housing options, and service providers. Each lodge would have a community board, as well as a planning department, and would need to use performance contracts or vouchers as devices for coordinating the local system of services for the homeless. Although some of these lodges might be established as new agencies, in other cases, they might be a branch or unit of an existing organization which has demonstrated particular expertise in working with the homeless. If the average homeless person used such a lodge for various purposes 10 hours a week, and 100 to 150 individuals could be accommodated at one time, the typical lodge could serve between 1,000 to 1,500 homeless persons who patronize a given lodge, between 250 and 400 such lodges would be needed throughout the nation, or perhaps three in a city the size of Boston.

So far it has been proposed that the competency-building component consist of a community lodge or lodges, which would provide the central entry point for the homeless to the service system, as well as plan for a larger system of contracted housing and social supports. One final component which would be needed in many areas is an independent unit, perhaps a branch of a state mental health authority, which would specialize in providing intensive case management for people under outpatient or inpatient psychiatric commitment, guardianship, or other similar legal provisions. In large urban areas with many seriously disordered individuals, there is often no agency or professionals willing to assume the legal liabilities involved in providing such services. In developing such units, it may be necessary to develop specific legal provisions to address the problems of professional liability, as well as in many states, providing for the possibility of outpatient commitment. While the vast majority--perhaps as many as 80%--of the homeless can best be reached through purely voluntary means, such as the drop-in oriented Community Lodges, there is a smaller subgroup of highly disabled persons, perhaps 5% to 15% of the homeless, depending on the locale--who represent clear dangers to either themselves or others, often simply because of their inability to care for themselves. This group requires the specialized services of intensive case managers, who would be assigned only very small caseloads of perhaps 8 to 12 clients, trained in the use of relevant legal provisions and associated services, to provide the necessary security and structure. But it would be important that such units be as independent as possible from the Community Lodges as well as traditional social and mental health services so as not to undercut the delicate trust between homeless clients and their service providers.

These units should be closely associated with state mental health authorities, as well as law enforcement agencies, and loosely connected with service agencies. Although such programs might require their wards to attend a traditional medication clinic, a support group at a lodge, or a day program, only bare bone attendance reports back from their service providers should be expected, with the client's permission, and with personal disclosures omitted. And it should be noted, that there will be some homeless individuals who will opt not to use community lodges or other services, and who would not qualify to have their freedoms diminished through commitment procedures, but it is expected that this would be a fairly small group.

Community-Building Component. Many social policy analysts tend to support large-scale, European-style social insurance programs, including myself. Yet, one thing that we have learned in this country is that there has generally been little support for such approaches, except in unusual circumstances such as during the Depression. We have also learned that when significant programs have developed, they have done so incrementally, sometimes as a result of the indexing of benefits, as was the case with old age benefits which resulted in the elimination of above average poverty rates in older adults over the last 25 years. As a strategy, I would therefore recommend the initiation of new social insurance programs on an initially targeted demonstration basis, in perhaps 5 to 20 cities, but in a manner which supports their expansion to new populations and localities, such as through the indexing of benefits. This strategy has the well-known disadvantage of often adding to program fragmentation, however, once benefits become sufficiently wide-scale, then it becomes increasingly feasible to consolidate programs without significant additional expense. With the gradual expansion of Medicaid and Medicare, along with free-care pools and private insurance, we appear to be approaching this point in the health care arena. Such consolidations are beginning to happen on the state-level, and these waiver programs will no doubt set the stage for larger-scale integrations of the competing health care programs. The following are a few such program initiatives which may be candidates for such strategies:

1. Top priority should be the expansion of employment and training programs. William J. Wilson's recommendations for expanded job programs in private business, and failing that, in the public sector as community service jobs, are excellent ones. An important variation of this strategy would be Rossi's recommendation for day labor pools for some of the subgroups among the homeless, and these would best operate out of the community lodges discussed in the previous section. In return for half a days labor, vouchers would be given for food and a simple hotel room, and for a full days work, additional compensation. Such programs should be designed as stepping stones to longer-term job training and employment, with temporary income supports for enrollees, which would focus on development of substantial skills. A major problem with current employment and training programs is that the training provided is often at a very minimal level; rather than training for a few weeks, many jobs require one to two year training programs.

    A critical part of such a jobs strategy would be the linkage of training programs with areas of industry which are clearly expanding. This linkage could be accomplished not only by concentrating training funds in such fields, but also by budgeting significant amounts for relocation of chronically unemployed, and sometimes homeless, individuals and families, to areas where such positions exist. Conversely, a program of support might be developed to encourage businesses to move to or open up branches in areas where there are labor pools, but few jobs exist.

2. Closely linked with job training should be education, specifically the design

340

of programs which create the incentives for non-academically inclined youth to complete high school and gain substantial vocational preparation, a major deficit in the nation's secondary and community college systems. Closer partnerships should be developed between industry and the appropriate educational institutions, to permit a private-public sharing of the costs of enhanced vocational preparation, and a promise of employment upon graduation. For older students who have dropped out, these programs would need to offer a diploma or GED as part of the education-training package. In some cases, the partnerships may be three way, involving perhaps a high school, local community college, and an auto maker in an integrated high school/associate degree program for preparing skilled auto workers. But to permit such partnerships to work, a greater level of control of such programs would need to be shared with the industries willing to commit the required investments in infrastructure and in the programs' graduates. Both state and Federal policy makers will need to create their own programs to foster such relationships, if through no other means than the use of seed monies as stimulative leverage for the development of such partnerships.

3. Another important initiative should be the indexing of the minimum wage to a fixed percent of the median wage, at a level above the value of a typical package of welfare benefits, such as AFDC, food stamps, etc. This would simplify the political problems involved in having to periodically adjust the minimum wage, as well as being responsive to changing economic conditions. During the first ten years of the program, an additional adjustment factor would need to be built in to gradually raise the minimum wage to one that is also a beginning living wage, perhaps around $7 to $8 in 1996 dollars. If this could be accomplished, it would greatly simplify welfare reform, as such benefits could be improved, and yet be kept below the minimum wage, so as to preserve work incentive, a major concern of the

341

electorate. Small businesses would fight any such initiatives, but with the targeting of subsidized work programs to small and medium businesses, such political trade-offs might be a necessary means for assuring its passage.

4.   Substantial welfare reform should ultimately involve a consolidation of the many current, disparate programs, including food stamps, housing assistance, social security, and unemployment insurance. To begin to close some of the gaps so as to make such an integration economically and politically feasible, specific programs should be gradually extended, in particular, unemployment insurance. Exemptions of businesses for inclusion under this program need to be eliminated; to do so, may involve a major restructuring of the premiums. Under this program, there should be a major expansion of job finding, training, and relocation services. In addition, a parallel program is needed for persons who rent, and this might be referred to as *rent insurance*, in contrast to renters insurance for protecting the effects of an apartment. Rent insurance should be compulsory, in the same way that mortgage insurance is compulsory for owners with a mortgage and insufficient equity in their homes. It should be shared, with the majority of the premium being paid for by the landlord. It would protect replacement rental payments for up to six months or a year for tenants who become unable to pay their rent. Criteria for the inability might be similar as for unemployment insurance, that the crisis is not their intentional making, and may be due to such factors as unemployment, extreme medical costs, crime, or natural disaster. Eviction for whatever cause would be insufficient to trigger the insurance as long as the person is employed. But eviction for cause would not preclude the tenant from collecting the insurance, as a voucher, and spending it on new housing, as long as there was some unemployment or similar financial emergency. Low-income housing or residential hotels should not be exempt from such a program as it would be specifically targeted to such populations.

342

5.   As enhanced unemployment and rent insurance, as well as Section 8 housing certificates, are extended and adapted to homeless and persons-at-risk of homelessness, it will become increasingly economically feasible to consolidate all these programs in a single, universal guaranteed income or perhaps a negative income tax system. These changes would be increasingly feasible as the minimum wage is improved through indexing, as described previously. By doing so, perverse incentives which are set up when individuals receive benefits from several well-designed individual programs would be eliminated, especially if such benefits were to be made negatively continuous with the existing semi-progressive tax system. However, in the foreseeable future it is unlikely that the electorate will support on-going income guarantees.

A second best strategy would then be to assure that such a comprehensive guarantee might be available for no more than two years at a time, with a longer life-time cap. After that, supports would be voucherized, i.e. food stamps, housing vouchers, rather than being eliminated as planned under the many of the recent welfare reforms of 1996. Thus, minimum ongoing support is provided at the same time that incentives are maintained to use the system for emergency purposes only. Exceptions would be made for retirees, seriously disabled persons, and anyone else incapable of working, and these would involve ongoing cash assistance.

6.   A key recommendation regarding housing policy would be for the establishment of a legal basis for the regulation of local zoning laws. This is a difficult legal problem, one which is interwoven with the way that federalism has been defined and implemented in this country. There are certainly a range of individual rights established not only by the Bill of Rights and the Constitution, but also by more recent laws, such as The Civil Rights Acts of the 1960s and the Americans with Disability Act of 1990, which could be a basis for establishing laws protecting access to housing by

low-income groups. This could be done through the regulation of low-density zoning laws which exclude multifamily rental units or otherwise set standards which, on a *de facto* basis, have the unintended but adverse impact of discriminating against various protected populations such as minorities, women, or the disabled.

7.   One final recommendation which would have a preventative impact on reducing the incidence of homelessness is support for families and individuals who double-up, after an initial one to two month period. If such a benefit was linked with services and Section 8 housing vouchers, and perhaps admin-istered through existing welfare programs, such as AFDC and general assistance, a clear impact on levels of homelessness could be anticipated, especially among families. The program should include the provision of special priority for doubled-up families and individuals in the application process for Section 8 housing certificates and vouchers.

Each of the above recommendations would involve some combination of redirected existing resources as well as new resources generated incrementally through lowered rates of homelessness and higher levels of employment. To the extent that new resources can be invested into such programs at the start, a larger pump-priming effect could be expected, especially since there are no doubt critical thresholds of programmatic intensity which are required for success. Rather than attempting to evenly distribute new resources to all areas in need, all new resources which can be generated should be concentrated in as many cities or other areas as can provide for the minimum conditions for program success. These would include organizational integration, political support, a solid foundation of existing programs, demonstrated motivation and creativity in development of homeless programs, and the ability to meet minimum thresholds of required program intensity, both in the local system as a whole, and in various service and rehabilitative components. Thus, the central recommendation of this chapter would be to direct all new McKinney Act funds into developing between 5 and 20 *demonstration systems of emergency and transitional services* along the lines recommended here, something akin to the Community Service System project conducted by the National Institute of Mental Health in the late 1970s. Such large scale demonstrations have a seed effect in building political support for workable programs across the nation, whether or not the federal government is able to continue to fund them..

The Linkage Component. At the heart of the recommendations advanced here is the notion of providing a multi-pronged yet fully integrated attack on the conditions perpetuating contemporary homelessness. While such an ideal is by no means new, several of the methods for doing so represent a new approach to historic problems of programmatic coordination. The underlying aim is to convert dys-functional interdependencies into synergistic partnerships and linkages through the development of multiple micro- and meta-linkages between program components.

The microlinkages involve linkage of the motivations and capabilities of particular homeless individuals with documented opportunities in the economic, service, and housing environments. For example, just as training slots would be carefully linked with areas of needed hiring, other rehabilitative programs would be designed to link or bridge the interests and beginning skills of the homeless individual with such training programs in a staged fashion. Supporting such microlinkage systems would be the development of large-scale computerized databases on job opportunities and on vocational inventories of unemployed individuals. These would need to be not only internet based, but employ a full-range of user friendly multi-media capabilities so as to afford a greater sense of reality to all opportunities identified, enhancing motivation of job seekers. The systems would need to provide for wide-spread public access, through computer terminals in community lodges, shelters, bus terminals, public libraries, and post offices in a similar fashion that tourists can access visitor information through CD-ROMs in hotel and airport lobbies, through the touch of the screen. Initially, the federal government should support the development of such systems, in the same way that the National Science Foundation supported the development of the Internet backbone, and then turned its operations over to private vendors. Similarly, large-scale user friendly housing databases are needed to reduce the massive stock of vacant units. Such an approach assumes that when individuals are armed with sufficient information, individual-level coordination of services and resources becomes an organic process, greatly diminishing the demands and stresses placed on higher level coordinative mechanisms.

The other form of linkage which this model relies on is the metalinkage of the various higher level coordinative mechanisms. Most program planners now recognize that any well organized service system requires individual level coordinators--typically case managers concerned with linking clients with services--and higher level coordinative mechanisms, such as agency-level boards, community level councils, or state or federal level agencies. The problem is that each of these 'coordinators' take on a life of their own, and there is no master controller for the diverse coordinative mechanisms. The proposal for a Presidential Council of Social Advisors would be a important linkage and coordinative mechanism. Another of the most important forms of metalinkage recommended here is the aggregation of individual level service plans developed by case managers for each of their clients, so as to generate profiles on an agency or community level of needed services; such aggregation needs both political and technical support through sufficiently versatile information systems. Conversely, as administrators or policy-makers solve interagency problems or generate new resources, there needs to be ways to translate general changes in the structure of opportunities into possible implications and scenarios for each and every client who may have a related interest. Again, this is a task, while at heart an administrative and political one, that would be greatly facilitated through technological means involving large-scale, real-time database technologies. Development of many of these technologies has been severely hampered by the administrative and legal fragmentation of existing services, especially through concerns about the protection of privacy.

Other supports for both micro- and meta-linkages would need to involve creative financing mechanisms, such as use of vouchers by case managers,

346

performance contracting, and in general integrating the funding of services through the community lodges. These would require specialized planning departments to staff the participatory boards, providing for real-time assessment of population needs and quick redirection of funding streams as population needs change, a task which would only be possible through interactive 'real-time' information systems which are required for any truly participatory planning processes. Another important coordinative mechanism, especially on the community-building level, would be the indexing of benefits to changing social problems and opportunities. Legislation for demonstration system projects for the homeless would need to carefully specify national, state, city, agency, and individual-level coordinative mechanisms and support the political integration, staffing, and technological developments required for their success.

Concluding Comments

The safety net for homeless and indigent persons needs to be woven strand-by-strand. This should be done according to a larger plan, one which simultaneously addresses the immediate needs of currently homeless persons and the need for building communities and the range of educational and economic opportunities which sustain them.

One of the key findings of the research reported here is that contemporary homelessness is symptomatic of long-term fundamental shifts in the structure of educational and economic opportunities, such as the shift of jobs to the service sector, which have disproportionately devastated traditionally oppressed populations in urban areas. The fragmentation of the family has both added to and been severely aggravated by the impact of the shift to a global economy. Such fundamental transitions have also severely taxed the adaptive capabilities of both disabled and healthy individuals, as well as the secondary income support and service systems intended to aid them. The main symptom has been both personal and service system fragmentation.

Our response to homelessness, thus, needs to involve the integration of both competency and community-building efforts around the focus of an institutionalized social development strategy, one which is organically-driven. This can be accomplished through the enhancement of planning capabilities on both the most decentralized and also the federal levels, as well as the creative use of a range of micro- and meta-linkage strategies, supported by state-of-the-art information technologies. In the final analysis, homes are interdependent partnerships between individuals and their communities. The elimination of homelessness, thus, requires the strategically-focused nurturing of individuals, their competencies and communities, and the intricate tapestry of their interdependent partnerships.

APPENDICES

Appendix 1

The Data and Research Strategy

The central aim of this research has been the development and testing of the interdependency model of homelessness which was presented in the introductory chapter. It has sought to do this primarily through the secondary analysis of 1990 Census data and a variety of other databases, using techniques of structural equation modeling. Its scope includes the United States, specifically, the 50 states and the District of Columbia, in total, 3,141 counties. The decision to model variations in the size of homeless populations throughout the nation, rather than in just cites or in particular regions, was made not only because of the availability of the data, but also because more restricted areas would have precluded the comparison of urban and rural areas, and of jurisdictions with various types of social programs. There is insufficient variation in key policies, such as deinstitutionalization, when multiple states are not included.

A project such as this necessarily requires data on a wide array of conditions and areas, more than any single individual or organization could possibly collect afresh. Fortunately, many governmental agencies and private organizations which regularly collect data disseminate it on computer tape and most recently on CD-ROM disks, with only minimal descriptive analyses completed, and with the expectation that independent researchers will conduct in depth analyses. For this reason, this project has relied on the analysis of the variety of governmental and private data sources listed in table A1-4, merging them whenever possible using the Federal Information Protocols (FIPs) or other common geographic coding schemes.

To date the analysis of governmental databases for the purposes of

351

understanding contemporary homelessness has been restricted mostly to descriptive statistics, and only occasionally have researchers concerned with homelessness, such as Belcher, Burt, Elliott and Krivo, Hudson, or Tucker[796], used conventional techniques of multiple regression. These approaches, however, forego the many advantages inherent in the field of structural equation modeling (SEM). This is a family of statistical techniques developed in recent years which is specifically designed for testing causal models with latent variables, measurement error, data with violates assumptions of normality, or with significant levels of multicolinearity.[797] Most important, these techniques permit the simultaneous test of a system of hypothesized causal pathways implied by a model, as exemplified by a path diagram, in contrast to the conventional approach to path analysis which tests the separate groups of paths in a piecemeal fashion. When they restrict themselves to the conventional multivariate analyses, researchers risk being misled by correlations which occur by chance. Thus, the data in this study were analyzed not only through conventional descriptive and multivariate approaches using the Statistical Package for the Social Sciences (SPSS-PC), but also with techniques of structural equation modeling as implemented under LISREL8 which was developed by Jöreskok and Sörbom[798].

Until recently, causal modeling has not been possible in research on homelessness. The main barrier has been the lack of comparable data from a sufficient

---

[796] John Belcher, Helping the Homeless; Martha Burt, Over the Edge (New York: Russell Sage Foundation, 1992); Tucker, "Where do the homeless come from?" National Review, September 25, 1987; Christopher G. Hudson, "The Homeless of Massachusetts: An Analysis of the 1990 U.S. Census S-Night Data," New England Journal of Public Policy 9 (1): 79-100.

[797] Latent variables are non-observed features of cases under study which can take a range of different values, such as 'Socioeconomic status' or 'deindustrialization'. These variables typically require several indicators for proper measurement. "Assumptions of normality" refer to the assumption which many conventional statistical procedures require which involve the requirement that the distribution of values for a variable assume the proverbial 'bell-shaped' curve. "Multicolinearity" refers to the situation in which a number of variables are so highly intercorrelated that their simultaneous use as a set of predictors for some phenomenon of interest is either severely compromised or rendered impossible.

[798] LISREL 8 & PRELIS 2 Documentation, Version 8.12, (Chicago: Scientific Software International, 1993).

352

number of jurisdictions to allow the use of statistical methods that require large samples. This need has been addressed through the release of the results of the U.S. Census Bureau's S-Night enumeration, conducted on the night of March 20 and 21, 1990. This was a mammoth attempt to enumerate observable homeless persons throughout the nation using over 22,722 enumerators. This enumeration, to be reviewed in the next section, was beset with a wide range of problems which some believe totally invalidated the use of this "fatally flawed"[799] data. The use of this data, thus, has required the use of independent sources of data to assess the extent and types of errors involved.

Some policy researchers prefer a purist approach to analysis which assumes reliable and untainted data. However, one of the most important findings of a preliminary study of this researcher[800] was that it is feasible to adjust census data using known sources of variation and bias to produce synthetic estimates, which in turn can be confirmed or disconfirmed using independent sources of data. Paleontologists, astronomers, and criminologists all have been effective predicting the existence of unobserved but later-to-be-verified phenomenon by using the flimsiest of data, the most disreputable of informants, or the most abstract theoretical conjectures as their starting point. The ability of social scientists to use the "fatally flawed" data from the census to study the dimensions of homelessness should not be an insurmountable task. The preliminary analysis of Massachusetts data produced results remarkably similar to several independent counts and estimates.[801] This preliminary study, as well as the approach used here, relies on what has been referred to as "triangulation" which is a method which surveyors use involving several independent methods to check their readings.[802] Likewise, in this project research data with known

---

[799] See National Coalition for the Homeless, Fatally Flawed, 1991.

[800] Christopher G. Hudson, "The Homeless of Massachusetts: An Analysis of the 1990 U.S. Census S-Night Data".

[801] Ibid., p. 94

[802] See Todd Jick, "Mixing qualitative and quantitative methods: Triangulation in action," Administrative Science Quarterly, 24 (December 1979): 602.

or unknown levels of error is compared with independent sources of data and research to construct a model or picture of contemporary homelessness with which some confidence can be placed.

The Unit of Analysis

Another key decision in this project has been the unit of analysis. Many policy studies use the states as the unit of analysis as they are some of the more important policy-making bodies in the country. The problem with such an approach is the small number of available states and the considerable intra-state variation, both of which preclude all but the most unrevealing multivariate analyses. Other studies use some version of the metropolitan statistical areas, e.g. MSAs. However, these are unsuitable for inter-state or urban-rural comparisons. The unit selected for this investigation is the county, of which there are 3,141 throughout the nation. These have the advantage that they are not only numerous, permitting a full range of multivariate statistical techniques, and that there is considerable data on them. They are also not so small, with an average population of 79,182, that a single homeless shelter or other institution will appreciably skew the homeless rates, especially in the larger urban counties. Furthermore, using counties does not preclude urban-rural comparisons as data is readily available on the proportion of the county population which is urbanized as well as its population density. In some parts of the country these are meaningful policy-making units with their own service systems, but in other areas they are somewhat arbitrary, with little authority. The use of counties does not preclude the use of state-level policy data, as data on such conditions can be spread or assigned to each of a state's constituent counties. Because most of the data used in this project is on demographic, economic, or housing conditions, the use of counties represents a more appropriate unit of analysis than does the state. The other level of aggregation considered was the census tract, but with an average population of four thousand these would be clearly inappropriate as the rates of homelessness would be unduly influenced by the presence of a single shelter.

354

Dependent Variables

This particular analysis focuses on what Rossi has referred to as the 'literal homeless',[803] those individuals of any age who are found in either shelters for the homeless, shelters for runaway children or battered women, or who are observed living on the street, in abandoned buildings, in public facilities such as bus depots, or staying in 'flop houses' known to charge less than $12 a night. This, in short, is the definition of the population that the Census Bureau used in its S-Night special enumeration in 1990.[804] It excludes those in locations not searched, the well-hidden homeless, those doubled up with friends or relatives, and those in institutions who do not have a domicile. However, whenever data permits, the project does consider separately several of these other subgroups, including people staying in group quarters such as migrant dormitories and group homes who have "no usual home elsewhere".

The U.S. Census S-Night Operations.[805] During the evening of March 20 and early morning hours of March 21, 1990, the United States Bureau of the Census attempted to include homeless persons as part of the 1990 census. This effort included counts of persons in emergency shelters, on the streets, hotels and motels used for the homeless, and at the exits of abandoned buildings. Other components of the homeless populations, such as doubled-up families, were enumerated as part of the regular census. In all, over 20 thousand locations throughout the country were reported to have been canvassed.[806] In preparation for this count, the Bureau surveyed local government officials in the 39 thousand legal jurisdictions in the United States, requesting information about shelter, street, and other locations where the homeless are likely to be found. Because of a very low response of only 14,200

---

[803] Peter Rossi, Down and Out in America: The Origins of Homelessness (Chicago: The University of Chicago Press, 1989), p. 9.

[804] Bureau of the Census, Fact Sheet, 1992.

[805] Parts of the following material have been adapted from Hudson, Christopher, "The Homeless of Massachusetts...".

[806] U.S. Bureau of the Census.

(36.4%), the Bureau was reported to have made systematic attempts to enumerate the homeless on the streets only in areas with populations over 50 thousand, and only occasional attempts in smaller areas[807]. The effort to enumerate the homeless in shelters, however, was not limited to the larger cities.

Many observers believe that the Census Bureau failed to include the majority of the homeless and have severely criticized both the conceptualization and implementation of S-night. Preliminary field tests suggested that a day-time count would have been more effective. In addition, excessive caution was reflected in the failure to include a range of groups of homeless, such as those hidden, and in seeking any information other than the most rudimentary demographics. The most critical problems, however, lay in the implementation of the excessively modest goals of the project. Despite a budget of $2.7 million and the employment of 22,644 enumerators for the count, widespread reports indicate there was poor field training and support for staff. A debriefing survey of the enumerators conducted by the Census Bureau indicated that most of these respondents were satisfied with the training (see table A1-3). However, 64.2% of their suggestions for improvement and 70% of the problems experienced were considered by the Bureau to be too general to be coded[808]. There were also widespread violations of Bureau procedures by the enumerators. Many of these violations appear to have arisen out of fear of the homeless. Enumerators sometimes teamed up in groups of four instead of two (thus, reducing coverage of the assigned locations), failed to leave their vehicles, or failed to show up at assigned locations. There was an attempt to employ homeless persons as enumerators, but administrative regulations, such as the requirement for several forms of identification,

---

[807] National Coalition for the Homeless, Fatally Flawed. Census Bureau officials report not making any systematic decision to exclude areas with fewer than 50,000 people, and it is clear, at least in Massachusetts, that there were occasional counts of homeless persons in smaller areas. Yet all available reports, as well as the data themselves, indicate that no efforts were made in areas of fewer than 50,000 population.

[808] J.H. Thompson, Memorandum, "Preliminary Results of the S-Night Enumerator Debriefing Questionnaire for the S-Night 'Assessment' Cities" (Washington, D.C.: Bureau of the Census, May 2, 1991).

are reported to have diminished this effort.[809]

Reliability of Shelter Counts. Because of the widespread concerns prior to the Census about the possibility of an undercount, several monitoring studies were organized by the Bureau and by independent advocates prior to the Census. Most of these involved the street count, however, two involved the implementation of the shelter count. A Census commissioned study by the Center for Survey Methods Research, for instance, found that despite the restrictive definition of shelters used by the Bureau, it generated lists with over twice as many shelters as advocates and local experts were able to[810]. This finding, although increasing confidence in the shelter counts, does not speak to the issue of how well individuals in those shelters were counted. The other Census Bureau study, unfortunately, did not address this issue either as it involved a survey of the Bureau district office personnel as to the degree of cooperation received from shelter providers and other groups.[811]

There were, however, two independently conducted surveys of the number of persons in homeless shelters in selected cities at around the time of the Census. Burt, of the Urban Institute, conducted a systematic telephone survey of shelters in 147 cities in 1989.[812] In addition, the U.S. Conference of Mayors in 1990 surveyed 30 cities as to their shelter bed rates.[813]

---

[809] See National Coalition for the Homeless, Fatally Flawed.

[810] W.T. Friskics-Warren, "The Independent Compilation of Shelter Lists by Local Experts for the 1990 S-Night Enumeration: Project Design and Recommendations," Council of Community Services, January 31, 1991.

[811] U.S. Bureau of the Census, "The Shelter Component of S-Night," March 18-20, 1991.

[812] Burt, Over the Edge.

[813] United States Conference of Mayors, A Status Report on Hunger and Homelessness in America's Cities: 1990: A-30 City Survey (Washington, DC: Author, December 1990).

357

Table A1-1. Comparison of 1990 Census and Independent Counts of Shelter Beds in Selected Cities with More than 100,000 Population, 1990 (per 10,000)

City[a]	U.S. Census	U.S. Conference of Mayors[b]	Urban Institute[c]
Mean[d]	27.3	25.4	28.4
Standard Deviation	17.1	13.8	19.7
Median	28.0	17.6	23.2

SOURCES: U.S. census figures computed from U.S. Bureau of the Census, 1990 Census, Summary Tape File 1-A; U.S. Conference of Mayors, A Status Report on Hunger and Homelessness in America's Cities, 1990: A 30 City Report (Washington, D.C., December 1990), 35; Martha Burt, Over The Edge: The Growth of Homelessness in the 1980s (New York: Russell Sage Foundation; Washington, D.C.: Urban Institute Press, 1992).

[a] The cities include Alexandria, Boston, Charlotte, Chicago, Cleveland, Kansas City, Louisville, Minneapolis, Nashville, New Orleans, New York, Norfolk, Phoenix, Portland, Providence, St. Paul, Salt Lake City, San Diego, San Francisco, Seattle, and Washington, D.C. The first two columns below indicate the level of covariation between these ratings, not agreement, and these indicate a correlatioan between the Census Bureau and the Urban Insitute findings, not with the Mayors' estimates.   The last two columns report on paired t-tests and reflect the level of agreement, indicating that none of the three pairs represents significantly different levels.

	Pearson r	p	T	p
Census and Mayors	.35	.12	.25	.81
Census and Urban Institute	.81	.00	-.60	.56
Mayors and Urban Institute	.67	.00	-.94	.36

[b] Figures represent total shelter beds and family shelter beds converted to population rates per 10,000.
[c] Figures from Burt, Over The Edge, Appendix A, "1989 Homeless Rate."
[d] Philadelphia and San Antonio, as well as other unlisted cities, are not included in the computation of the various statistics (except median), since data from the Conference of Mayors' estimates are unavailable.

358

Table A1-1 above summarizes the counts for the 21 cities for which all three counts were available and provides a basis for comparison of the Bureau's findings with those of the other two studies. The table is based on counts in the form of rates per10 thousand so as to control for differences in population size and permit inter-city comparisons. An examination of the figures for individual cities indicates much variability, however, the means of all three counts fall within the 25 to 28 per 10 thousand range. The Bureau's rates are not significantly different from either of the two other figures at the 0.05 level using paired t-tests. The Urban Institute and Census Bureau's counts compare relatively well, with means of 28.4 and 27.3, which are not significantly different, and which are highly correlated ($r = 0.81$; $p = 0.00$). However, the correlation with the Mayor's estimate is not statistically significant, though in aggregate, the levels are not significantly different. The Mayor's estimate represented a less systematic effort than Burt's as it involved city-level estimates on the part of diverse municipal officials.

It is clear that there is much random error involved in one or more of these measurements due to the considerable differences within individual sets of figures. However, both these figures and the Nashville study do not provide evidence of systematic error or bias in under counting homeless persons in shelters who adhere the Bureau's implicit definition.

Reliability of The Street Counts. The question of the reliability of the street counts is considerably more problematic than that of the shelter counts. Fortunately, the street counts represent only about a fifth of the actual homeless enumerated. In addition, both advocates and the Bureau paid greater attention to assessing any systematic bias or possible undercount in selected locations. The Bureau contracted with five private research groups to monitor the street count using one or both of two types of methodology. Four of these groups used recapture methods which involved placing between 57 and 127 volunteers as "plants" at the predefined locations where the census bureau would be counting homeless.[814] Each of these volunteers would record whether or not a census enumerator counted them, thus permitting an assessment of the percentage of eligible persons enumerated. The other kind of methodology employed involved personal interviews with homeless persons in the few days following the census, likewise, to determine the percentage of them who say that they were interviewed by a census enumerator.[815] In addition to the contracted studies, private groups in Tucson and San Francisco independently conducted two of the most substantial monitoring efforts and these involved interviews with 300 and 1,008 homeless persons, respectively.[816]

The results of the ten studies conducted, summarized in table A1-2, indicate that only 42.6% of the combined total of the plants and homeless persons were enumerated, indicating a severe undercount in the seven urban areas studied. This percentage is calculated using the 1,508 out of the total 1,701 subjects who were able to say they definitely were or were not counted, and excluding all those who equivocated with a 'Maybe', 'Probably Yes', or 'Probably Not'. An analysis of variance indicated that the results did not significantly differ depending on either the method used (recapture vs. homeless survey) or auspices (contracted vs. independent study), however, they did vary significantly depending on the city. An examination of the findings in individual cities indicate that the studies with large samples all had findings in the 40% to 46% range, whereas the studies with small samples in Chicago, Los

---

[814] M.R. Cousineau, and T.W. Ward, "An Evaluation of the 1990 Census of the Homeless in Los Angeles," The Los Angeles Homeless Health Care Project, June 8, 1990; J.D. Wright and J. A. Devine, "Assessment of the Street Enumeration Procedures during the Census 'Shelter and Street Night' in New Orleans," Tulane University (undated); Kim Hopper, "Final Report: Monitoring and Evaluating the 1990 S-Night Count in New York City," Nathan S. Kline Institute for Psychiatric Research, January 1991; Louisa Stark, "An Evaluation of the 1990 Census of Homeless People in Phoenix," The Community Housing Partnership, Phoenix, AZ, July 30, 1990.

[815] See Edin, Kathryn, "Assessment of S-Night 1990 in Chicago, IL", North Park College, Chicago, IL, May 1990.

[816] Coalition on Homelessness, The Newsletter of the Coalition on Homelessness, "Alternate Homeless Survey Finds Severe Under Count by Census Bureau," San Francisco, CA, April 1990, p. 3; Primavera Foundation, (press release), "Monitoring the U.S. Census Bureau Shelter/Street Count of Tucson: A Survey by the Primavera Foundation," March 28, 1990.

Angeles, New Orleans, and Phoenix almost all varied dramatically from a low of 20% to a high of 74% For this reason, the 99% confidence interval for the aggregate percentage counted--39.2% to 46.0%--represents a fair estimate of the percentage of homeless living in non-hidden street locations who were counted in major urban areas,[817] but not in rural areas where it is undoubtedly considerably greater.

Since contracting for these studies, officials of the Census Bureau have argued that the results can not be used as a measure of the degree of undercount.[818] The Bureau's own analysis of these studies, however, indicated that the enumerators, "may have missed half the street sites in Chicago and Los Angeles, and a third in Phoenix, and that, "Substantial departures from standard procedure appear to have occurred to varying degrees in all 5 cities..."[819] Statistical and probability theory precludes untested generalizations from the monitoring studies. Nonetheless, the cumulative results of the ten studies do constitute persuasive evidence that, regardless of auspices and method of study, a consistent pattern of undercounting of persons in the identified locations occurred.

Reliability of Overall Counts. The conclusion that the S-Night resulted in a serious undercount of the homeless is also supported by a comparison of counts and estimates for various cities, states, and the nation as a whole with those from independent sources. Table 8-2 (chapter 8) compares the aggregated figures from the S-Night--including both the street and shelter counts--with a variety of independent sources. In only a few instances, such as with Alameda, Orange, and Yolo counties, California, were the Census figures higher than the surveys. In most instances, especially when service provider estimates or aggregation

---

[817] Since the Census Bureau did not chose these sites randomly, statistical generalization--without empirical testing--can not be made to the nation or urban areas as a whole. Since this study goes beyond mere statistical generalization and investigates the fit of these generalizations and projections with independent observations, the assumption of random selection here and elsewhere is not made.

[818] B.E. Bryant. Report on the 1990 Census S-Night Operations. United States Senate & United States House of Representatives, May 9, 1991.

[819] Ibid.

Table A1-2. Meta-analysis of Results, Monitoring Studies of 1990 U.S. Census Street Counts in Selected Cities

City (Investigator)	Studies Using Recapture Methods							Follow-up Studies of Homeless							TOTAL
	n	Yes	Prob- ably	May be	Prob- ably Not	No	% Ctd[a]	n	Yes	Prob- ably	May be	Prob- ably Not	No	% Ctd[a]	
Chicago (Edin)	—	—	—	—	—	—	—	18	5	—	—	—	13	28	28.0%
Los Angeles[b] (Cousineau)	63	21	—	11	—	31	40	50	17	11	—	16	6	74	51.0%
New Orleans (Wright & Devine)	58	38	—	3	—	17	69	10	5	—	1	—	4	56	67.0%
New York[c] (Hopper)	127	46	15	4	19	56	45	—	—	—	—	—	—	—	45.0%
Phoenix (Stark)	57	17	—	4	—	36	32	10	2	—	—	—	8	20	30.0%
San Francisco[d] (HTF & COH)	—	—	—	—	—	—	—	1008	353	—	122	—	533	40	40.0%
Tucson[d] (Primavera)	—	—	—	—	—	—	—	300	138	—	—	—	162	46	46.0%
Aggregate	305	122	15	18	10	140	47	1396	520	11	123	16	726	42	42.6%

F tests for main and interaction effects:	F	p
Method (recapture vs. homeless survey)	1.399	.237
Funding (census contracted vs. advocacy)	3.130	.077
City	4.609	.000
Method by City	3.583	.028

SOURCES: Kathryn Edin, "Assessment of S-Night 1990 in Chicago, IL," North Park College, Chicago, May 1990; M.R. Cousineau and T.W. Ward, "An Evaluation of the 1990 Census of the Homeless in Los An geles," Los AngelesHomeless Health Care Project, June 8, 1990; J.D. Wright and J.A. Devine, "Assessment of the Street Enumeration Procedures during the Census Shelter and Street Night in New Orleans," Tulane University, n.d.; Kim Hopper, "Final Report: Monitoring and Evaluating the 1990 S-Night Count in New York City," Nathan S. Kline Institute for Psychiatric Research, January 1991; Louisa Stark, "An Evaluation of the 1990 Census of Homeless People in Phoenix," Community Housing Partnership, Phoenix, July 30, 1990; Coalition on Homelessness, The Newsletter of the Coalition on Homelessness, "Alternative Homeless Survey Finds Severe Under Count by Census Bureau," San Francisco, April 1990; Primavera Foundation, press release, "Monitoring the U.S. Census Bureau Shleter/Street Count of Tucson: A Survey by the Primavera Foundation," March 28, 1990.

[a] The percentage of homeless persons counted on the streets is calculated in each case by dividing the Yes's (counted) by the n for the particular study, excluding any May be's or Probablys. This percentage does not consider the "hidden homeless" or other classes of homeless persons, but only those fitting the U.S. Census criteria for the street count; [b]Only the figures for street locations selected for the census counted are used here; [c]Hopper computed a more specific figure of 53 percent, but to enhance comparability with other studies, the percentage based on the raw data is retained here. This researcher also reports having conversations with 22 homeless persons in the weeks after the census, of whom four reported being interviewed. These data, however, are not included owing to their informality; [d]In contrast to the first two studies, these two studies were conducted by independent advocacy associations which were under contract with the U.S.s Bureau of the Census. While the mean positive count rate for the census studies was 47%, in contrast to 41% for others, this, as noted below, was not a significant effect.

of service provider estimates were used, the independent figures were dramatically greater than those counted by the Census Bureau. With the exception of the S-Night results which placed the number of homeless counted at 240,140, all the national estimates ranged from 324 thousand to 735 thousand, with most estimates in the area of 500 to 600 thousand. Despite their rational basis, most of these estimates rely on numerous assumptions which, however plausible, preclude any of them from being treated as hard and fast figures. But collectively, they support the impression of a serious undercount, one which can not be explained merely by the 57.4% undercount figure reported earlier for the street studies, as the total street count represents only about 20% of the total. The other major source of undercounting no doubt involves that in rural areas which would not be reflected in the undercount monitoring studies which were all urban based.

Analysis of Enumeration Efforts. The findings discussed in the foregoing section, necessitated further analysis of possible sources of systematic error in the S-Night Census. Specifically these involved testing the hypothesis that the more the Census Bureau looked for homeless persons, the more they found. The author obtained through the Freedom-of-Information Act, and other sources, data files on selected facets of the S-Night enumeration process, including data from a survey of the 22,722 enumerators which was administered at the completion of the S-Night assignments. Variables pertinent to systematic error included the response rates from a preliminary survey of governmental units for the purpose of identifying homeless sites, the number of sites per 10 thousand persons, staffing levels, and training participation. Survey data from the enumerators themselves included such characteristics as their sex, age, experience in work with the homeless, in the local area, and with Censuses; satisfaction with their training and support; and special difficulties encountered, as locating sites.

Most of this data consisted of totals for various questionnaire items for each

Table A1-3. Characteristics of S-Night Enumeration and Their Zero-order Correlations with Homeless Rates

	Mean	Median	SD	r w/ Homeless Rate	r w/ Street Rate
PLANNING					
Governmental Response (%)	57.9	56.7	8.0	0.07[b]	-0.01
Sites per 10,000	1.2	0.9	1.1	0.81[b]	0.76[b]
STAFFING					
Total staffing per 10,000 Pop.	2.0	1.6	1.6	0.67[b]	0.71[b]
Staff per Site	2.4	1.7	7.5	-0.01	0.03
Staff per Team	2.6	2.9	0.9	0.19[b]	0.20[b]
CHARACTERISTICS OF ENUMERATORS					
Percent Male	57.4	57.1	12.0	-0.04[a]	-0.02
Median Age	41.0	39.8	7.2	-0.26[b]	-0.20[b]
Percent Experienced with:					
Other census work	13.2	10.0	11.8	-0.23[b]	-0.21[b]
Being homeless	4.8	3.9	4.6	0.17[b]	0.17[b]
Work with homeless	10.7	10.5	5.7	-0.02	-0.06
Area assigned	66.7	67.0	12.0	-0.05[b]	-0.07[b]
TRAINING & SUPPORT					
Percent staff trained	94.4	100.0	15.0	0.12[b]	-0.01
Mean # assignment types	1.3	1.3	2.4	-0.17[b]	-0.16[b]
Enumerator satisfaction with:					
Training (1–Low; 3–High)	2.6	2.6	1.6	-0.25[b]	-0.21[b]
Job Guide (1–Low; 3–	2.3	2.3	2.6	-0.13[b]	-0.20[b]
SPECIAL DIFFICULTIES					
Percent reporting any	27.5	27.6	10.7	0.14[b]	0.09
Mean # problems reported	1.1	1.0	1.4	-0.01	-0.04[a]
% problem finding locations	7.0	6.6	4.8	-0.03	-0.04[a]
WEATHER					
Mean Low temperature	31.6	31.0	7.9	0.11[b]	0.10[b]
Precipitation	0.034"	.000"	.002"	.10[b]	.02

NOTES: Table is based on reported rates in 451 District Offices of the U.S. Census Bureau, with all enumerator statistics weighted on relative number of enumerators in each office. Govern-mental response data and weather data are asigned to counties and correlated with homeless rates.
[a]. $\alpha < 0.05$; [b]. $\alpha < 0.01$

364

of the Census Bureau's 451 district offices. These were first converted to proportions, means, or medians, as was appropriate (see table A1-3). A computer algorithm was then developed which used a supplemental file of district office, tract, county, and state codes for each of the nation's 62,190 census tracts, to, (i) assign the district rates for the survey responses to each of the component census tracts, and then, (ii) after appropriate re-weighting and sorting to, (iii) re-aggregate the tract rates to the county level.

The above procedure was necessary as there is little overt relation between the Census Bureau's district office structure, set up for administering the census, and the geographic hierarchy to which the census data is eventually aggregated and disseminated. In some parts of the nation, there are many district offices per county, but more commonly, there are many counties covered by a single district office. Fortunately, all 62,190 census tracts, with one exception, could be uniquely associated with both a single county and a single district office. This was done with a computer file which associates the code for each tract with the correct county and district office. This re-aggregation was tested through a comparison of the national means of the county level estimates with the means for each of the same items on the district office level, prior to the procedure described above, and this revealed that all means were nearly identical, within rounding error.

Another computer program was developed which calculated a separate linear regression model for interpolating temperature and precipitation levels for each county center point for the early morning of March 2.[820] This procedure used data on each of the nation's 3,141 counties' distance and direction from the three closest weather stations (n=290)--computed from its published geographic coordinates--and their temperature and precipitation levels at the time of the S-Night effort, as recorded

---

[820] Available from the author.

by the U.S. Weather Service.[821]

The foregoing transformations produced county estimates for each of the methodological variables, descriptive statistics for which are listed in table A1-4. This allowed for the merging and computing of their correlation with the rates of homeless persons on the county level. Systematic error or basis is suggested by a significant correlation with any one of these variables. Such correlations, however, do not prove systematic error. For instance, more enumerators or a higher rate of sites per 10 thousand people may be associated with higher homeless rates because the Census Bureau had good reason to believe that more homeless would be found and thus made greater efforts to search. Those that had strong correlations, such as enumeration sites per 10 thousand population and staffing levels and rate of homeless, were further analyzed. A strong correlation between the staff levels and homeless rates was accounted for in an analysis of partial coefficients by the rate of sites. In the initial modeling efforts two methodological variables were included--site rate and homeless experience of enumerators--the second of which was included because of its likely relevance to the assigned task.

The hypothesis was strongly supported that the more extensive the search or enumeration effort, the more homeless were found, even after controlling for a range of socioeconomic and other environmental conditions which the Census Bureau may have considered in assigning its enumerators to various district offices and sites. At lower levels there is an approximately linear relationship between the siting rate and homeless findings. However, if three counties with outlying values are excluded, the relationship levels off, indicating a saturation point: the more the Bureau looked for homeless persons, the more they found, *but only up to a point*. After this point, it did not matter whether there were three, six, or ten sites per each 10,000 persons in the general population.

---

[821] These estimates were constrained to fall between the upper and lower readings recorded for the set of three stations involved so as to prevent extreme and implausible estimates in locations falling at some distance from the periphery of the stations involved.

Preparation of Data on Homelessness. The initial step in preparation of the homeless rates involved totalling for each county the Census Bureau's reported counts for: (i) homeless persons visible on street locations, (ii) those enumerated in shelters for the homeless, (iii) shelters for battered women and their children, and, (iv) shelters for runaway youth.[822] Final figures for each of these were obtained from an extract of the STF-2C tape series, as well as separate versions from the STF-1C (i & ii) and STF-3C tape series (i-iv). Totals for each state were compared with totals published by the Census Bureau, a procedure which indicated small disparities for a few of the states. After several written and telephone communications with Census Bureau officials, it was determined that the earlier published totals were in error and that the totals derived from the STF-2C and STF-3C tape files had already been corrected by the Bureau.

After the four sub-counts were totalled for each county, the resulting figure was divided by the county's 1990 population, and then multiplied by 10 thousand, to produce the number or rate of homeless for each 10 thousand persons, permitting

Table A1-4. Means and Standard Deviations of Selected Predictor Variables and Their Zero-Order Correlations with Homeless Rate (n=3,141)

Variable	Mean	Standard Deviation	Zero-order r w/ Homeless
DEMOGRAPHIC RISK FACTORS			
Population, 1990* (1a)	79,182	263,812	0.28[b]
Baby Boom: % Persons between 25-44 (1a,2)**	0.32	0.03	0.33[b]
Change in Population, '80-'90 (1a,2)**	0.12	0.18	-0.02
Change in 65+ Population, '8--'90 (1a,2)**	0.27	0.21	-0.29[b]

---

[822] For further details see, Census of Population and Housing, 1990: Summary Tape File 3 Technical Documentation / prepared by the Bureau of the Census. --Washington: The Bureau, 1991

Variable	Mean	Standard Deviation	Zero-order r w/ Homeless
Population Density (Persons/Sq. Mile)[*](1a)**	220	1,431	0.43[b]
% Nonwhite Population (1a)**	0.20	0.16	0 42[b]
% Males (1a)**	0.49	0.01	-012[b]
% Foreign Born (1c)**	0.08	0.09	0.42[b]
% Born in state of residence (1c) **	0.62	0.17	-0.29[b]
% In same house as in 1985 (1c)**	0.53	0.09	-0.10[b]
Median Age (1a)**	33.60	2.90	-0.20[b]
Change in Median Age, '80--'90 (1a,2)**	0.18	0.07	-0.29[b]

EDUCATION AND DISABILITY

Variable	Mean	Standard Deviation	Zero-order r w/ Homeless
% With BA degree (1c)	0.18	0.07	0.35[b]
% With HS diploma (1c)	0.75	0.08	0.03
% With no HS degree (1c)**	0.25	0.08	-0.03
Rate of Violent Crimes	661.46	278.71	0.29[b]
Suicide Rate	12.39	2.63	-0.17[b]
Hard core cocaine users per 1,000 pop.	9.84	5.88	0.35[b]
Change in % completing HS, '80-'90 (1c)	0.08	0.04	-0.22[b]
Disabled: % 16+ Civilian Non-institutional Population who have a mobility or self-care limitation (1c)**	0.07	0.02	0.21[b]
% Disabled who are male (1c)**	0.38	0.03	-0.12[b]
% Disabled who are unable to work (1c)**	0.63	0.08	-0.34[b]

ECONOMIC OPPORTUNITY

Variable	Mean	Standard Deviation	Zero-order r w/ Homeless
Proportion adults employed, 1990 (1c)**	0.50	0.06	0.07[b]
Change in % adults employed, '80-'90 (1c, 2)**	0.19	0.22	0.00

Variable	Mean	Standard Deviation	Zero-order r w/ Homeless
Civilian Unemployment, 1990 (1c)**	0.05	0.02	-0.07[b]
Change in Unemployment, '80-'90 (1c, 2)**	0.83	0.14	-0.06[b]
Proportion Jobs semi- or unskilled (1c)	0.37	0.08	-0.24[b]
Median commute time to work (min.) (1c)**	19.80	4.80	0.34[b]
Manufacturing Employment as % of total (1c)**	0.15	0.09	0.00
Change in Manufacturing employment '79-'89 (2)**	-0.02	0.41	-0.10[b]
Individual Infl. Adjusted Earnings in Manufacturing, 1988 (2)**	$33,848.00	$19,268.00	0.04
Change in Earnings in Manufacturing, 1979-1989 (2)**	0.06	0.50	-0.02
Service Employment as % of total (2)**	0.20	0.11	0.70[b]
Change in Service Sector employment, '79-'89 (2)**	0.60	0.65	-0.09[b]
Individual Infl. Adjusted Earnings in Service sector, 1988 (2)**	$31,163.00	$25,280.00	0.06
Change in Services Earnings, '79-'89 (2)**	-0.11	0.33	0.08[b]
Family Income (1c)	$28,476.00	$7,164.00	0.22[b]
Family Income Change, '79-'89 (1c, 2)	-0.06	0.11	0.13[b]
% Families with no workers (1c)	0.13	0.05	0.11[b]
Change in Per Capita Income, '80-'90 (1c, 2)**	0.80	0.09	0.07[b]
JOBS-EDUCATION FIT Ratio of semi-skilled and unskilled jobs to non-high school graduates (1c)**	0.84	0.27	-0.19[b]
PRIMARY SUPPORTS			
% of Persons in Families (1a)	0.82	0.05	-0.57[b]

Variable	Mean	Standard Deviation	Zero-order r w/ Homeless
Median Family Size (1a)**	3.88	0.29	0.57[b]
% of Households One Person (1a)**	0.24	0.04	0.59[b]
% Adults 15+ Separated, Widowed, Divorced (1a)	0.18	0.03	0.28[b]
% Households Female Headed (1a)**	0.12	0.04	0.31[b]
Median Size Family Households (1a)**	2.94	0.21	0.01
Median Size Non-Family Households (1a)**	1.11	0.05	0.18[b]
% Family Households Persons Non-relatives (1a)**	0.02	0.01	0.50[b]
Teenage Birth Rate, 1980 (2)	211.20	89.70	0.02
% of Aged in Family Households (1a)	0.64	0.04	-0.35[b]
SECONDARY SUPPORTS--SERVICES			
Deinstitutionalization: % reduction in MH populations, '55-'90 (3)	86.40	5.40	0.06a
Total hospitalization rate in MI, 1990 per 100,000 (1a)	51.70	158.90	0.05[b]
Outpatient MH additions, 1990 (4)	1215.00	371.00	0.027[b]
MH Professionals (social workers, psychologists, psychiatrists) (5)	88.30	41.50	0.34[b]
Groups Homes for MI (1b)	1.30	3.25	0.11[b]
Physicians per 100,000 (2)	195.51	138.32	0.57[b]
Primary Care Centers (2)	5.13	2.67	-0.08[b]
SSI Mean Payments, in 1986 (inflation adjusted) (2)	$275.39	$67.85	0.35[b]
General Assistance Benefits, 1987 (inflation adjusted)(6)	$195.39	$49.64	0.21[b]
Mean AFDC Benefit, 1980 (inflation adjusted)(2)	$419.38	$170.85	0.05[b]
% Households with public assistance, 1990 (1c)	0.08	0.04	0.22[b]

Variable	Mean	Standard Deviation	Zero-order r w/ Homeless
Medicaid per capita, 1986	$173.97	$93.98	0.35[b]
McKinney support /homeless person, 1989	$2,649.70	$1,488.71	-0.30[b]
Per Capita Receipts social service organizations, 1987 (2)	$33.89	$19.90	0.30[b]
POVERTY			
Overall Individual Poverty Rate (1c)	0.13	0.63	0.12[b]
Rate of Extreme Poverty: Persons With Income < .5 Povety Line (1c)	0.06	0.03	0.20[b]
Rate of Minorities who are poor (1c)	0.26	0.11	-0.02
% Poor who are Minorities (1c)	0.36	0.23	0.38[b]
% Poor who are children (1c)	0.35	0.05	0-.03
HOUSING			
Ratio of Rooms for rent to homeless (1a,1b)	156.20	311.90	-0.25[b]
Percent Occupied Units Rentals (1a)	0.36	0.11	0.66[b]
Gross rent/Income in households with under $10,000 Income (1c)	0.57	0.06	0.18[b]
Median Gross rent, 1990 (1c)	$473.00	$138.00	0.26[b]
% 0-1 bedroom units under $250 (1c)	0.31	0.21	-0.34[b]
Vacancy rate for 0-1 bedrm rentals (1a)	0.16	0.01	-0.23[b]
Ratio of 1990 to 1980 mean rent, adjusted for inflation (1c,2)	1.02	0.15	0.29[b]
Rate of Board and Care rooms (1b)	5.12	8.00	0.38[b]
Vacancy rate for all rentals (1a)	0.08	0.04	-0.13[b]
Total Section 8 Units (as rate) (7)	44.70	10.60	0.33[b]
Presence of Rent Control laws* [1--Yes(188); 0--No(2,953)] (8)	0.06	0.00	0.37[b]
Length of Period of Rent* Control (years) (8)	5.60	0.50	0.22[b]

Variable	Mean	Standard Deviation	Zero-order r w/ Homeless
% Change in rental units under $250 (infl.adj.), 1980-1990 (1c)	1.1	0.38	0-.31[b]

NOTES:
* The statistics for these variables are not weighted for relative population size of county.
** Base-10 log transformations were computed for these variables when they were used in structural equation modeling. [*Decisions have not been made yet regarding the Secondary Support, Poverty, and Housing variables in this regard.*]
SOURCES:
1a. U.S. Bureau of the Census. (March 1991). 1990 Census of Population and Housing–Standard Tape File 1C (CD-ROM).
1b. U.S. Bureau of the Census. (August 1991). 1990 Census of Population and Housing–Standard Tape File 2C.
1c U.S. Bureau of the Census. (December 1991). 1990 Census of Population and Housing– Standard Tape File 3C. (CD-ROM).
2. U.S. Bureau of the Census. (1992). USA Counties. (CD-ROM).
3. The 1990 figure was obtained from: U.S. Department of Health and Human Services, Substance Abuse and Mental Health Services Administration. (1993). Additions and Resident Patients at End of Year, State and County Mental Hospitals, by Age and Diagnosis, United States, 1990. The 1955 figure was taken from: National Institute of Mental Health. (1955). Patients in Mental Institutions. These are based on state level figures and the subsequent calculated percentage is then assigned to each county within the state.
4. Center for Mental Health Services and National Institute of Mental Health. (1992). Mental Health, United States, 1992. Edited by Manderscheid, R.W. and Sonnenschein, M. A.
5. Number of mental health professionals represent the combined rates for social workers, psychologists, and psychiatrists as given in: E. F.Torrey, K. Erdman, S. M. Wolfe, & L. M. Flynn. (1990). Care of the Seriously Mentally Ill: A Rating of State Programs, Third Edition. Public Citizen Health Research Group and National Alliance for the Mentally Ill. These were cited as coming from the American Psychological Association, the national Association of Social Workers. The number of psychiatrist were listed in the second edition of this publication (1988) and were cited as coming from: American Medical Association. (1988). Physician Characteristic Distribution in the U.S. (figures are for 1986).
6. Burt, M. R. (1992). Over the Edge: the Growth of Homelessness in the 1980s. New York: Russell Sage Foundation, pp. 102-104.
7. U.S. Department of Housing and Urban Development. (1992). Unpublished tables.
8. U.S. Department of Housing and Urban Development. (September 1991). Report to Congress on Rent Control; The Heritage Foundation. (January 12, 1989). America's Homeless: Victims of rent control. The Backgrounder.

more meaningful inter-county comparisons than would the raw counts. Both these rates and the raw counts were used when descriptive statistics are presented on the homeless, especially in Chapter 2. The STF-2C tape series also permitted the computation of sub-counts and associated rates for the following breakdown groups: (i) male and female; (ii) age 0-18, 19-34, 35+, (iii) white and non-white, as well as, (iv) gender by race, and, (v) type of setting (street, homeless shelter, battered women's shelter, and runaway shelter), by each of the foregoing breakdowns (see tables 2-2 to 2-3). The rates for each subgroup are population specific rates. For instance, the homeless rate for white females is the number of white females who are homeless for each 10 thousand white females in the population of the county (or, region, state, nation, etc.).

Most of the analyses of the homeless rates used the overall rate for each county as the primary dependent or criterion variable, unless otherwise noted. In the final testing of the model, rates for subgroups, such as for men and women, whites and non-whites, were substituted for the overall rate.

Predictor Variables

Table A1-4 lists details of key predictor variables that were obtained from the 1990 Census and several other public data sources. Data from 1990 was extracted from the CD-ROMs for both the STF-1C and STF-3C tape series for each of the nation's 3,141 counties. Figures for earlier dates, especially 1980, were extracted from the USA Counties CD-ROM (1992), also published by the U.S. Census Bureau. Data pertinent to the deinstitutionalization and several other mental health services on the state level were obtained from the National Institute of Mental Health publications,[823] and after being converted to proportions, rates, or means, they were assigned to counties within each of the states. Information on the Section 8 housing program was obtained through unpublished correspondence with the U.S. Department of Housing.[824]

Extensive data transformations were involved in collapsing the multiple categories in which many of the census counts are recorded. For instance, the counts for the various age groups were used to compute, through a grouped data formula,

---

[823] Center for Mental Health Services and National Insitute of Mental Health. Mental Health, United States, 1992. Manderscheid, R.W., and Sonnenschein, M.A., eds. DHHS Pub. No., (SMA) 92-1942. Washington, D.C.: Supt. of Docs., U.S. Govt. Print. Off., 1992.

[824] U.S. Department of Housing and Urban Affairs, "Section 8 Certificate units reserved by state (as of 4/30/92)", "Section 8 Housing Voucher units reserved by state (as of 4/30/92)", Benoitz, Prepared 5/13/92.

the median age for each county. In other cases, several counts, such as for separated, widowed, and divorced, were totalled, and divided by an appropriate denominator, in this case, the number of adults over 15, to obtain the proportion of adults which were separated, widowed, or divorced. In several cases, ratios were computed to measure the scarcity of jobs or housing for persons at risk of homelessness. For instance, the number of semi-skilled or unskilled jobs in a county was divided by the number of adults who had less than a high school education, or the median rent was divided by the median income for households with less than $10,000 annual income. Rent control laws were measured not only by their presence (1--Yes; 0--No), but also by the number of years that they have been in place. Whenever data transformations were used, the results were tested through inspection of results for individual counties and comparison of sample results with those obtained manually through use of a hand calculator.

Missing data rarely was a problem as most variables were complete for all 3,141 counties. However, in a few of the services variables data was missing for 10% to 20% of the cases. In these counties, the mean of the counties for which data was available was used as an estimate for the missing data. This procedure has the limitation that it reduces the natural variability in the data, making it less likely to detect any significant relationships with the variables concerned. However, it enables a much more efficient and accurate use of the data which is available than would be possible had the counties for which any data was missing were entirely eliminated.

Whenever rates, proportions, or means are presented for groups of counties (such as for a state or region) or used in correlational analyses, each county is weighted for its relative share of the U.S. population. The proportional weighting factor was calculated by dividing the county population by the total U.S. population, and then multiplying the result by the total number of counties, usually 3,141. Thus, a county of strictly average size would have a weight of 1, and smaller or larger counties would have smaller or larger weights accordingly. If this had not been done, rates for states and regions would be in error, as the many small rural counties would

374

out weigh and camouflage the conditions in the more populous urban areas. Had conclusions been sought only about, say, global political characteristics of each of the counties, such weighting would be counter-indicated. However, data on county populations and conditions are being used to infer and model the rate or risk of homelessness, thus population weighting becomes a necessary procedure. When global characteristics of counties are considered, such as presence of rent control laws, these are not weighted in descriptive statistics, and in correlational analysis only when the rate or risk of homelessness is being analyzed as the central dependent variable.

Data Analysis

The strategy of the data analysis involved both extensive descriptive statistics and procedures for exploratory model development and confirmation using structural equation modeling techniques. Descriptive statistics involved not only examination of standard univariate statistics, but also the extensive examination of bivariate statistical relationships (between pairs of variables) through cross tabulations, means procedures, and graphs such as scattergrams and 3-D bar charts. In some cases, such as with the services statistics, non-linear measures turned out to be most revealing, although it was not feasible to extend these procedures into the multivariate analyses. The overall analysis proceeded in an incremental fashion from first testing the impact of the demographic predictors while controlling for the extensiveness of the enumeration effort (Chapter 2), and then to the addition of each of the other groups of predictors in a stagewise fashion (Chapters 3 through 8). At each stage, predictors which failed to enhance the explanatory power of the model were dropped. After the final model was specified, the models for each of the previous stages were rerun with uniform subsets of variables so as to fully understand the utility of each subject in improving the overall model. In presenting the results of the multivariate analyses, generally several regression statistics are reported to provide alternative views of the relationship, most commonly, the standardized regression coefficient (Beta or β), the percentage of the variation explained[825], the partial, and in a few cases, the "level importance".[826]

Throughout the structural analyses, the assumption is made that the homeless rates have at least a moderate degree of random error, thus an error estimate of 10% was randomly used for this variable. While the true value may be higher or lower than this, it is believed that this figure represents a considerably better estimate than the 0% error which has been assumed in most past research using homeless rates.[827] Likewise, modest estimates of random measurement error, typically 1% to 2%, were used for each of the independent variables based on the difficulties in measuring the particular variable (see chapter 8, table 8-1). While these are only general estimates, they are considerably less arbitrary than the conventional assumption of zero measurement error which is made in most regression analyses. By including estimates of measurement error for both the dependent and independent variables, it was possible to compute disattenuated regression coefficients which are not artificially reduced by the effects of random error.

Structural equation modeling techniques are especially suited for exploration and model development because, unlike conventional regression techniques, they require an explicit initial theory. But more important, the global goodness-of-fit and other tests of significance and parsimony used provide powerful protections against

---

[825] This was computed with the following formula so as to normalize it and permit totalling percentage of variation explained among various predictor subgroups.

Absolute Variation Explained = $| \beta r | * (R^2 / \sum | \beta r |)$

[826] These are reported in Chapter 9, and reflect the contribution of the independent variable to the level of the dependent variable, according to the following formula:

Level Importance = $\bar{x}\beta$

See Christopher H. Achen. Interpreting and Using Regression Series: Quantitative Applications in the Social Sciences, No. 29. (Newbury Park, CA: Sage, 1982). p. 72.

[827] John Belcher, Helping the Homeless ; Martha Burt, Over the Edge (New York: Russell Sage Foundation, 1992); William Tucker, "Where do the homeless come from?" National Review, September 25, 1987, p. 35; Christopher G. Hudson, "The Homeless of Massachusetts: An Analysis of the 1990 U.S. Census S-Night Data," New England Journal of Public Policy 9 (1): 79-100.

being misled by chance correlations which are routinely uncovered in the extensive use of multivariate statistical techniques.

Because of high levels of skewness and kurtosis in several of the variables, such as the homeless rates, it was necessary to use the generally weighted least squares method which does not assume multivariate normality or homoscedasticity. Thus, both covariance and asymptotic variance-covariance matrices were computed using LISREL8. Standard criteria were used in screening for acceptable models, namely that the model converges on an admissible and stable solution, one with an absence of anomalous statistical output, such as negative error variances or R^2s over 1.00. Indices of goodness-of-fit and covariance residuals were then examined to evaluate the apparent strength and plausibility, as well as the weaknesses, of the computed model. This process was repeated in the process of specification search until a theoretically acceptable model was found which substantially fit the available data.

Several attempts were made to test the interdependency model as originally diagramed in chapter 1. This proved impossible for what was probably a combination of reasons: high levels of multicolinarity, which were exacerbated by the large sample size and which served to make almost any relationship between otherwise unrelated indicators statistically significant, as well as the extreme model complexity which would have been required to achieve a well fitting model between so many variables. Ultimately it was decided to use a multiple regression strategy which would serve simply to illuminate the relationship of each of the predictors with the homeless rates, and set aside the problem of disentangling the many interrelationships among the predictors. However, as mentioned above, this was using estimates of measurement error, both random and systematic, as diagrammed in chapter 8, figure 8-2. Following the development of this model, a simplified model was also computed using only the four most important predictors for estimation purposes, and it is this model which was used in the projections described in the next section.

The use of goodness-of-fit indices based on chi-square is widely believed to

377

be unduly generous in the evaluation of goodness-of-fit in very large samples. Therefore, as recommended by Hayduk[828], each provisional model was recomputed with a specification of a reduced sample size of 200, and none of the indices revealed a model with a lower goodness-of-fit, and several cases, a better one. Another test regularly used involved that of the possibility that the LISREL algorithms were converging not on the best possible solution, but only on what is referred to as a 'local minima' or second best solution, determined by the starting values used in the iterative process. This involved, at each stage, the use of several sets of very different randomly chosen starting values. If the algorithm continues to converge on the same solution regardless of where it begins, considerably greater confidence can be placed in the solution.

Further Testing and Application of Final Model. When a model is generated based on an exploratory specification source, further validation of the model is particularly important. Confirmation of the trimmed model in this project was sought not only through its cross-validation, using the Expected Cross Validation Index when ever possible,[829] but also by re-computing the final model using the extended LISREL model which uses additional information consisting of variable means. This enabled the computation of intercepts for each dependent variable and the prediction of homeless rates for each county. Thus, a more indepth examination of model fit was possible than simply through an examination of the model residuals. Newly computed estimates could then be adjusted and compared with the original rates, essentially, permitting an examination of the same type of residuals as are used in traditional regression diagnostics. The residuals between the predicted and the observed values of the homeless rates of each county for the final model were then

---

[828] Leslie A. Hayduk, Structural Equation Modeling with LISREL: Essentials and Advances (Baltimore: John Hopkins Press, 1987).

[829] Traditionally cross validation was accomplished by computing the model on one randomly chosen half of the data, and validating it on the other half. However, the development of new cross validation indices, such as the ECVI, makes this process superfluous as this type of index is designed to accomplish the same task.

mapped so as to identify patterns in the fit of the model.

In addition, predicted estimates of actual homeless levels for each of the nation's 3,141 counties were computed with adjustments made for systematic error, or the differential search effort.[830] The adjusted estimates were based on the assumption that had the Census Bureau deployed enumerators to sufficient sites such that there would be no evidence of enumeration error, they would have obtained accurate counts. This level, the reader may recall, represents a saturation point where additional search efforts would make no difference in the results, and this was computed from the data to be 2.9 sites for each 10,000 persons. Estimates derived from entering the 2.9 figure into the model and re-computing the predicted rates (see endnote 34) are then compared not only with the original data, but also with independent estimates and counts. These results are also plotted on a map of the United States to permit full visual inspection of the results.

The final step consisted of computing estimates of the homeless rates for each county for 1995. The same formula was used, but with alternative data for each county. Population density was recomputed from the Current Population Estimates for 1995[831]. Projections of services employment were computed, based on an

---

[830] The formula used for this was (in SPSS syntax):
if (siterate lt 2.9)homadj=((.3782*empser89)+(.0600*(density*.01))-(.1023*(mckinhom*.0001))+(.0439*2.9)+.0043)*100.

if (siterate ge 2.9)homadj=((.3782*empser89)+(.0600*(density*.01))-(.1023*(mckinhom*.0001))+(.0439*siterate)+.0043)*100.

KEY: siterate=Rate of sites enumerators visited
      homadj=Adjusted homless rate, per 10,000
      empser89=% Working in services sector
      density=Population density
      mckinhom=Rate of McKinney spending
NOTE: .01, .0001, and 100 figures were for rescaling data after scale had been changed by LISREL8 program. .0043 is the intercept term.

[831] Obtained from the U.S. Bureau of the Census computer bulletin board.

extrapolation using 1979 and 1989 data to 1994.[832] Although 1995 McKinney expenditure amounts were not available for each state, a total was available.[833] State McKinney expenditures 1995 were not available, so they were estimated based on the average state percentage of McKinney funds for 1992 and 1993. The percentage for each state was then applied to the 1995 national total. Finally, the 2.9 site enumeration rate was again used as a correction for the inadequate enumeration efforts made by the Census Bureau in most areas of the nation.

Limitations

Despite the extensive statistical controls and testing involved in this analysis, this project is confronted with inherent limitations which future research will need to address. Most of the data is cross-sectional, taken at one point in time. Thus, although inferences can sometimes be made as to time order in the similar way a geologist infers time order in vertical strata, less certainty can be attached to these inferences than in such a hard science. A similar problem arises out of the multivariate analysis of aggregated county data. Without replication in individual-level studies, there is no assurance that results from an aggregated analysis will also apply to, or necessarily should apply to, the individual level. For example, indicators of individual disabilities were found to have only very weak correlations with the homeless rates, despite their manifest importance in surveys of homeless individuals, and the reason may be that such disabilities most typically develop symptomatically as a result, rather than the cause, of the life histories leading to homelessness. Finally, the attempt to test the model by comparing its predictions with independent estimates and counts is an imperfect test, as most of these counts or estimates are based on different definitions and methodologies.

---

[832] U.S. Bureau of the Census, USA Counties CD-ROM, 1990. This extrapolation was based on a compounding formula which assumes a constant annual rate of change. The extrapolation was made to 1994, a year prior to the target date of 1995, since 1989 data had been used to model the 1990 rates.

[833] Interagency Council on the Homeless, "McKinney Act Funding Data", 12/94. 1995 total for the nation obtained in phone conversation with an official of this agency.

APPENDIX 2

Statistics on Good-of-Fit Indices for Structural Models

Table A2-1. Goodness-of-Fit Indicators for Each Sub-Model, In Isolation

Goodness of Fit Indicator	Demo-graphic (Chapter 2)	Disability (Chapter 3)	Economic Opportunity (Chapter 4)	Primary Supports: Family (Chapter 5)	Secondary Supports: Services (Chapter 6)	Housing (Chapter 7)
Chi-Squared	0.19	1.02	0.17	1.74	0.17	0.05
Degrees of Freedom	6	5	4	4	7	8
α Probability[a]	0.99	0.96	1.00	0.78	1.00	1.00
Goodness of Fit Index	--	1.00	1.00	1.00	--	--
Adjusted Goodness of Fit	--	1.00	1.00	1.00	--	--
Parsimony Normed Fit	--	0.24	0.40	0.40	--	--
Comparative Fit	--	1.00	1.00	1.00	--	--
Multiple R^2 for Rate of	0.62	0.27	0.59	0.50	0.32	0.55
STANDARDIZED						
Smallest	--	-0.32	-0.40	-0.39	--	--
Median	--	0.00	0.00	0.00	--	--
Largest	--	0.51	0.01	0.44	--	--
Root Mean Square Error	--	0.00	0.00	0.00	--	--
Expected Cross Validation	--	0.01	0.01	0.01	--	--

NOTES: These models were tested using the generally weighted least squares procedure, as implemented under LISREL 8.0. The solutions converged typically after 3 iterations and all were found admissible.
-- Indicates these statistics are either not relevant or uncalculatable given the high degree of fit.
[a]. This measures the probability that the sample and model covariance matrices come from different populations, thus, a .06 level indicates that these matrices are not significantly different at the .05 level. The interpretation of these significance levels is opposite that of conventional tests, with numbers larger than the conventional .05 level indicating significance and smaller ones indicating non-significance of the tested model.

Table A2-2. Goodness-of-Fit Indicators for Each Sub-Model, Controlling for Effects of Preceding Models

Goodness of Fit Indicator	Demographic & Measurement (Chapter 2)	Disability Including Demographic & Measurement (3)	Economic Opportunity & Ch. 2-3 (4)	Primary Supports: Family & Ch. 2-4 (5)	Secondary Supports: Services & Ch. 2-5 (6)	EX-PLANATORY MODEL Housing & Ch. 2-6 (7)	PREDICTION MODEL
Chi-Square	0.19	1.59	1.76	4.95	5.53	6.89	26.02
Degrees of Freedom	7	11	15	19	26	36	2
α Probability[a]	1.00	1.00	1.00	1.00	1.00	1.00	0.00
Goodness of Fit	--	1.00	--	1.00	--	--	0.99
Adjusted Goodness	--	1.00	--	1.00	--	--	0.91
Parsimony Normed	--	0.12	--	0.09	--	--	0.20
Comparative Fit	--	1.00	--	1.00	--	--	1.00
Multiple R^2 for Rate	0.84	0.89	0.93	0.94	0.95	0.97	0.80
STANDARDIZED							
Smallest	--	-0.02	--	-1.10	--	--	-5.10
Median	--	0.00	--	0.00	--	--	5.09
Largest	--	0.33	--	1.06	--	--	5.10
Root Mean Square	--	0.00	--	0.00	--	--	0.06
Expected Cross Validation Index (ECVI)	--	0.05	--	0.14	--	--	0.02

NOTES: These models were tested using the generally weighted least squares procedure, as implemented under LISREL 8.0. The solutions converged typically after 3 iterations and all were found admissible.
– Indicates these statistics are either not relevant or uncalculatable given the high degree of fit.
[a]. This measures the probability that the sample and model covariance matrices come from different populations, thus, a .06 level indicates that these matrices are not significantly different at the .05 level. The interpretation of these significance levels is opposite that of conventional tests, with numbers larger than the conventional .05 level indicating significance and smaller ones indicating non-significance of the tested model.

APPENDIX 3

Nonlinear Relationships of Service Indicators with Rates of Homelessness

Table A3-1. Homelessness and Indicators of Income Maintenance Benefits: Nonlinear Regression Statistics

Type of Measure	n	Mean	SD	Standardized Coefficients			R^2
				Linear	Quadratic	Cubic	
AFDC							
Mean Payment, 1980	3,141	$419.3	$170.85	-4.0[c]	8.98[c]	-4.61[c]	.23[c]
Change in Individuals, 1980-1985	3,081	-20.0	49.88	-.13[c]	-.38[c]	.22[c]	.11[c]
% Population on AFDC	3,141	3.41	4.28	.30[c]			.19[c]
GENERAL ASSISTANCE							
Mean payment, 1987	35	$206.5	$64.19	-2.14[c]	5.33[c]	-3.04[c]	.09[c]
Change in mean payment	21	5.55	42.81				.00
SSI							
Mean Payment, 1990	3,141	$275.3	$67.85	.69[c]	-.41		.14[c]
% Population on SSI,	3,141	1.72	1.15	.71[c]	-.59[c]		.08[c]
Change mean payment, 1980-1986	3,141	71.11	27.74	-.15[c]	08[b]		.01[c]
Change % Population	3,141	8.05	15.01	-.05[a]	-.09[a]	.06[a]	.01[c]
SSDI							
% Population covered	3,141	1.10	.43	.45[c]	-.88[c]	.43[c]	.02[c]
Change in coverage, 1980-1986	3,141	.43	17.67	-.27[c]	.17[c]		.07[c]
OVERALL							
% Households on public assistance	3,141	.08	.04	.49[c]	-.28[c]		.06[c]
Mean per capita transfer	3,141	$2,352.	$574.15	.18[c]	.23[c]		.16[c]
Total transfer payment	3,141	83.54	21.49	-1.59[c]	2.18[c]	.88[c]	.07[c]

Table A3-2. Homelessness and Indicators of Deinstitutionalization of Mental Health Services: Nonlinear Regression Statistics

Type of Measure	n	Mean	SD	Standardized Coefficients			R^2
				Linear	Quadratic	Cubic	
INPATIENT SERVICES							
Total inpatients, 1988		43.36	27	-1.42[c]	2.98[c]	-1.43[c]	.20[c]
% Decline in State & County inpatients, '55-'88 (pop. adjusted)		.86	.05	-.07[c]	.24[c]	.24[c]	.02[c]
COMMUNITY SERVICES							
Community Mental Health Centers		3.8	6.2	-.91[c]	.84[c]		.04[c]
Total Outpatient Additions, 1988		1215.1	371.1	1.62[c]	-2.55[c]		.02[c]
Partial Care, 1988		112.7	49.5	1.06[c]	-2.13[c]	1.13[c]	.02[c]
Group Homes for MI, 1990		1.3	3.3	.52[c]	-1.20[c]	.79[c]	.06[c]
OTHER INDICATORS							
Rated Quality of State MH Services		9	2.82	-1.16[c]	3.12[c]	-1.97[c]	.01[c]
Index of Restrictiveness of Emergency Commitment Laws		.45	.27	.56[c]	-1.80[c]	1.15[c]	.02[c]
Index of Restrictiveness of Judicial Commitment Laws		3.63	1.18	2.39	-4.85[c]	2.39[c]	.05[c]
Rate of MH Professionals		88.3	41.5	1.08	-2.00[c]	1.44[c]	.13[c]
OVERALL							
Total mental health expenditures, 1988				-.69	1.54[c]	-.56[c]	.14[c]
% Change total mental health expentures, '83-'88		.43	.27	.06	-.84[c]	.73[c]	.04[c]

Table A3-3. Homelessness and Other Human Services: Nonlinear Regression Statistics

Type of Measure	n	Mean	SD	Standardized Coefficients			R²
				Linear	Quadratic	Cubic	
SUBSTANCE ABUSE							
Drug and Alcohol Admissions, 1990	3043	8	4	-.33[a]	1.77[c]	-1.32[c]	.06[c]
MEDICAL							
Access Index	3140	22	12	.42[a]	-1.51[c]	.91[c]	.05[c]
Medicaid Coverage	3126	174	95	2.39[c]	-6.35[c]	4.42[c]	.15[c]
Primary Care	2829	5	3	-.36[c]	.23[c]		.02[c]
Physicians per 100,000	3118	196	138	.63[c]	-.07[c]		.32[c]
EDUCATION							
School spending per Pupil,1987	3141	$4,043	$984	-1.68[c]	3.74[c]	-1.81[c]	.09[c]
Student-Teacher Ratio, 1990	3077	17	3	-1.61[c]		1.68[c]	.07[c]
GENERAL SOCIAL SERVICES							
Social service agency receipts, per capita	1590	$37.68	$20.78	.45[c]	-.24[c]		.07[c]
SPECIFIC HOMELESS SERVICES							
Percentage of homeless in shelters	3141	84%	19%	.72[c]	-.99[c]		.11[c]
McKinney homeless funds per capita, 1987-1991	3141	$9.18	$3.79	1.46[c]	-3.30[c]	2.39[c]	.15[c]
McKinney homeless funds per homeless person, per year	3141	$2,650	$1,489	-.30[c]			.09[c]

REFERENCES

Achen, C. H. (1982). *Interpreting and using regression series: Quantitative applications in the social sciences. No. 29.* Newbury Park, CA: Sage.

Adams, C. (1986) Homelessness in the postindustrial city: Views from London and Philadelphia. *Urban Affairs Quarterly, 21* (4), 527- 549.

American Medical Association. (1988). Physician Characteristic Distribution in the U.S.

Anderson, N. (1961). *The hobo: The Sociology of the homeless man.* Chicago: University of Chicago Press.

Apgar, W. C., & Brown, H. J. (1989). *The state of the nation's housing: 1988 Cambridge.* Boston: Harvard University, The Joint Center for Housing Studies of Harvard University.

Appleby, L., & Desai, P. N. (1987). Residential instability: A perspective on system imbalance. *American Journal of Orthopsychiatry, 57,* 515-524.

Appleby, L., & Desai, P. N. (1985). Documenting the relationship between homelessness and psychiatric hospitalization. *Hospital and Community Psychiatry, 36*(7), 732-737.

Bachrach, L. L. (1987). Geographic mobility and the homeless mentally ill. *Hospital and Community Psychiatry, 38,* 27-28.

Bachrach, L. L. (1984). *The homeless mentally ill and mental health services: An analytical review of the literature.* Unpublished manuscript.

Backgrounder. (1989). America's Homeless: Victims of Rent Control , Jan. 12, 1989.

Bahr, H. (1990). Introduction. In J. Momeni (Ed.). (1990). *Homelessness in the United States: State surveys.* (pp.xxi). New York: Praeger.

Baker, S. G. & Snow, D. A. (1990). Homelessness in Texas: Estimates of Population Size and Demographic Composition. In J. Momeni (Ed.). (1990). *Homelessness in the United States: State surveys.* (pp.xxi). New York: Praeger.

Ball, F. L. J., & Havassy, B. E. (1984). A survey of the problems and needs of homeless consumers of acute psychiatric services. *Hospital and Community Psychiatry, 35*(9), 917-921.

Barak, G. (1991). *Gimme shelter: A social history of homelessness in contemporary America.* New York: Praeger.

Barth, R. (1990). On their own: The experiences of youth after foster care. *Child and Adolescent Social Work, 7*(5), 419-440.

Bassuk, E. L. (1984). The homelessness problem. *Scientific American, 251*(1), 40-45.

Bassuk, E. L., Buckner, J. C., Weinreb, L. F., Browne A. Bassuk, S. S., Dawson R., and Perloff, J.N. (1977). Homelessness in Female-Headed Families: Childhood and Adult Risk and Protective Factors. American Journal of Public Health, 87(2), 241-248.

Bassuk, E. L., & Rosenberg, L.(1988). Why does family homelessness occur?: A case-control study. *American Journal of Public Health, 78*(7), 783-788.

Bassuk, E.L., & Rubin, L. Homelessness: Critical issues for policy and practice. In L. Orr (Ed.). *The homeless: Opposing viewpoints*. San Diego: Greenhaven.

Bassuk, E. L., Rubin, L., & Lauriat, A. (1984). Is homelessness a mental health problem?. *American Journal of Psychiatry, 141*, 1546-1550.

Bassuk, E.L.,Rubin,L.,& Lauriat, A. (1986). Characteristics of sheltered homeless families. *American Journal of Public Health, 76*, 1097-1101.

Baum, A. S., & Burnes, D. W. (1993). *A nation in denial*. Boulder, CO: Westview Press.

Baxter, E., & Hopper, K. Private Lives/Public (New York: Community Service Society, 1981).

Baxter, E., & Hopper, K. (1982). The new mendicancy: Homeless in New York City. *American Journal of Orthopsychiatry, 52*(3), 406.

Belcher, J. R. (1991). Moving into homelessness after psychiatric hospitalization. *Journal of social Service Research, 14*(3-4), 63.

Belcher, J. R. (1991). Three stages of homelessness: A conceptual model for social workers in health care. *Health and Social Work, 16*(2), 87-93.

Belcher, J. R., & DiBlasio, F. A.(1990*). Helping the homeless: Where do we go from here?*. Lexington, KY: Lexington Books.

Belcher, J. R., & Toomey, B. G. (1988). Relationship between the deinstitutionalization model, psychiatric disability, and homelessness. *Health and Social Work, 134* (2).

Belsie, L. (1986). U.S. jobs tide rises, but many workers are still aground. *Christain Science Monitor* (Jan. 9, 1986), p. 9.

Benda, B. B., & Hutchison, E. D. (1990). Homelessness and alcohol. In Belcher, J. R., & DiBlasio, F. A. (1990*). Helping the homeless: Where do we go from here?*. Lexington, KY: Lexington Books.

Benson. (1980). Labeling theory and community care of the mentally ill in California: The relationship of social theory and ideology to public policy. *Human Organization, 39*(2).

Blau, J. (1992). *The visible poor: Homelessness in the United States*. New York: Oxford Press.

Blau, J., & Kleiman, B. (1985). Homeless youth in the New York city municipal shelter system: The project A.I.D. Final Report New York: Human Resources Administration.

Block, M. A. (1962). A program for the homeless alcoholic. *Quarterly Journal of Studies on Alcoholism, 23*(4), 644-649.

Bluestone, B., & Harrison, B. (1988). The growth of low-wage employment: 1963-86. *American Economic Review, 78*(5), 124-128.

Bohanon, C . (1991). The economic correlates of homelessness in sixty cities. *Social Science Quarterly, 72*(4), 817-821.

Borg, S. (1965). Homeless men and the community, *Australian Journal of Social Issues* 2 (3), pp. 27-33 (1965)

Borg, S. (1978). Homeless men: A clinical and social study with special reference to alcohol abuse. *Acta Psychiatric Scandia Supplement, 276*.

Breakey, W. R. (1991/1992). Mental health services for homeless people. p. 101. In M. Robertson

& M. Greenblatt (Eds.). *(1992). Homelessness: A national perspective* (pp.245). New York: Plenum Books.

Breakey, W. R. (1987). Treating the homeless. *Alcohol, Health and Research World, 11*, 42-46.

Brenner, M. H. (1973). *Mental illness and the economy.* Cambridge: Harvard University Press.

Breton, M., & Bunston, T. (1992). Physical and sexual violence in the lives of homeless women. *Canadian Journal of Community Mental Health, 11* (1), 29-44.

Bromlesy, B. B., Johnson, D. M., Hartman, D., & Ruffin, A. L. (1990). Homelessness in virginia: Dimensions of the problem and the public reaction. In J. Momeni (Ed.). (1990). *Homelessness in the United States: State surveys.* (pp.xxi). New York: Praeger.

Browne, A. (1993). Family violence and homelessness: The relevance of trauma histories in the lives of homeless women. *American Journal of Orthopsychiatry, 63* (3), 370-384.

Bryant, B. E. (1991). Report on the 1990 Census S-Night Operations. United States Senate & United States House of Representatives, May 9, 1991.

Burnam, M. A. (1991). Estimation of the number of homeless and mentally ill persons in three California counties. In Tauber, C. (Eds.). *Conference proceedings for enumerating homeless persons: Methods and data needs.* U.S. Bureau of the Census, March 1991.

Burt, M. R. (1991). Developing the estimate of 500,000-600,000 homeless people in the United States in 1987. In, Tauber, C. (Eds.). *Conference proceedings for enumeration homeless persons: Methods and data needs.* Bureau of the Census. March 1991.

Burt, M. R., & Cohen, B. E. (1988). *America's homeless: Numbers, characteristics, and the programs that service them.* Washington, D.C.: Urban Institute Press.

Burt, M. R. (1992). *Over the edge: The growth of homelessness in the 1980s.* New York: Russell Sage Foundation; Washington, D.C.: Urban Institute Press.

Carter, E., & McGoldrick, M. (Ed.). (1980). *Family life cycle: A framework for family therapy.* New York: Gardner Press.

Castro, J. (1992, March). *The disposable workers.* Time, pp. 43-47.

Caton, C. L. M., Shinn, M., & Gillespie, C. (1994). The roles of changing housing and poverty in the origins of homelessness. *Journal of Social Issues, 46*(4), 157-174.

Caton, C. L. M., Shrout, P. E., Eagle, P. F., Opler, L. A., Felix, A., & Dominguez, B. (1994). Risk factors for homelessness among schizophrenic men: A case-control study. *American Journal of Public Health, 84*(2).

Caton, C. L. M. (1990). *Homeless in America.* New York: Oxford University Press.

Caton, C. L. M. Wyatt, R. J. Felix, A., Grunberg, F., & Dominguez, B. (1993). Follow-up of chronically homeless mentally ill men. *American Journal of Psychiatry, 150*(11), 1641.

Coalition on Homelessness, The Newsletter of the Coalition on Homelessness, Alternate Homeless Survey Finds Severe Under Count by Census Bureau, San Francisco, CA, April 1990, p. 3;

Cohen, C. I., & Sokolovsky, J. (1990). Alcoholism contributes to homelessness. In L. Orr (Ed.). *The homeless: Opposing viewpoints.* San Diego: Greenhaven.

Cohen, C. I., & Sokolovsky, J. (1989). *Old men of the bowery: Strategies for survival among the homeless.* New York: The Guilford Press.

Comprehensive Homeless Assistance Plan, 1987, cited in Momeni, J. (ed.) Homelessness in The

United States.

Corrigan, E. M., & Anderson, S. C. (1984). Homeless alcoholic women on skid row. *American Journal of Drug and Alcohol Abuse, 10* (4).

Cousineau, M. R., & Ward, T. W. (1990). *An evaluation of the 1990 census of the homeless in Los Angeles.* The Los Angeles Homeless Health Care Project,

Covey, S. R. (1989). *The 7 habits of highly effective people.* New York: Simon and Schuster.

Crystal, S., Ladner, S., & Towber, R. (1986). Multiple impairment patterns in the mentally ill homeless. *International Journal of Mental Health, 14*(4), 61-73.

Cuomo, A. (1992). *The way home: A new direction in social policy.* New York: New York City Commission on the Homeless. p. c-2.

Dear, M. J., & Wolch, J. R. (1987). *Landscapes of despair: From deinstitutionalization to homelessness.* Princeton, NJ: Princeton University Press.

DeParle, J. (1991, December). Poor are increasingly facing a tough choice on housing. *New York Times,* A1 & A13.

DeParle, J. (1992, March). Why marginal changes don't rescue the welfare state. *New York Times,* E3.

Devine, D. J. (1988). Homelessness and the social safety net. Doctoral dissertation, University of Michigan. Ann Arbor, MI: University Microfilms International, 1989.

Dixon, L., Meyers, P., & Lehman, A. (1994). Clinical and treatment correlates to Section 8 certificates for homeless mentally ill persons. *Hospital and Community Psychiatry, 45*(12), 1196.

Dockett, K. H. (1989). Street homeless people in the District of Columbia: Characteristics and service needs. Washington D.C.: University of the District of Columbia.

Dolbeare, C. N. (1991). Out of reach: Why everyday people can't find affordable housing, Second Edition. Washington, DC: Low Income Housing Information Service, p. 7.

Dooley, J.A., Parry, J.W. (Editors), *Involuntary Civil Commitment: A Manual for Lawyers and Judges,* Commission on the Mentally Disabled, American Bar Association, 1988; pp. 90-121.

Dreir, P., & Applebaum, R. (1990). Nobody home: The housing crisis meets the nineties. *Tikkun, 5,* 15-18.

Durham, M. L., & Pierce, G. L. (1986). Legal intervention in civil commitment: The impact of broadened commitment criteria. *The Annals, 484,* 42-55.

Eagle, P. F., & Caton, C. L. M. (1990). Homelessness and mental illness. In L. M. Caton. *Homeless in America* (pp.61). New York: Oxford University Press.

Easterlin, R. A. (1987). The new age structure of poverty in America. *Population and Development Review, 13*(2), 195-208.

Edin, K., Assessment of S-Night 1990 in Chicago, IL , North Park College, Chicago, IL, May 1990.

Edsall, T. B. (1988). The Reagan legacy. In S. Blumenthal & T. B. Edsall (Eds.). *The Reagan legacy* (pp. 3-49). New York: Pantheon Books.

Eitzen, D. S., & Zinn, M. B. (1993). *In conflict and order: Understanding society.* Boston: Allyn & Bacon.

Elliot, M., & Krivo, L. J. (1991). Structural determinants of homelessness in the United States. *Social Problems, 38* (1), 113-131.

Fabricant, M. (1986). Creating survival services. *Administration in Social Work, 10* (3), 71.

Fabricant, M., & Epstein, I. (1984). Legal and welfare rights advocacy: Complementary approaches in organizing on behalf of the homeless. *The Urban and Social Change Review.*

Farr, R. K., Koegel, P., & Burnham, A. (1986). *A study of homelessness and mental illness in the skid row area of Los Angeles.* Los Angeles: Los Angeles County Department of Mental Health.

First, R. J. (1992). *Final Report on Ohio Homeless Study* (Columbus, OH: Ohio State University, Feb. 13, 1992).

First, R. J., Roth, D., & Arewa, B. D. (1988). Homelessness: Understanding the dimensions of the problem for minorities. *Social Work, 33* (2), 120-124.

Fischer, P. J. (1988). Criminal activity among the homeless: A study of arrests in Baltimore. *Hospital and Community Psychiatry, 39*(1), 51.

Fischer, P. J., & Breakey, W. R. (1986). Homelessness and mental health: An overview. *International Journal of Mental Health, 14,* 6-41

Fischer, P. J., & Breakey, W. R. (1991). *The epidemiology of alcohol, drug, and mental disorders among homeless persons. American Psychologist, 46*(11), 1116.

Fischer, P. J. (1992). The criminalization of homelessness. In M. Robertson & M. Geenblatt (Eds.). (1992). *Homelessness: A national perspective* (pp.245). New York: Plenum Books.

?Fischer, P. J. Chapter 6, Criminal behavior and victimization among homeless people, p. 90.

Fischer, P. J., Shapiro, S., Breakey, W. R., Anthony, J., & Kramer, M. (1986). Mental health and social characteristics of the homeless: A survey of mission users. *American Journal of Public Health, 76*(5), 519-521.

Foster, C. D., Landes, A., & Jacobs, N. R. (Eds.). (1993*). Homeless in America: How could it happen here?.* Wylie, Texas: Information Plus.

Freeman, R. B., & Hall, B. (1986). *Permanent homelessness in America?.* Cambridge, MA: National Bureau of Economic Research.

Friends Committee on National Legislation. (1988, July). *Washington Newsletter.*

Friskics-Warren, W. T. (1991, January). The independent compilation of shelter lists by local experts for the 1990 S-Night enumeration: Project design and recommendations. Council of Community Services.

Gelbert, L., & Linn, L. S. (1988). Social and physical health of homeless adults previously treated for mental health problems. *Hospital and Community Psychiatry, 39*(5), 516.

Gelbert, L. Linn, L. S., & Leake, B. D. (1988). Mental health, alcohol, and drug use, and criminal hx among homeless adults. *American Journal of Psychiatry, 145,* 191-196.

Germain, C. (1980). *The life model of social work practice.* New York: Columbia University Press.

Goodman, L. A. (1991). The prevalence of abuse among homeless and housed poor mothers: A comparison study. *American Journal of Orthopsychiatry, 61* (4), 489-500.

Gore, A. (1990). Public policy and the homeless. *American Psychologist, 45.*

Gronfein, W. (1985). Incentives and intentions in mental health policy: A comparison of the Medicaid and community mental health programs. *Journal of Health and Social Behavior, 26,*

192- 206.

Hafner, H., & Heiden, W. (1989). Effectiveness and cost of community care for schizophrenic patients. *Hospital and Community Psychiatry, 40* (1), 59.

Hagan, J. L. (1989). Participants in a day program for the homeless: A survey of characteristics and service needs. *Psychosocial Rehabilitation Journal, 12*(4), 29-37.

Hagen, J. L. (1987). Gender and homelessness, *Social Work 32*, pp. 312-16.

Hayduk, L. A. (1987). *Structural equation modeling with LISREL: Essentials and advances.* Baltimore: John Hopkins Press.

Heritage Foundation. (January 12, 1989). America's Homeless: Victims of rent control. *The Backgrounder.*

Heritage Foundation. (May 6, 1985). A Strategy for Helping America's Homeless, *The Backgrounder.*

Hirschl, T., & Momeni, J. A. (1990). Homelessness in New York: A demographic and socioeconomic analysis. In J. Momeni (Ed.). (1990). *Homelessness in the United States: State surveys.* New York: Praeger.

Hoch, C., Slayton, R. A. (1989). New homeless and old: Community and the skid row hotel Philadelphia: Temple University Press.

Hope, M., & Young, J. (1986). *The faces of homelessness.* Lexington, KY: Lexington Books.

Hopper, K. (1991). Final Report: Monitoring and Evaluating the 1990 S-Night Count in New York City, Nathan S. Kline Institute for Psychiatric Research, January 1991

Hopper, K., & Hamberg, J. (Dec. 1984). *The Making of America's Homeless: From Skid Row to New Poor, 1945-1984.* New York: Community Service Society.

Hopper, K., Baxter, E., Cox, S., Klein, L. (June 1982). *One Year Later: the Homeless Poor in New York City, 1982.* Community Service Society

Hopper, K., Susser, E., & Conover, S. (1985). Economies of makeshift: Deindustrialization and homelessness in New York city. *Urban Anthropology, 14*(1-3), 183-236.

Horvath, F. E. The pulse of economic change: Displaced workers of 1981-1985. *Monthly Labor Review, 110*, 3-12.

Hudson, C. G. (1993). The homeless of Massachusetts: An analysis of the 1990 U.S. Census S-Night Data. *New England Journal of Public Policy, 9*(1), 79-100.

Hudson, C. G. (1988). The development of policy for the homeless: The role of research. *Social Thought, XIV*(1), 3-15.

Hudson, C. G. Socioeconomic status and mental illness: Implications the research for policy and practice. *Journal of Sociology and Social Welfare, 15*(1), 27-54.

Hudson, C. G., Flory III, C. B., & Friedrich, R. M. (Feb. 1, 1995). Trends in psychiatric hospitalization and long term care: A plan for ongoing advocacy and monitoring. (National Alliance for the Mentally ill, Hospital and Long Term Care Network).

Hudson, C. G., Salloway, J., & Vissing, Y. M. (1992). The impact of state administrative practices on community mental health. *Administration and Policy in Mental Health, 19*(6), 417-436.

Hudson, R. A. (Ed.). (1993). *Foreverness: The collected poems of Jean Barlow Hudson.* Yellow Springs, OH: Fallen Timbers Press.

Institute of Medicine, Homelessness, Health, and Human Needs (Washington, D.C.: National Academy Press, 1988).

Jackson-Wilson, A. G., & Borgers, S. (1993). Disaffiliation revisited: A comparison of homeless and nonhomeless women's perceptions of family of origin and social supports. *Sex Roles, 28*(7-8), 361-377.

Jahiel, R. I. (1992). Homeless-making processes and the homeless-makers. In Jahiel (Eds.). *Homelessness: A prevention-oriented approach* (pp. 284). Baltimore: John Hopkins press.

Jahiel, R. I. (Ed.). (1992). *Homelessness: A prevention-oriented approach.* Baltimore: John Hopkins Press.

Jahiel, R. I. (1992). Health and health care of homeless people. In M. Robertson & M. Greenblatt (Eds.). (1992). *Homelessness: A national perspective* (pp.245). New York: Plenum Books.

Jencks, C. (1994). *The homeless.* Cambridge: Harvard University Press.

Jick, T. (1979). Mixing qualitative and quantitative methods: Triangulation in action. *Administrative Science Quarterly, 24*, 602.

Johnson, A. B. (1990). Out of Bedlam: The truth about deinstitutionalization. New York: Basic Books.

Johnson, A. K. K. (August 1990). Homeless shelter services in St. Louis, Dissertation, Washington University.

Joreskog, K.G. & Sorbom, D. *(1993). LISREL 8 & PRELIS 2 Documentation,* Version 8.12. Chicago: Scientific Software International.

Kahn, M. et al, (1987). Psychopathology on the streets: Psychological assessment of the homeless, *Professional Psychology: Research and Practice* 18, pp. 580-86.

Kaufman, N. (1986). Homelessness: A comprehensive policy approach. In J. Erickson & C. Wilhelm (Eds.). *Housing the homeless.* New Brunswick, NJ: Rutgers University Press.

Keigher, S., & Greenblatt, S. (1992). Housing emergencies and the etiology of homelessness among the urban elderly. *The Gerontologist, 32*(4), 464.

Kiesler, C. A. & Sibulkin, A. E. (1987). *Mental hospitalization: Myths and facts about a national crisis.* Beverly Hills: Sage.

Koegel, P., & Burnham, M. D. (1992). Problems in the assessment of mental illness among the homeless: An empirical approach. In M. Robertson & M. Greenblatt (Eds.). (1992). *Homelessness: A national perspective.* New York: Plenum Books.

Kovisto, in Momeni, J. (ed.). (1990). In J. Momeni (Ed.). (1990). *Homelessness in the United States: State surveys.* (pp.xxi). New York: Praeger, p. 63.

Kozol, J. (1988). *Rachel and her children.* New York: Fawcett Columbine.

Kurgman, P. (1990). *The age of diminished expectations.* Cambridge: MIT Press.

Lamb, H. R. Deinstitutionalization and The Homeless Mentally Ill. In H.R. Lamb, (ed.), *The Homeless Mentally Ill: A Task Force Report of the American Psychiatric Association.* Washington, D.C.: American Psychiatric Association.

Lamb, H. R. (1984). Deinstititionalization and the homeless mentally ill. *Hospital & Community Psychiatry, 35*, 899-907.

Lamb, R. H., & Lamb, D. M. (1990). Factors contributing to homelessness among the chronically and severely mentally ill. *Hospital & Community Psychiatry, 41*(3), 301-305.

Lang, M. H. (1989). *Homelessness amid affluence: Structure and paradox in the American political economy.* New York: Praeger

Leach, J., & Wing, J. (1980). *Helping destitute men.* London: Tavistock.

Leda, C., & Rosenheck, R. (1992). Mental health status and community adjustment after treatment on in a residential treatment program for homeless veterans. *American Journal of Psychiatry, 149*(9), 1219.

Lee, B. (1990). Homelessness in Tennessee. In J. Momeni (Ed.). (1990). *Homelessness in the United States: State surveys.* New York: Praeger.

Litan, R. E. , Lawrence, R. Z., & Schultze, C. E. (1988/1989). Improving American living standards. *Brookings Review, 7*(1), 78.

Locke, B. Z., & Regier, D. A. Chapter 1, Prevalence and selcted mental disorders, in National Institute of Mental Health. Mental Health, United States, 1985. Taube, C.A., and Barrett, S.A., (eds.) DHHS Pub. No. (ADM) 86-1378. Washington, D.C.:

Maine, T. (1983, September). New York City's lure to the homeless. *Wall Street Journal.*

Manderscheid, R.W., and Sonnenschein, M.A. (Eds.). (1992). *Mental Health, United States, 1990.* U.S., Center for Mental Health Services & National Institute of Mental Health. DHHS Publication No. SMA 92-1942). Washington, DC: Supt. of Docs., U.S. Government Printing Office.

Mare R. D., & Winship, C. (1991). Socioeconomic change and the decline of marriage for blacks and whites. In C. Jencks & P. Peterson (Eds.). *The urban underclass* (pp. 175-202). Washington, DC: The Brookings Institution.

Massachusetts, Executive Office of Human Services. (1990). *Comprehensive Homeless Assistance Plan 3,* Winter 1991-1992.

Maurin, J. & Russell, L. S. (1987). *Homelessness in Utah: Utah homeless survey final report.* Salt Lake City Utah: The Task For Force for Appropriate Treatment of the Homeless Mentally Ill (Unpublished Report).

Mavis, B. E., Humphreys, K., & Stoffelmayr, B. E. (1993). Treatment needs and outcomes of two subtypes of homeless persons who abuse substances. *Hospital & Community Psychiatry, 44*(12), 1187.

McCarthy, D., Argeriou, D., & Huebner, R. (1991). Alcoholism, drug abuse, and the homeless. *American Psychologist 46*(11), 1139-1148.

McChresney, K. Y. (1992). Absence of a family safety net for homeless families. *Journal of Sociology and Social Welfare 19*(4), 55-72.

McChresney, K. Y. (1992). Homeless families: Four patterns of poverty. In M. Robertson & M. Greenblatt (Eds.). (1992). *Homelessness: A national perspective* (pp.245). New York: Plenum Books.

McChresney, K. Y. (1987). *Characteristics of the residents of two inner-city emergency shelters for the homeless.* Los Angeles: University of Southern California, Social Science Research Institute.

McGarrell, E., & Flanagan, T. (1985). *Sourcebook of Criminal Justice Statistics--1984,* Washington, D.C.: U.S. Department of Justice, Bureau of Justice Statistics.

McKnight, J. (1989). Do no harm options that meet human needs. *Social Policy 20* (1), 5-15.

McMurray, D. (1990). Family breakdown causes homelessness. In L. Orr (Ed.). *The homeless: Opposing viewpoints.* San Diego: Greenhaven.

McWirter, W.(1992, March). The temping of America. *Time,* pp. 40-41.

Meher Baba. (1967). *Listen, humanity.* New York: Dodd, Mead, & Company.

Mehrten, J. (1990). A national housing policy would harm the homeless. In L. Orr (Ed.). *The homeless: Opposing viewpoints.* San Diego: Greenhaven.

Merton, R. (1976). *Contemporary Social Problems.* New York: Harcourt Brace.

Michel, R. C. Economic growth and income inequality since the 1982 recession. Washington, D.C.: Urban Institute, 1990 .

Molnar, J., Rath, W. R., Klein, T. P., Lowe, C., & Hartman, A. (1991). *Ill fares the land: The consequences of homelessness and chronic poverty for children and families in New York City.* New York: Bank Street College of Education.

Morse, G. A., & Calsyn, R. J. (1990). Mental health and other human service needs of homeless people. In M. Robertson & M. Greenblatt (Eds.). (1992). *Homelessness: A national perspective* (pp.245). New York: Plenum Books.

Morse, G. A., & Calsyn, R. J. (1986). Mentally disturbed homeless people in St. Louis: Needy, willing, but underserved. *International Journal of Mental Health, 14,* 74-94.

Morse, G. A. (1992). Causes of homelessness. In M. Robertson & M. Greenblatt (Eds.). (1992). *Homelessness: A national perspective.* New York: Plenum Books.

Morse, G. A., Shields, C., Hanneke, C., Calsyn, R. J., Burger, G., & Nelson, B. (1985). *Homeless people in St. Louis: A mental health program evaluation field study & follow-up investigation.* Jefferson City: Missouri Department of Mental Health.

Mowbray, C. Bybee, D., & Cohen, E. (1993). Describing the homeless mentally ill: Cluster analysis results. *American Journal of Community Psychology, 21* (1), 67-93.

Mowbray, C., Solarz, A., Johnson, S. V., Philips-Smith, E., & Combs, C. J. (1986). *Mental health and homelessness in Detroit: A research study.* Lansing, MI: Michigan Department of Mental Health.

Mulkern, V., Bradley, V. J., Spence, R., et al (1985). *Homeless needs assessment study: Findings and recommendations for the Massachusetts Department of Mental Health.* Boston: Human Research Institute.

Mulroy, E., & Lane, T. (1993). Housing affordability, stress and single mothers: Pathways to homelesseness. *Journal of Sociology and Social Welfare, 3,* 29-34.

National Coalition for the Homeless, *Fatally Flawed,* 1991.

Neubauer, R. (1993). Housing preferences of homeless men and women in a shelter population. *Hospital and Community Psychiatry, 44,*(5), 492-494.

New York Times, Despite a 5-year upturn, 9.7 million jobs are lost, December 13, 1988, A12.

North, C. S., & Smith, E. M. (1993). A comparison of homeless men and women: Different populations, different needs. *Community Mental Health Journal, 29*(5), 423-441.

North, C. S., Smith, E. M., & Spitznagel, E. L. Violence and the homeless: An epidemiological study of victimization and aggression. *Journal of Traumatic Stress, 7*(1), 95-110.

O'Reilly, B. (1992, August). The job drought. *Fortune,* pp. 62-74.

Olshansky, S. J., & Ault, A. B. The fourth stage of the epidemiological transition: The age of delayed degenerative diseases. *Milbank Quarterly, 64*(3), 355.

Opler, I. A., Caton, C. L., Shrout, P., Domingues, B., & Case, F. I. (1994). Symptom profiles and homelessness in schizophrenia. *Journal of Nervous & Mental Diseases, 3*, 174-178.

Palmer, J. L., & Sawhill, I. V. (1984). *The Reagan record*. Cambridge, MA: Ballinger.

Passero, H. J. M., Zax, M., & Zozus, R. T. (1991). Social network utilization as related to family history among the homeless. *Journal of Community Psychology, 19*, 70-78.

Pelton, L. H. (1978). Child abuse and neglect: The myth of classlessness. *American Journal of Orthopsychiatry, 48*(4), 608-617.

Peterson, P. E. (Ed.). (1985). *The new urban reality*. Washington, DC: Brookings Institution.

Peterson, R. A., & Weigand, B. (1985). Ordering disorderly work careers on skid row. In R. L. Simpson & I. H. Simpson (Eds.). *Research in the sociology of work: Unemployment*. Greenwich, CT: JAI Press.

Piliavin, I., Sosin, M., & Westerfelt, H. (1987). *Conditions contributing to long-term homelessness: An exploratory study*. (IRP Discussion paper no. 853-87). Madison, WI: University of Wisconsin, Institute for Research on Poverty.

Piven, F. & Cloward, R. (1972*). Regulating the poor: The functions of public welfare*. New York: Random House, Vintage Books.

Piven, F. & Cloward, R. (1985). *The new class war*. New York: Pantheon Books.

Primavera Foundation, (press release), Monitoring the U.S. Census Bureau Shelter/Street Count of Tucson: A Survey by the Primavera Foundation, March 28, 1990.

Reamer, F. (1989). The affordable housing crisis and social work. *Social Work, 34* (1), pp. 5-9.

Redburn, F. S., & Bus, T. F. (1986). *Responding to America's homeless: Public policy alternatives*. New York: Praeger.

Reich, R. B. (1992). *The work of nations: Preparing ourselves for 21st century capitalism*. New York: Vintage Books.

Reilly, F. E. (1993). Experience of family among homeless individuals. *Issues in Mental Health Nursing, 14*(4), 309-321.

Rife, J. C., First, R. J., Greenlee, R. W., Miller, L. D., & Feichter, M. A. (1991). Case management with homeless mentally ill people. *Health and Social Work, 6*(1), 58-67.

Ripple, L. (1969). *Motivation, capacity, and opportunity: Studies in casework theory and practice*. Chicago: University of Chicago, School of Social Service Administration.

Robertson, M., & Greenblatt, M. (Eds.). (1992). *Homelessness: A national perspective*. New York: Plenum Books.

Robertson, M. Ropers, R. H., & Boyer, R. (1985). *The homeless of Los Angeles County: An empirical assessment*. Los Angeles: University of California, School of Public Health.

Rochefort, D. A., & Cobb, R. W. (1992). Framing and claiming the homelessness problem. *New England Journal of Public Policy, 8*(1), 49-65.

Ropers, R. H. (1988). The invisible homeless: A new urban ecology. *Human Sciences Press*, p. 212.

Rose, S. M. (1979). Deciphering deinstitutionalization: Complexities in policy and program analysis. *Milbank Quarterly, 57*, 429-60.

Rosenheck, R., Frisman, L., & Chung, L. The proportion of homeless among veterans. *American Journal of Public Health, 84*(3), 466-469.

Rossi, P. H. (1989). *Down and out in America.* Chicago: University of Chicago Press.

Rossi, P. H., Wright, J. D., Fisher, G. A., & Willis, G. (1987). The urban homeless: Estimating composition and size. *Science, (235),* 1336-1341.

Roth, B. and Bean, J. (1985). Alcohol problems and homelessness: Findings from the Ohio study. In F. D. Wittman (Ed.). *The homeless with alcohol-related problems.* Rockville, MD: U.S. Department of Health and Human Services.

Roth, D. (1992). Homeless veterans: Comparisons with other homeless men. In M. Robertson & M. Greenblatt (Eds.). (1992). *Homelessness: A national perspective.* New York: Plenum Books.

Roth, D. (1990) Homelessness in Ohio: A statewide epidemiological study. In J. Momeni (Ed.). (1990). *Homelessness in the United States: State surveys.* New York: Praeger.

Roth, D., Toomey, B. G., & First, R. J. (1992). Gender, racial, and age variations among homeless persons. In M. Robertson & M. Greenblatt (Eds.). (1992). *Homelessness: A national perspective* (pp. 207). New York: Plenum Books.

Sakano, D. (Nov. 19, 1981). Testimony given at New York State Assembly Hearings, Homeless New Yorkers: The Forgotten Among Us.

Sawhill, I.V. (1989). Rethinking employment policy. In Bawden & Skidmore (Eds.). *Rethinking employment policy* (pp.23). Washington, DC: Urban Institute Press.

Schutt, R. K., & Garrett, G. R. (1986). *Homeless in Boston in 1985: The view from Long Island.* Boston: University of Massachusetts, Sociology Department.

Schutt, R. K., & Garrett, G. R. (1992). *Responding to the homeless: Policy and practice.* New York: Plenum Press.

Schutt, R. K. (1988). *Boston's homeless, 1986-1987: Change and continuity. report to the Long Island shelter.* Boston: University of Massachusetts, Sociology Department.

Scull, A. (1984). *Darceration: Community treatment and the deviant--A radical view* (2nd ed.). New DecBrunswick, NJ: Rutgers University Press.

Segal, S. P., & Baumohl, J. (1980). Engaging the disengaged: Proposals on madness and vagrancy. *Social Work, 25*(5), 358-365.

Segal, S. P., Baumohl, J., & Johnson, E. (1977). Falling through the cracks: Mental disorder and social margin in a young vagrant population. *Social Problems, 24,* 387-400

Shaiken, H. (1987). Globalization and the worldwide division of labor. Monthly Labor Review, 110, (8), 47.

Shapiro, I., & Nichols, M. E. (1989). *Unprotected: Unemployment insurance and jobless workers in 1988.* Washington, DC: Center on Budget and Policy Priorities.

Shelter Partnership, Inc. (May 1992). *The number of homeless people in Los Angeles City and County, July 1990 to June 1991.*

Shinn, M., Knickman, J. R., & Weitzman, B. C. (1991). Social relationships and vulnerability to becoming homeless among poor families. *American Psychologist, 46,* (11), 1180-7.

Shlay, A., & Rossi, P. (1992). Social science research and contemporary studies of homelessness. *Annual Review of Sociology, 18,* 129-160.

Silverstein, K. (1994). Homelessness commands attention. *American City and County, 109,* 10.

Simons, J. M., Finlay, B., & Yang, A. (1991). *The adolescent and young adult fact book.* Washington, DC: Children's Defense Fund.

Slagg, N. B., et al. (1994). A profile of clients served by a mobile outreach program for homeless mentally ill persons. *Hospital and Community Psychiatry, 45*(11), 1139.

Smith, E. M., North, C. S., & Spitznagel, E. L. (1992). Alcohol, drugs, and psychiatric comorbidity among homeless women: An epidemiological study. *Journal of Clinical Psychiatry, 4*(2), 111-120.

Smith, R. E., & Vavrichek, B. (1987). The minimum wage: Its relation to incomes and poverty. *Monthly Labor Review, 110* (6), 24-30.

Snow, D. A., & Anderson, L. (1990). *Down on their luck: A study of homeless people.* Berkeley: University of California Press.

Snow, D. A., Baker, S. G., & Erson, L. (1986). The myth of pervasive mental illness among the homeless. *Social Problems, 33,* 301-317.

Snyder, M., & Hombs, M. E. (1983). *Homelessness in America: The forced march to nowhere.* Washington, DC: The Community for Creative Nonviolence.

Solarz, A. (1985, November). An examination of criminal behavior among the homeless. Paper presented at the annual meeting of the American Society of Criminology, San Diego, CA.

Sosin, M., Colson, P., & Grossman, S. (1988). *Homelessness in Chicago: Poverty and pathology, social institutions and social change.* Chicago: University of Chicago, School of Social Service Administration.

Sosin, M., Piliavin, I., & Westerfelt, H. (1990). Toward a longitudinal analysis of homelessness. *Journal of Social Issues, 46*(4), 157-174.

Stark, L. (1990). An evaluation of the 1990 census of homeless people in Phoenix. The Community Housing Partnership, Phoenix, AZ, July 30, 1990.

Stefl, M. E. (1988). The new homeless. In R. D. Bingham, R. E. Green, & S. B. White (Eds.). *Homeless in contemporary society* (pp. 46). Beverly Hills, CA: Sage.

Stern, M. (1984). The emergence of homeless as a public problem. *Social Service Review. (June),* 299-301.

Stevens, O'Brien, A., Brown, L., Colson, P., & Singer, K. (1983). *When you don't have anything: A street survey of homeless people in Chicago.* Chicago: Chicago Coalition for the Homeless.

Stroup, A. L., & Manderscheid, R. W. (1988). The development of the state mental hospital system in the United States: 1840-1980. *Journal of the Washington Academy of Sciences, 78,* 64.

Susser, E., Lin, S. P., Conover, S. A., & Struening, E. (1990, May). Childhood antecedents of homelessness in psychiatric patient. Paper presented at the meeting of the American Psychiatric Association, New York, NY.

Susser, E., Streuning, E., & Conover, S. (1987). Childhood experiences of homeless men. *American Journal of Psychiatry, 144,* 1599-1601.

Susser, E., Struening, E., & Conver, S. (1989). Psychiatric problems in homeless men. *Archives of General Psychiatry, 46,* 845-850.

Sutherland, E., & Locke, H. (1936). Twenty thousand homeless men. Chicago: Lipincott.

Taeuber, C. (1991). *Statistical handbook on women in America.* Phoenix, AZ: Oryx Press.

Tessler, R. C., & Dennis, D. L. (Feb. 9, 1989). *A synthesis of NIMH-funded research concerning persons who are homeless and mentally ill.* Amherst, MA: University of Massachusetts, Social and Demographic Research Insitute.

Thompson, J. H. (1991). Memorandum, Preliminary Results of the S-Night Enumerator Debriefing Questionnaire for the S-Night 'Assessment' Cities (Washington, D.C.: Bureau of the Census, May 2, 1991).

Thorman, G. (1988). Homeless families, Springfield, IL: Charles C. Thomas.

Timmer & Knotterus (1990). In J. Momeni (Ed.). (1990). *Homelessness in the United States: State surveys.* New York: Praeger.

Timmer, D. A. D., Eitzen, S., & Talley, K. K. (1994). *Paths to homelessness: Extreme poverty and the urban crisis.* Boulder, CO: Westerview Press.

Toomey, B., & First, R. (1985, February). *Homelessness in Ohio: A study of people in need.* Columbus, OH: Ohio Department of Mental Health.

Torrey, E. F. Erdman, K., Wolfe, S. M., & Flynn, L. M. (1990). Care of the seriously mentally ill: A rating of state programs (3rd ed.). Public Citizen Health Research Group and National Alliance for the Mentally Ill.

Torrey, E. F., Burt, M. R., Beirne, K., & Tucker, W. (1988). Who are the homeless and why are they on the streets?. *The Heritage Lectures: Rethinking Policy on Homelessness*, December 14, 1988.

Tucker, W. (1987, September). Where do the homeless come from?. *National Review*, p. 35.

Tull, J. (1992). Homelessness: An overview. *New England Journal of Public Policy, 8*(1), 25- 48.

U.S. Conference of Mayors. (1987). *The continuing growth of hunger, homelessness and poverty in America's cities: 1987. A 26-city survey* Washington, DC: U.S. Government Printing Office.

U.S. Congress, Joint Hearing before the Subcommittee on Housing and Urban Development of the Committee on Banking, Finance, and Urban Affairs and the Subcommittee on Manpower and Housing of the Committee of Government Operations, HUD Report on Homelessness.

U.S., Bureau of the Census, Fact Sheet, 1992.

U.S., Bureau of the Census, Fact sheet for 1990 decennial census counts of persons in selected locations where homeless persons are found, (CPH-L-87), pp. 3-4.

U.S., Bureau of the Census, The Shelter Component of S-Night, March 18-20, 1991.

U.S., Bureau of the Census, 1982, Characteristics of the Population Below Poverty Levels: 1980 (Washington, D.C.: CPS Reports).

U.S., Bureau of the Census, 1990 Census, Summary Tape File 1-A.

U.S., Bureau of the Census, Census of Population and Housing, 1990: Summary Tape File 3 Technical Documentation / prepared by the Bureau of the Census. --Washington: The Bureau, 1991.

U.S., Bureau of the Census. (1992). *USA Counties.* (CD-ROM).

U.S., Bureau of the Census. (August 1991). 1990 Census of Population and Housing--Standard Tape File 2C.

U.S., Bureau of the Census. (December 1991). 1990 Census of Population and Housing-- Standard

Tape File 3C. (CD-ROM).

U.S., Bureau of the Census. (March 1991). 1990 Census of Population and Housing--Standard Tape File 1C (CD-ROM).

U.S., Bureau of the Census. (1985). *Money Income and Poverty Status of Families and Persons in the United States.* Washington, D.C.: CPS Reports.

U.S., Conference of Mayors. (June 1984). *Homelessness in America's Cities: Ten Case Studies.*

U.S., Conference of Mayors. (1990). *A status report on hunger and homelessness in America's cities: 1990. A-30 city survey.* Washington, DC: Author.

U.S., Conference of Mayors. (November 1991). *Mentally Ill and Homeless: A 22- City Survey,* pp. 44-45.

U.S., Department of Health and Human Services, Substance Abuse and Mental Health Services Administration. (1993). *Additions and Resident Patients at End of Year, State and County Mental Hospitals, by Age and Diagnosis, United States, 1990.*

U.S., Department of Housing and Urban Affairs, Section 8 Certificate units reserved by state (as of 4/30/92), Section 8 Housing Voucher units reserved by state (as of 4/30/92).

U.S., Department of Housing and Urban Affairs. (1989). *A report to the secretary on the homeless & emergency shelters* (Washington, D.C.: HUD Office of Policy Development and Research, Division of Policy Studies.

U.S., Department of Housing and Urban Development. (1992). Unpublished tables.

U.S., Department of Housing and Urban Development. (Sept. 1991). *Report to Congress on Rent Control.*

U.S., General Accounting Office. (April 9, 1985). *Homelessness: A Complex Problem and the Federal Response* (GAO/HRD-85-40).

U.S., H.U.D, A Report to the Secreatary on the Homeless and Emergency Shelters, p. 4.

U.S., House of Representatives, Committee on Ways and Means, Background Material and Data on Programs within the Jurisdiction of the Committee on Ways and Means, Washington, D.C., Government Printing Office, 1990, p. 563.

U.S., House of Representatives, Committee on Ways and Means. *(1990). Overview of Entitlement Programs: The 1990 Green Book,* Washington, D.C.: Government Printing Office.

U.S., Interagency Council on the Homeless, McKinney Act Funding Data , 12/94.

U.S., Interagency Council on the Homeless, Federal Progress Toward Ending Homelessness. (Sept. 1992). The 1991/1992 Annual Report of the Interagency Council on the Homeless, Washington DC

U.S., National Institute of Mental Health (NIMH), Additions and Resident Patients at End of 1990, p. x.

U.S., National Institute of Mental Health. (1955). Patients in Mental Institutions.

Vernex, G. et al. (1988). *Review of California's program for the mentally disabled.* Santa Monica, CA: Rand Corporation.

Vissing, Y. M. (1996). *Out of sight, out of mind.* Lexington: University of Kentucky.

Webster's New World Dictionary of the American Language (1962). Cleveland: World Publishing Company.

Weitzman, L .J. (1985). *The divorce revolution*. New York: Free Press.

Weitzman, B. C., Knickman, J. R. and Shinn, M. (1992). Predictors of shelter use among low-income families: Psychiatric history, substance abuse, and victimization. *American Journal of Public Health, 82*(10), 1547-1550.

Wenzel, S. L. (1993). The relationship of psychological resources and social support to job procurement self-efficacy in the disadvantaged. *Journal of Applied Social Psychology, 23*(18), 1471-1497.

Westerfelt, H. (1990). The ins and outs of homelessness: Exit patterns and predictions. (Doctoral dissertation, University of Wisconsin at Madison, 1990).

Whitbeck, L. B., & Simons, R. L. (1993). A comparison of adaptive strategies and patterns of victimization among homeless adolescents and adults. *Violence and Victims, 8*(2),1394-1398.

Whitman, B. Graves, & Accardo, P. (1989). Parents learning together: Training parenting skills for retarded adults. *Social Work, 34,* 431-434.

William T. (1990). *The excluded Americans: Homelessness and housing policies*. Washington DC: Regnery Gateway.

Wilson, W. J. (1967). *The truly disadvantaged*. Chicago: University of Chicago Press.

Winkleby, M. A. (1990). Comparison of risk factors for ill health in a sample of homeless and nonhomeless poor. *Public Health Reports, 105*(4), 404.

Winkleby, M. A., Rockhill, B., Jatulis, D., & Fortmann, S. P. (1992). The medical origins of homelessness. *American Journal of Public Health, 82*(10), 1395.

Wletman, K., Poveromo, L., & Nofi, R. (1988). Impact of community-based psychosocial treatment on clients' level of functioning. *Hospital and Community Psychiatry, 39*(5), 550.

Wood, T.N., Valdez, Hayashi, T., and Shen, A. (1990). Homeless and housed families in Los Angeles: A study comparing demographic, economic, and family function characteristics. *American Journal of Public Health 80* (9), pp. 1049-52.

Wright, J. D. (1989). *Address unknown: The homeless in America*. New York: Aldine.

Wright, J. D., & Devine, J. (1995). Housing dynamics of the homeless: Implications for a count. *American Journal of Orthopsychiatry, 65*(3), 326.

Wright, J. D., & Devine, J. A. Assessment of the Street Enumeration Procedures during the Census 'Shelter and Street Night' in New Orleans. Tulane University. (undated)

Wright, J. D., & Weber, E. (1988). Determinants of benefit-program participation among the urban homeless: Results from a 16-city study. *Evaluation Review, 12*(4), p. 39.

Wright, J. D., & Weber, E. (1987). *Homelessness and health*. New York: McGraw-Hill.

Wyatt v. Stickney, 325 F. Supp. 781 (1971).

Zozus, R. T., & Zax, M. (1991). Perceptions of childhood: Exploring possible etiological factors in homelessness. *Hospital & Community Psychiatry, 42* (5), 535-537.

INDEX

SYMPOSIUM SERIES

1. Jïrgen Moltmann *et al.*, **Religion and Political Society**

2. James Grace, **God, Sex, and the Social Project: Glassboro Papers on Religion and Human Sexuality**

3. M. Darroll Bryant and Herbert W. Richardson (eds.), **A Time for Consideration: A Scholarly Appraisal of the Unification Church**

4. Donald G. Jones, **Private and Public Ethics: Tensions Between Conscience and Institutional Responsibility**

5. Herbert W. Richardson, **New Religions and Mental Health: Understanding the Issues**

6. Sheila Greeve Davaney (ed.), **Feminism and Process Thought: The Harvard Divinity School / Claremont Center for Process Studies Symposium Papers**

7. A.T.D./Fourth World, **Children of Our Time: Words and Lives of Fourth World Children**

8. Jenny Yates Hammett, **Woman's Transformations: A Psychological Theology**

9. S. Daniel Breslauer, **A New Jewish Ethics**

10. Darrell J. Fasching (ed.), **Jewish People in Christian Preaching**

11. Henry Vander Goot, **Interpreting the Bible in Theology and the Church**

12. Everett Ferguson, **Demonology of the Early Christian World**

13. Marcia Sachs Littell, **Holocaust Education: A Resource Book for Teachers and Professional Leaders**

14. Char Miller, **Missions and Missionaries in the Pacific**

15. John S. Peale, **Biblical History as the Quest for Maturity**

16. Joseph Buijs, **Christian Marriage Today: Growth or Breakdown**

17. Michael Oppenheim, **What Does Revelation Mean for the Modern Jew?**

18. Carl F.H. Henry, **Conversations with Carl Henry: Christianity for Today**

19. John Biermans, **The Odyssey of New Religious Movements: Persecution, Struggle, Legitimation. A Case Study of the Unification Church**

20. Eugene Kaellis and Rhoda Kaellis (eds.), **Toward a Jewish America**

21. Andrew Wilson (ed.), **How Can the Religions of the World be Unified?: Interdisciplinary Essays in Honor of David S.C. Kim**

22. Marcia Sachs Littell *et al.*, (eds.), **The Holocaust Forty Years After**

23. Ian H. Angus, **George Grant's Platonic Rejoinder to Heidegger: Contemporary Political Philosophy and the Question of Technology**